Foreword

Foreword - by Franz Krauth

IT teachers are challenged in their mission to help students master the complexities of Graphics Programming and Games Development considering the great quantity of information and the near daily changes that occur in the world of real time 3D. Creating relevant and timely course content is difficult and IT teachers must also accommodate various learning styles, competencies and interests for the myriad of subtopics in game development. Virtools has proven to be a great asset to manage this variety in the classroom. One of the biggest benefits of Virtools has been its ability to include both technical and creative students into the game development mix. They have Virtools as the development environment and simply work in different areas of the software. Virtools has also proven to be a great tool for us in other ways, a few of which I have listed below;

- Create impressive visual results measured in hours rather than days;
- Use Virtools' intuitive Building Block scripting system to create, test and debug complex behaviors without writing a single line of code;
- Technical students can learn complex game programming techniques with Virtools' extensive and well-documented Software Development Kit (SDK);
- The Virtools internal scripting language (VSL) is a great way for non-technical students to get an introduction to the basics of programming.

This book, Virtools Fundamentals, provide teachers with new and interesting ways to offer tutorials, exercises, and classroom content for beginners and advanced students alike, leaving more time to do what we like best: 'Virtooling'.

Franz Krauth
Certified Virtools Instructor
Academy of Information Technology, Sydney, Australia

Table of contents

Chapter01 Introduction

1.0 An Introduction to Virtools

Welcome to Virtools Fundamentals. This book is a practical guide for those starting out in the world of Real-Time 3D and for those with previous experience who want to learn the Virtools application. We feel most people learn best by doing, so after a brief introduction in Chapter 1, the rest of the book takes you through various exercises to help you build you skills around the basic operations of Virtools. The best way to learn Virtools is by experimenting; we would encourage you after finishing each exercise, to take some time to modify your project on your own. If you, get stuck, there are a wide variety of resources available to help you including a very detailed context-sensitive help file included with Virtools (just hit the F1 key).

In Virtools, there are usually a number of ways to accomplish any given task, some ways are simple but require more computing power, whilst others are more complex, code-based solutions that may yield a higher frame rate but usually require more time to develop. That being said, this book focuses on the simplest way to get the job done; once you are confident with the basic development toolset in Virtools, you can move up to VSL (Virtools Scripting Language), the Shader Editor and the Software Development Kit (SDK) to further refine and tweak your work.

Although each lesson builds in complexity, there is no requirement for you to follow each lesson in order. Feel free to jump into a lesson that you find interesting and see what you can learn. If you find it too difficult, try to figure out which skills you need to build and complete the appropriate lesson.

In sum, whilst Virtools is a complex application covering many areas of expertise, from 3D Modeling and Level Design to Programming and Networking, don't feel you need to be a technical and creative guru to turn your ideas into reality. With this in mind, take your time to learn the core concepts and components of Virtools and most importantly, have fun doing it.

1.1 About Virtools & Dassault Systèmes

Before we get started on learning the software, let's first take a look at the history of Virtools (now Dassault Systèmes) as a company.

Virtools launched its commercial activities in 1993 as a consulting and services company targeting the Virtual Reality sector. The core team primarily developed cutting-edge interactive applications for industrial groups such as EADS, Airbus Industry, PSA and IFP. With the needs of this and other key markets in mind, Virtools built the company's initial software solution, Virtools.

As an Independent Software Vendor since 1999, Virtools specialized in providing comprehensive software development environments for creating highly interactive 3-D content. The Virtools software suite is used for creating offline and online applications in many fields such as virtual reality, video games, industrial simulation, visualization, and marketing multimedia.

The most recent change has been the acquisition of Virtools (the company) by Dassault Systèmes. The Dassault Group is a large enterprise based in France with interests the Aerospace and Automotive industries. A subsidiary of the Dassault Group, Dassault Systèmes, specializes in 3D and PLM (Product Lifecycle Management) solutions; the Virtools package falls under their '3D For All' solution, which aims to let everyone create and experience 3D ubiquitously.

1.2 What is Virtools?

Virtools is not simply another 3D engine. Virtools is an integrated 3D development environment with numerous components used to build interactive behaviors in real-time 3D. Using Virtools you can create a wide variety of applications such as 3D web sites, computer games, 3D multimedia, architecture presentations, interactive television, e-learning software, idea prototypes and product demos.

In addition to the front-end development software, Virtools also provides an SDK for programmers to develop new functionality, Building Blocks and custom drivers as well as extend the user interface of Virtools. The SDK is also used to create an executable wrapper (or '.exe' file) that allows users to natively run your project without having to install additional plug-ins.

In addition to executable files, Virtools can also export your project to a web-compatible format. You can then upload the '.html' file and '.vmo' (exported project file) to your website for others to view. The web deployment method is in fact the most common way to publish your work and is compatible with both PC and Mac browsers. To create an even better user experience, you can integrate your Virtools project with Adobe (Macromedia) Flash™ content in the same webpage to create a truly amazing experience. (Note that the licensing system for creating executables and web-based projects are different; you should check the Virtools website for more information).

The Building Blocks (BB's) concept in Virtools realizes the ideal of visual programming by enabling drag-and-drop 'precompiled' modules (or code blocks) onto appropriate objects or characters and uses flow charts to decide the sequence of processing these modules. Each BB has input and output parameters (PIn's and POut's) and a number of behavior inputs and outputs (BIn's and BOut's) to determine the program flow. Virtools 3.5 contains more than 500 BB's, each of which has its own distinct use relating to a certain area of functionality (i.e. BB's that are related to sound processing, or mesh modification etc). A configuration of a number of BB's that perform a certain function (such as fading a light based on the characters distance to it) can be grouped together to form a new reusable module called a Behavior Graph. This module can later be updated, exchanged with others or even sold.

Virtools also includes special BB's that allow you to add LAN and Internet functionality to your project. You can create LAN based games where multiple player characters interact, or use specific Internet BB's to send and retrieve data from the Internet and even develop persistent-world online multiplayer games.

1.3 A Brief History of Features and Improvements

At the time of writing, Virtools 3.5 was the most current iteration of the software and Virtools 4.0 was just a few weeks away from release, thus we decided to include a section on some of the major improvements in Virtools since the 3.0 release. Virtools 3.0 was a major step forward with the inclusion of a full Shader Editor feature that was compatible with HLSL (High Level Shader Language) v2.0.

- Virtools 3.0 key new features;
  - Pixel and Vertex Shader Editor

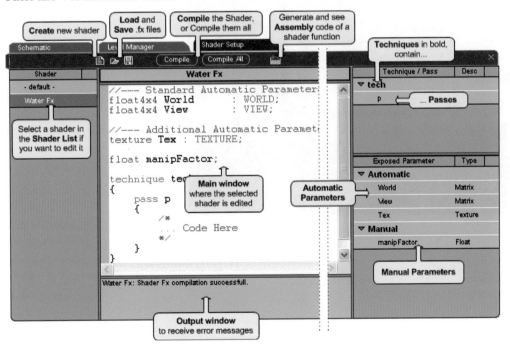

•NXN Alien Brain Integration

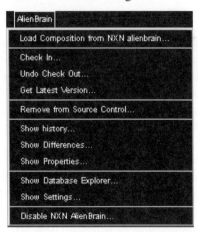

•Action Manager for creating automation scripts
•A range of new Building Blocks, including;
　　•Web Download and Web Get Data BB's for dynamic interaction with web pages and online files.
　　•Cloth System (Spring & Mass System) for creating realistic hanging materials with collision detection and deflection.
　　•DirectX Dependency Checker
　　•Mark System used to create marks on surfaces (like bullet holes, skid marks etc)
　　•Ray Intersection \ Ray Box Intersection \ 2D Picking

Virtools 3.5 key new features;
　　•New Video Engine for playback of video files or real-time streaming from a live source. The output of the video can be set to playback to the screen, a 2D Frame or a Texture.

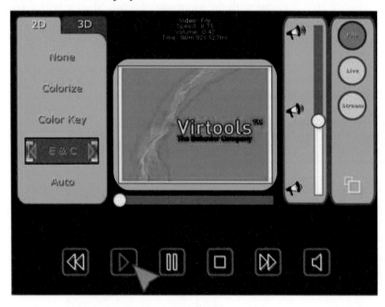

·New OpenGL 1.5 Rasterizer features better performance and compatibility.
·Point Clouds and 3D Textures for advanced visualization

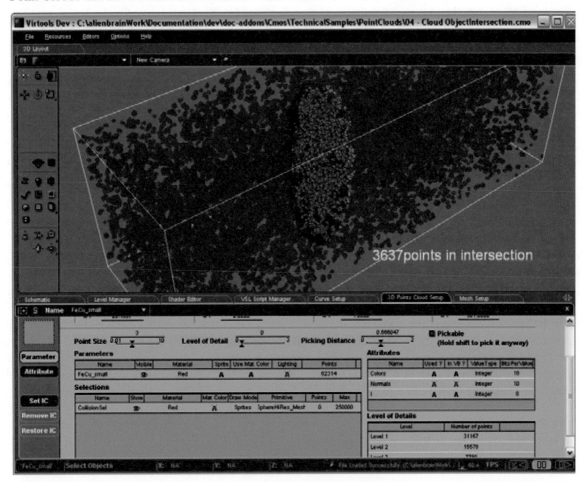

·Shader Material Examples including drag-and-drop Shader scripts to allow you to simply drag a shader onto an object to apply it.

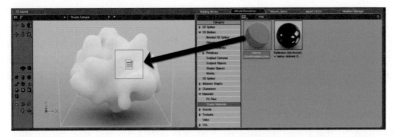

·New Microsoft Visual Studio .NET 2003 SDK (Note: With Virtools 3.5, support for Visual Studio 6 has been ended)

Virtools Dev 4.0 key new features;
The release of Virtools 4.0 was the first new version since Dassault had acquired Virtools and many of the improvements relate directly to integration with Dassault's existing range of software. Rather than introducing a large number of new features, the 4.0 release focuses more on fixing bugs and improving usability. One important change to note is the renaming of the "Virtools Web Player" to "3D Life Player".
·3DXML Support
    ·3DXML is now seamlessly integrated in Virtools 4.0. The purpose of 3DXML is to act as a lightweight XML-based format to share 3D between applications. Dassault has signed an agreement with Microsoft to jointly collaborate in the specification of 3DXML and to include compatibility for XAML (Extensible Application Markup Language). XAML was developed by Microsoft to simplify development of the presentation subsystem in Windows Vista.

•CgFX Support
>   •CgFX is now supported for OpenGL 2.0. CgFX is a shader programming language developed by NVidia and Microsoft. The Microsoft implementation is called HLSL (High Level Shader Language) for DirectX on Windows platforms; CgFX is the NVidia implementation and runs on any platform supporting OpenGL.

•COLLADA v1.4 Support
>   •COLLADA 1.4 files can now be directly imported into Virtools. COLLADA is an open format that allows DCC (Digital Content Creation) vendors to support data interchange between otherwise proprietary applications. COLLADA is based on the XML format and was originally created by Sony, but is now maintained by an open consortium called the Khronos Group.

•Xbox 360 Controller Support
>   •New Building Blocks have been added to natively support Xbox 360 controllers and rumble features. In addition, generic joystick support has also been improved to test if the joystick is still connected or if new ones have been added.

1.4 The Basics of Virtools

To get an idea of the overall framework of the Virtools suite, let's look at the 5 basic elements, which are;

1) The Authoring Application (the software you run and work with) is used to build your interactive 3D composition by combining media created using 3rd party software such as 3ds Max and Maya.

2) The Behavioral Engine is the core component of Virtools that sits behind the scenes and allows you to add automation and interactivity to your application. Building Blocks (BB's) are the basic units of behaviors and are linked together to achieve a certain result or perform a particular function. Virtools includes over 500 BB's grouped into categories such as Characters, Lights, Cameras, Narrative, Particles and Shaders etc. The Virtools Scripting Language (VSL) can also be used to add further, more granular, customization to your application.

3) The Rendering Engine is used by Virtools to render all the visible components of your scene to the screen in real-time. The default Rendering Engine can be replaced by a customized version or modified using the Software Development Kit.

4) The Web-based Player consists of a playback-only version of the Behavioral Engine and the complete Rendering Engine all in a downloadable package for both PC and Mac. The Web Player can play '.cmo' files (editable versions of Virtools compositions) and '.vmo' files (exported non-editable Virtools compositions).

5) The Software Development Kit (SDK) is a set of low level development tools that allow you to extend Virtools' functionality. Using the SDK developers can create stand-alone executables, customized building blocks, media import\export plug-ins, custom Rasterizers and extensions to the Virtools GUI (Graphical User Interface).

1.5 Installing the Virtools Evaluation Version

Now that you've had a brief introduction to the basic architecture of Virtools let's get the application up and running on your PC. The installation is similar to most Windows-based applications and doesn't require too much technical wizardry to get working.

The minimum system requirements of Virtools are;
1) Pentium 500 or faster (PIII or higher recommended)
2) Windows 98\2000\XP\2003
3) 128Mb RAM (256Mb recommended)
4) DirectX or OpenGL compatible 3D graphics card with 32Mb RAM 5) (DirectX9 compatibility is required for Shader support)
5) Sound Card (not required, but highly recommended)
6) Internet Explorer 4 or greater

Ok, let's get started on installing Virtools;
1) Firstly, insert the disc included with this book into your CDROM.

2) If Autorun is enabled, an installation dialog will automatically open. If you don't have Autorun, navigate to the root folder of the CD and run the file 'setup.exe'.

3) From the dialog, select Virtools.

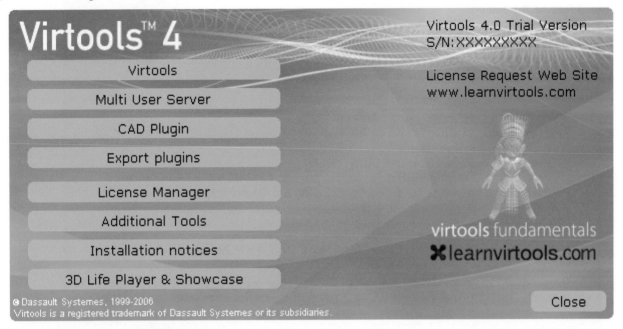

4) A welcome dialog will appear, press Next.

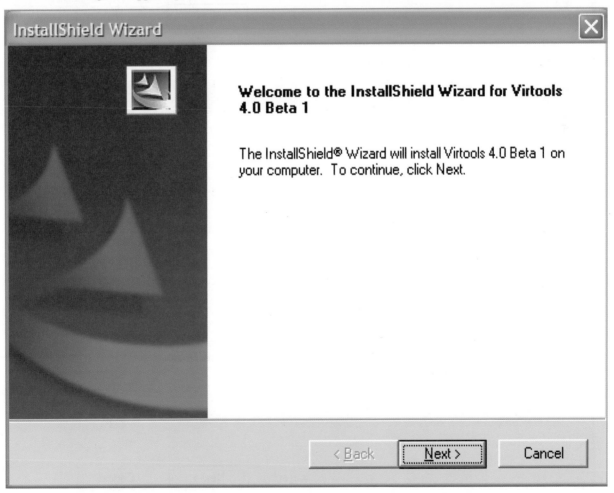

5) The license agreement window appears next, read it and click Next.

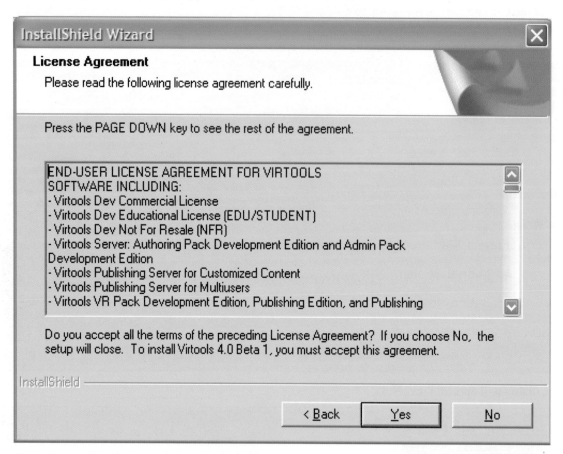

6) Click Next when the Information dialog appears.

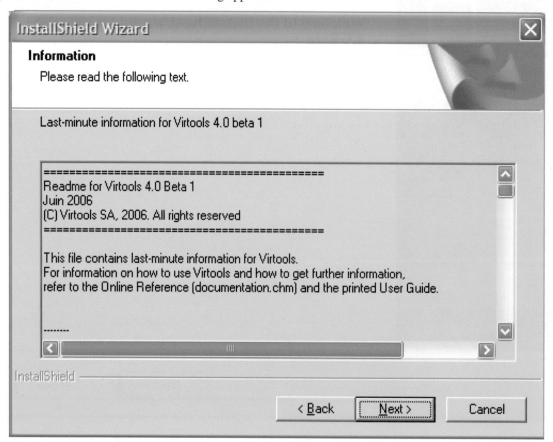

7) The registration dialog will appear, enter your name, company (if you have one) and the following serial number 'khwzep22kf-NFR1P3524'.

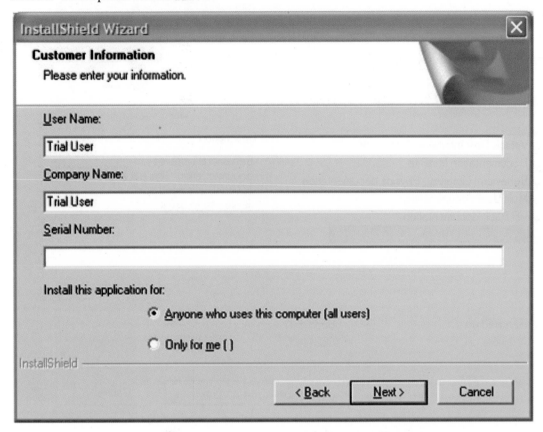

8) In the location dialog, select the folder in which Virtools will be installed. (We recommend you keep the default location). Click Next.

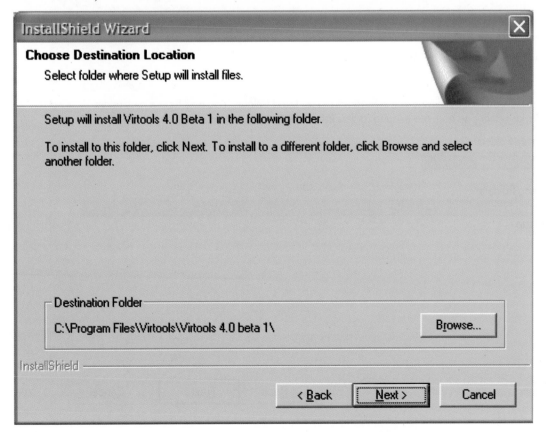

9) A check-box dialog appears asking which components you want to install. Check all the boxes and click Next.

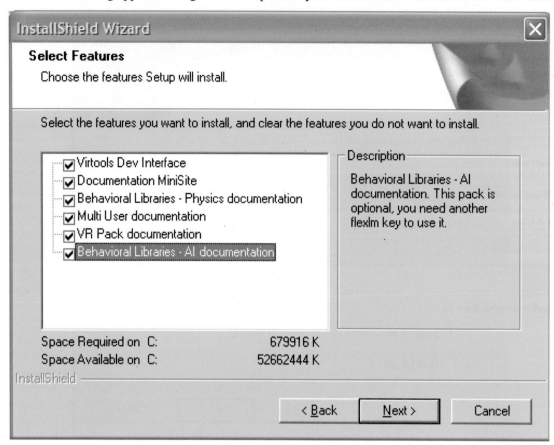

10) The shortcut location dialog appears; just leave it as default and click Next

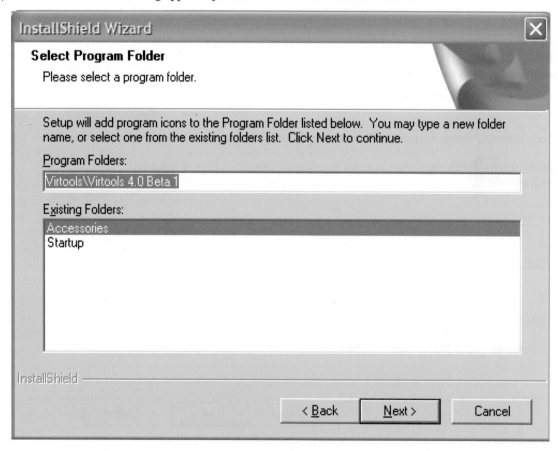

11) The installer will begin loading Virtools onto your system. The full install is just over 700Mb, so it may take a few minutes to complete.

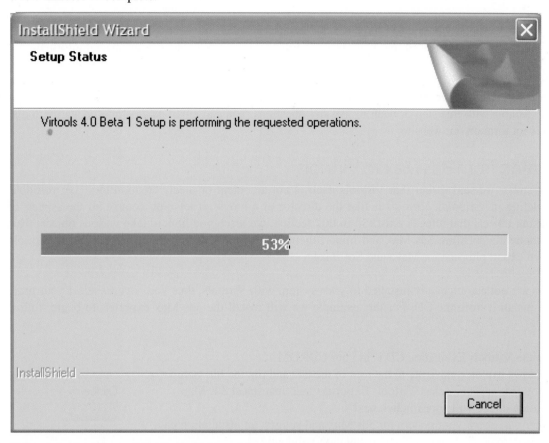

12) When it is complete a 'Finished' dialog will appear; click Finish.

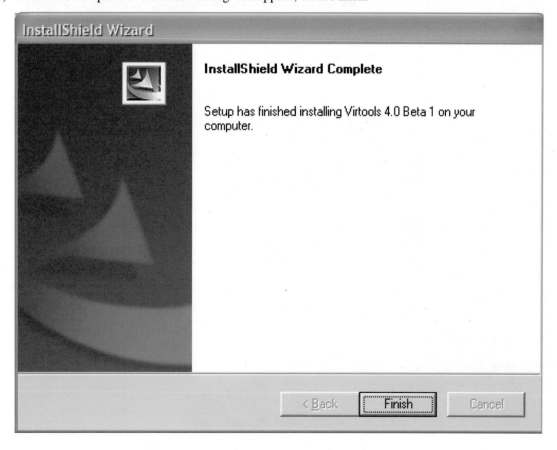

13) Virtools has been successfully installed on your system. There are still a couple of extra tasks we need to complete before you can get started.

To be able to use Virtools, you need to have a valid license installed on your system. The license comes in a special ".lic" file format that is placed into your Virtools folder. This file is created using special information about your computer to make it unique and non-transferable. To obtain the file, you need to log into our website, <u>www. learnvirtools.com</u> (go to the Register section), register your details and some information about your computer (our privacy policy will ensure your details are only known to us and Virtools) and the file will be emailed to you. If you have any trouble with this step or want to ask any questions, you can email us at <u>support@learnvirtools.com</u> or use the contact form on our website.

1.6 Exporting from 3ds Max to Virtools

You will remember we said earlier that Virtools itself is not a content or media creation tool (i.e. you don't do your 3D modeling in Virtools); Virtools is like the director of a movie, it lets you control all the aspects of the production using objects that already exist. So in this section, we teach you how to take various objects from the popular 3D modeling software 3ds Max and import them into Virtools. If you don't use 3ds Max, Virtools has also developed export plug-ins for Maya and Softimage.

The exporters are not automatically installed to your system with Virtools, thus you have to select your preferred exporter and install it from the CD. For this example we will install the 3ds Max exporter, to begin, follow the steps below;

1) Make sure the Virtools Evaluation CD is in your CDROM
2) Using windows explorer, navigate to the root of the CD and run the file 'setup.exe'
3) In the dialog that appears, select Virtools Exporters and then select 3ds Max
4) An installation dialog will appear, click next
5) The installer will check your system for 3ds Max and suggest an installation path
6) If the path is correct, click next and the installation will begin
7) Once finished, click the close button to exit; we can now start 3ds Max and export our models to Virtools

1.6.1 Exporting a Single Static Object to Virtools

1) Open 3ds Max and select Open from the file menu
2) Navigate to the CD included with this book open the file Sample CMOs\Chapter 1\Anchor.max

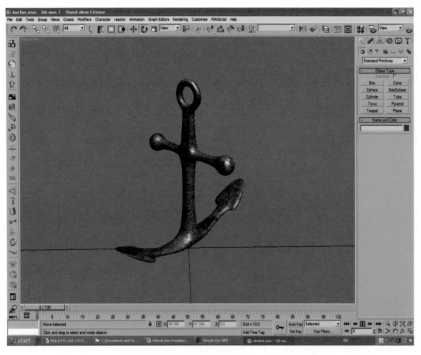

3) Select Export from the File menu. In the dialog that appears, change the Type to 'Virtools *.NMO *.VMO'. Set the name of the file to 'Anchor'. Select an appropriate folder to store the file and click Save.

4) A configuration dialog will appear. You can use this dialog to adjust the settings of the object or scene you are exporting

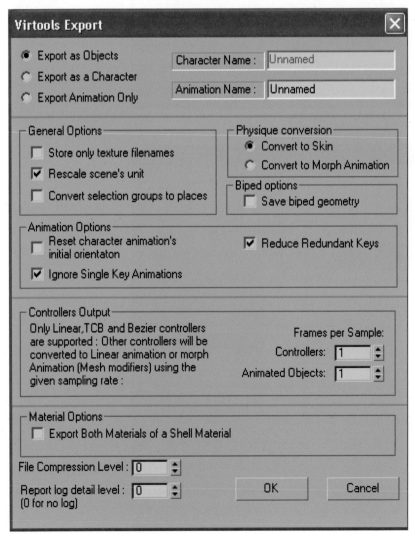

5) In the first section, select 'Export as Objects' Since there is no animation and the object is not a Character we don't need to modify any other settings Click OK and we are finished with first part of our export

Now that the object has been converted from the 3ds Max format to a Virtools compatible (NMO) format, the second set of steps is to get the object into Virtools. Follow the steps below to import the object;
1) Start Virtools and select Resources \ Import File.

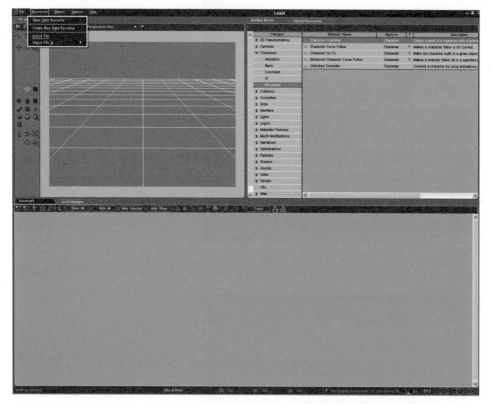

2) Now locate the file you just exported from 3ds Max, select it and click OK.

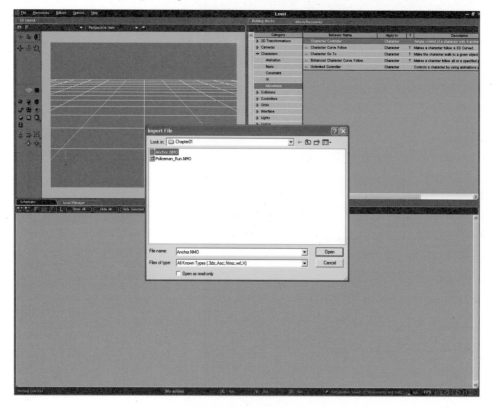

3) You will see the object appear in the Virtools 3D Layout window. The object is not centered in the window and is completely black. We need to center the object on screen and add a light to our scene in order to see the texture.

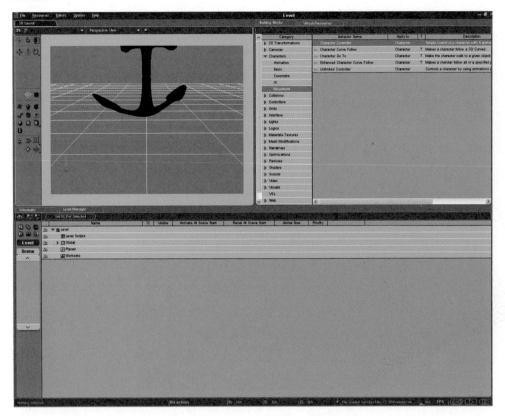

4) Click the Pan icon and move the Anchor so that it is centered in the viewport. Next click the light bulb icon to add a light. A completed version of this composition is available in Sample CMOs \ Chapter01 \ Lesson06_01_Finished.cmo

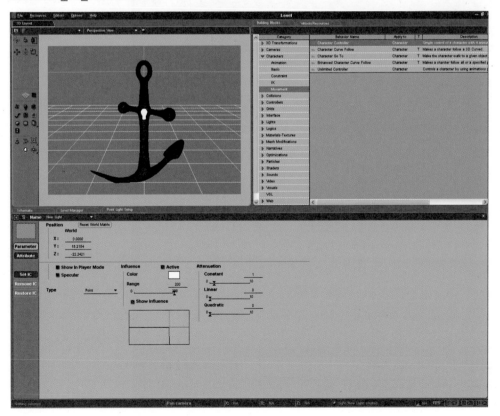

1.6.2 Exporting an Animated Character to Virtools

1) Start 3ds Max and select Open from the file menu.

2) On the CD open the file Sample CMOs\Chapter 1\Policeman_Run.max.

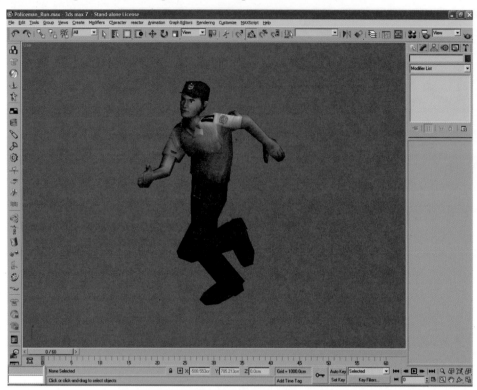

3) You will see a character appear in the 3ds Max view port – click the play button to view the characters animation; this activates the run loop which we will export to Virtools. Select File \ Export and change the type to Virtools *.NMO .VMO

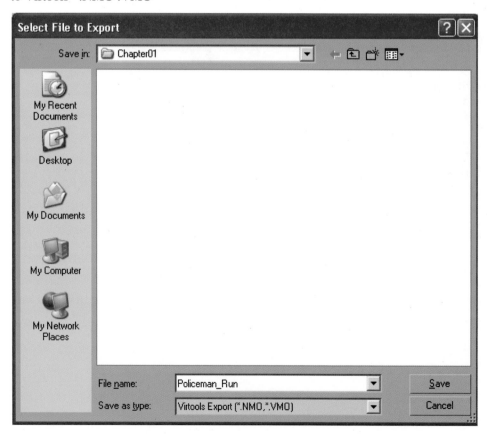

4) Enter ' Policeman_Run' into the name textbox and select a location to save the file.

5) The configuration dialog will appear; select Export As Character.

6) Change the Character Name to 'Policeman' and the Animation Name to 'Running'. In the Controllers Output section, set the Samples Per Frame settings to 1 for both Controllers and Animated Objects. This will ensure our animation is smooth and matches what we see in 3ds Max.

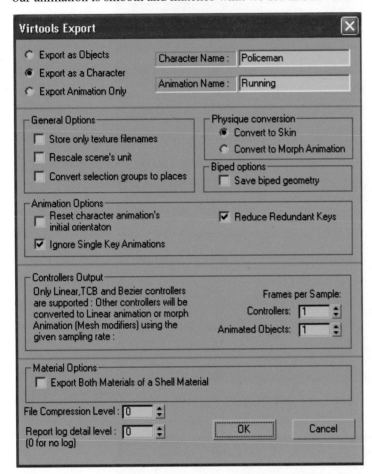

7) Start Virtools and select File \ New Composition to clear our workspace then Select Resources \ Import. In the Import dialog, select 'Policeman_Run.NMO' and click Open.

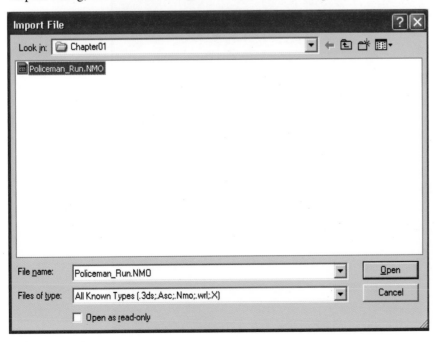

8) Our Policeman appears in Virtools, but he is rather small and dark. To fix this, click the light bulb icon next to the 3D Layout Window to create a light. Then click the Zoom button and move the camera closer to the character.

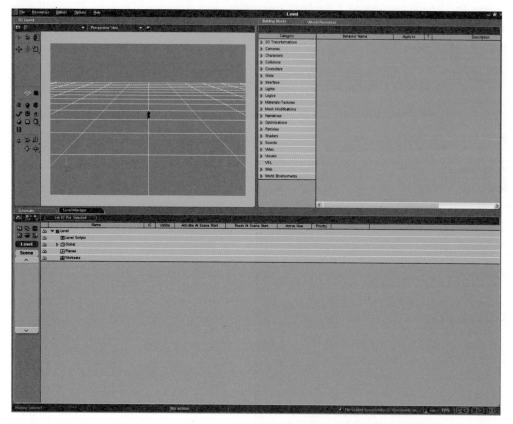

9) Right click the character in the 3D Layout window and select Create Script On \ Policeman(Character) from the popup menu.

10) In the Building Blocks menu, select Characters \ Movement and drag the Character Controller BB into the Script window.

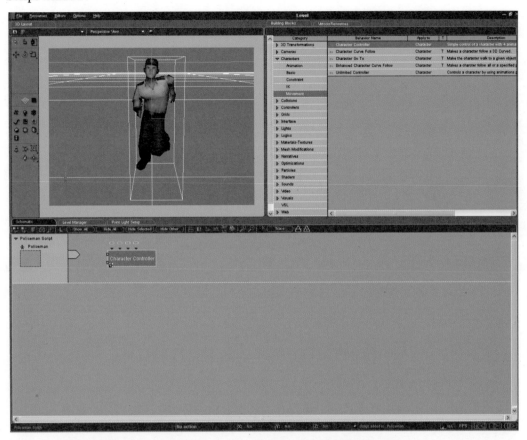

11) Drag a connector from the Start Node to the Character Controller On Pin.

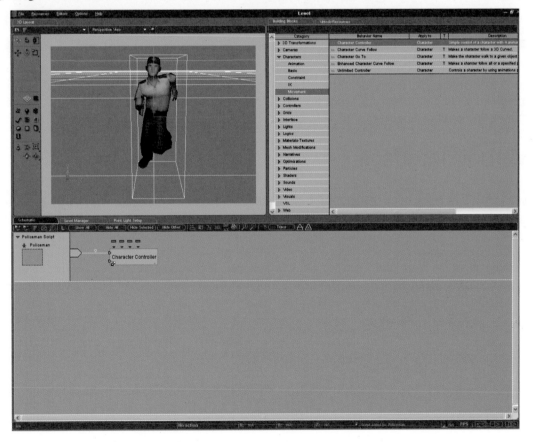

12) Double click the Character Controller BB and the configuration dialog will appear. Change the Stand Animation parameter to Running.

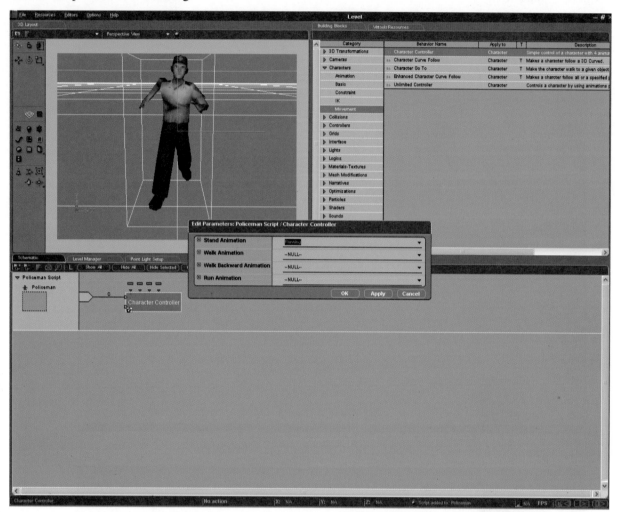

13) Click the Play button and our Policeman starts running. You have just successfully exported a 3ds Max physique character including its bones into Virtools where you can modify all of its parameters in real-time. If you had problems getting this working, Open the file Sample CMOS \ Chapter01 \ Lesson06_02_Finished. cmo to learn how to configure the scene.

2.0 The Virtools Interface

Virtools has a similar look to many other 3D applications, but that's where the similarities end. Virtools is a real-time 3D development environment and as such has a lot of panels and options you won't find in applications like 3ds Max and Maya.

Let's start by learning about the main user interface areas in Virtools. The workspace of Virtools can be divided into five distinct sections; the Menu Bar, 3D Layout panel, Building Blocks panel, Level Manager panel and the Status Bar.

Each area has one or more special functions which you will quickly become familiar with as you begin using Virtools. The Building Blocks and Level Manager areas are used as a docking station for various configuration dialogs whereas the 3D Layout area is used specifically for laying-out and visualizing your scene.

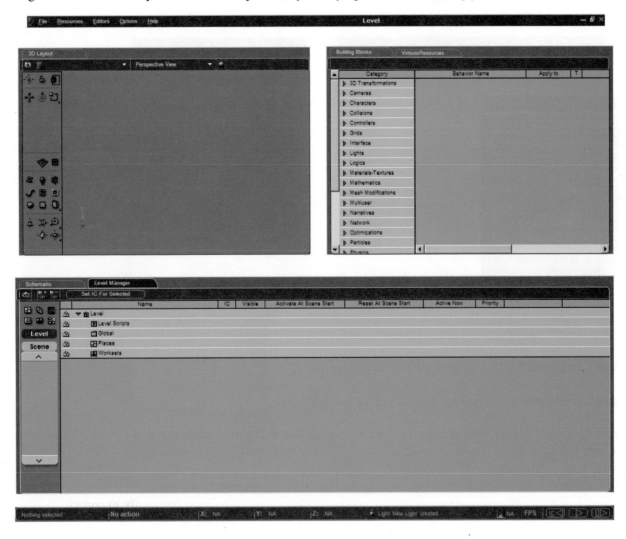

In the next section, we will introduce each of the main areas and describe their uses and options.

2.1 The Menu Bar

The Menu Bar contains all the options for loading, saving and exporting your compositions as well as access to the various editors and managers. In this section we will look at the most important menu options and explain their various functions.

2.1.1 The File Menu

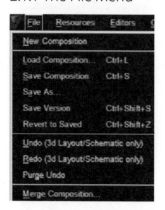

New Composition resets the Virtools workspace, unloads all previous level data and creates an empty level for you to begin working in.

Load Composition allows you to load a saved project file.

Save Composition saves the level you are currently working on.

Save As is used to save the project to another file name. Use this option when you don't want to overwrite an existing file.

Save Version functions much the same as Save As except that it appends a sequential number to the end of the file.

Revert to Saved is used in conjunction with the Save Version option to restore the last version of your project.

Merge Composition is used to merge other projects into the current project.

Merge Composition as New Scene takes an existing project and adds it as a new scene to your current project. This makes it easier to identify which assets belong to your current scene and which assets were added from your loaded project.

Export to Virtools Player creates a version of your project that can be viewed using the Web Player component. The exported file (known as a VMO) is not editable.

Create Web Page functions much like the Export to Virtools Player option, but it also creates a HTML page configured specifically for viewing your project. This page can be run on any PC or Mac that meets the minimum specifications and has the Virtools Web Player component installed. (If it is not installed, the browser will try to automatically download it).

Print Schematic allows you to print out your scripts schematic data for analysis. This is useful if you have large, complex schematics that don't fit on your screen.

Exit unloads your project and exits Virtools.

2.1.2 The Resources Menu

When creating your project in Virtools it is common to put all your media and assets into a common database or resource pool for easy access and to keep things organized. The Resources menu is used to create such a database and for loading external media.

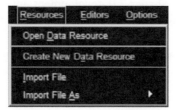

Open Data Resource loads an existing database and makes it available as a tab in the Building Blocks area.

Create New Data Resource is used to create a new database for all the resources used by your project. Once your Data Resource is created, it will be available as a tab in the Building Blocks area.

Import File is used to import external media such as 3D models and Virtools NMO files.

Import File As allows you to import a file as a specific type such as a Character, Scene or Place.

2.1.3 The Editors Menu

The editors menu gives you access to various configuration and setup dialogs used to control both the Virtools environment and your project. Let's take a brief look at what each manager does;

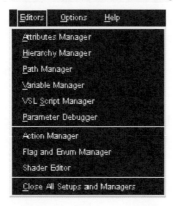

Attribute Manager is used to set various attributes of entities within your project. E.g. setting a plane entity as a floor or setting a 3D Frame as a particle emitter.

Hierarchy Manager is a parent\child style manager that contains a hierarchical list of all the entities within your project. You can use to manually adjust Z-Order and entity relationships.

Path Manager is used to specify default file paths for Virtools related data (like sounds, textures and objects).

Variable Manager configures Virtools environment variables such as anti-aliasing and number of Undo levels.

VSL Script Manager is used to edit and debug your VSL scripts within Virtools. VSL Scripts are often used to perform calculations or functions that would otherwise be overly complicated if created using BB's.

Parameter Debugger can be used to track the values of various Building Block inputs and outputs. Think of it as a central window to view any input\output values from any Building Block in your project.

Action Manager is a recent addition to Virtools and allows you to use VSL to script actions (similar to Macros in Microsoft Word) that can be used to automate almost any aspect or entity in Virtools in design-time (not runtime)

Flag and Enum Manager was added in Virtools 3.5. The Flag and Enum manager allows you to define user parameters which have a name and integer value; Both Flags and Enum's are available to Schematic's and VSL Scripts.

Shader Editor is a full Pixel and Vertex Shader 3.0 development environment where you can create, load, edit and debug Shader code directly in Virtools, of course all updated in real-time.

Close All Setups and Managers does exactly what it says. It leaves only the default tabs open; good for quickly cleaning up your workspace.

2.1.4 The Options Menu

The options menu is used to configure Virtools' preferences and customize the development environment to suite your project.

General Preferences is used to configure the Virtools environment. You can modify Virtools default parameters such as Preview Resolution and Schematic Color Coding.

Check for Updates at Next Startup forces Virtools to connect to the Internet and check for newer versions of its components the next time you start.

Activate Trace Mode enables you to see the execution progress of Building Blocks in your Schematic by coloring the active links and BB's red (very useful for checking scripts, but a large number of complex scripts can use a lot of CPU power to trace).

Unused Object Explorer displays a list of assets or media in your project that are not used by any other entity or active at any time.

Refresh Windows refreshes all the active windows in your composition and resets the 3 main panels to their default sizes.

Reset Interface docks all separated windows and resets the 3 main panels to their default sizes.

Building Block Version Test checks all the default and custom Building Blocks used by Virtools to ensure their compatibility with your current version.

Installed Plug-ins shows a categorized list of all the various plug-ins used by Virtools from Bitmap Readers to Building Blocks.

2.1.5 The Help Menu

The Help menu gives you access to the online reference, which is one of Virtools' strongest features. You will likely use the context sensitive help often as it contains explanations and examples of every Building Block in Virtools.

Online Reference opens the main help document for Virtools and contains a myriad of information and examples on every aspect of the application.

About Virtools opens a dialog that shows the version information of Virtools and gives you access to the system information of your computer.

2.2 The 3D Layout Panel

The 3D Layout Panel contains a toolbar for creating various entities, manipulating the 3D world and a preview window. It can further be divided into several subsections; the top toolbar, selection and transformation controls, guide controls, object creation controls, camera manipulation controls and the preview panel.

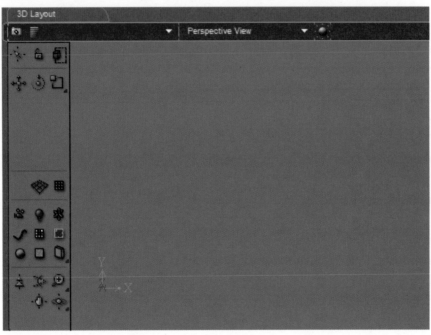

2.2.1 The Top Toolbar

Snapshot is used to capture the preview panel. This icon can then be assigned to a script or object to visually identify it.

3D Layout Explorer gives you a tree like view of all the objects in your project and allows name based selection instead of using the 3D view which is useful if your scene contains a lot of small or hidden objects.

Selection Groups is a drop-down list box that displays groups defined in the Level Manager. For example you could have a group called 'Obstacles' and use the Selection Groups panel to quickly select all the objects for editing.

Available Cameras contains a list of all the default and custom defined cameras in your level. Selecting a camera from this list changes the active camera in the preview panel.

General Preferences opens Virtools' configuration dialog. It can also be accessed through the Top Menu by clicking on Options \ General Preferences.

2.2.2 Selection and Transformation Controls

Select lets you select an object to manipulate by left clicking on it.

Lock Selection disables the selection of any other objects other than the currently selected object or objects.

Selection Mode sets the type of object selection; to be selected either the object must be completely inside the selection rectangle or alternatively the object needs only to intersect with the selection rectangle to be selected.

Translate moves an entity in 3D space. It also includes options for constraining the movement axis and plane and using a different axis referential.

Rotate rotates an object in 3D space. Much like translate it also includes the same constraint and referential options.

Scale adjusts the size of the object and has 3 modes of operation. Uniform Scale scales the object equally along all three axes. Volumetric Scale keeps the volume of the object the same but scales the object along an axis or plane constraint. Normal Scaling allows you to scale the object along any axis or plane but the volume and aspect of the object will not be respected.

2.2.3 The Guide Controls

Toggle Reference Guide turns the 3D reference grid on and off.

Toggle Screen Guide turns the 2D layout grid on and off.

2.2.4 Object Creation Controls

Create Camera creates a configurable camera in your scene.

Create Light creates a point light source in your scene.

Create 3D Frame creates a 3D Frame that is used as a reference in 3D space. A 3D Frame has a position, orientation and scale, but it not visible at runtime.

Create Curve creates a curve or spline which can be used as a path or guide for other entities.

Create 2D Grid creates a special kind of grid in which each unit can be customized and referenced by other entities. The 2D Grid is useful for path finding and creating player boundaries.

Create 2D Frame creates a 2D Frame that is used as a reference for 2D operations.

Create Material creates a material that can be assigned to a 3D entity or have a Shader applied to it.

Create Texture creates an empty texture entity.

Create Portal creates a portal in the front of your scene. Portals are used along with Places to avoid unnecessary calculations for objects that are not in the cameras field of view.

2.2.5 The Camera Manipulation Controls

Dolly moves the camera forwards or backwards

Field of View adjusts the camera's cone of visibility much the same as using a wide-angle or zoom lens on a traditional camera.

Zoom lets you get closer or further away from objects in your scene.

Pan moves the camera along it's local XY plane

Orbit Target \ Orbit Around moves the camera around its target keeping the same distance at all times.

2.2.6 The Preview Panel

The preview panel is the visual window into your scene. The preview panel lets you manipulate objects at design time and preview the output at runtime.

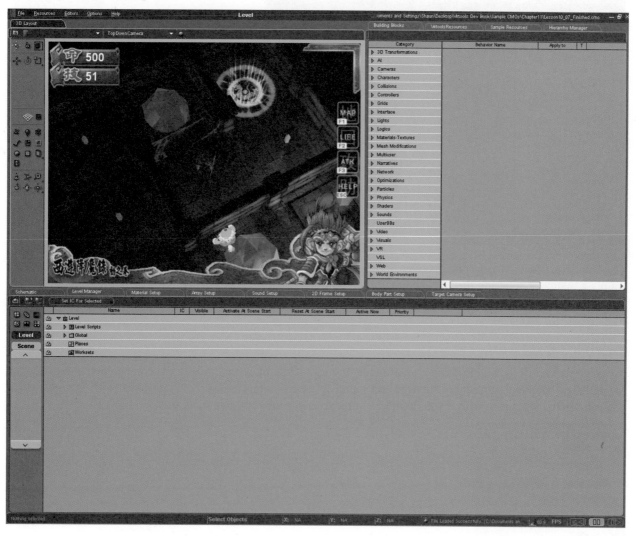

2.3 The Building Blocks panel

The Building Blocks panel is in fact just a docking area that by default has the first tab as Building Blocks. This panel can contain any tabbed dialog, which can be dragged from one area to another. We have used the name 'Building Blocks panel' because it was easier than calling it the 'upper right-hand tabbed dialog area'.

2.3.1 Building Blocks

Building blocks are one of the key features that make Virtools so different from any other 3D development application. The best way to think of Building Blocks is as small pieces of compiled code that can be linked and configured to give you the result you want. To simply illustrate this explanation, imagine you have a 3D cube object and you want to be able to move it around using the keyboard. Using other 3D engines, this is a reasonably complex task involving many steps and a lot of code. But in Virtools, you can use a few BB's to accomplish the same task all in under a minute. Of course there are other factors to consider and everything is not always this simple, but Virtools certainly makes the basic tasks in developing 3D applications a lot less time consuming.

Of course there are benefits with writing custom code for certain elements of your application and this is where VSL and the Virtools SDK are useful.

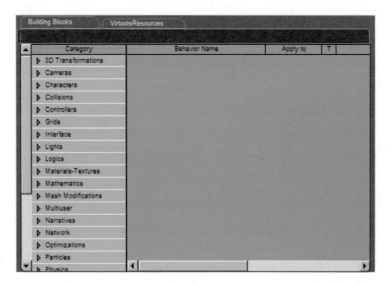

The Building Blocks panel contains over 500 different BB's all categorized into various groups. Using a BB is simply a matter of selecting the BB and dragging it onto your objects script (some BB's can only be dragged onto certain types of objects). From there you set its input parameters and link it with other BB's to get the result you want.

2.3.2 Virtools Resources

Every project needs to contain some kind of media to make it useful; a typical Virtools composition would contain 3D models, characters, animations, images and sounds. A set of default resources is provided with Virtools which you can use to experiment with if you don't have time to create all your own media.

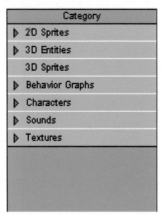

Using Virtools you can also create your own Resources database. In fact the Resources database is reasonably simple; it is basically a set of folders which each contain files categorized by their type. For example, all textures ('.tga', '.png' and '.jpg files) are stored under the Textures folder.

2.4 The Level Manager Panel

The Level Manager Panel takes up the lower half of the Virtools workspace and by default contains two tabs; Level Manager and Schematic. The Level Manager panel functions in exactly the same way as the Building Blocks panel in that you can drag any tabbed dialog into the area and dock it.

2.4.1 Level Manager

The Level Manager is a hierarchical list of all of the elements of your project; from the 3D models and Materials to the Scripts and Scenes.

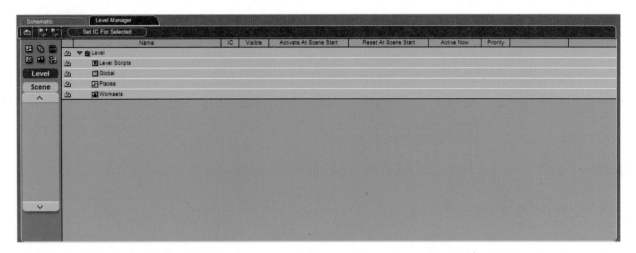

In the left hand section of the Level Manager you will see a number of buttons and a list style control. The toolbar contains six icons with the following functions;

Create Place is used to create separate locations in your level in order to increase performance.

Create Group allows you to group types of objects together.

Create Array is used to create a data array similar to a row and column database (it can also store objects and parameter for any entity in Virtools).

Create Scene lets you divide your level up into discreet narrative elements, like introduction, main menu and end scene etc.

Create Workset allows you to group together any kind of entity regardless of its type.

Create Script creates a new script for the object selected in the Level Manager.

The list style control allows you to change the scope of view in the Level Manager. There are two options; Level view and Scene view. Using the Level view allows you to edit objects and scripts for your entire level and Scene view modifies objects and scripts only for a particular scene. The up and down arrows let you navigate your available scenes if you have more than the list can display.

2.5 The Status Bar

The status bar basically has two main functions. The first is to give you feedback about the currently selected object, tool and debug data of your level, the second is to access the playback controls.

Selection shows you the currently selected object.

Action displays the name of the currently selected tool.

XYZ Coordinates displays the world position of the current object.

Event Log displays an output window containing Virtools events, warnings and error messages. By default, the status bar displays the last line of event output. Clicking on the icon opens a list window containing all event messages.

FPS displays the number of frames Virtools is processing per second in runtime. In design time, it will display the word 'FPS' as nothing is being processed.

Reset IC resets the Initial Conditions of all entities and stops level playback.

Play \ Pause starts and suspends the playback of your level.

Step One Frame allows you to advance frame-by-frame through the execution of your level.

3.0 Naming Conventions and Best Practice Concepts

In this section we start by introducing Virtools' naming conventions for entities, concepts and methodologies that you will need to understand before going further. As with most technical software, Virtools has some unique features and conventions that once you understand, will make learning the software much easier.

3.1 Virtools Naming Conventions

Let's start by introducing the basic objects and elements typically used in a standard project;

Media is any external asset used within Virtools. Media could be a 3D Mesh, texture or sound. All media is loaded into Virtools either from a Resource database or using the Resources \ Import or Import As menu.

3D Entities are objects that exist within the 3D environment of your project. For example; a character, light, camera or 3D Frame.

3D Frames can be considered the simplest form of 3D Entities and are not visible at runtime. 3D Frames contain data like position, orientation and scale but have no visible properties.

Characters are special entities in Virtools and have a unique set of sub-categories such as Animations and Body Parts. Despite its name, a Character object is not necessarily a character as such, but could be a car or plane; in fact any 3D Object can be a character. Characters are 3D Objects which fall under the category of 3D Entities.

Cameras come in two different flavors; a Free Camera which merely has a position and orientation and a Target Camera which always looks to its target vector.

Lights in Virtools have 3 types; the Point Light, the Spot Light and the Directional Light.

Curves in Virtools are similar to splines in typical 3D modeling applications and can be used as paths for 3D Entities.

2D Entities are elements in Virtools that have only 2 dimensions of scale. 2D Frames and 2D Sprites are the two kinds of 2D Entities available in Virtools.

Groups contain sets of same-type entities and are used to make multi-object operations more efficient. The entities in a group are references to the originals and not copies.

Places are similar in concept to layers in Photoshop and are used to spatially divide areas within your Scene or Level. An entity can only belong to one place at one time; if an entity needs to be in multiple places you can make it 'global' so it is part of the Level.

Scenes are used to add narrative partitions to your project. To illustrate the concept more clearly, Scenes are used to organize time segmentation whereas Places are used to segment areas of space. Unlike Places, entities can belong to many Scenes at any one time.

Levels are the parent object of the entire composition. There can only be one Level in a composition and to create another level is to create another composition.

3.2 Considerations for Importing from 3ds Max

Virtools supplies a set of importers for the most recent versions of Autodesk's 3ds Max. For the examples in this book we use 3ds Max version 7. Using the exporter we can very quickly bring models, cameras, lights and other objects directly into Virtools.

The export utilities are updated independently of Virtools releases; you should check the Virtools web site for the latest version which will likely include new export options and bug fixes.

3.2.1 3D Model Data

Before exporting your 3D models from 3ds Max you should first ensure that they have been converted to a mesh. The exported parameters are;

- Mesh data
- Mapping coordinates
- Smoothing groups
- Normals
- Materials
- Vertex color including alpha value

3.2.2 Resetting the Models Transform

To avoid problems importing your objects into Virtools, the transformations of your 3D objects should be reset using the Reset XForm utility in 3ds Max. The Reset XForm utility aligns pivot points and bounding boxes with the World Coordinate system and places any modifications in an XForm modifier at the top of the object modifier stack.

To use the Reset XForm on an object;

1) Select the object
2) Click the Utilities panel and click the Reset XForm button
3) In the Reset XForm rollout, click the Reset Selected button

An XForm modifier is now at the top of the selected objects modifier stack. You can absorb the modifications into the mesh or delete the modifier to completely remove transformations.

3.2.3 Exporting Materials

The following material data of 3ds Max objects is exported;

1) Diffuse Map; although not a requirement, you should try to ensure your texture size is to the power of 2 (i.e. 2,4,8,16...256,512,1024 etc).
2) Diffuse Color; this color influences the materials response to light unless its value is 255,255,255.
3) Ambient Color
4) Specular Color

5) 2-Sided Flag
6) Opacity
7) Texture Cropping; Note that you cannot crop and tile a texture at the same time.
8) Texture U/V Offset
9) Face Map Flag
10) Both Materials of a Shell Material

When selecting textures for your models don't think that a compressed JPG file will be more efficient than an uncompressed BMP of the same size. When a JPG is loaded into video memory it is converted into an uncompressed format (unless you configure the Texture parameters differently in Virtools) and takes the same amount of memory with a lower quality than the equivalent BMP file. Also avoid using 8bit files as they are not supported and may cause problems in Virtools.

Note that both DirectX and OpenGL support the Direct Draw Surface (DDS) file format; Textures saved in a compressed DDS format can actually be sent directly to the graphics card without conversion or decompression; i.e. they are stored natively in the graphics cards memory and can considerably reduce texture memory usage.

3.2.4 Exporting Lights
All lights in your 3ds Max scene will be exported to Virtools; the following parameters are kept;
1) On/off flag
2) Color
3) Range; only the Attenuation, Far and End parameters are exported
4) "Affect Specular" flag
5) Hotspot and Falloff (for Spot lights only)
6) 3ds Max allows a Directional light to be bound to cylinder of influence. This cylinder does not exist in Virtools so the light will influence the entire scene.

3.2.5 Exporting Cameras
All cameras created within 3ds Max including free and target cameras are exported. Exported parameters are as follows;
1) Field of View (FOV)
2) Front and Back Clipping Planes

Note that camera animations are currently not exported to Virtools; you can work around this by animating a Dummy that will be exported and making it the Parent of your Camera in Virtools.

3.2.6 Exporting Dummy Objects
Dummy objects are converted to 3D Frames in Virtools.

3.2.7 Dynamic Animation Data
The animation data for objects and characters can be exported to Virtools. It is recommended that you use Linear, Bezier or TCB (Tension, Continuity and Bias) animation controllers. Linear controllers are preferred as they are the fastest. Remember that when exporting an animation, the higher the sampling rate the larger a file will be. Where possible you should try to use Virtools' internal animation BB's.
In order to export the animation correctly, the key frames of the parent object must be located on the first and last frame of the timeline.

The rotation scope of Virtools is limited to 360° whereas 3ds Max allows rotation to any angle value. Before exporting to Virtools, subdivide any greater than 360° rotations to avoid incorrect animations.

3.2.8 Exporting Curves
A Spline in 3ds Max is converted to a Curve in Virtools and only the Splines vertex data is exported.

3.2.9 Exporting Groups

Exporting a 3ds Max group will result in a 3D Frame being created as a Parent to the objects in the group. To convert a group to a place you can select the Convert Groups to Places option in the exporter. The places can then be used in Virtools for Portal management.

3.2.10 Exporting Bone Data

If the Bone setup in 3ds Max doesn't match the output expected by Virtools, chances are that the characters will not work correctly in Virtools even though there is no problem in 3ds Max. When constructing bones in Character Studio, you should complete the full bone structure before attaching to a mesh.

3.3 Best Practices when using Virtools

The following list contains some important guidelines to keep in mind when using Virtools.

1) Undo / Redo Command

   The Undo and Redo commands only work in the 3D Layout Panel and the Schematic. This is where Initial Conditions (IC) settings become important. If you modify entities in any way within Virtools (and want to keep the changes), you should set their IC. Doing this allows you to use the Reset IC button in the status bar to revert all entities in your scene to their initial conditions.

2) Curves

   Although you can use Virtools to create Curves, a better approach is to use 3ds Max's Spline function and then export them to Virtools.

3) World-Space Units

   In the 3D Layout window you can see a 3D grid that represents 'ground zero' of your 3D space. It is important to remember that one square of this grid represents one Meter in the real world. This becomes useful when using physics in your project as the size of objects affects the weight when the physic engine is calculating the scene dynamics.

4) Animated GIF Files

   Virtools does not support animated GIFs. If you want to animate a series of images there is a movie play function that reads the slots of a sprite.

5) Image Compression

   Don't be deceived by using highly compressed images to keep your CMO files small. A JPG and equivalent TGA file will take the same amount of space in your CMO file as Virtools performs its own internal compression when saving media. Note that this can be changed in Virtools using the General Preferences panel or on a per-texture basis.

6) Object Manipulation

   Where possible try to use Virtools' internal BB's for transformation, rotation and scaling as importing these kinds of animations from your 3D modeling software will use a considerable amount of space.

7) Mesh Deformation

   Basic mesh deformations can be performed in the Virtools environment rather than being imported as an animation from your 3D modeling application. BB's exist for functions such as Bend, Noise, Taper and Twist. Using these BB's saves space and gives more real-time editing scope.

8) Un-exportable Effects

   The Explode effect in 3ds Max is not supported in Virtools. Instead, use the Explode BB in Virtools to create a similar effect.

9) Material Effects

3ds Max material effects such as transformation, rotation and scaling are not exportable to Virtools, again there are built in BB's that give you equivalent functionality.

10) Referencing Materials

When copying objects within Virtools, the objects Material will not be copied, but will reference the original.

11) Arrays

Get used to using Arrays. Arrays allow you to store a wide variety of data and objects and make it possible to create complex games using sophisticated data structures. Arrays are an essential part of almost every project you will create in Virtools. We recommend you get as familiar as possible with Arrays; it will make your time in Virtools a lot more enjoyable.

12) Save Version

Try to use Save Version often as this gives you an easy option to do a point-in-time restore if you make a serious mistake and don't realize until later.

13) Portals

Portals provide a good way to hide areas that are not visible to the user and can save a lot of processing power.

Chapter02 getting started with virtools

1.0 Data Resources and Initial Conditions

In this lesson we show you how to create a new Data Resource and load an existing Data Resource from the file system. The Data Resource concept in Virtools is basically a way to categorize various media in a way that can be easily accessed from within the Virtools interface. Think of a Data Resource as a categorized list that points to physical files (like mesh files, images and sounds) on your hard disk drive.

1.1 Creating a Data Resource

1) Click the Resources menu and select Create New Data Resource.

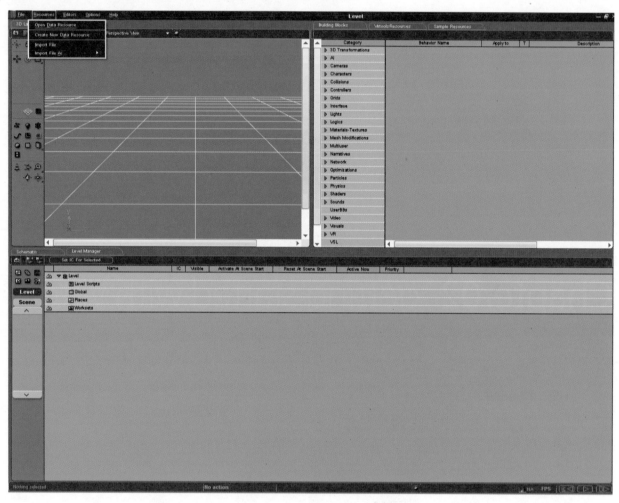

2) Select an appropriate folder in which to create the data resource. Enter "Test Resource" in the File Name box as we will only use this resource for this lesson. Click Save to finish.

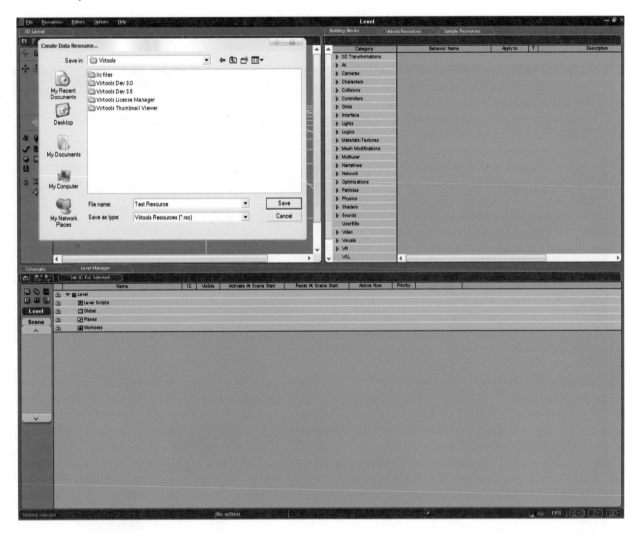

3) Test Resource now appears as a tab in the top-right window. Any data from external applications can be saved in the corresponding directory within the resource folder for easy access via Virtools.

To better understand the use of resources in Virtools, open Windows Explorer and navigate to the folder where you created Test Resource, look at the names of the subfolders and you will see they match the categories of the Test Resource tab in Virtools.

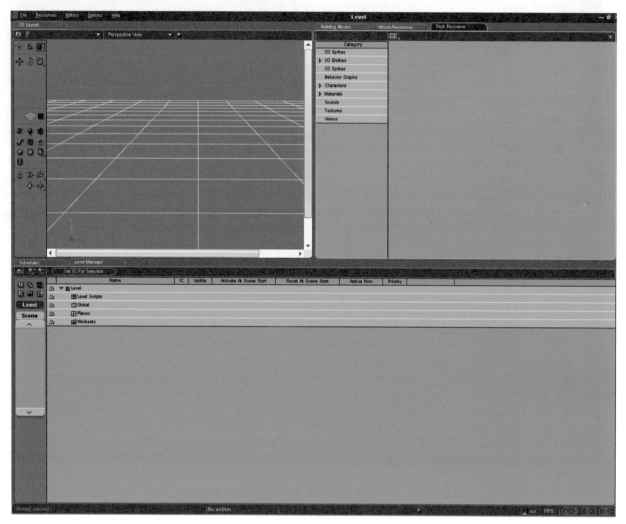

1.2 Loading a Data Resource

1) Click the Resources menu and select Open Data Resource.

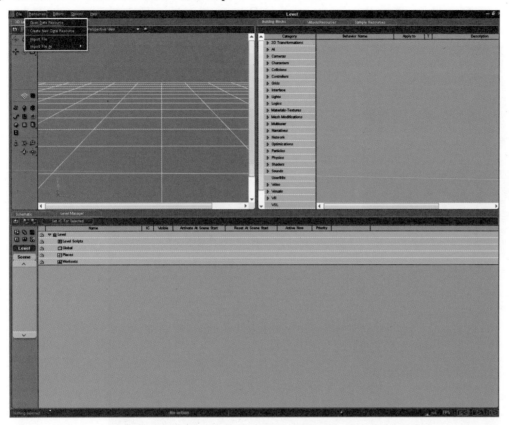

2) Ensure you have the CD included with this book in the drive then navigate to the folder called Sample Resources. Click on the file called "Sample Resources.rsc" and click Open.

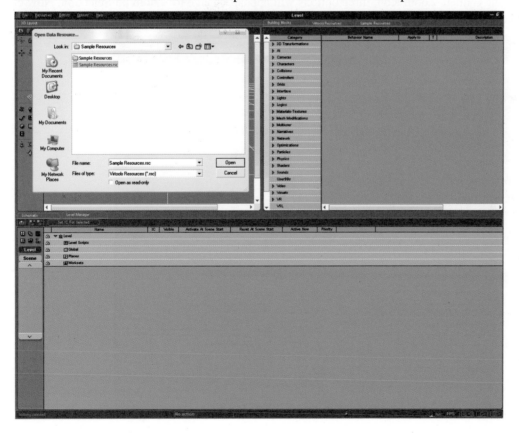

1.3 Loading an Object and Adjusting its Properties

1) Make sure the Sample Resources tab is selected then click on the Characters item in the list. You will see an object called Treasure Chest.nmo. Drag the object into the 3D layout window. The object appears to be too close to the screen and is obscuring our view.

2) From the left hand toolbar, click the Select icon (or press 'A') and click on the object in the 3D layout window. Click and hold on the Camera Zoom icon, three options will appear, change to Zoom on Selection. Now click the Zoom on Selection icon (or press Shift+'Z') and the object will fit within the window boundaries.

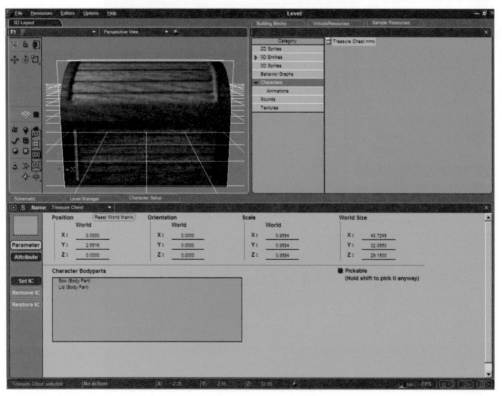

3) To avoid problems with object selection, click the Lock Selection Icon (or press 'Space Bar'). This is useful when you have a lot of objects in your level and need to manipulate them from various views.

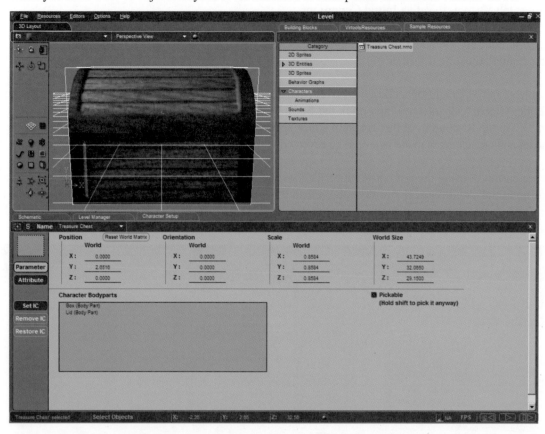

4) Using the Select and Translate tool, adjust the object to match the picture below. You can also use the Camera Dolly tool to move the Camera back from the object.

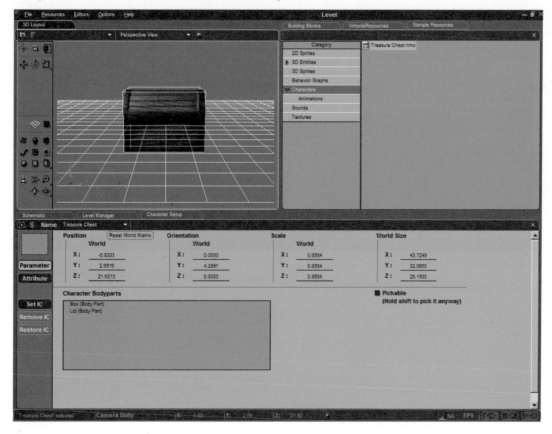

5) The above adjustments have changed the object from its initial state (the state at load time) to another state (state after rotation, transformation and scaling). Since we want to use this current state as the new initial state of the object, we must tell Virtools to set its Initial Conditions.

The Initial Conditions (IC) concept is very important as it gives us a kind of "Undo" function if we want to reset the object after adjusting it further.

To set the objects Initial Conditions, click the Level Manager tab and navigate to the Treasure Chest object (it is located under Global \ Characters) then click the Set IC for Selected button. When you click on Set IC for Selected an "X" in the IC column of the Treasure Chest appears. This means the initial state data for the object has been saved and any changes made later can be reversed using the Restore Initial Conditions command.

(Note: We are currently using the default Perspective view to display our scene; this view is not a real camera and thus has no Initial Conditions. If you save and reload this scene, the position of the Perspective Camera will be reset – if you create a camera and set its IC, its position and orientation will be restored when you reload the composition).

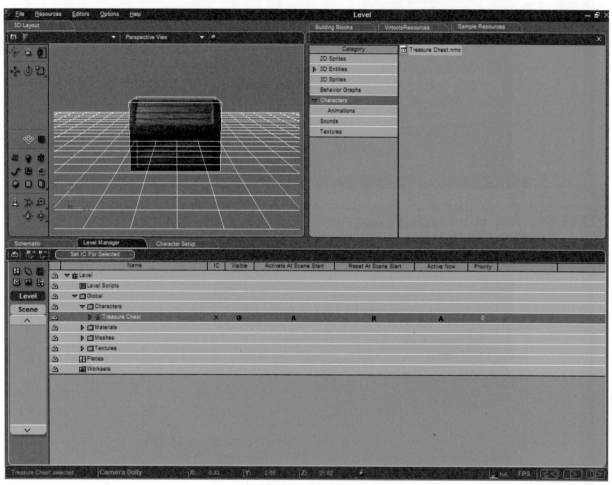

2.0 Object Transformation, Rotation, Scaling

Before getting started on the more advanced features of Virtools, we need to first cover the basics; making an object move. In this lesson we will discover how to use the Virtools environment to add a behavioral script to an entity, create some building blocks in that script and then link everything together to make the object move by itself.

2.1 Adding a Movement Script to a 3D Entity

1) You can use the work from the previous lesson or open the file Lesson02_01_Start.CMO in the Chapter02 folder to get started.
2) Right click the Treasure Chest and select Create Script on Selection in the pop-up menu.

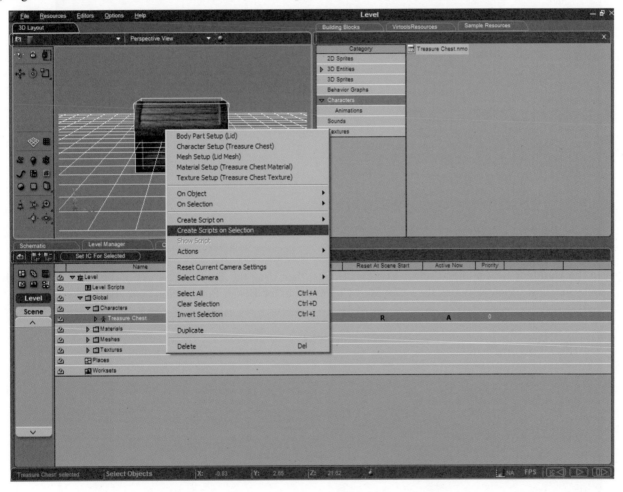

3) Click on the Schematic Window tab to view the Script that is now linked to the treasure chest.

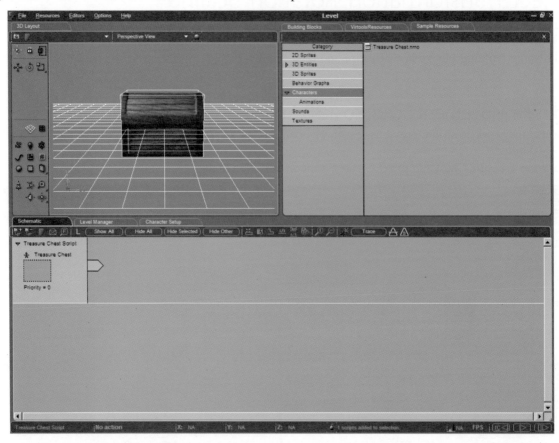

4) In the Building Blocks menu select Logics \ Loops, then drag the Bezier Progression building block to the treasure chest script. Now link the script Start Connector to the Bezier Progression "On" BIn.

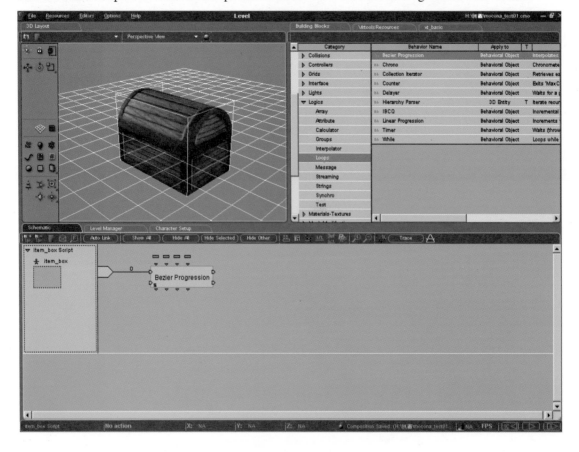

5) In the Building Blocks menu select 3D Transformations \ Basic then drag the Translate building block to the treasure chest script.

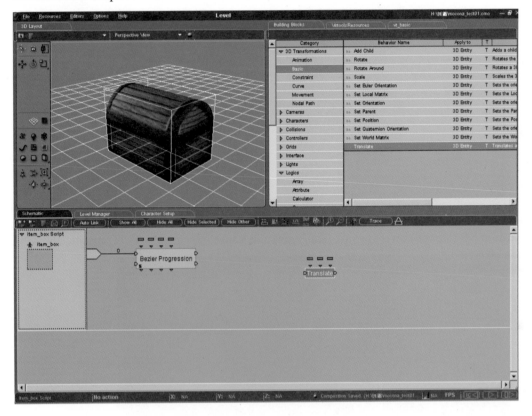

6) Right click in the treasure chest script area (in a blank space) and select the Add Parameter Operation option in the pop-up menu. The Edit Parameter Operation dialogue box will appear, now select Float for the left Input and Vector for the right Input. Next, select Multiplication for the Operation parameter and Vector for the Output parameter.

Note: You can resize the scripting area by dragging the white line down. You can also 'Maximize' the entire Schematic panel, or any panel for that matter, by simply double-clicking on the tab.

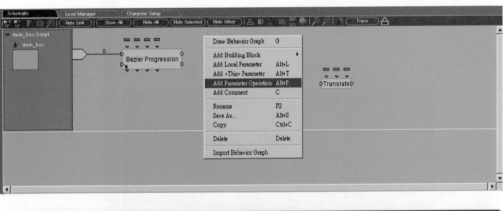

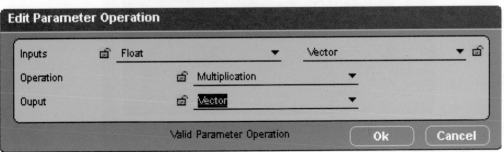

7) Now connect the Loop Out BOut of the Bezier Progression BB to the BIn of the Translate BB. Then connect the BOut of the Translate BB to the Loop In BIn of the Bezier Progression BB to complete the calculation loop.

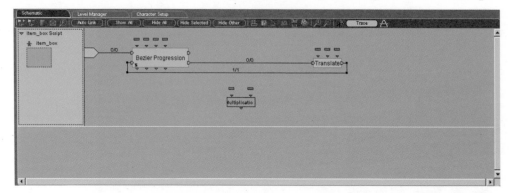

8) Connect the Delta POut of the Bezier Progression BB with Pin 0 (Left PIn) of the Parameter Operation, then connect it's POut to the Translate Vector PIn of the Translate BB. This connection multiplies the data sent from the Bezier Progression BB into the correct format (data type) and Range expected by the Translate BB.

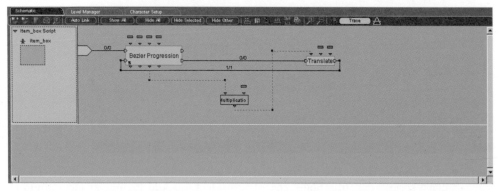

9) Double click the Bezier Progression BB to open the Edit Parameters dialog. Set the Duration to 3 Seconds. Make sure the A value is set to 0 and B value to 1, click OK to confirm and close the panel.

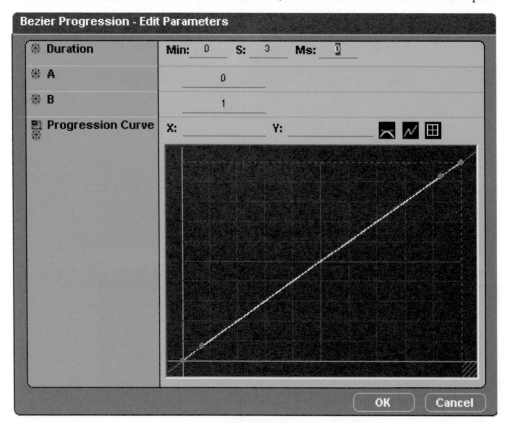

10) Double click the Pin 1 Variable (the block above the right pin) of the Parameter Operation to edit its value. Set the Y parameter to 30.

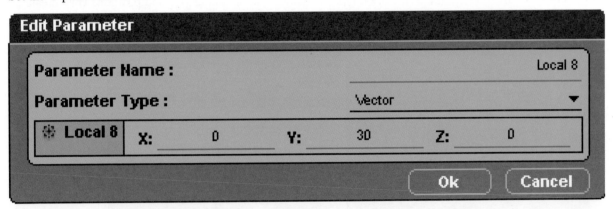

11) Now Click Play to see the Treasure Chest rise upwards.

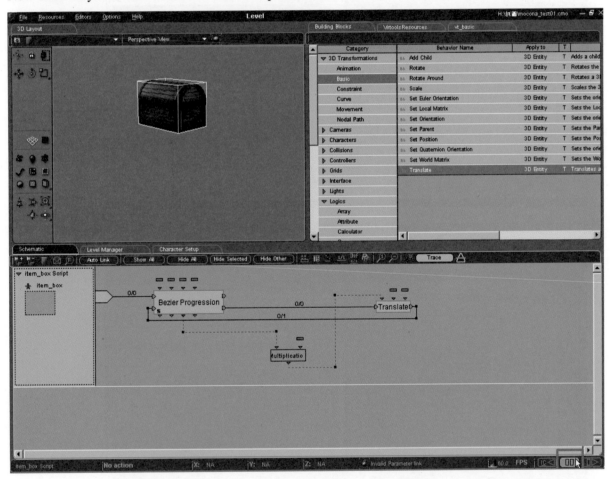

The time parameter of the Bezier Progression BB can be used to control the movement velocity of the object; the shorter the time duration the faster the object moves and vice-versa. This is because we are using the delta value of the Bezier Progression BB to set the amount of movement of the object on the Y axis. The Delta value is equal to the subtraction between the current Bezier-interpolated value and the previous one; the sum of the Delta value at the end of the Duration is always equal to Value B.

During the calculation loop, the Delta value of the Bezier Progression BB is multiplied by 30 and set to the Y Vector value using the Multiplication Parameter Operation. This value is then passed to the Translate BB which moves the treasure chest by the resulting amount and is independent of the computers frame rate.

2.2 Simple Object Rotation

1) First drag the treasure chest into the 3D Layout window to set its initial size and position. Then create a script for the object.

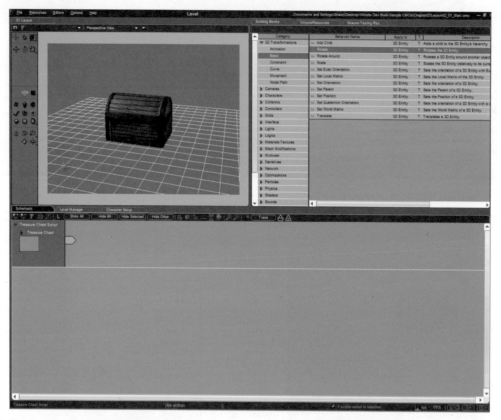

2) In the Building Blocks menu select Logics \ Calculator and drag the Per Second BB into the treasure chest script. Now link the script Start Connector to the Per Second BB BIn.

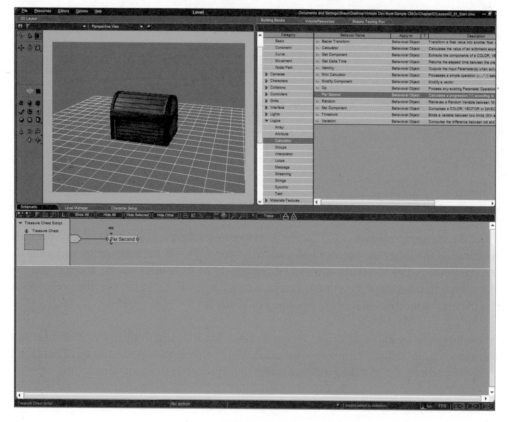

3) In the Building Blocks menu select 3D Transformations \ Basic and drag the Rotate BB into the treasure chest script. Now link the Per Second BB BOut to the Rotate BB BIn. Connect the Rotate BB BOut to the Per Second BB BIn to form a loop.

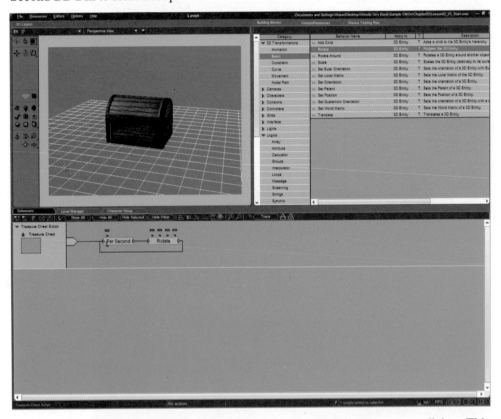

4) Double click the POut of the Per Second BB to open the Edit Parameters dialog. This will allow us to define the type of data that the Per Second BB will calculate. Choose the Angle Parameter Type, since we are dealing with rotation. Click OK to close.

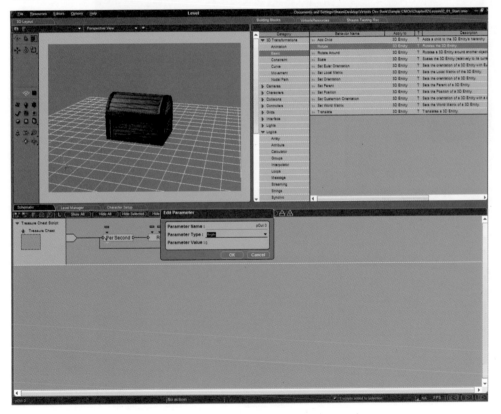

5) Double click the Per Second BB to open Edit Parameters Dialog, and you will see that we can set an angle value (the default is a numeric (float) value). Set the Degree's value to 45.

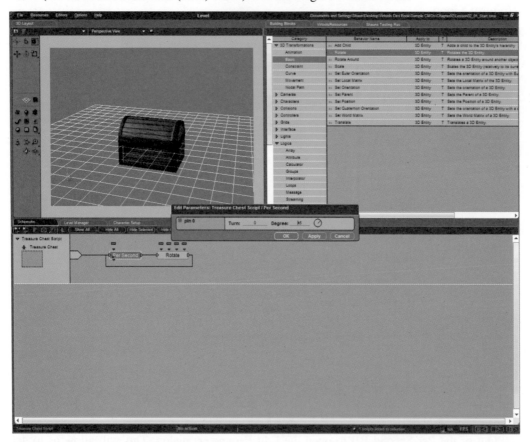

6) Connect the Per Second BB's POut to the Rotate BB's Angle of Rotation Pin. Click Play to test.

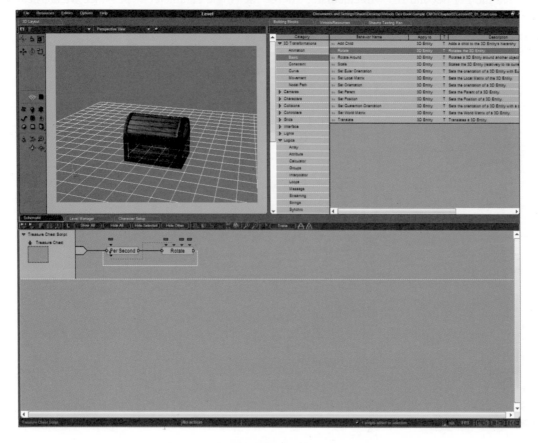

7) The treasure chest will rotate 45° every second, as per our setting in the Per Second BB. This concept is important to understand as not all computers will play your composition at the same frame rate. Just using the Rotate BB, setting a low value for the Angle or Rotation parameter and looping it will produce a similar result, until you play it on a slower or faster computer. The rotation would speed up at higher frame rates and slow down at lower frame rates as the amount of rotation is calculated every frame and not interpolated over time; that is the job of the Per Second BB. You can use it to control many kinds of translation, scaling and rotation behaviors.

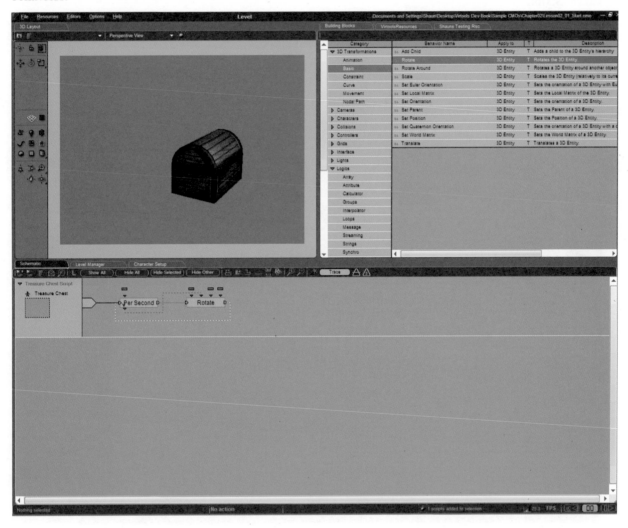

2.3 Advanced Object Rotation

In this lesson we use the Bezier Progression BB with more complex rotation to make the lid of the treasure chest open.

1) Drag the treasure chest into the 3D Layout window to set its initial size and position. Select the Level Manager tab and navigate to Global \ Characters \ TreasureChest \ Body Parts \ TreasureChestLid. Right click and select Create Script.

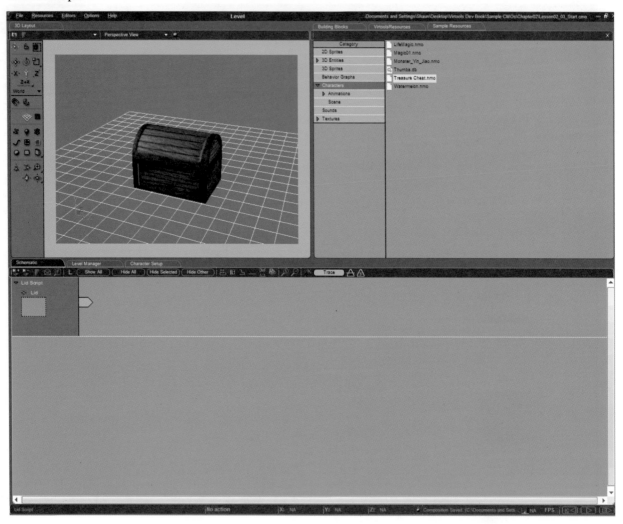

2) In the Building Blocks menu select Logics\Loops and drag the Bezier Progression BB into the treasure chest lid script. Now link the script Start Connector to the Bezier Progression "On" BIn.

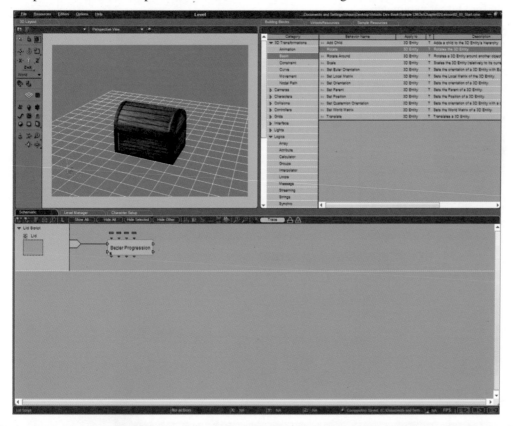

3) Again, in the Building Blocks menu select 3D Transformations\Basic and drag the Rotate BB into the treasure chest lid script. Now link the Bezier Progression "Loop Out" BOut to the Rotate "On" BIn. Connect the Rotate BB BOut to the Bezier Progression "Loop In" BIn to complete the script.

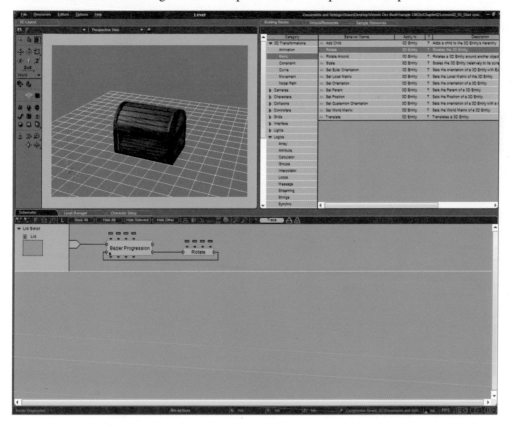

4) Right click in the script area and select Add Parameter Operation. In the parameter dialogue box, select Float for the left parameter Inputs and Angle for the right parameter Input. Select Multiplication for the Operation parameter, and Angle for Output parameter.

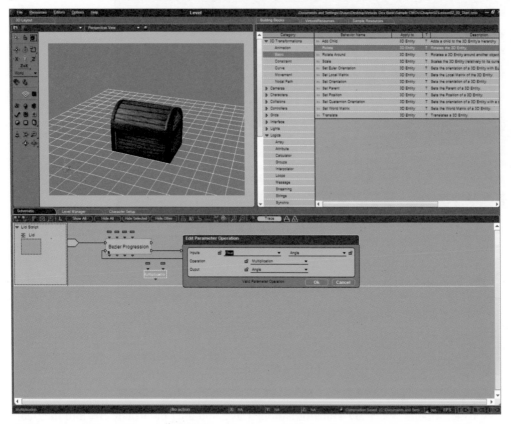

5) Connect the Delta POut of the Bezier Progression BB to Pin 0 of the Multiplication Parameter Operation and then connect the POut to the Angle of Rotation PIn of the Rotate BB.

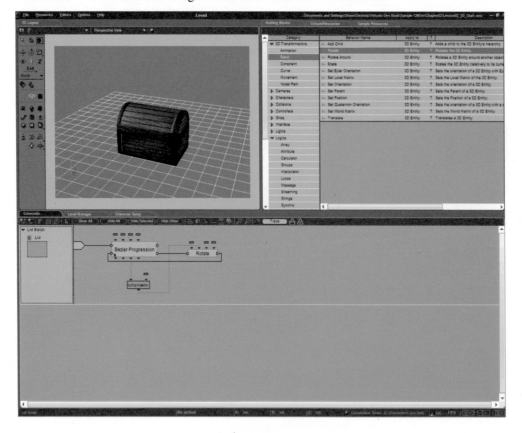

6) Double click the Rotate BB and set the Axis of Rotation to X=1, Y=0, Z=0. This will make the lid rotate around the correct axis.

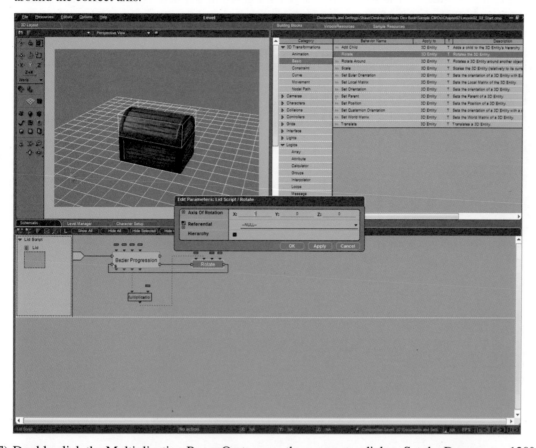

7) Double click the Multiplication ParamOp to open the parameter dialog. Set the Degrees to -120°.

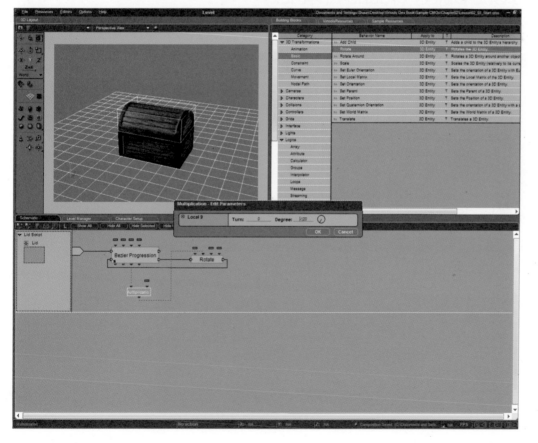

8) Now Click Play, you can see the lid opens by 120°. You can use the Time parameter of the Bezier Progression BB to control the rotation velocity. The role of the Bezier Progression BB here is to control the amount of movement per frame independent of the frame rate, over a given amount of time, using the Delta (time between the current frame and last frame) value.

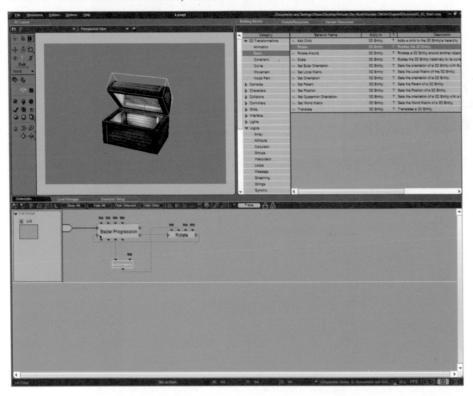

2.4 Revolving One Object Around Another

1) Drag the treasure chest and barrel objects into the 3D Layout window to set their initial size and position. Create a script on the barrel object.

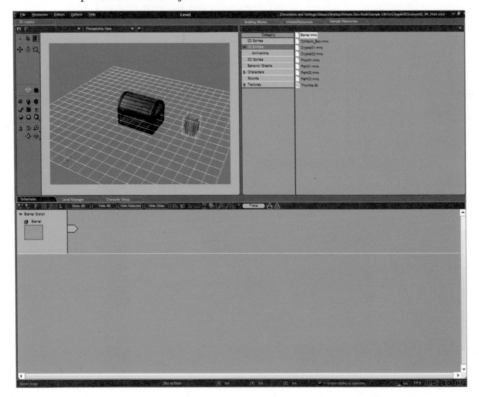

2) Add the Per Second and Rotate Around BB's to the script, connect them in sequence and then form a loop as per the screenshot. Don't forget to connect the Per Second BB's BIn to the Start Node.

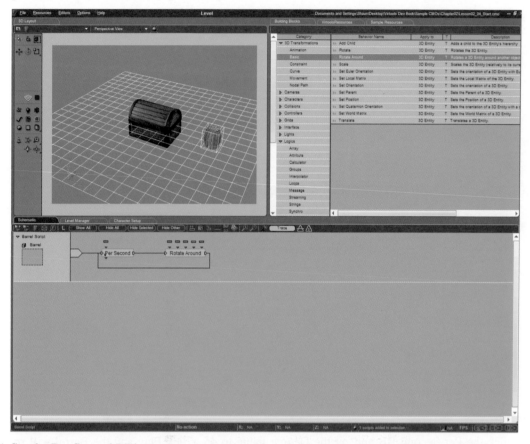

3) Set the Per Second BB's output parameter type to Angle by double clicking on the POut.

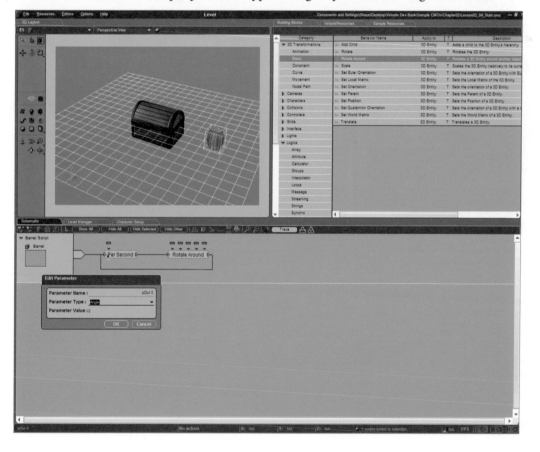

4) Connect the Per Second POut to the Angle of Rotation PIn. Double click the Rotate Around BB and set the Referential parameter to Treasure Chest. Click OK to close.

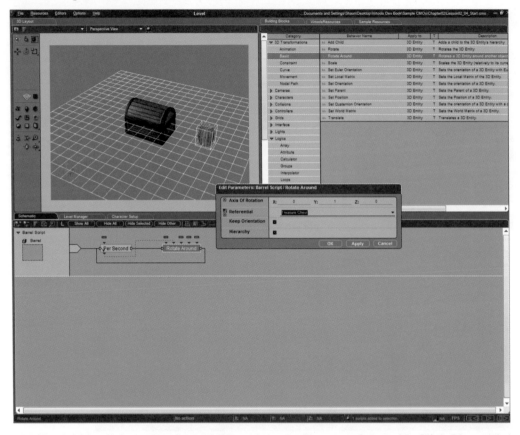

5) Finally, double click the Per Second BB and set the Degree value to 45. Click Play and the Barrel will rotate around our treasure chest.

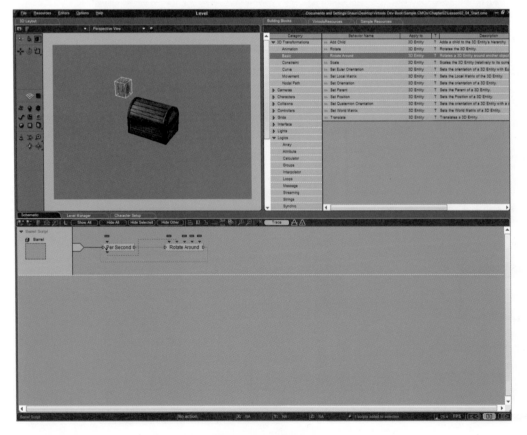

2.5 Object Scaling

1) In this lesson we use the Bezier Progression BB to scale a character. From Characters \ Animations \ Actors drag our character, YinJiao (YinJiao.nmo), into the 3D Layout window and set its initial size and position. Create a script on the object.

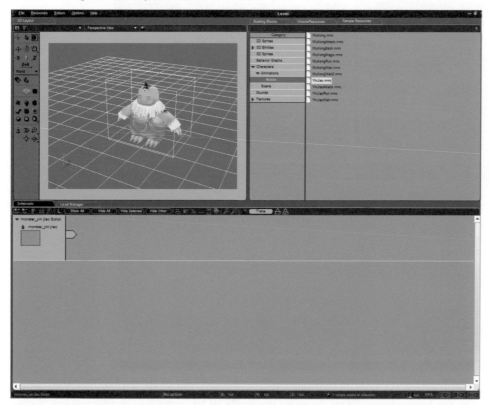

2) In the Building Blocks menu select Logics \ Loops and drag the Bezier Progression BB into the YinJiao script. Now link the script Start Node to the Bezier Progression "On" BIn.

3) In the Building Blocks menu select Logics and drag the Interpolation BB into the YinJiao script. Now link the Interpolation BIn to the Bezier Progression "Loop Out" BIn.

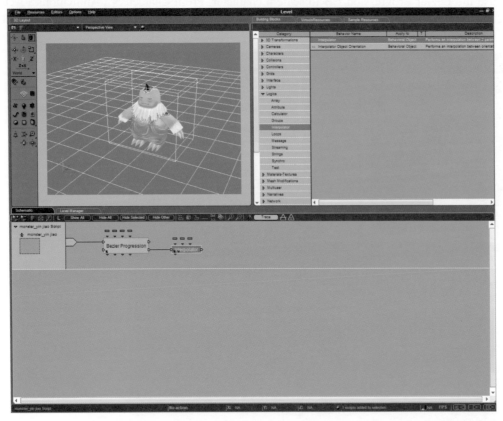

4) In the Building Blocks menu select 3D Transformations \ Basic and drag the Scale BB into the YinJiao script. Now link the Scale BIn to the Interpolation BOut. Connect the Scale BOut to the Bezier Progression "Loop In" BIn to complete the loop.

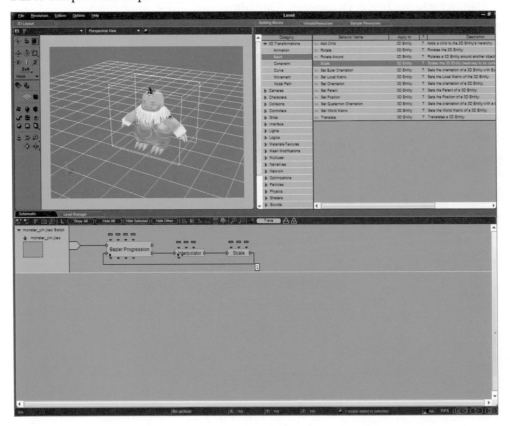

5) Connect the Percentage POut of the Bezier Progression BB to the Value PIn of the Interpolator BB.

6) Click the POut of the Interpolator BB and change the Parameter Type to Vector. Then connect the Interpolator POut to the Scale "Scaling Vector" PIn.

7) Double click the Scale BB and turn on the Absolute checkbox.

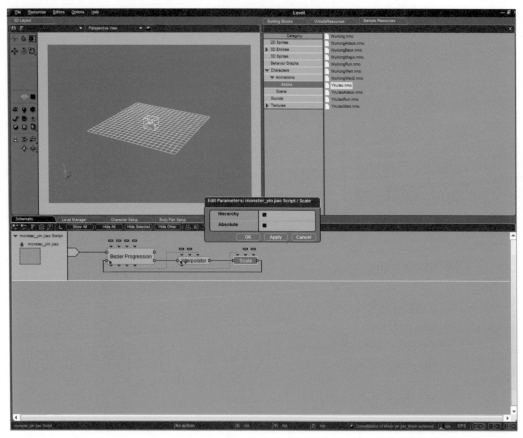

8) Double click the Interpolator BB to open its Edit Parameters dialog. Set A (Initial scale values) as: X=1, Y=1, Z=1, and B (Final scale values) as: X=2, Y=2, Z=2.

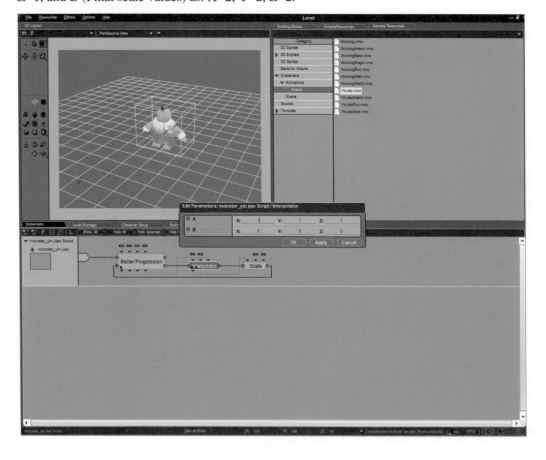

9) Click Play to test the behavior script. The character will immediately fill the screen and get larger. This is because the default size of the YinJiao is set to a scale factor of less than 1.0. Just zoom out to see the full character. It is important to remember to export your characters and objects from your 3D application at the correct scale to avoid rescaling in Virtools.

10) In this lesson, we used the Percentage parameter of the Bezier Progression BB to control the scaling speed. The difference between the Interpolator BB's A and B parameters controls the scale result. Be careful: if the A or B value is 0, the object will disappear.

2.6 Making an Object Move Along a Path

1) From Sample Resources \ 3D Entities drag the Barrel object into the 3D Layout window to set its initial size and position. Create a script on the object

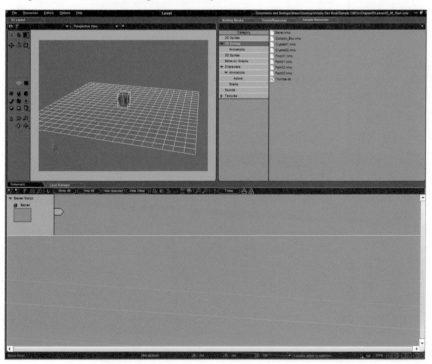

2) From Samples Resources \ 3D Entities drag the Path03 object into the 3D Layout window and set its initial size and position.

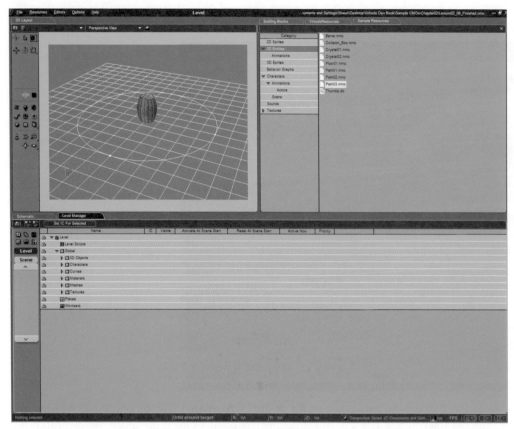

3) In the Building Blocks menu select Logics\Loops and drag the Bezier Progression BB into the Barrel script. Now link the script Start Connector to the Bezier Progression "On" BIn.

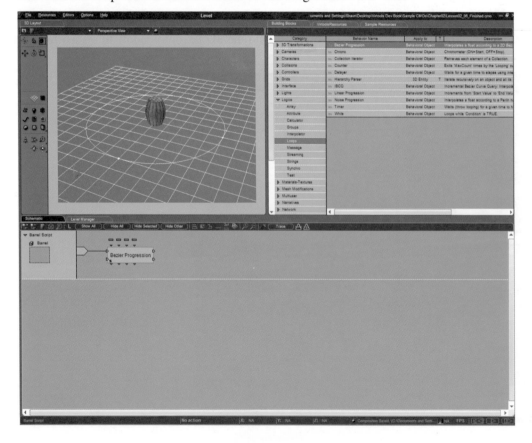

4) In the Building Blocks menu select 3D Transformations \ Basic \ Curve and drag the Position On Curve BB into the Barrel script. Link the Bezier Progression "Loop Out" BOut to the Position On Curve BIn, then connect the Position On Curve BOut to the Bezier Progression "Loop In" BIn to complete the loop.

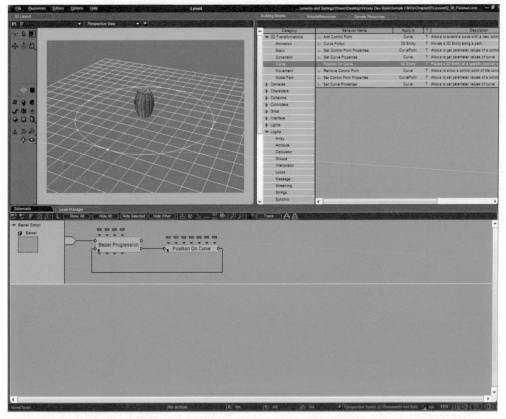

5) Connect the Percentage POut of the Bezier Progression BB to the Progression PIn of the Position On Curve BB to send the value that will determine the objects' position on the curve.

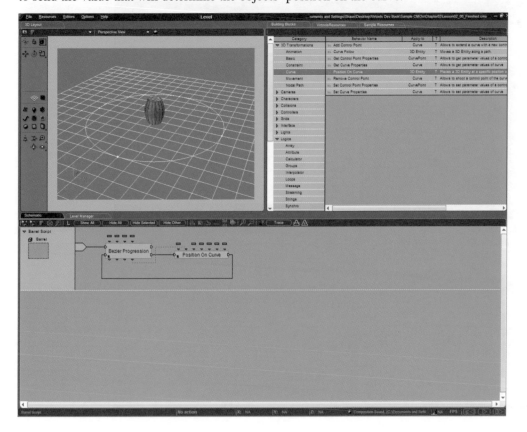

6) Click the Position On Curve BB to open the parameter dialog. Set the Curve value to Circle01 and enable the Follow checkbox. Click Play to see the result. The Barrel moves once around the curve.

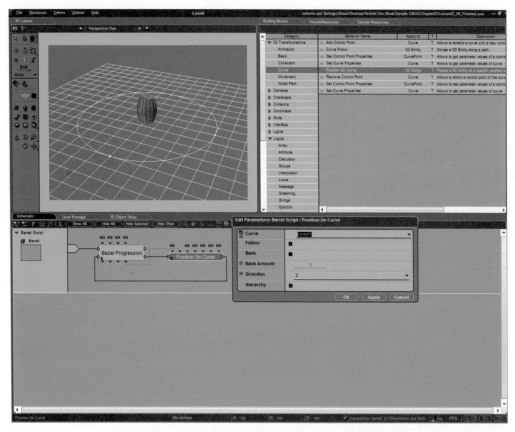

7) To make the Barrel move continuously around the curve, just connect the BOut and BIn of the Bezier Progression BB to form a loop. This will cause the Bezier Progression BB to restart upon completion.

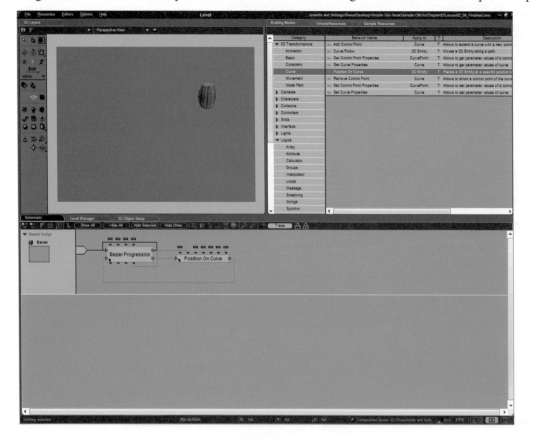

2.7 Controlling an Object Using the Keyboard

1) First drag the treasure chest into the 3D Layout window to set its initial size and position. Then create a script for the object.

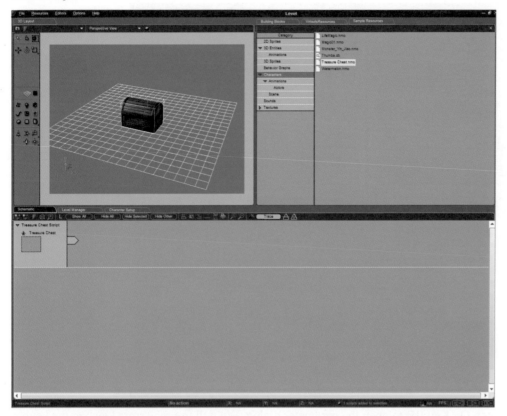

2) In the Building Blocks menu select Controllers \ Keyboard and drag the Switch On Key BB into the Treasure Chest script. Now link the script Start Connector to the Switch On Key "On" BIn.

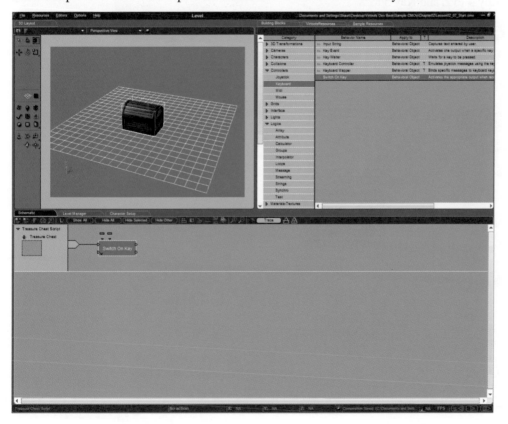

3) We need to create 6 keyboard equivalents for the 6 actions that will be applied to the treasure chest which includes movement, rotation and scaling. Right Click the Switch On Key BB and select Construct \ Add Behavior Output and create an extra 4 BOuts.

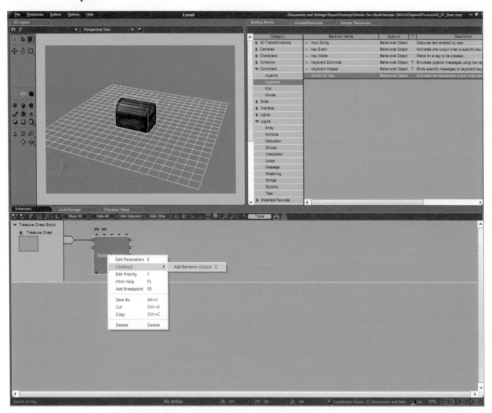

4) Double click the Switch On Key BB to open the parameter dialog. We will use the arrow keys on the keyboard to control movement and rotation, so set Key 0 to Up, Key 1 to Down, Key 2 to Left and Key 3 to Right. For scaling control, set Key 4 to Z and Key 5 to X.

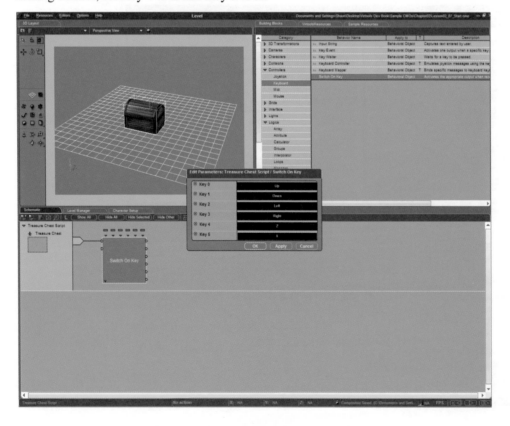

5) In the Building Blocks menu select Logics \ Calculator \ Per Second and drag the Switch On Key BB into the Treasure Chest script. Then select 3D Transformations \ Basic and add the Translate BB into the script. Connect the Switch On Key "Up" BOut to the Per Second BIn, then connect the Per Second BOut to the Translate BIn.

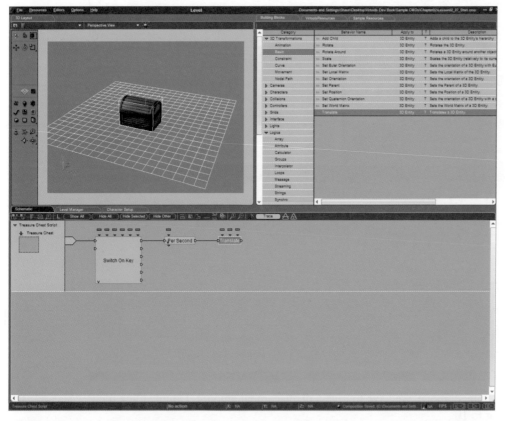

6) Click the POut of the Per Second BB to open its parameter dialog and change the Parameter Type to Vector.

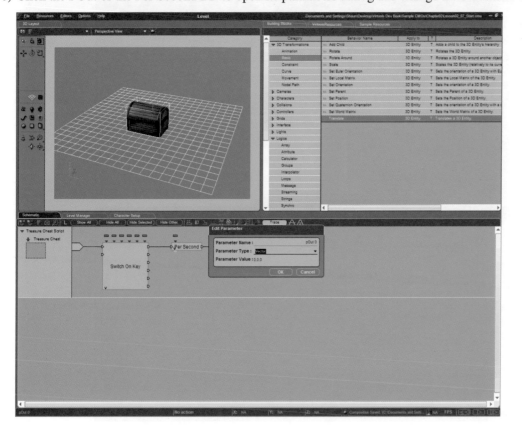

7) Connect the Per Second POut to the Translate Vector PIn of the Translate BB.

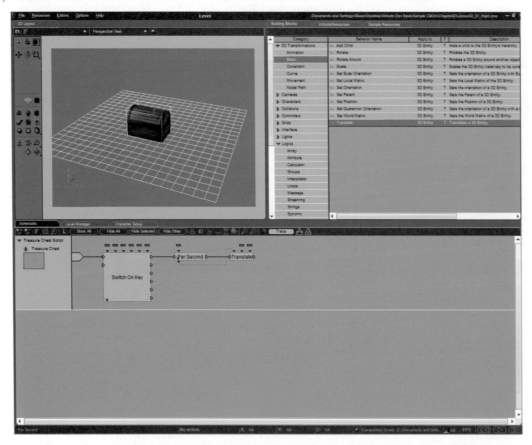

8) In order to make the object move, we have to give a displacement amount. Double click the Per Second BB and change the Y Vector to 10.

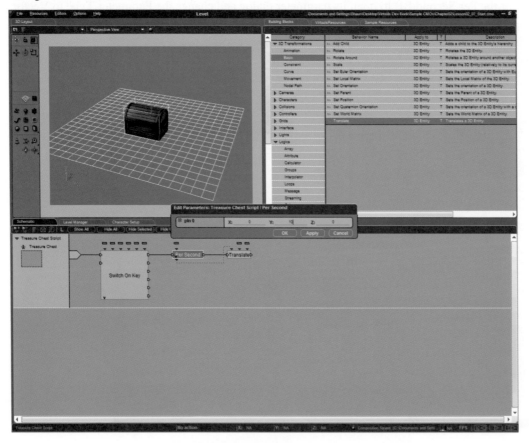

9)　Repeat steps 5 to 7 but connect the Per Second BB to the Switch On Key Out1 (Down) to allow us to move the object down. For Step 8, set the Y Vector to -10. Click Play and press the Up and Down keys to make the object move.

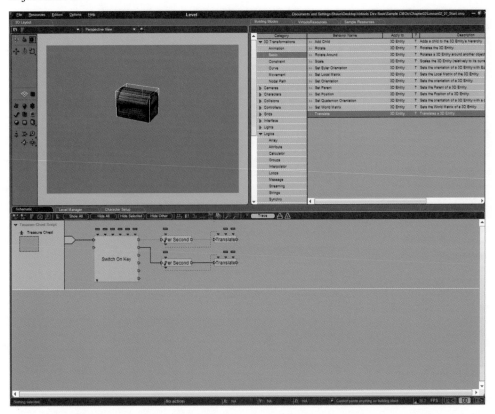

10)　Add another Per Second BB and from the Building Block menu select 3D Transformations \ Basic and add the Rotate BB to the script. Connect the Per Second BB BIn to the Switch On Key Out2 (Left), then connect the Per Second BB BOut to the Rotate BIn.

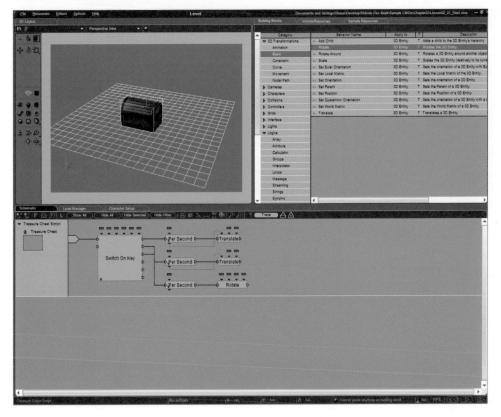

11) Double click the Per Second BB POut and in the parameter dialog set the Parameter Type to Angle. Then Double click the Per Second BB and set the Degree value to -30. Finally, connect the Per Second BB's POut to the Rotate BB's Angle Pin.

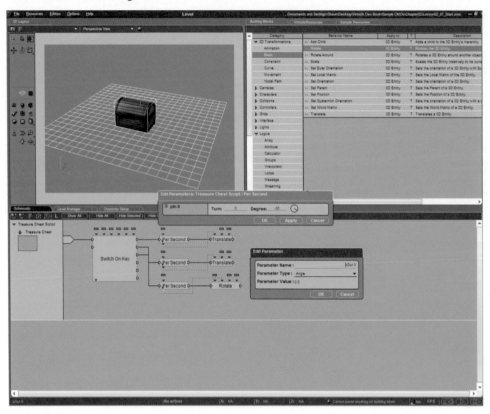

12) Now repeat Steps 10 and 11 to add the same functionality to Switch On Key Out3 (Right). Remember to set the Degree value in the Per Second BB to 30. Click Play and press the Left and Right keys to make the object rotate.

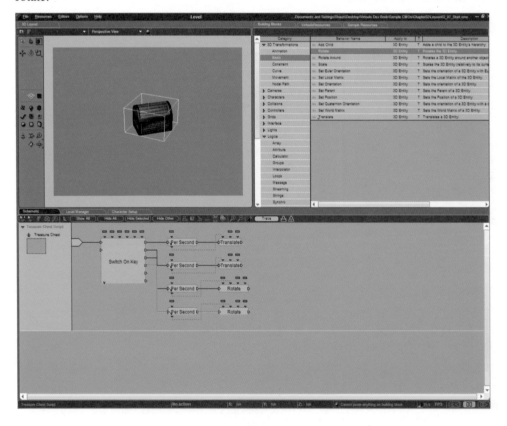

13) Add the Per Second BB to the script then add the Interpolator BB and Scale BB. Connect the Switch on Key Out 4 ("Z") to Per Second, and Per Second to Interpolator and finally connect Interpolator to Scale.

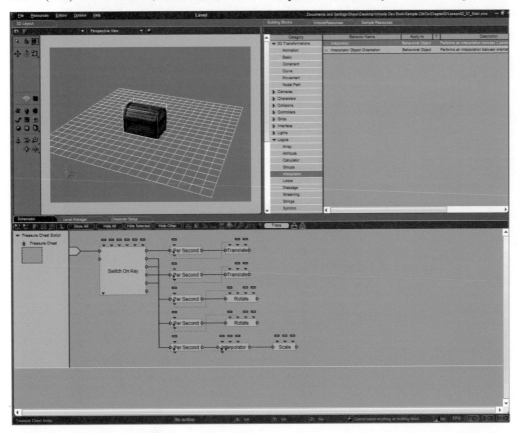

14) Click the POut of the Per Second BB and set the Parameter Type to Percentage. Double Click the Per Second BB and change the Percentage value to 50%.

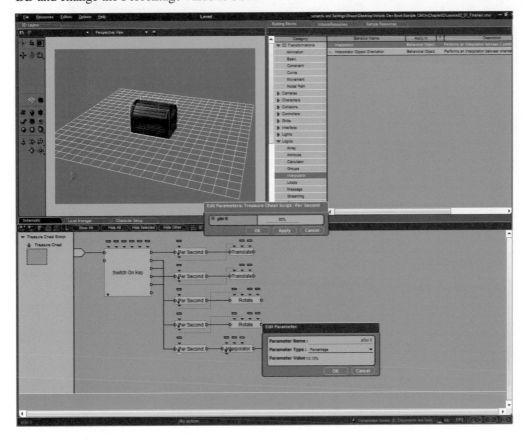

15) Double click the Interpolator BB's POut and change the type to Vector.

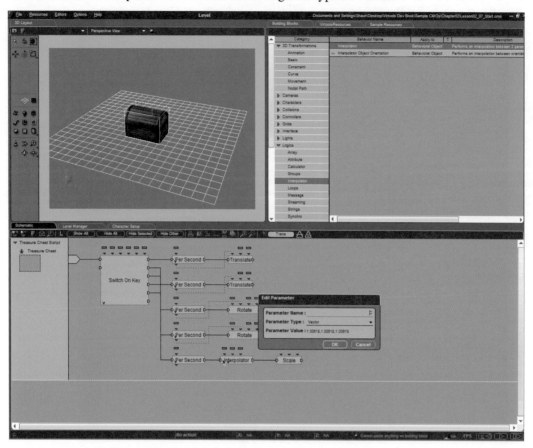

16) Connect the POut of Per Second to the Value PIn of Interpolator.

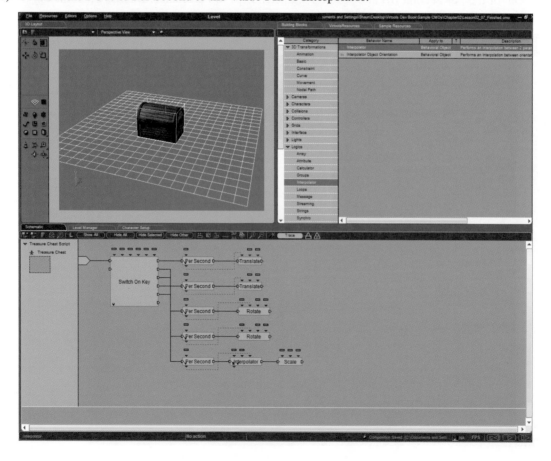

17) Double click the Interpolator BB and change the A Vector to X=1, Y=1, Z=1 and set A Vector to X=2, Y=2, Z=2. Then connect the Interpolator POut to the Scale "Scaling Vector" PIn.

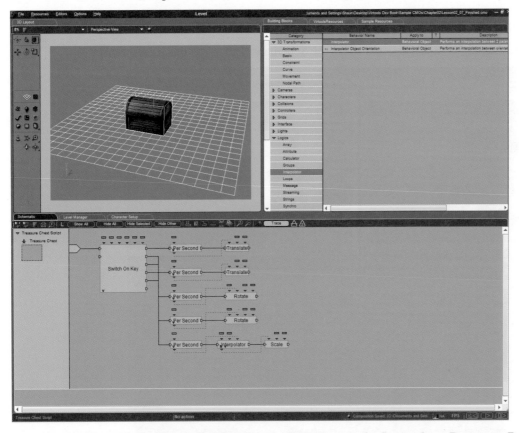

18) Repeat steps 13 to 17 for Switch On Key Out 5 ("X"). But set the Interpolator Parameter B to 0. Click Play and use the X and Z keys to scale the object.

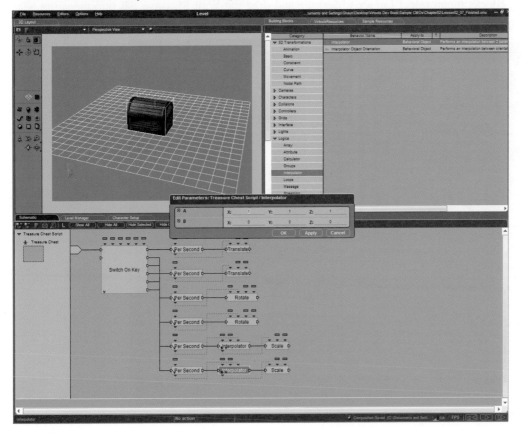

3.0 Using Virtools Messaging

3.1 Using Messages to control objects

1) Open the file Lesson03_01_Start.cmo and select the Schematic Tab to see the objects Script.

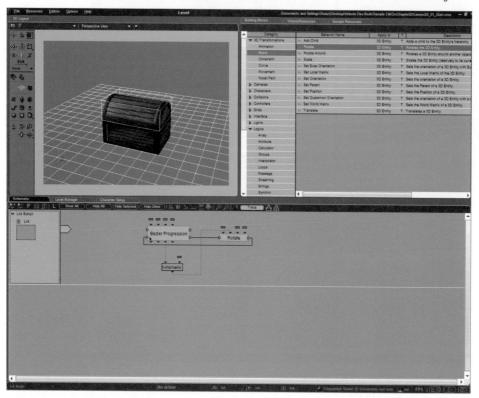

2) In the Building Blocks menu select Logics \ Message and drag the Wait Message BB into the script. Connect the BIn to the Script Start Connector and the BOut to the Bezier Progression "On" BIn.

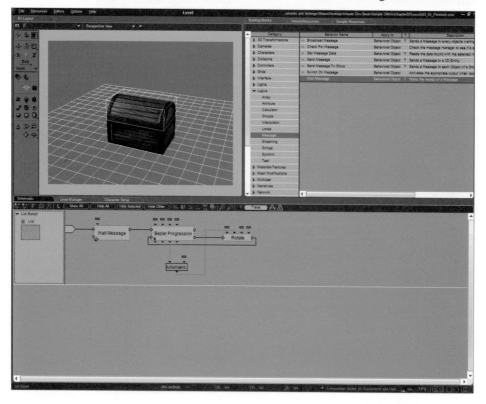

3) Double click the Wait Message BB to open the parameter dialog and set the Message parameter to "OnClick".

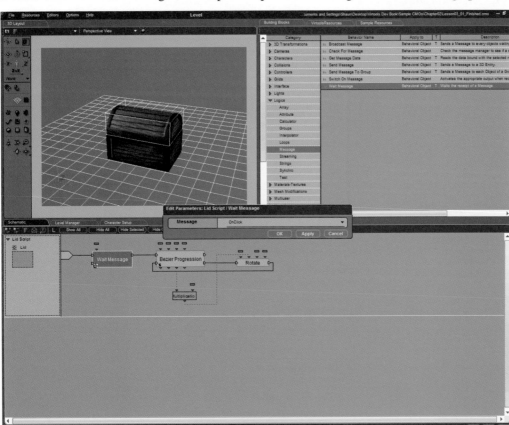

4) Click Play and then Click on the Treasure Chest lid, which will then open. The Wait Message BB is activated by our mouse click event and then allows our script to continue processing.

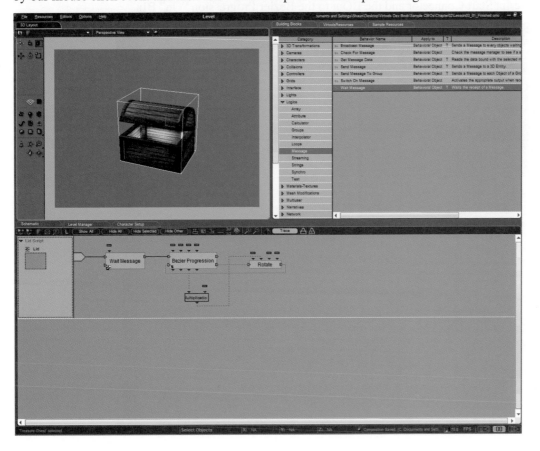

3.2 Using Keyboard Input

1) Open the File "Lesson3_2_Start.cmo" and select the Schematic Tab to see the objects Script

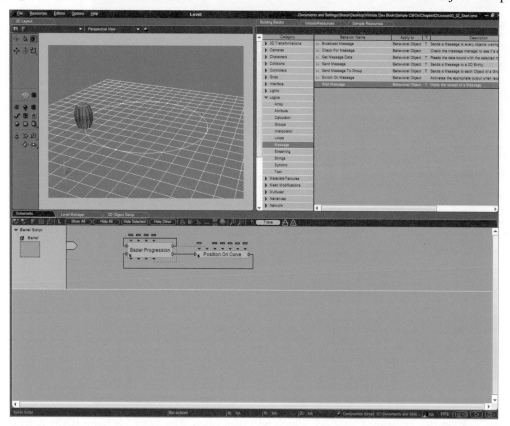

2) In the Building Blocks menu select Logics \ Message and drag the Wait Message BB into the script. Connect the BIn to the Script Start Connector and the BOut to the Bezier Progression "On" BIn.

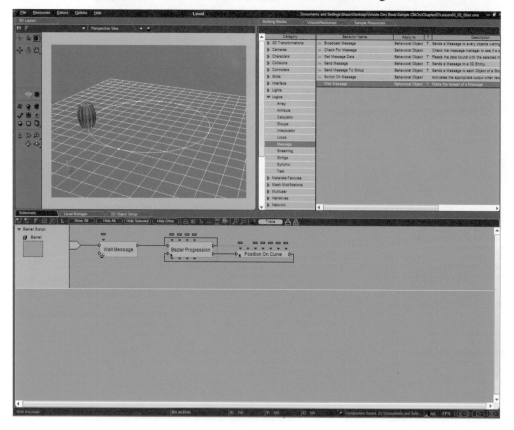

3) In the Building Blocks menu select Controllers \ Keyboard and drag the Key Waiter BB into the script. Connect the BIn to the Script Start Connector.

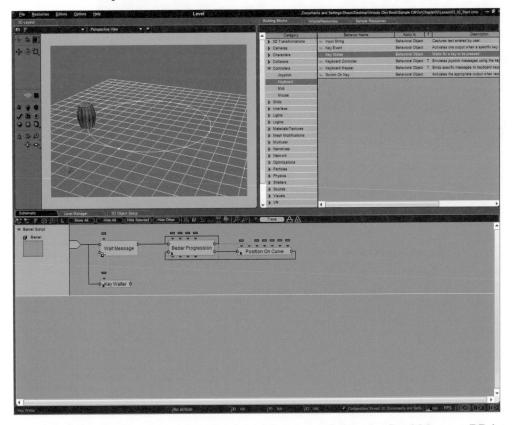

4) In the Building Blocks menu select Logics \ Message and drag the Send Message BB into the script. Connect the BOut of the Key Waiter BB to the BIn of the Send Message BB. Next, connect the BOut of the Send Message BB to the BIn of the Key Waiter BB to form a loop.

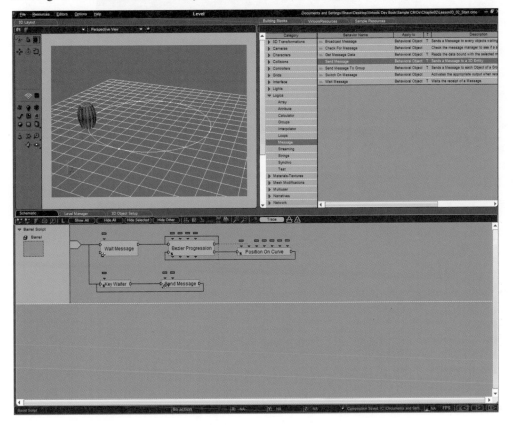

5) Open the parameter dialog of the Key Waiter BB and set the Key value to "Space".

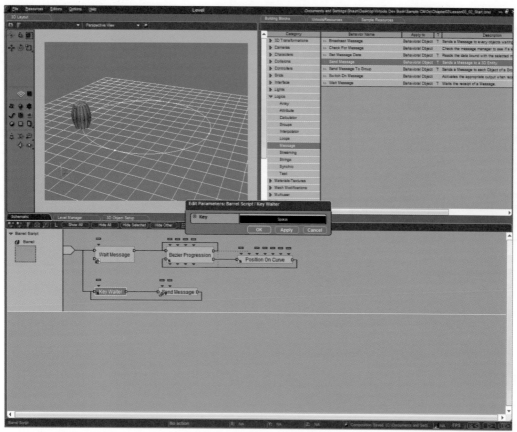

6) Now open the parameter dialog of the Send Message BB and set the Message value to "Start" and set the Dest value to Barrel.

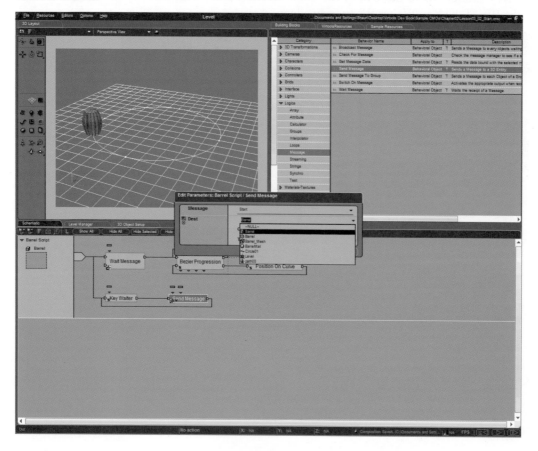

7) Open the parameter dialog of the Wait Message BB and set the Message value to "Start" which is now available as a selection in the drop down menu. Also, delete the loop connecting the Bezier Progression BB's BIn and BOut as we will create our own behavior for looping,

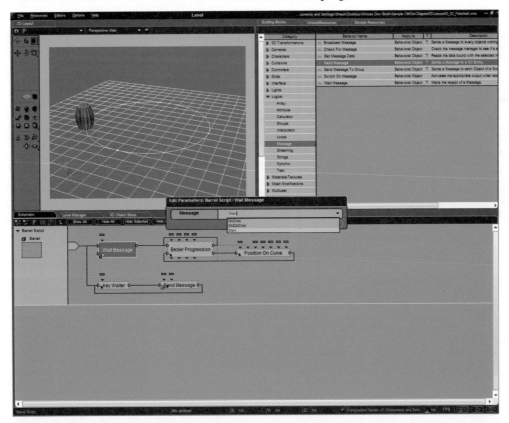

8) Click Play and the Barrel will initially do nothing. Press the Space bar and the Barrel will move around the ellipse once.

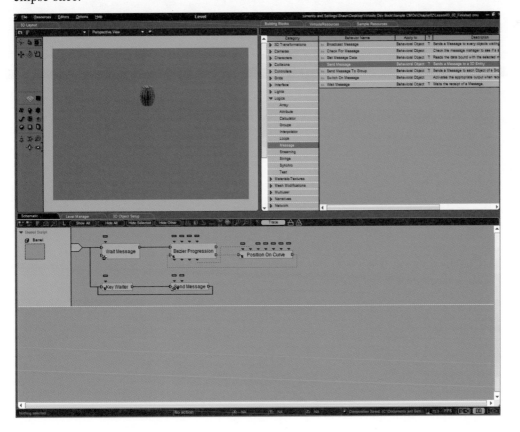

9) The Barrel only moves once around the ellipse, pressing Space again has no effect as the Wait Message BB has already received a message and is now inactive. To reactive the Wait Message BB we need to link the BOut of the Bezier Progression BB to the BIn of our Wait Message BB. Click Play and the Barrel will loop around the ellipse every time you press space.

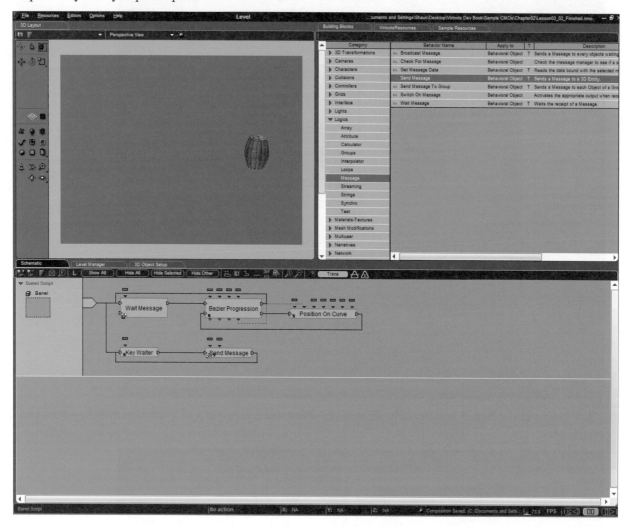

4.0 An Introduction to the Camera

4.1 Cameras in Virtools

In this lesson, we introduce the camera entity and its configurable parameters. The camera provides a window into our composition. A composition can contain any number of cameras that can be used to give the user different viewpoints. We will explore some advanced functionality of the camera in later chapters, but let's have a look at some of the basics now.

1) Open the File "Lesson4_1_Start.cmo" and select the Target Camera Setup tab.

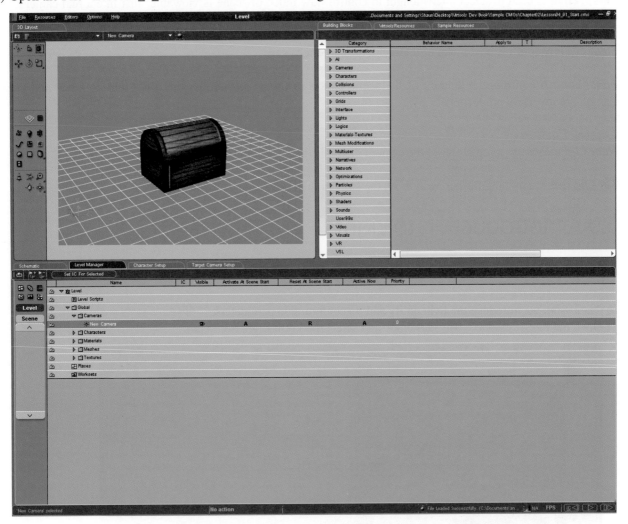

Now, lets take a look at some of the options that we can configure;

Position is the vector of the camera's position in relation to the rest of the world.

Orientation controls the direction of the camera.

Show in Player Mode makes the wireframe of the camera visible when our scene is playing.

Show Cone shows the viewable range of the camera.

Target is used to select an entity to target, or "look at".

Projection Types
Perspective Projection sets the mode to perspective where the further away an object is, the smaller it gets, just like in the real world.

Orthographic Projection sets the camera to an Isometric style view, where all objects retain their original size regardless of distance to the camera.

Aspect Ratio lets us control the width and height proportions of the screen. Options are Normal (4/3), Extended (16/9), Widescreen (7/3), Panoramic (20/7) and Custom which is set by the user.

Perspective is used to select a lens length to control how much of scene is viewable. Just like a real camera, the lower the lens value, the more "light" or scene is allowed into the camera lens.

Field of View controls how much of the scene the camera can see.

Focal Length controls the amount of the scene that is in focus. Remember that the Field of View and Focal Length are inversely proportional.

Clipping Controls
Near Clip means anything closer to the camera than this distance is not displayed.

Far Clip means anything further away from the camera than this distance is not displayed.

5.0 An Introduction to Lights

5.1 Introducing the Light

In this lesson, we introduce the light entity and its configurable parameters.
1) Open the File "Lesson05_01_Start.cmo" and select the Point Light Setup tab.

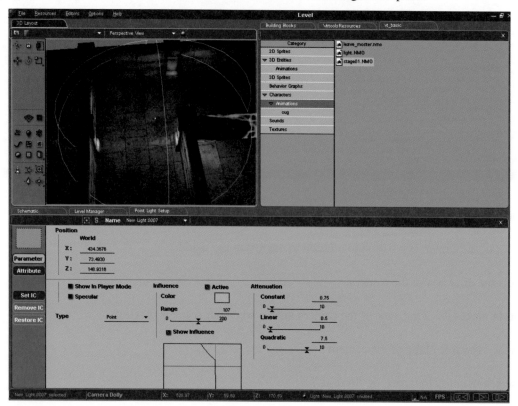

Now, let's take a look at some of the options that we can configure;

Position The position of the light in relation to the rest of the world.

Show in Player Mode makes the wireframe of the light visible when our scene is playing.

Specular allows hotspots (or white spots) to be created on objects where the light is directly reflecting into the camera.

Point - A point light is just like a regular light bulb that can be hung from anywhere in your scene. The Point light can also be used for as a sun.

Spot - A spot light is has a cone of influence and direction, similar to a desk lamp.

Directional - A directional light travels in only one direction, doesn't spread out over distance and has no attenuation. Commonly used for panoramic scenes.

Influence is used to control the color and range of the light. If Active is checked, the light will affect other objects; if it is unchecked the light has no effect on the scene.

Color controls the RGB color of the light.

Range is the sphere of influence or distance the light can travel. Higher values let the light travel further.

Show Influence displays a wireframe of the lights boundaries in the 3D Layout view.

The table below shows the attenuation or falloff of the light and allows you to visualize the light configuration.

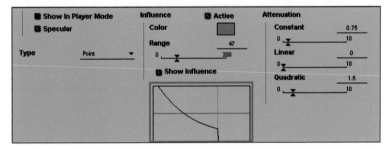

Attenuation Controls
Constant is the overall intensity or brightness of the light.

Linear sets a linear falloff for the light. The light attenuates at a constant value over distance.

Quadratic attenuation makes the light intensity falloff faster the further away the light travels. The higher the value, the more aggressive the attenuation is over a shorter distance.

Chapter03 Importing and animating characters

1.0 Importing a Character and Assigning a Controller

1.1 Importing the Character

1) Drag character YinJiao from Sample Resources\Characters and adjust the viewport so that you can see the entire character.

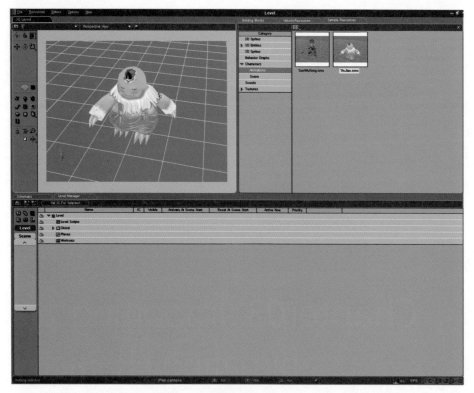

2) Drag the three YinJiao animations (Walk, Stand and Attack) from Sample Resources\Characters\Animations onto the YinJiao character. This will add the bones animations to YinJiao, which we can control using BB's.

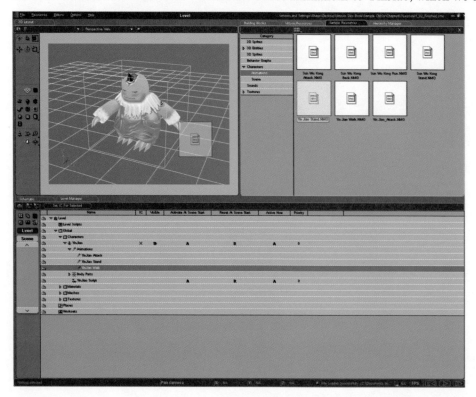

3) In the Level Manager, navigate to Global \ Characters \ YinJiao and open the Animations and Body Parts sections. Here you will see that the YinJiao character has 3 kinds of animations (Attack, Stand and Walk) and a large number of bones. The animations control the movement of bones and bones in turn modify the form of the object (or Character).

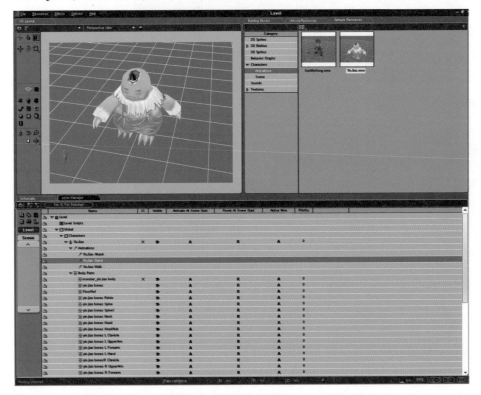

1.2 Adding the Animation Controller

1) Create a Script on the YinJiao Character. Double click the script to open it in Schematic View. Drag the "Character Controller" BB from "Building Blocks\Characters\Movement" and drop it into the script. Connect it with the Start Node.

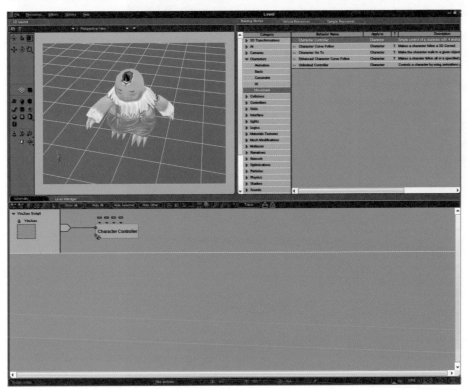

2) Double Click the Character Controller BB to open its parameters editing window. Select the corresponding animation for each option as follows; Stand Animation = YinJiao Stand; Walk Animation = YinJiao Walk; Walk Backward Animation = Null; Run Animation = YinJiao Attack.

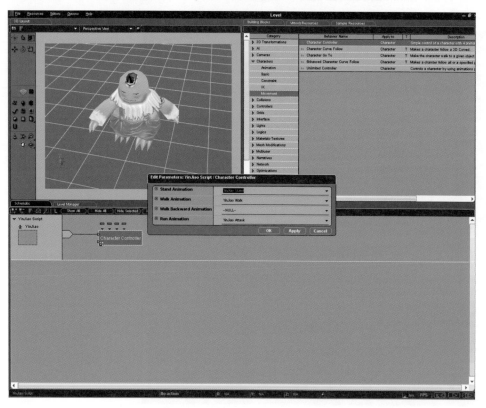

3) Click Play to test the animation. You can see YinJiao's Stand animation is playing in a continuous loop. No matter which keys are pressed the character will not change its animation. At this point Virtools has no way of knowing which keys should be assigned to activate which animation. To solve this problem we use the Keyboard Controller BB.

4) Drag the Keyboard Controller BB from Building Blocks\Controllers\Keyboard to the script of YinJiao. Then connect it with the Start node.

5) Click Play to test. Use the numeric keypad to move the character. i.e. Key #8 for "Forward", #4 for "Left", #6 for "Right", and Insert for "Attack". The Keyboard Controller BB automatically assigns the numeric keypad as the default input configuration. Later we will learn how to map specific keys to play any animation.

2.0 Floors and Object Collision

2.1 Creating Characters and Floors

1) Drag and drop the object "Scene01" from the path Sample Resources\Characters\Scene and position it in the center of the viewport.

2) Drag and drop the character Sun WuKong from the path Sample Resources\Characters. Resize and position the character to match the screenshot. Now drag the 4 Animations (Stand, Run, Attack and Back) onto Sun WuKong from the Sample Resources\Characters\Animations folder.

3) Create a Script on Sun WuKong and add a Character Controller and Keyboard Controller to the Script.

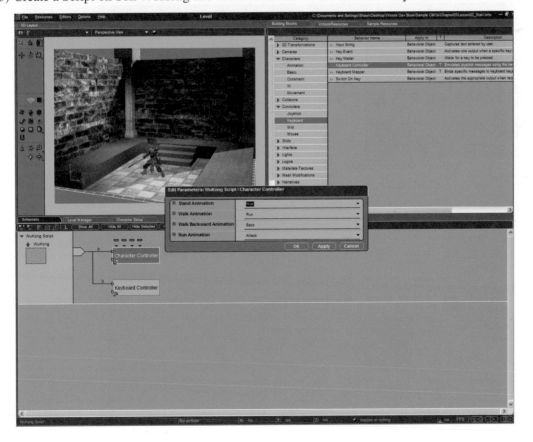

4) Drag the "Enhanced Character Keep On Floor" from Building Blocks\Characters\Constraint to the script of Sun WuKong. Connect it with Start node.

5) Right click the floor object and select Body Part Setup (Floor).

6) In the Setup panel, click Attribute and then click Add Attribute. Select Floor Manager \ Floor and click Add Selected. You will see a new line called 'Floor' is added to the Attribute list for the object.

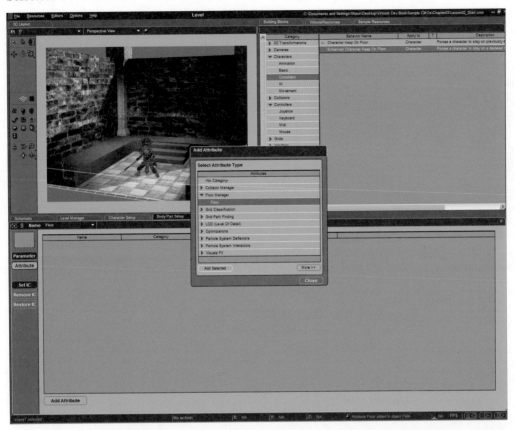

7) Click Play and use the numeric keypad to move WuKong. You will find WuKong 'sticks' to the floor, however, once he walks outside of the floor boundary he drops out of the scene.

8) Double click the "Enhanced Character Keep On Floor" BB to open its configuration window. Check the item "Keep In Floor Boundary". Sun WuKong is now limited to moving within the extents of the floor object.

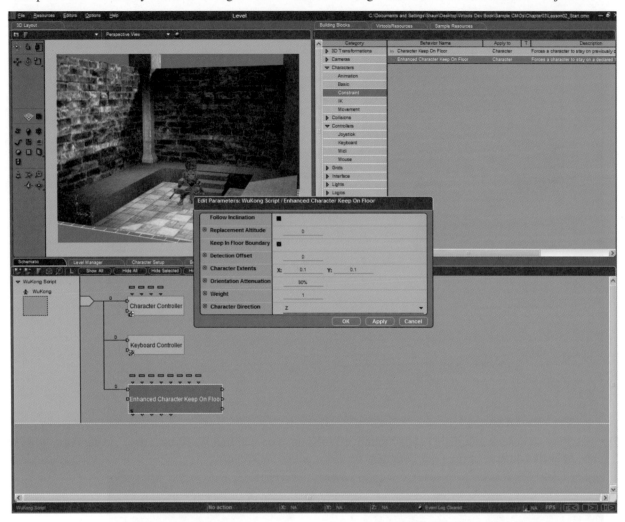

9) You may have noticed that when Sun WuKong moves down from a higher level he seems to float rather than drop to the floor; this is because the character doesn't have enough 'weight'. To correct this, open the "Enhanced Character Keep On Floor" BB configuration and increase the value of the Weight parameter to around 5. Now WuKong will fall down naturally.

2.2 Basic Collision

1) Drag and drop the Prevent Collision BB from Building Blocks\Collisions\3D Entity and connect it to the Start Node.

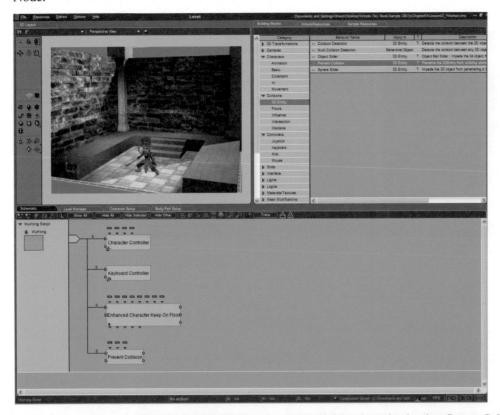

2) Open the Attribute settings of the Wall object by right clicking it and selecting Setup. Select Collision Manager \ Fixed Obstacle and click Add Attribute. Then click Play to test. Now, when Sun WuKong collides with the wall he no longer passes through it.

2.3 Advanced Collision using Collision Groups

1) Using the scene from the last exercise, drag the Barrel object from Sample Resources \ 3D Entities into the scene. Next, right click the barrel and select Duplicate from the menu. Create a total of 3 barrels and place them anywhere (as long as they are on the floor).

2) Select the three barrels in Level Manager \ 3D Entities. Click Create Group in the left hand panel. The new group appears in Level Manager \ Groups. Name the Group 'Barrels'.

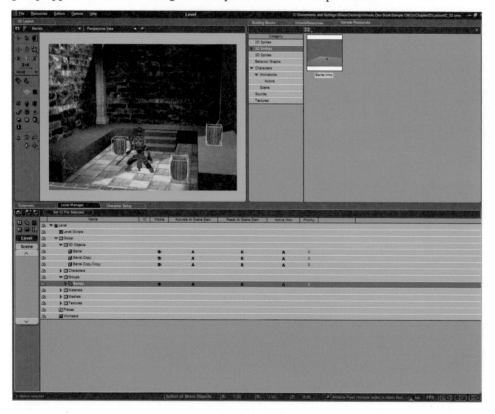

3) We need to define each of the barrels as a collision object. Select each barrel and in its Attributes panel select Collision Manager \ Fixed Obstacle and click Add Selected.

4) In the Schematic view add the Object Slider BB from "Building Blocks\Collisions\3D Entity" and connect it with the Start Node.

5) Double click the Object Slider BB. In the parameter window change the Group to Barrels. Click Play to test the scene.

6) The character may become stuck occasionally; you can fix this by increasing the value of the radius parameter in the Edit Parameters window. Normally the Prevent Collision BB and Object Slider BB are used together. If only the Prevent Collision BB is used, the character will tend to get stuck often.

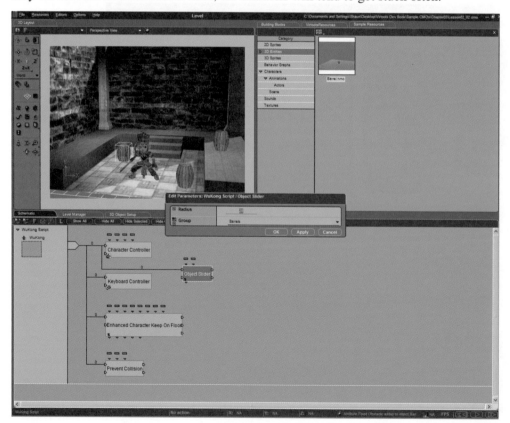

2.4 Triggering Events using Collision Detection

1) Using the same scene from the last exercise, add a Script to one of the Barrel objects.

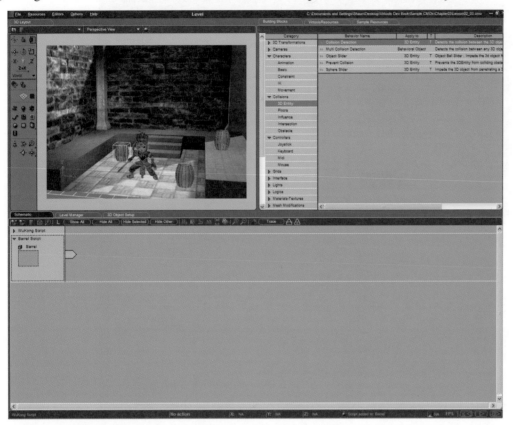

2) Drag the Collision Detection BB from Building Blocks\Collisions\3D Entity\Collision Detection" to the Barrel script. Connect it with the Start Node.

3) Connect the False BOut with the In BIn of the Collision Detection BB so that the detection process will loop continuously until collision occurs.

4) Drag and drop Send Message from Building Block\Logics\Message\Send Message. Connect Send Message with the True BOut of the Collision Detection BB.

5) Double click the Send Message BB and change the parameter "Select Message" to "Move" and the Destination to the Barrel you want to move.

6) Select the Barrel you chose as the destination for the Send Message BB and create a script for it. Add the Wait Message BB from Building Block\Logics\Message\Wait Message and connect it with the Start Node.

7) Double click the Wait Message BB and change the Message parameter to "Move".

8) Add the relevant BB's to make the Barrel move 50 units along the Y axis. (Please refer to Chapter2 Exercise 2.1). Connect the Bezier Progression In BIn with the Out BOut of the Wait Message BB.

9) In order to let the Barrel return to the original spot after moving, open the Edit Parameters dialog of the Bezier Progression BB and double click the curve to add a control node. Drag the 2nd and 3rd nodes of the curve to be a symmetrical peak at the center and ending at the original level. This effectively creates a loop that allows the Barrel to return to its original position.

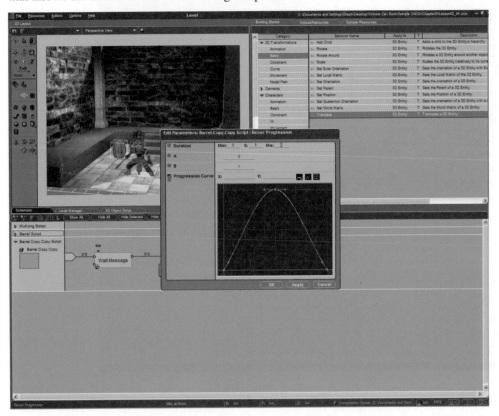

10) Connect the Out BOut of the Bezier Progression BB to the In BIn of Wait Message. This will make the script wait for the Move message again after finishing the Translation loop.

11) To finish off, we need to reset the Send Message script after the collision has occurred. To do this, connect the Out BOut of Send Message to the In BIn of Collision Detection.

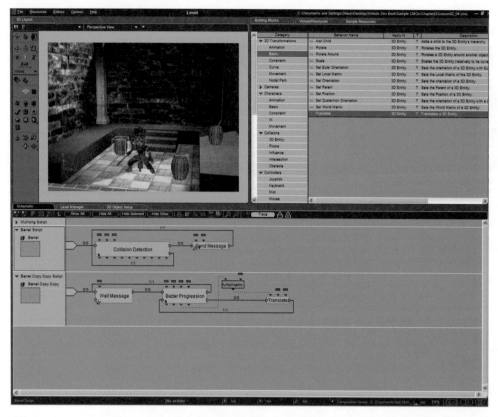

12) Click play to test the scene. You will see that when Sun WuKong touches the Barrel with the Collision Detection script, the Barrel waiting for the message will activate the Bezier Progression loop. Tip: To get a better idea of what is happening within your scripts during runtime, click the Trace button in the toolbar; the currently active BB's and connectors will turn red when you play the composition.

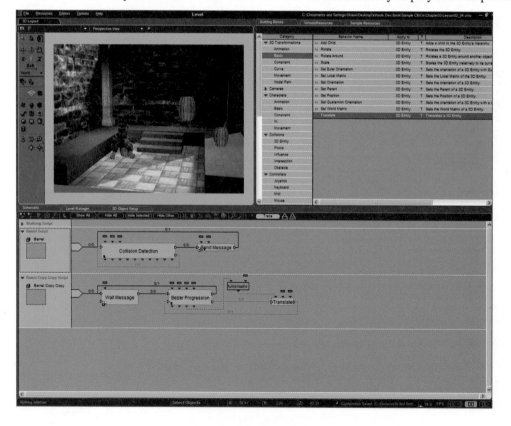

3.0 Creating Targeted Character Movement

3.1 Using the Character Go To Building Block

1) In this lesson we continue with our progress from the last section. Start by dragging the Character Go To BB from Building Blocks\Characters\Movement and connect it with the Start Node. Then Connect the Loop Out with the Loop In to form a loop. This will ensure the BB is 'live' for more than just a single frame.

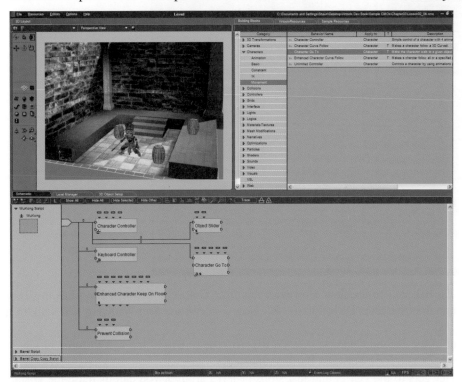

2) Double click the Character Go To BB to open its configuration dialog. Choose any Barrel as the Target Object. Change the Character Direction to -Z.

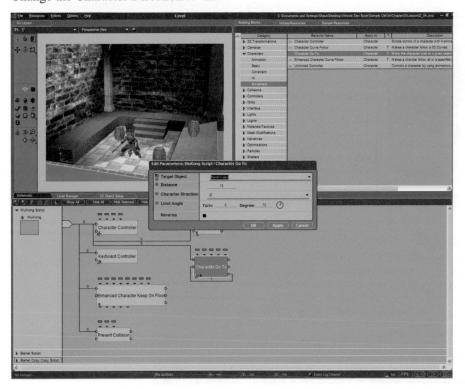

3) Click play; you can see the character runs to the position of the Barrel you chose.

4) Add another Character Go To BB next to the first. However, this time choose a different Barrel as the Target Object (don't forget to change the Character Direction to –Z). Now you can see Sun WuKong will walk to the first Barrel and then the second.

If you link the Arrived BOut of the second Character Go To BB with the In BIn of the first to form a loop, you can see the character will go back and forth between Barrels repeatedly.

Tip: If you find your character gets to the Barrel and just stops or jerks around, you can increase the Distance parameter in the Character Go To BB's. This will allow the 'Arrived' flag to be triggered further from the object.

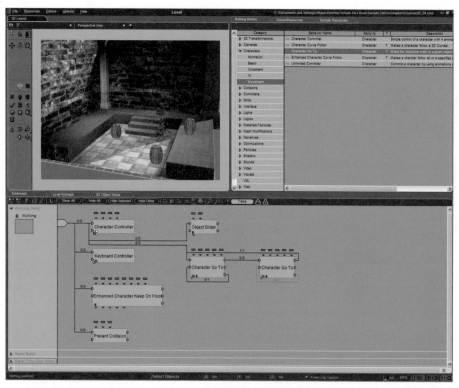

4.0 Camera Tracking

4.1 Click to Move Character Script

1) In this lesson we continue with our progress from the last section. Click the "Create Camera" button in the Toolbar Panel next to the 3D Layout Window. Next, create a Script on the camera.

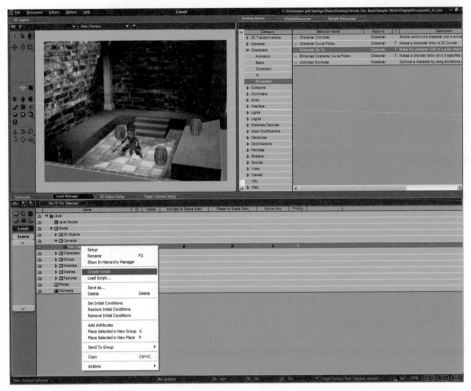

2) Add the Set Position BB from Building Blocks\3D Transformations\Basic. Add the Look At BB from Building Blocks\3D Transformations\Constraint. Connect both with the Start Node and create loops for each.

3) Open the configuration dialogs of the Set Position and Look At BB's and change the Referential parameter to Sun WuKong. Click Play and the Camera will zoom into Sun WuKong's body obscuring the rest of the scene from view. To fix this problem we need to offset the camera from the character.

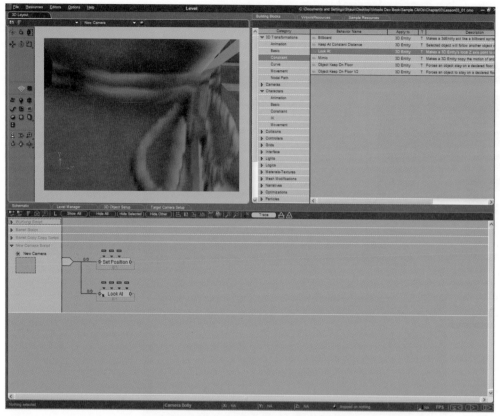

4) Reopen the configuration dialog for the Set Position BB and change the Position parameter to: X=100, Y=150, Z=-200. Click Play again. Now the camera is offset from the character and the scene is displayed normally.

5) This of setting position and focal point can also be applied to objects such as lights. For example, you could create a headlight to be fixed to the head of your character which will illuminate the path in front of the character.

5.0 Shadows

5.1 Creating Simple Shadows

1) In this lesson we continue with our progress from the last section. Select "Wukong Face" in the Level Manger and create a script for it.

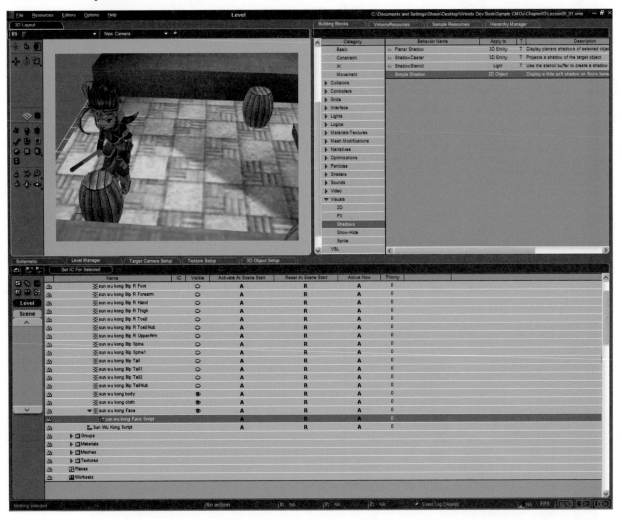

2) Drag the Simple Shadow BB from Building Blocks\Visuals\Shadows. Connect it with the Start Node.

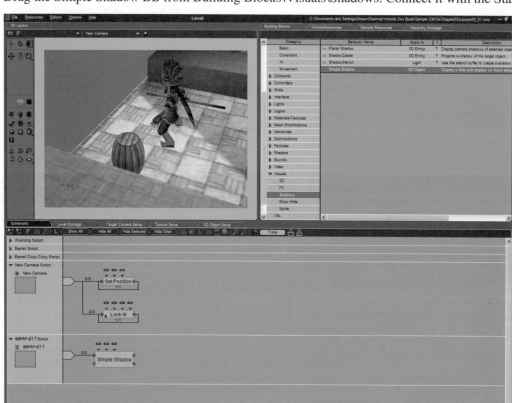

3) Select "SoftShadow.jpg" from Sample Resources\Textures. Add it to the scene by dragging it to an empty section of the 3D layout window.

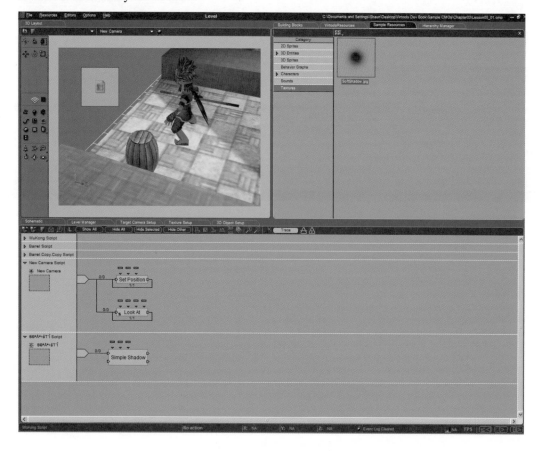

4) Double click the Simple Shadow BB to open its configuration dialog and change Texture to SoftShadow and Size Scale to 8.

5) Click play and a shadow will appear at Sun WuKong's feet.

   Note: The Simple Shadow BB can only be applied to objects and not characters. Furthermore, the shadow will only appear on objects with the Floor attribute.

5.2 Creating Planar Shadows

1) To begin this lesson, open the file Chapter03 \ Lesson05_02_Start.CMO. Add a light using the Create Light button and place it near the rear wall around the height of the roof.

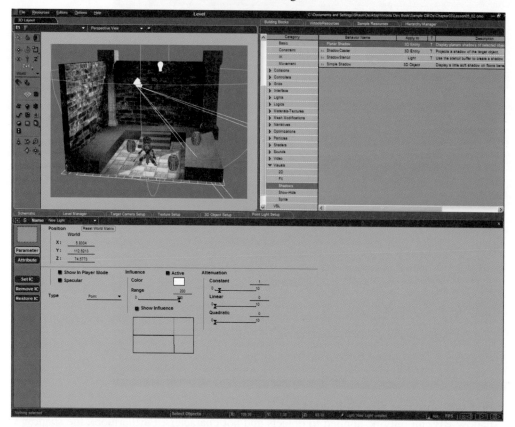

2) In the Level Manager select the Floor object located in Global\Characters\Scene1\Body. Create a script for it.

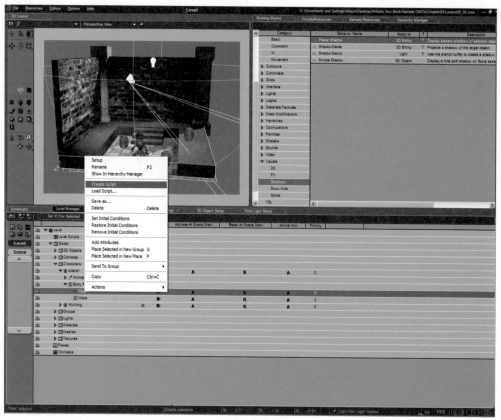

3) Drag the Planar Shadow BB from Building Blocks\Visuals\Shadows\ into the Floor Script. Connect it with Start Node.

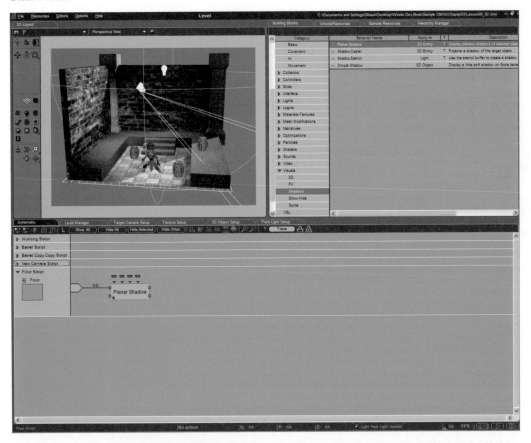

4) Double click the Planar Shadow BB and change the Light parameter to New Light, the light we just created.

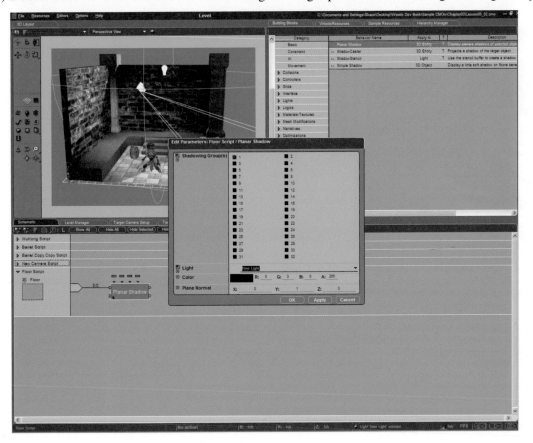

5) Right click WuKong and select Setup from the popup menu. In the Attributes panel, add the attribute Planar Shadow Object located in Visuals FX.

6) Click Play to test the scene. Now under Sun WuKong's feet a shadow appears that matches the outline of the character. One caveat of the Planar Shadow BB is that the shadow is cast on the flat surface of objects, so it is not suitable for 3D objects but can only displayed on planar objects.

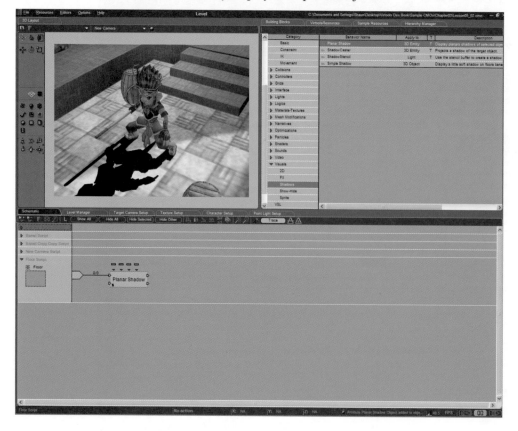

5.3 Creating Projected Shadows

1) To begin this lesson, open the file Chapter03 \ Lesson05_03_Start.CMO. To give more effect to the shadow casting we have placed the light in the center of the scene.

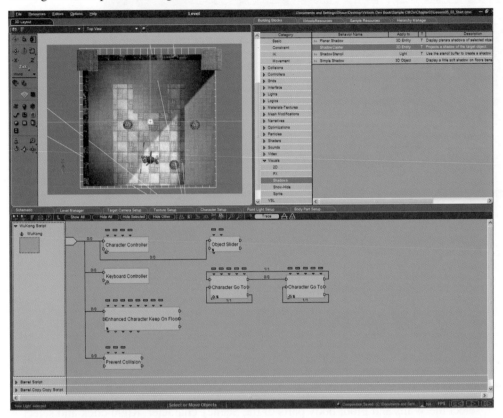

2) Add the Shadow Caster BB from Building Blocks\Visuals\Shadows into Sun WuKong's Script. Connect it with the Start Node.

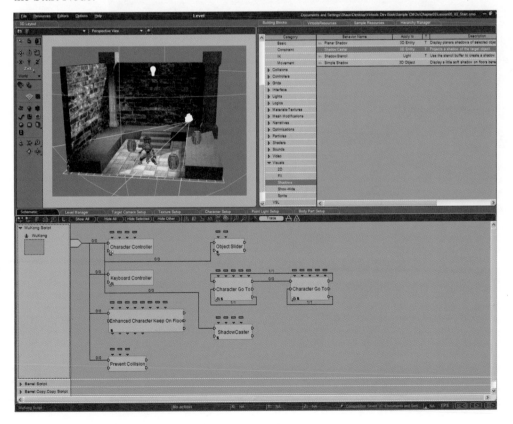

3) Double click the Shadow Caster BB to open its configuration dialog. Select New Light for the Light parameter and change the Max Light Distance to 200.

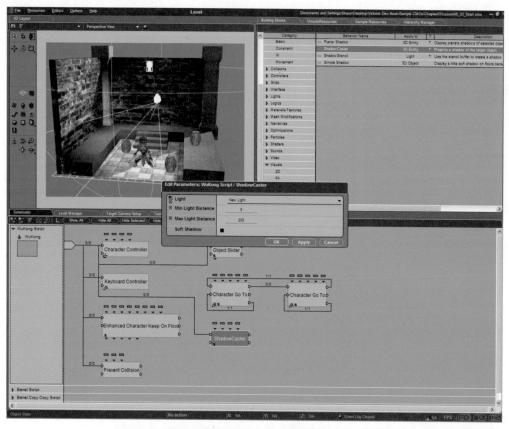

4) In the Level manager, select the Walls and Floor body parts of the Scene1 character. Right click and select Add Attributes from the popup menu. Then add Shadow Caster Receiver from the Visuals FX category.

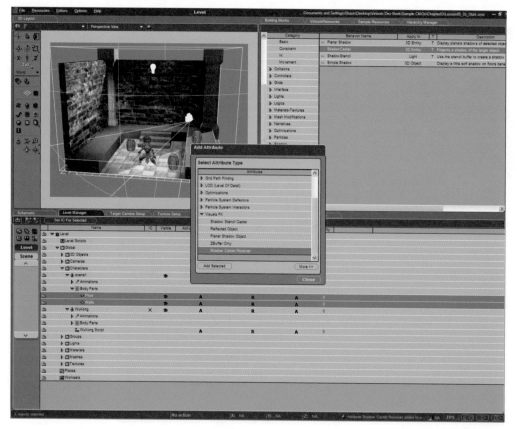

5) Click Play to test the scene. Now any object with the attribute of "Shadow Caster Receiver" receives the shadow of the character. The darkness of the shadow on different objects varies according to its distance from the light. Tip: If you Right click the Shadow Caster BB and select Edit Settings, then change Shadow Resolution Size to 512, you shadow will no longer have aliasing artifacts and will be much smoother. Be careful not to set it too high as this will waste valuable video memory. Although the result of the Shadow Caster BB is excellent it uses a considerable amount of resources, so use it cautiously.

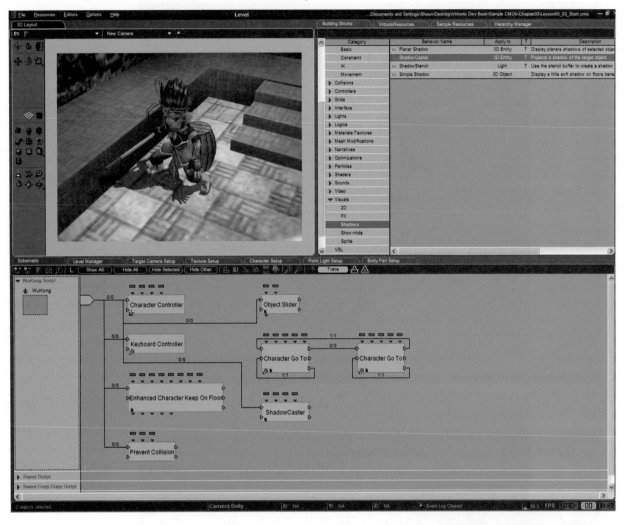

6.0 Using Grids in Virtools

6.1 Creating Grid Collisions

1) To begin this lesson, open the file Chapter03 \ Lesson06_01_Start.CMO.

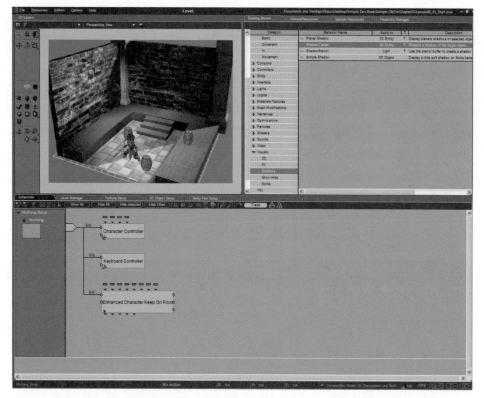

2) Change the 3D Layout Window to Top View. Click the Create Grid to create a new grid. Scale and Transform the grid to fit the boundaries of the room.

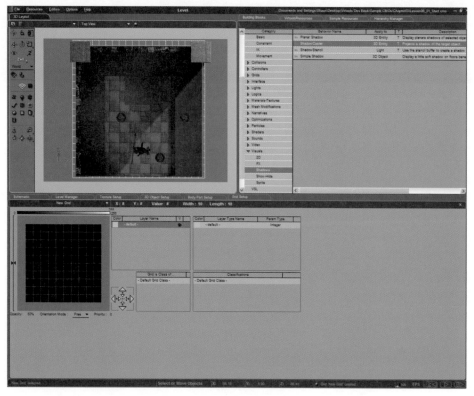

3) Right click in the Layer Database panel (on the right) and select New Layer Type on the pop-up menu to create a new Layer. Name it "Collision".

Tip: In the Grid Setup panel, you can use the Arrow controller to adjust the grid density on both the X and Y axis. Note that this will change the size of your grid. If you have scaled your grid correctly you should not need to use this.

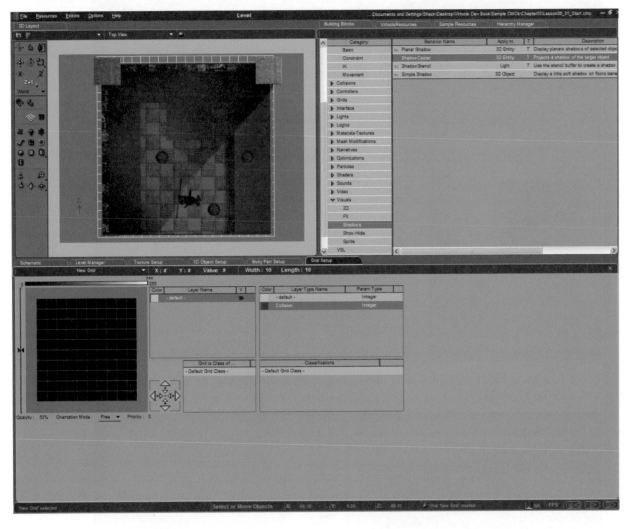

4) Drag the newly created Collision layer into the Execution Layer panel on the left.

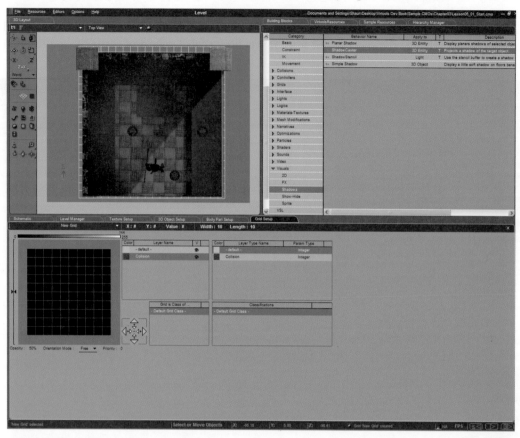

5) In the Execution Layer panel, left click the Collision layer. In the grid, fill in the blocks that intersect with the wall and the 3 barrels.

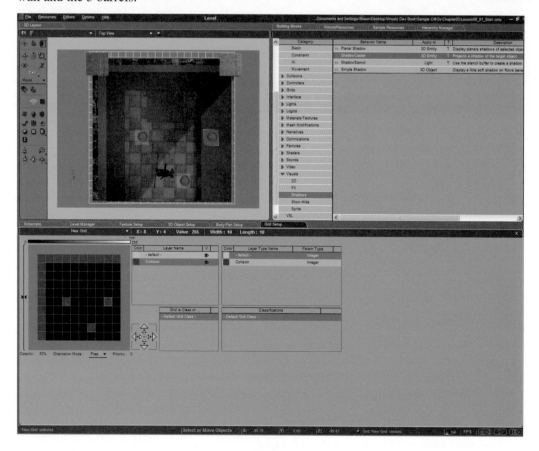

6) In the Schematic View, drag the Layer Slider BB from Building Blocks\Grids\Basic into WuKong's Script and connect it with the Start Node.

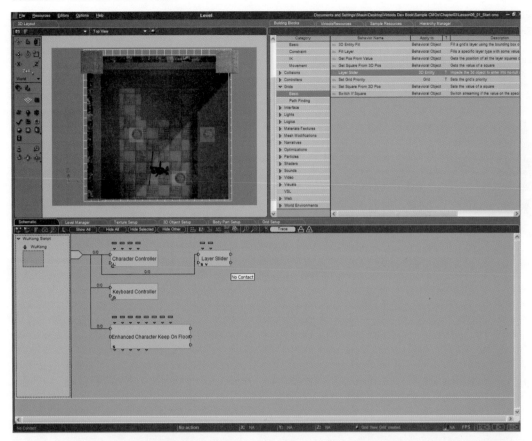

7) Double click the Layer Slider BB to open its configuration dialog and set "Layer To Slide On" to "Collision".

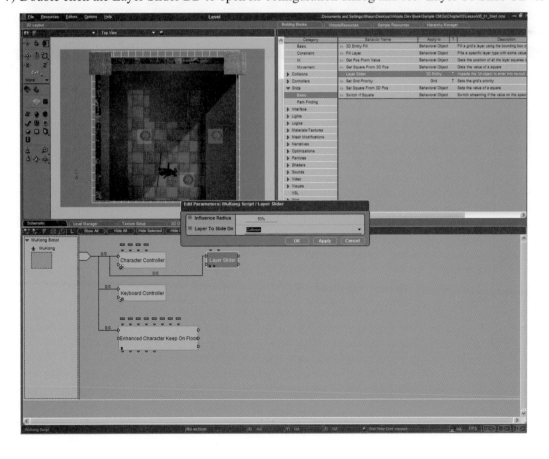

8) Click Play and test if the character can walk through the walls or barrels. The Grid based method is often easier to setup and manage than object based collisions.

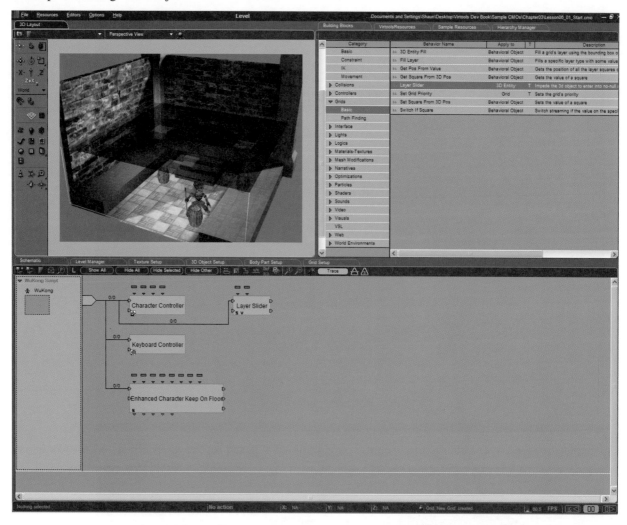

7.0 Creating a Background

7.1 Creating a Background Color

1) To begin this lesson, open the file Chapter03 \ Lesson07_01_Start.CMO. Right click Level in Level Manger and create a script for it.

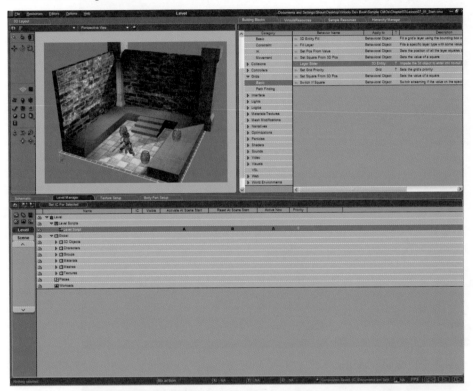

2) Insert the Set Background Color BB from Building Blocks\World Environments\Background\ into the Level script. Connect it with the Start Node.

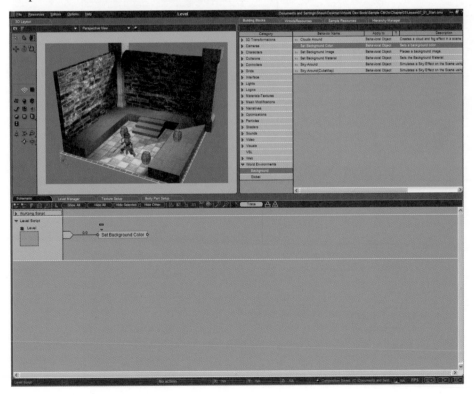

3) Double click the Set Background Color BB and change the Background Color.

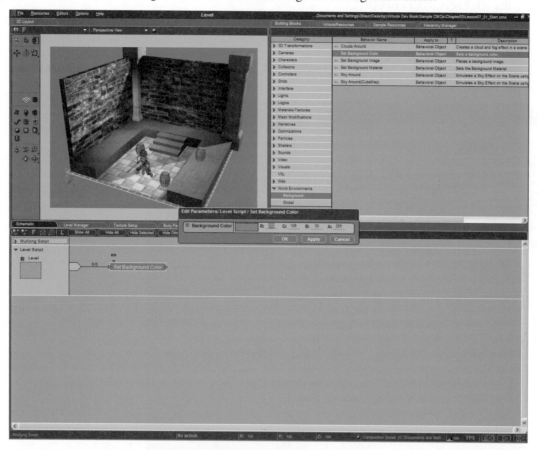

4) Click Play and the background will change color.

7.2 Using a Background Image

1) To begin this lesson, open the file Chapter03 \ Lesson07_02_Start.CMO. Right click Level in Level Manger and create a script for it.

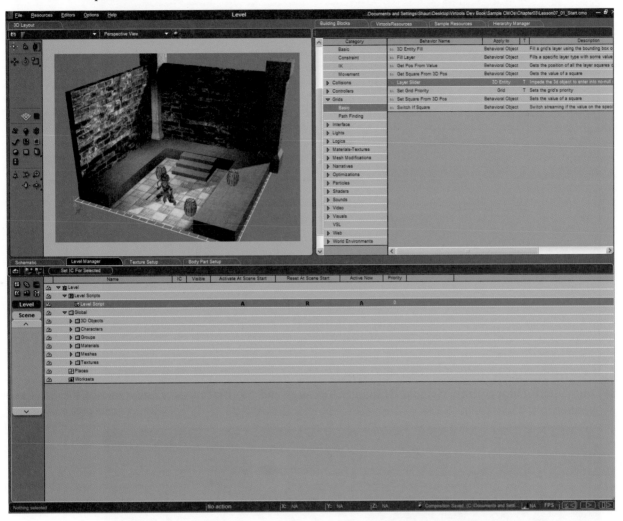

2) Add the Set Background Image BB from Building Blocks\World Environments\Background into the Level Script. Connect it with the Start Node.

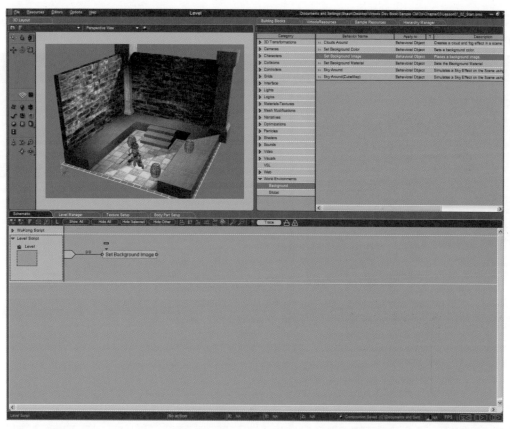

3) Drag "StarField.jpg" from Sample Resources\Textures and drop it into an empty area of the 3D Layout Window.

4) Double click the Set Background Image BB and change the Background Texture to StarField.

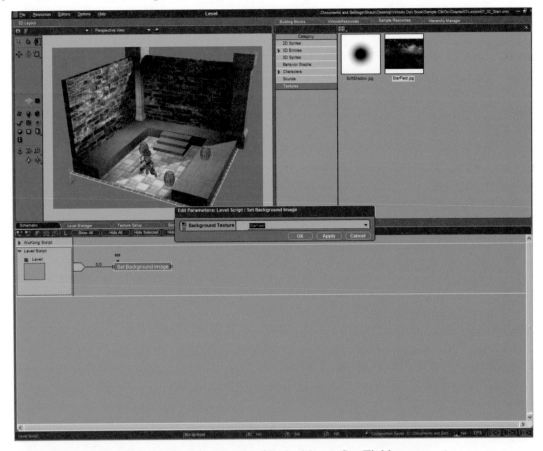

5) Click Play to test and the background is now filled with our StarField texture.

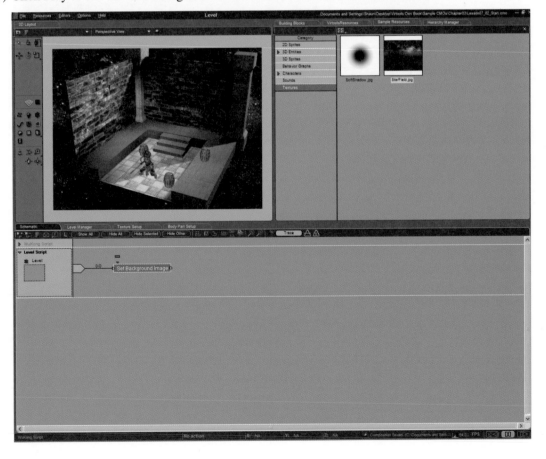

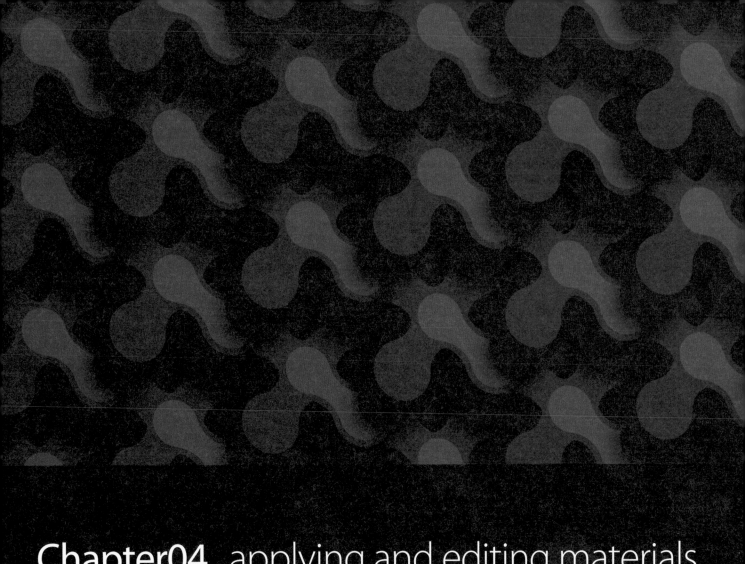

Chapter04 applying and editing materials

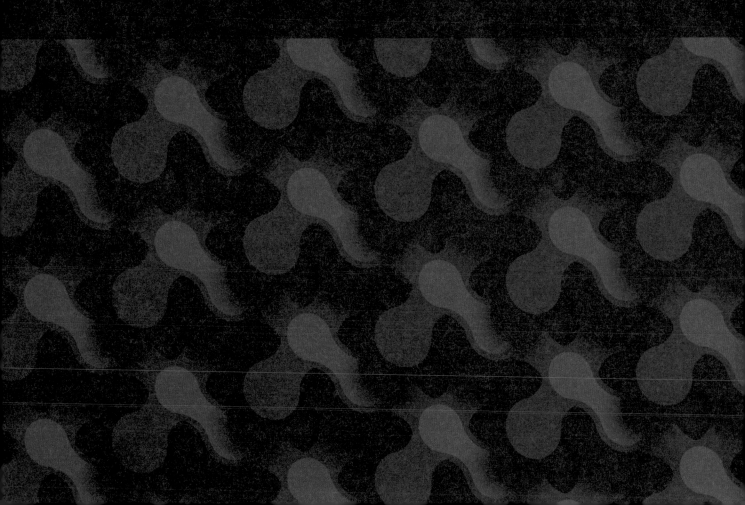

1.0 Material and Texture Basics

Let's start with a short introduction on Materials and Textures. A Material contains data that defines the appearance of a surface (or faces) of an object in the 3D world. Materials control properties that relate to the lighting of the object such as the ambient and diffuse color, texture (or textures), shading mode and transparency.

The images you assign to Materials are called Textures. Most Textures are normally bitmap files (such as ".jpg", ".tga" or ".dds" images) that are mapped onto an object to enhance its appearance. Textures can contain an Alpha channel that lets you define transparent and opaque areas separately (such as a fence texture). Objects generally contain mapping coordinates (UV Maps) that tell the renderer where certain parts of the Texture should appear on the object (for example, the position of the buttons on a shirt).

When a texture is mapped onto a 3D object, the renderer converts the pixels in the 2D Texture into a Texel (the most basic unit for a 3d surface) and performs a number of calculations to define what color that Texel should be; this is a relatively complex process that depends on the lighting, material, texture and a number of other variables.

1.1 Adding a Texture
1) Click Create Texture in the 3D Layout Toolbar to create a new empty texture.

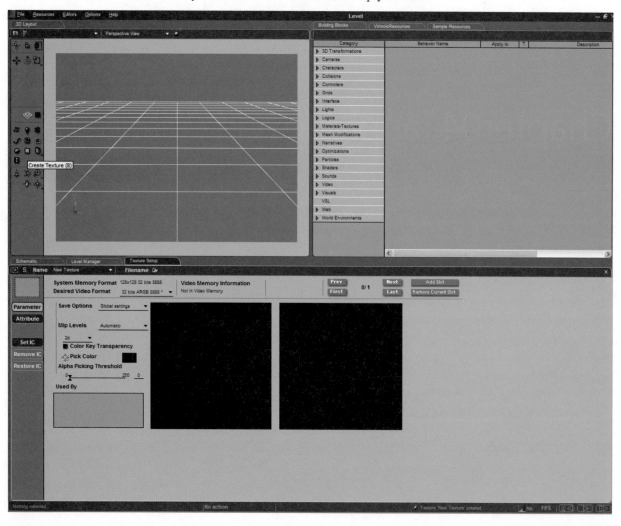

2) Click Add Slot and select the image Magic_Life.jpg located in Sample Resources\Textures.
This method of creating Textures has the limitation that image must be the same dimensions as the texture. For example, our texture size is 128x128, so we can only add images of a 128x128 resolution to the texture slots.

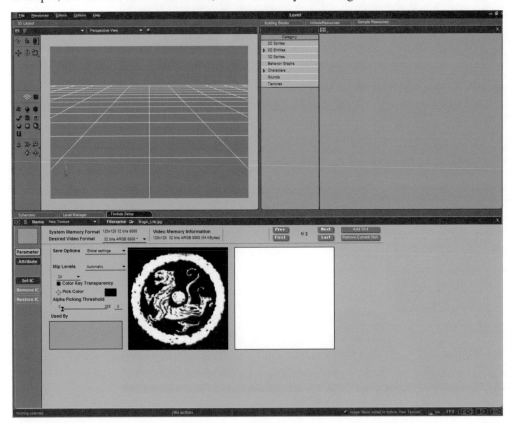

3) The next method is to simply drag in any image from a Resource database into the 3D Layout Window. Select StarField.jpg and add it to the scene as described above.

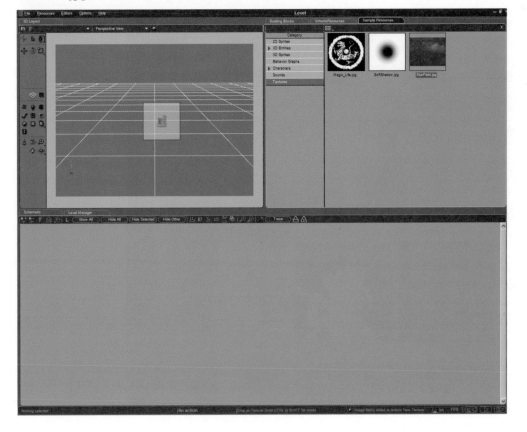

4) The textures Setup panel automatically appears and you can see the resolution of the texture has been automatically set to match the images' native resolution of 800x600.

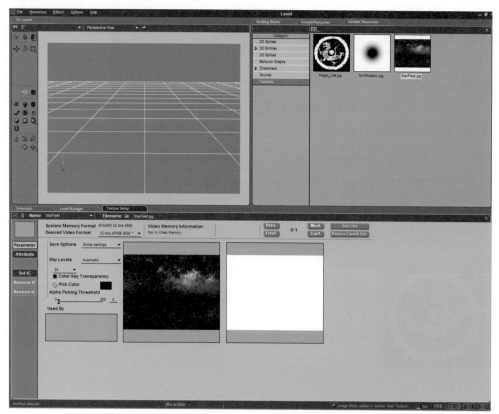

1.2 The Texture Setup Panel

1) Now, let's have a look at some of the options available within the Texture Setup panel.

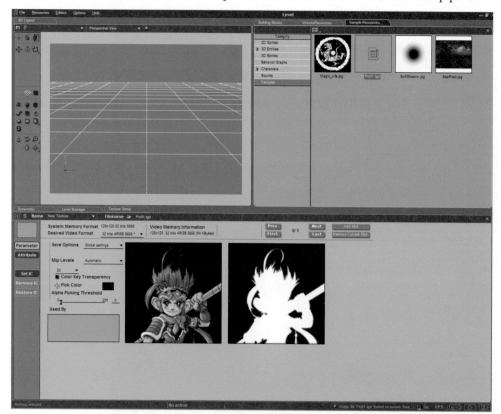

Name	The name of the texture
Filename	The filename of the texture in the current slot.
System Memory Format	The resolution, bit depth and mask information of the texture in your systems main memory.
Desired Video Format	The desired format for the image to be sent to the Video Memory. If an asterisk appears next to the Format name, this means it is natively supported by your 3D card.
Video Memory Information	The format and amount of memory used by the texture in your 3D cards memory.
Save Options	Allows you to configure how to store the texture when saving your composition
Mip Levels	Mip Mapping allows you to configure different resolution textures to use on objects at different distances from the camera.
2D \ Cube Map Volume Map	Allows the storage of different map types.
Color Key Transparency	Defines a single RGB value as the alpha color. You can use the Pick Color option to select the color to assign as the alpha value.
Used By	Shows all the entities currently using this texture.
Texture Preview Window	Displays the RGB version of the image
Alpha Channel Window	Displays the Alpha channel component of the image.

1.3 The Material Setup Panel

1) Lets go through the basic options for the Material Setup panel.

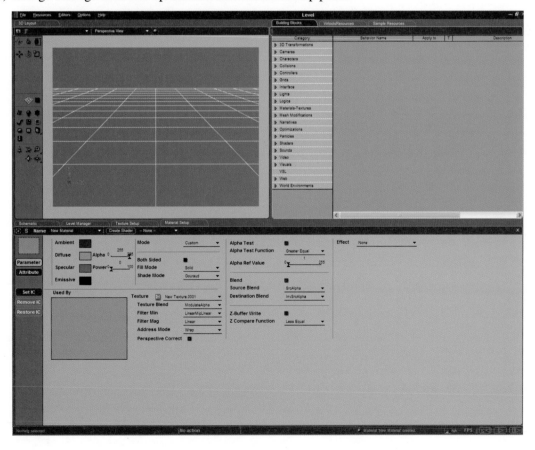

Color Parameters	The Ambient, Diffuse, Specular and Emissive options allow you to configure the basic lighting color configuration of the object.
	Alpha allows you to specify the objects transparency while Power sets the level of specularity (the "hot spot") for the object.
Mode Options	Allows you to set the material to support transparency, masking or other custom blending settings.
Both Sided	Renders the back faces of the object. i.e. faces of the object that are facing away from the camera.
Fill Mode	Point mode renders only the objects vertices, Wireframe renders the edges while Solid renders the faces (and is the normal mode of operation)
Shade Mode	Shade mode can be set to either Flat, which renders a single color value per face or Gouraud which linearly interpolates the light between the vertices of a face.
Used By	Shows all the objects using this Material.
Texture	The current Texture assigned to this Material.
Texture Blend	Allows you to define the way the Texture is affected by the Color Parameters of the Material.
Filter Min / Mag modes	Sets the way a Texel is interpolated when it is smaller or larger than its original size.
Address Mode	Defines how the texture is repeated on the object, for instance Wrapped or Mirrored.
Perspective Correct	This option helps avoid texture distortion and is automatically enabled by default on most 3D graphics cards.

2.0 Animating and Manipulating Materials

2.1 Basic Texture Animation

1) Click the Create 2D Frame button and configure the new frame so that it is 128x128 in size and centered on the screen.

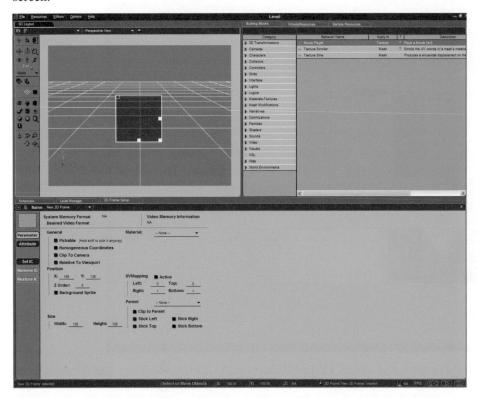

2) Click the Create Texture Button to create a new empty texture. Click the folder Icon next to Filename to open a new texture. From Sample Resources\2D Sprites add the file called Boom01.bmp.

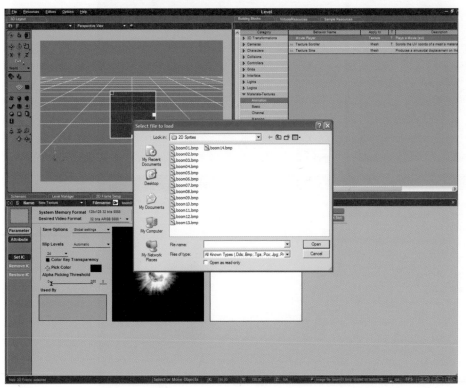

3) Click Add Slot button to add a sequence of pictures. Select Boom02.bmp through to Boom14.bmp then click Open. You should end up with a total of 14 slots.

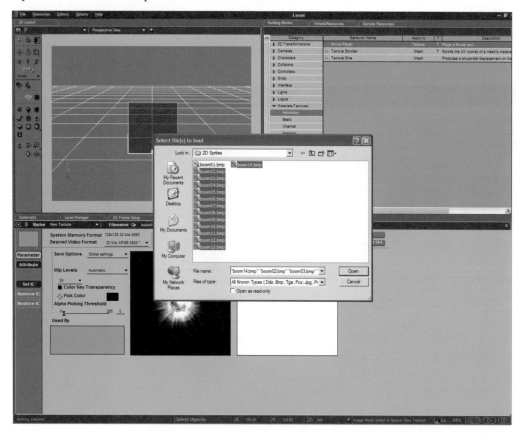

4) Next Click the Add Material button and set its Diffuse Color to 255,255,255 (white) and Texture to New Texture.

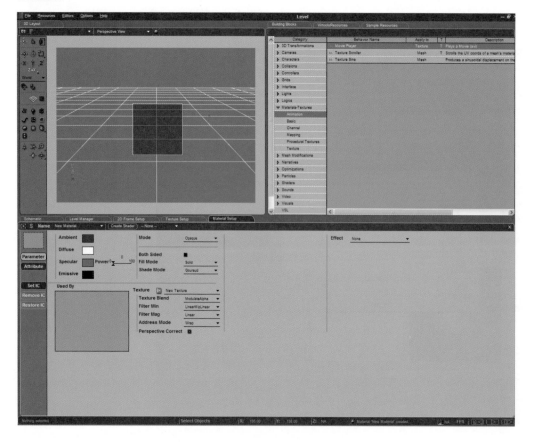

5) Right Click the 2D Frame and select Setup from the popup menu. Change the Material to New Material. The first slot of the Boom texture should appear in the 2D Frame.

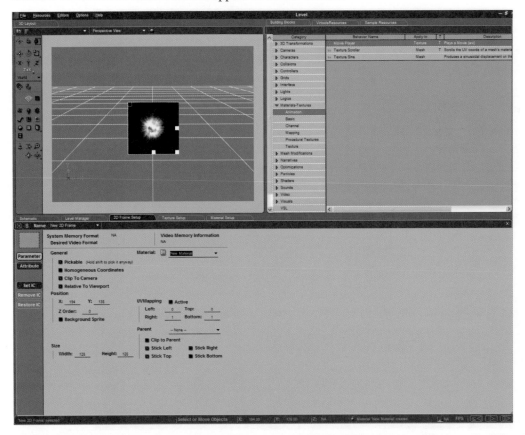

6) Right click the 2D Frame and create a Script for it. Drag the Movie Player BB from Building Blocks\Materials-Textures\Animation into the Script. Connect it with the Start Node.

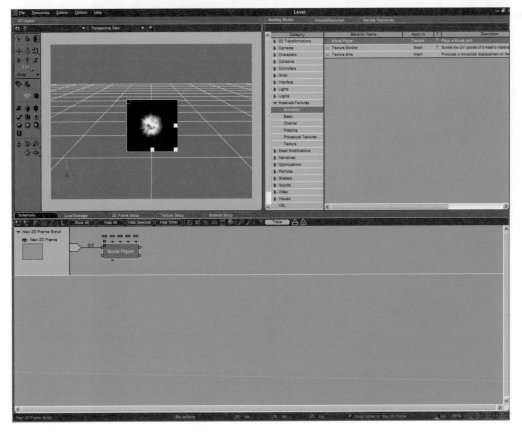

7) Double click the Movie Player BB and set the Target Texture to New Texture, Duration to 1 Second and Ending Slot to 14.

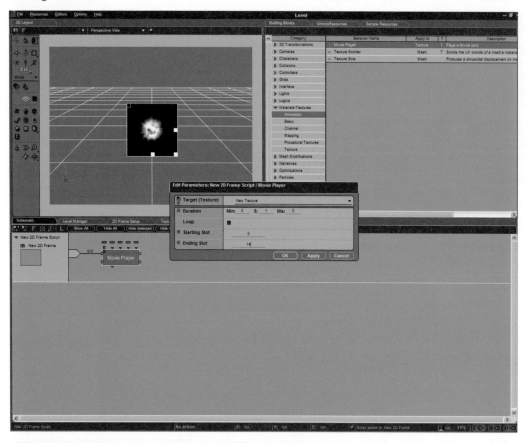

8) Click Play and the texture will loop inside the 2D Frame.

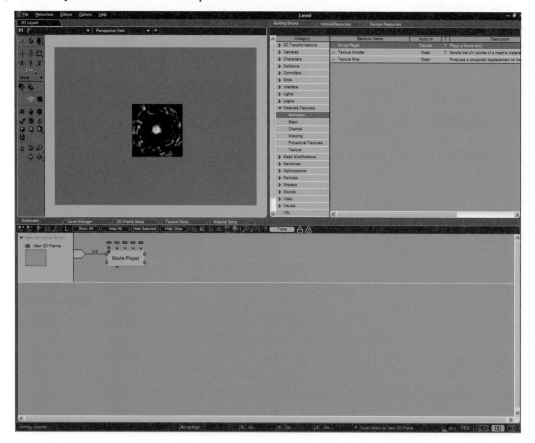

2.2 Creating Pseudo-3D Characters Using Sprites

1) Drag the image "animpic_f01.tga" from Sample Resources\3D Sprites in the 3D Layout Window and a 3D Sprite will be created containing the image.

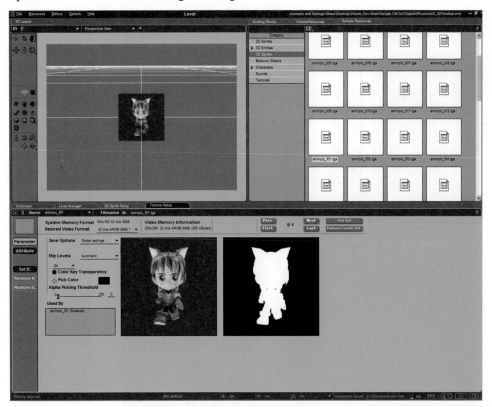

2) In Level Manager, open the Texture Setup panel for the Texture Animpic_f01. Use Add Slot to sequentially insert the images in the following order. animpic_f02-f12, b01-b12, l01-l12、r01-r12. You should end up with a total of 48 slots with the images in Front, Back, Left, Right order.

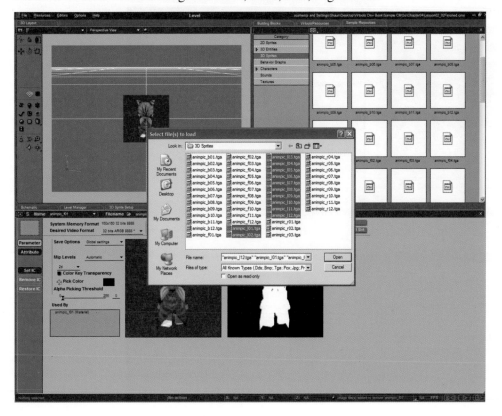

3) Now we need a scene. Add Sample Resources\characters\Scene\scene01. We also need to adjust the Size and Position of our 3D Sprite. Since the Sprite is not visible in the 3D Layout Window, use the Level manager to select open its Setup Panel and change the World Position to X=0, Y=20, Z=0 and set the Scale to X=40, Y=40.

4) Using the Level Manager panel open the Material Setup Panel and set the Material Mode to Transparent. This will enable the Alpha Channel of our Sprites texture.

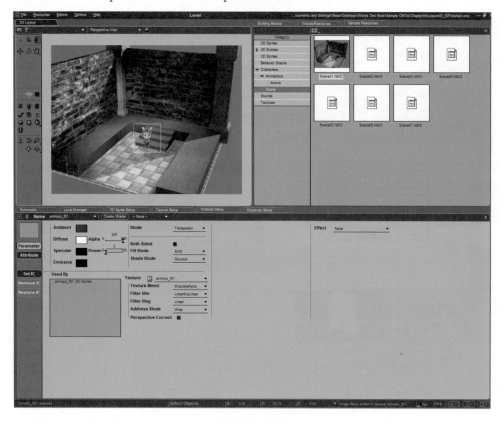

5) Because the 3D Sprite has no physical size in our 3D space we need to employ an invisible bounding box to use as a dummy character. To do this, add Sample Resources\3D Entities\Collision_Box into the scene. Create a Script for the Object.

6) Drag the Object Keep On Floor V2 BB from Building Blocks\3D Transformations\Constraint in the Script of our Collision Box and then connect it to the Start Node.

7) Add the Set Position BB from Building Blocks\3D Transformations\Basic to the Script of Animpic_f01 and connect to the Start Node. Connect the Out BOut to the In BIn to form a loop and set the BB's Referential parameter to Collision Box.

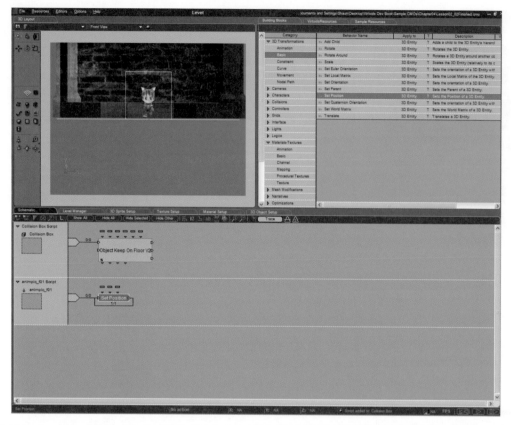

8) Create a Level Script and add the Switch on Key BB from Building Block\Controllers\Keyboard. Connect it to the Start Node.

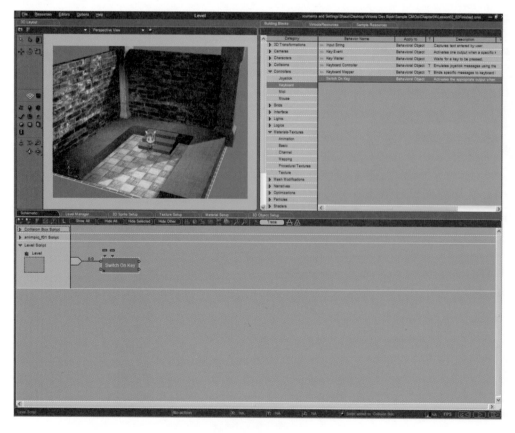

9)   Initially, Switch On Key has only two BOut pins. Since we need four keys (Up, Down, Left and Right) to set the characters four directions, right click Switch On Key and select Construct\Add Behavior Output from the popup menu and add two extra BOut pins.

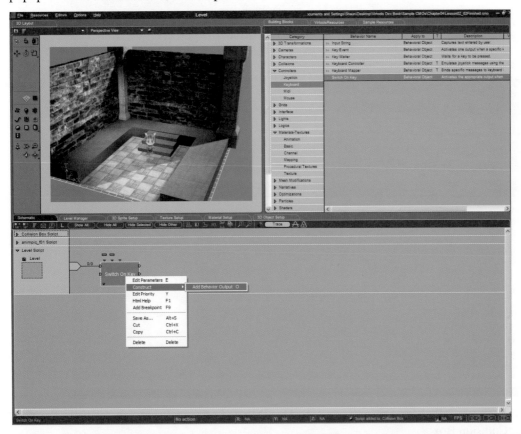

10) Double click the Switch On Key BB and set the corresponding keys to Up, Down, Left and Right.

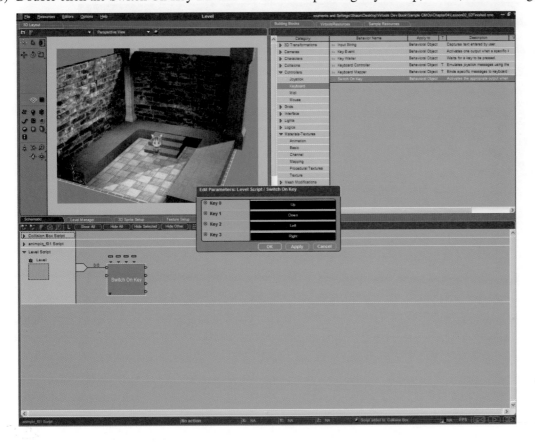

11) Now add four Send Message BB's and connect them to the four BOut pins of Switch On Key.

12) Set the Send Message BBs Message parameter to Up, Down, Left and Right respectively. Set the Dest parameter to 'Collision Box'.

13) Add a Wait Message BB to the Script of Collision Box. Set the Message parameter to Up.

14) Now, using what we learnt in Chapter two, add a Bezier Progression, Set Position and ParamOp BB to the Script. Set the Bezier Progression time to 1 second and the Set Position Referential to Collision Box. Next, Set the ParamOp to do a Float \ Vector Multiplication and set the Vector Z=30. Remember to connect the Out BOut of the Bezier Progression BB to the BIn of Wait Message to form a loop so we can move the character more than once.

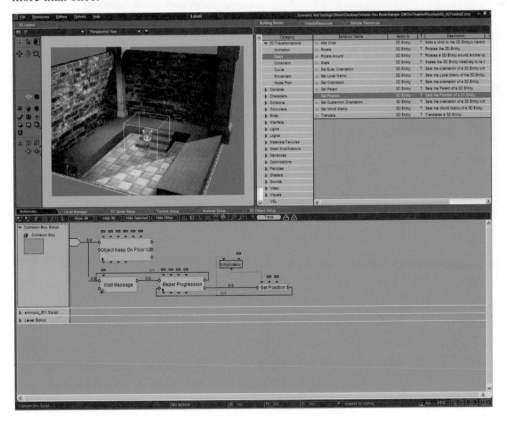

15) Add the Movie Player BB and configure it to play the texture Animpic_f01 for 1 second, the Start Slot to 12 and End Slot to 23.

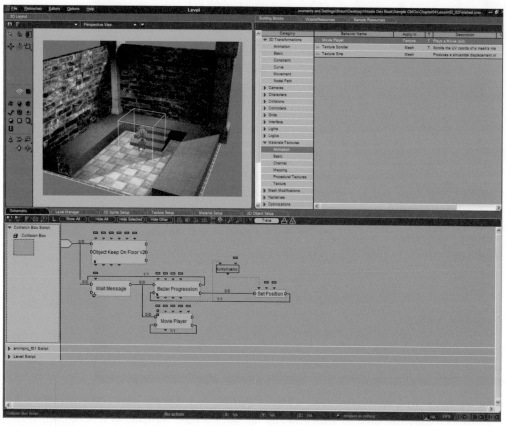

16) Remember to set the initial conditions for the Collision Box then Click Play. Press the "Up" key and the character moves up while the texture animation is player.

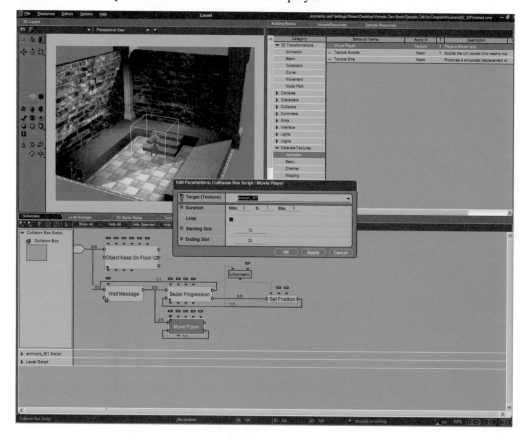

17) Following the same steps we just learnt, add the BB's for the characters other 3 directions, namely Down, Left and Right. Remember to change the Multiplication Param Op Vector values as follows: Down Z=-30; Right X=-30; Left X=30.

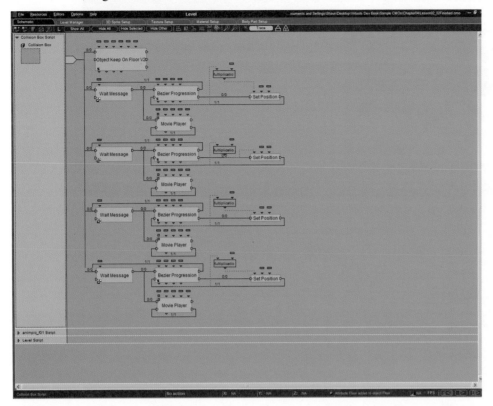

18) When one animation is being played, we want to stop the other Wait Message BB's from being activated; this will avoid two or three animations trying to be played at once. To do this, connect the Out of Wait Message "Up" to the Off of other the Wait Message BIn's. To restart the other Wait Message BB's once up has finished, connect the Bezier Progression BB's BOut to the In BIn of the other Wait Message BB's.

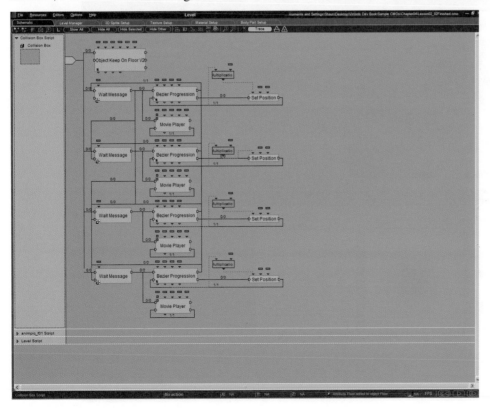

19) Now do the same for the other Wait Message BB's. The script is starting to get a little complicated!

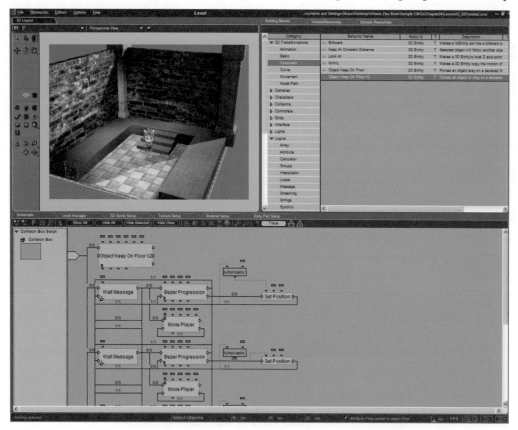

20) Finally, let's add a shadow to make the character seem like it is part of the scene. Drag the "SoftShadow. jpg" texture into the 3D Layout Window and add the Simple Shadow BB to the Collision Box Script. Set the Simple Shadow BB's Texture parameter to SoftShadow.

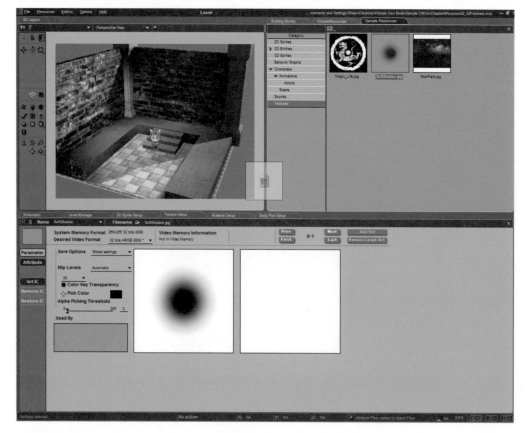

21) Click Play and try moving the character around the scene.

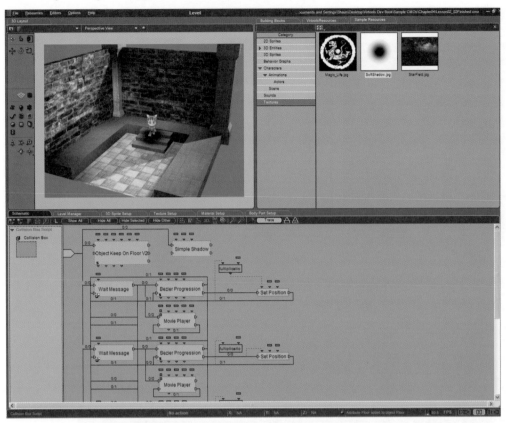

2.3 Animating Material Movement and Distortion

1) Drag "Scene03.nmo" from Sample Resources\Characters\Scenes. Resize and rotate the perspective view so that it's centered in the 3D Layout viewport.

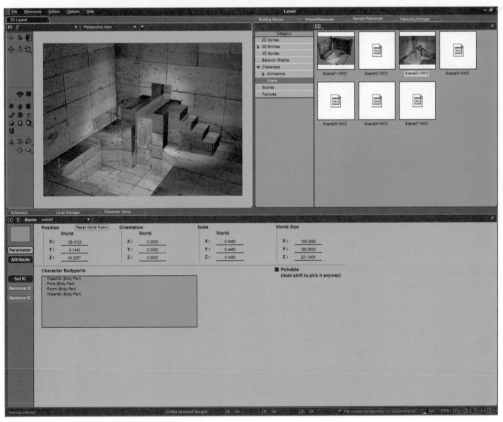

2) Find the Pool and Waterfall mesh objects in Level Manager\Global\Meshes and create Scripts for both.

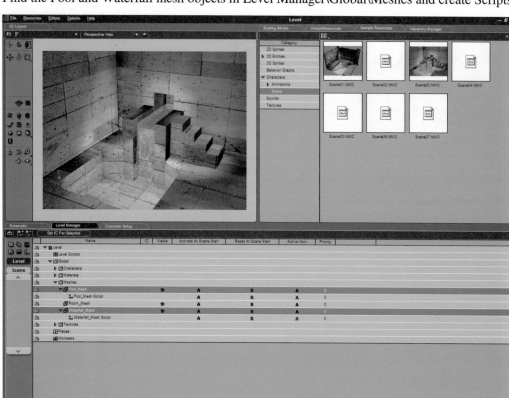

3) Add the Texture Scroller BB from Building Blocks\Materials-Textures\Animation to the Waterfall script and connect it to the Start Node.

4) Double click to open the Texture Scroller configuration dialog. Set the Scroll Vector to X=0、Y=0.01 and channel to −1. Connect the BOut of Texture Scroller to the BIn to form a loop. Click Play and the water should flow down into the Pool.

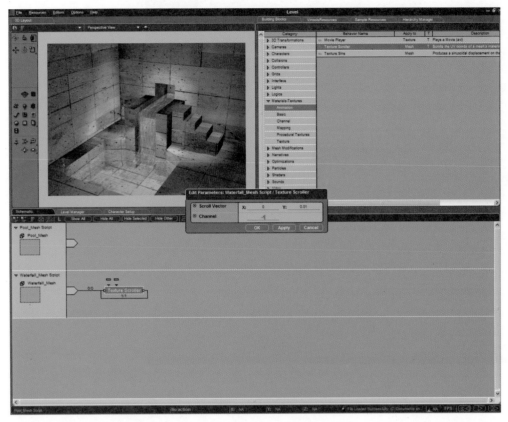

5) Next, add the Texture Sine BB from Building Blocks\Materials-Textures\Animation to the Pool Script and connect to the Start Node. Connect the BOut to the BIn to form a loop.

6) Open the Texture Sine configuration dialog window and set X Amplitude = 0.1, Y Amplitude = 0.1, Velocity = 3 and Channel = -1. Click Play and the water should oscillate on the Pool surface.

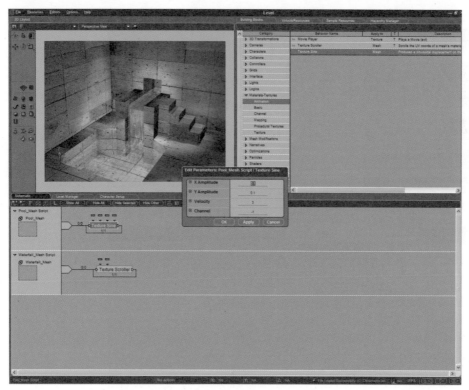

3.0 2D Interface

3.1 Creating a 2D Sprite

1) Drag the "Icon_Game.bmp" image from Sample Resources\2D Sprites into the 3D Layout Window.

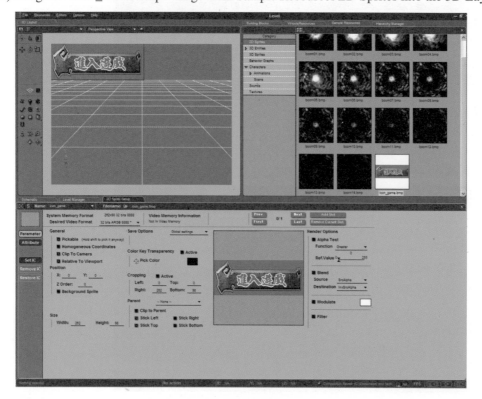

2) To process the Color Key, check the Color Key Transparency box and click Pick Color. In the image preview window, click the purple background color. The selected color is set to transparent and the change should be visible in the 3D Layout Window.

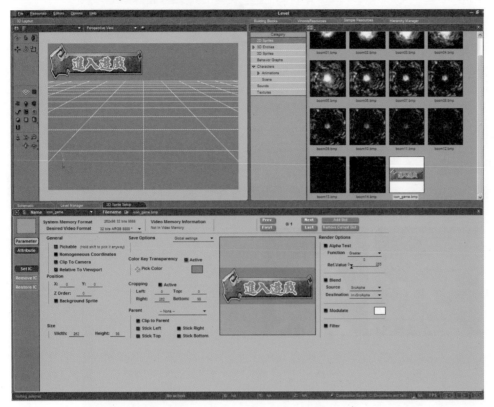

3.2 Creating a 2D Frame

1) Click Create 2D Frame to create an empty 2D Frame.

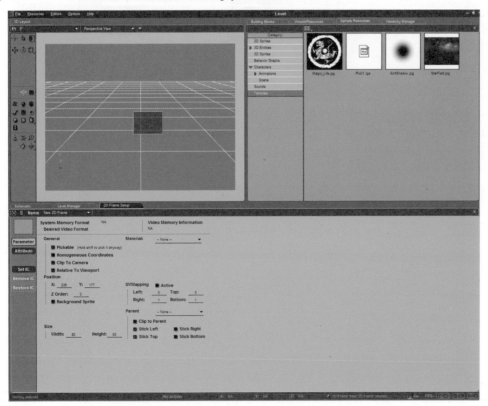

2) Add "Pic01.tga" from Sample Resources\Textures by dragging it into the 3D Layout Window.

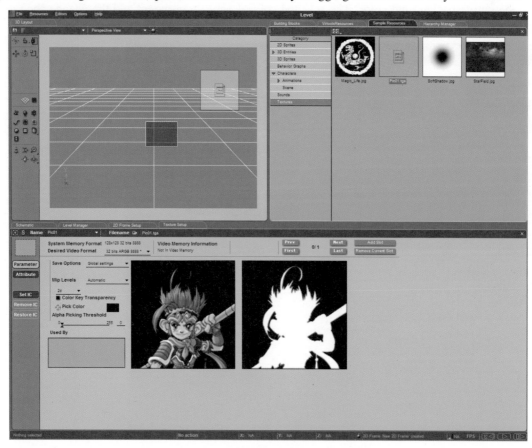

3) Click Create Material to add a new Material set its name to Pic01.

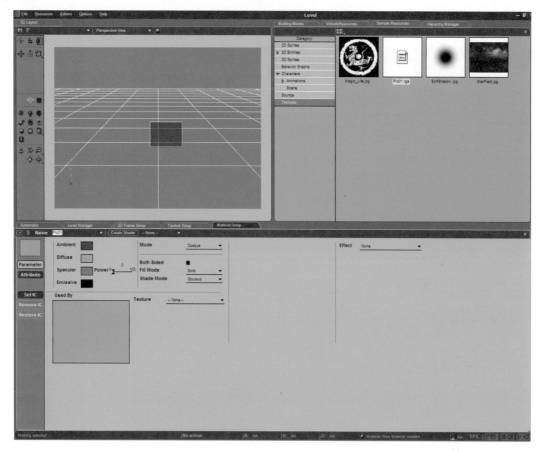

4) In the Material Setup panel, set Texture to Pic01 and set the Mode to Transparent.

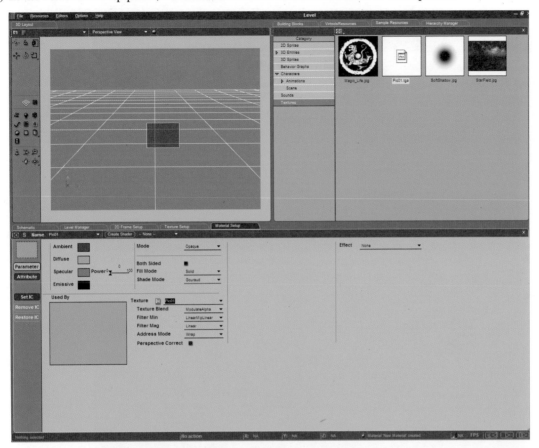

5) Open 2D Frame Setup panel and set its Material to Pic01. The texture will appear in the 2D Frame.

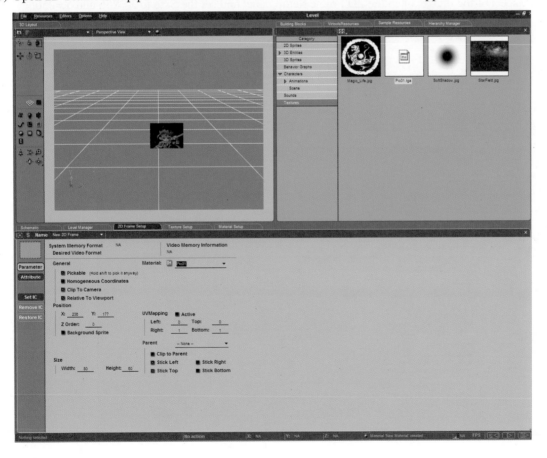

6) At this stage, the picture appears a little dark; this is due to the Diffuse setting of our Pic01 material. To make the image display correctly, in the Material Setup panel set the Diffuse color to RGB 255,255,255 (White).

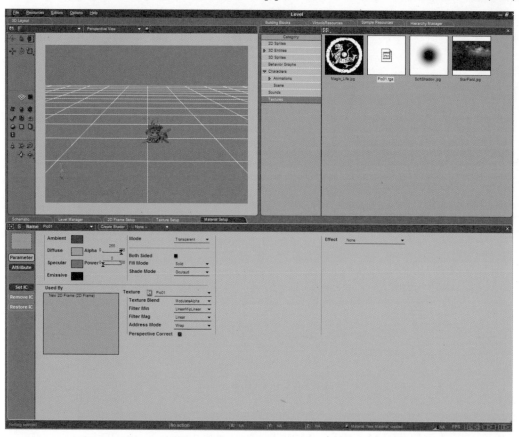

7) To correct the aspect of the image, open the 2D Frame Setup panel and set the Size to X=256 and Y=256.

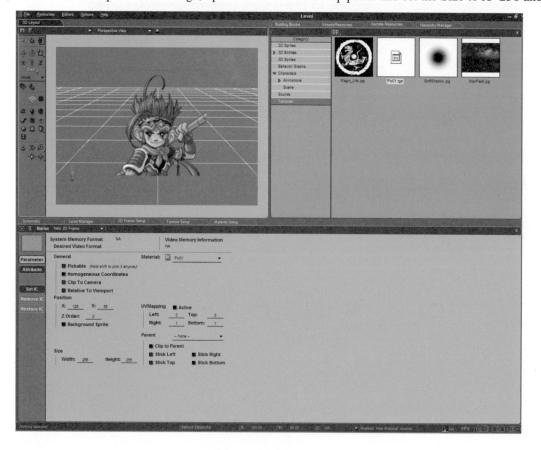

Chapter05 text messages

1.0 Basic Text Functions

Almost every game or 3D application, no matter how modern, needs to have some way of giving information or feedback to the user. This could be a textbox triggered by an event, a dialogue between two characters or even a few paragraphs describing a back-story to the player; the fact is, text is an important communication medium between your application and the person who is using it.

In this chapter we look at how to create two types of text feedback within your composition. The first lesson deals with setting up 2D text that is bound to a 2D Frame and the second with 3D text that is bound to a 3D Frame.

In the last lesson we set up a scene with two characters and create a dialogue between them; you will see that even this simple exercise adds a great deal of depth to the user experience.

1.1 Displaying 2D Text

1) Click the Create 2D Frame button and create a script for it. This 2D Frame will act as a placeholder for our text.

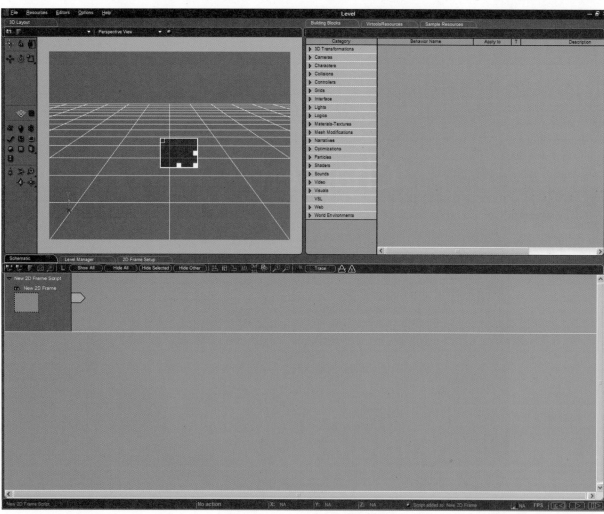

2) Insert the Create System Font BB from Building Blocks\Interface\Fonts into the script and connect it with the Start Node.

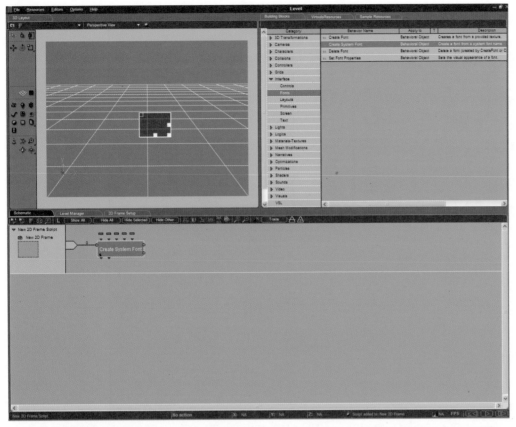

3) Double click the Create System Font BB and Set the parameters "Font Name" to "Font01", "System Font Name" to "Arial", "Font Weight" to "Normal" and make sure "Underline" is checked.

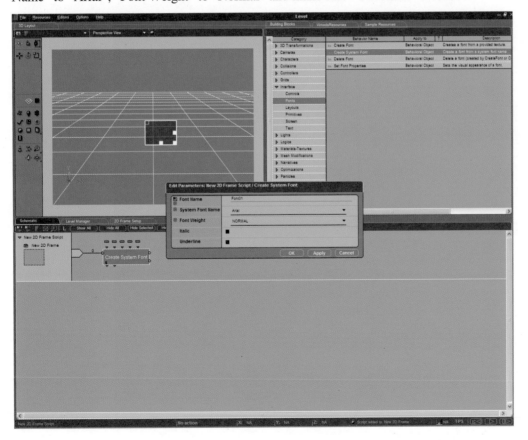

4) Insert the Set Font Properties BB from Building Blocks\Interface\Fonts and connect it with the "Success" BOut of the "Create System Font" BB.

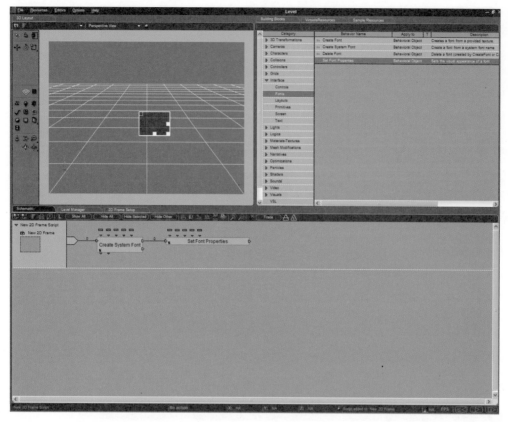

5) Connect the Font Type POut of the Create System Font BB with the Font Type PIn of the Set Font Properties BB. This will allow the Set Font Properties BB to automatically use the Font created by the Create System Font BB.

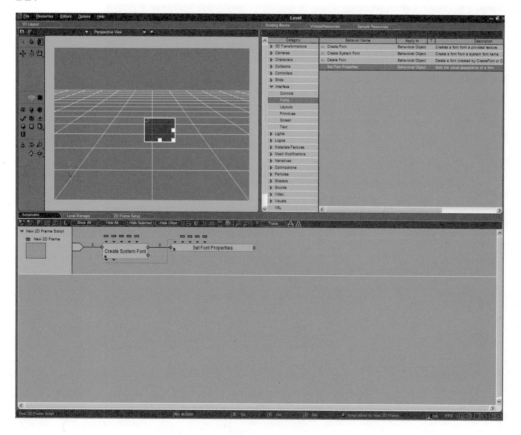

6) Open the Set Font Properties configuration dialog and set "Space" to "X=0, Y=0", "Scale" to "X=1, Y=1", "Italic Offset" to "0", and "Color" to "R=255, G=186, B=0, A=255".

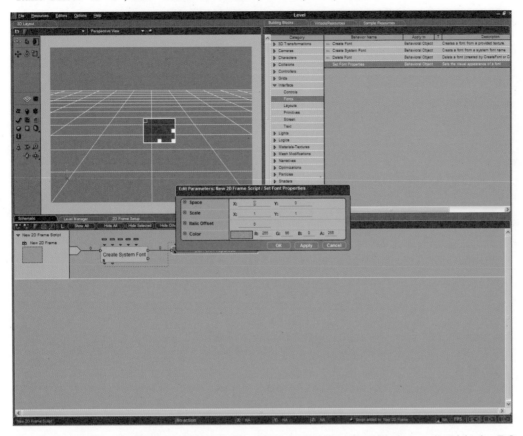

7) Insert the 2D Text BB from Building Blocks\Interface\Text and connect it with the BOut of the Set Font Properties BB.

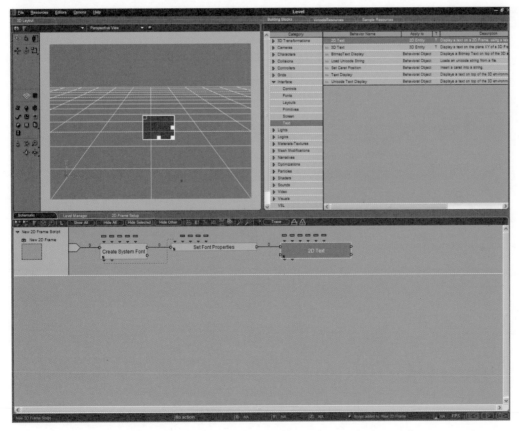

8) Connect the Font Created POut of the Create System Font BB to the Font Pin of the 2D Text BB. Again, this will use the Font created by the Create System Font BB by default.

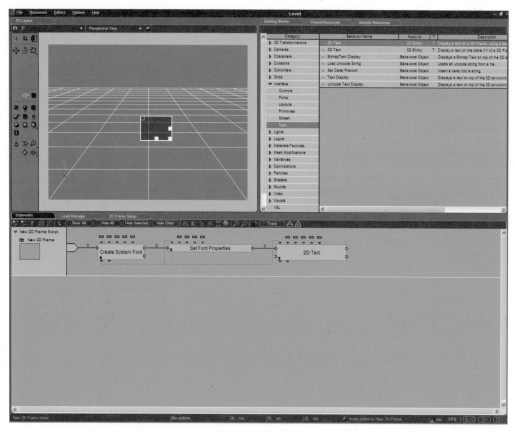

9) Open the Edit Parameters dialog of the 2D Text BB and set the Text to "Testing 2D Text". Leave the other parameters as they are for now.

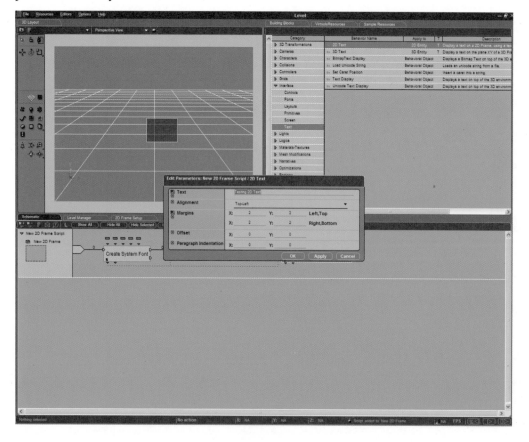

10) Click Play and the text we just entered will appear in the color we chose and at the location of our 2D Frame. You can adjust the parameters of the Set Font Parameters and 2D Text BB's to modify variables like the spacing, alignment, margins and scaling of your text.

1.2 Displaying 3D Text

1) Add a 3D Frame and create a Script for it.

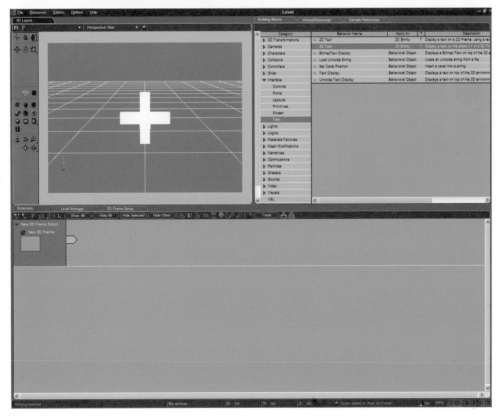

2) Add the Create System Font and Set Font Properties BB and connect them using the same method as we used in the last lesson (Steps 2 to 6).

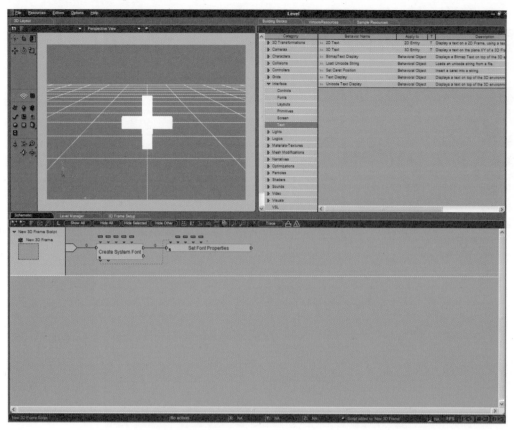

3) Add 3D Text BB from Building Blocks\Interface\Text, and connect it with the BOut of the Set Font Properties BB.

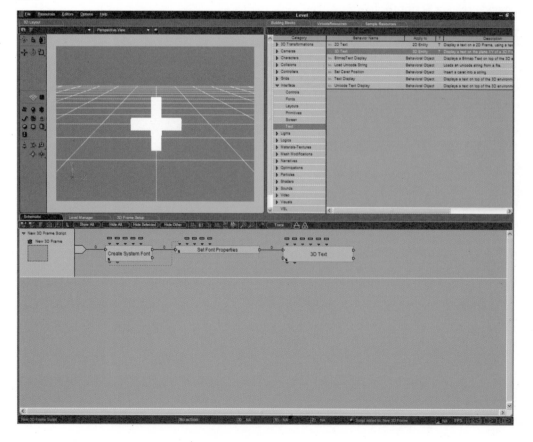

4) Connect the Font Created POut of the Create System Font BB with the Font Pin of the 3D Text BB.

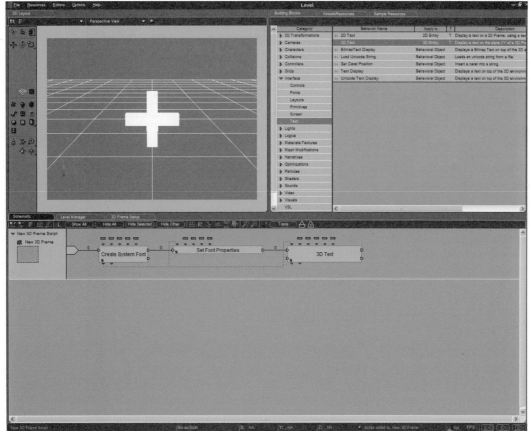

5) Open the Edit Parameters dialog of the 3D Text BB and set the Text to "Testing 3D Text".

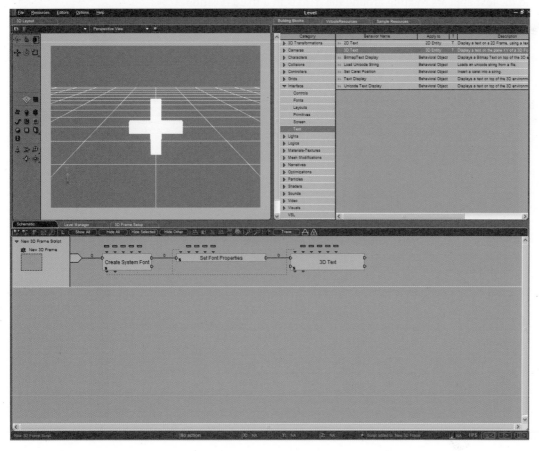

6) To really see the text in '3D' lets add the Rotate BB from Building Blocks\3D Transformations\Basic. Connect it to the Start Node and then connect it's BIn and BOut pins to form a loop.

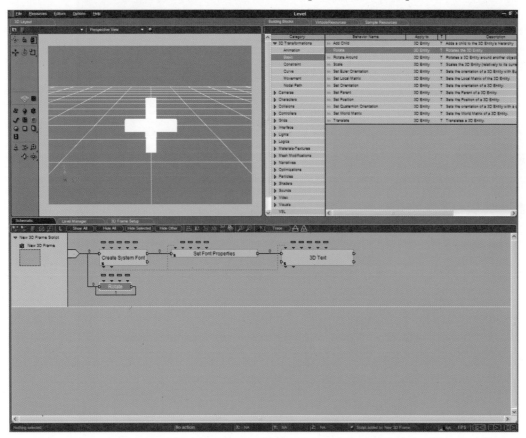

7) Click Play and the text appears rotating around the Y axis in a fixed position.

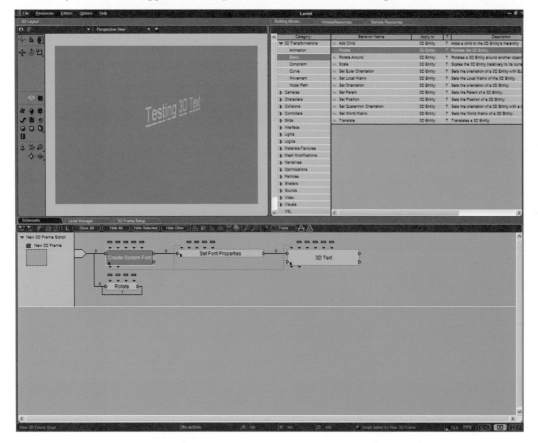

1.3 Displaying Text Messages

1) Create a 2D Frame and drag the image "Background.jpg" from Sample Resources\Textures into the 2D Frame.

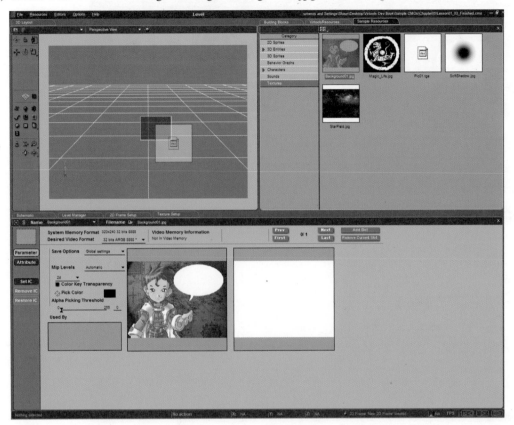

2) Create a new material and set its Texture to Background01. Set the materials Diffuse color to White (RGB 255, 255, 255).

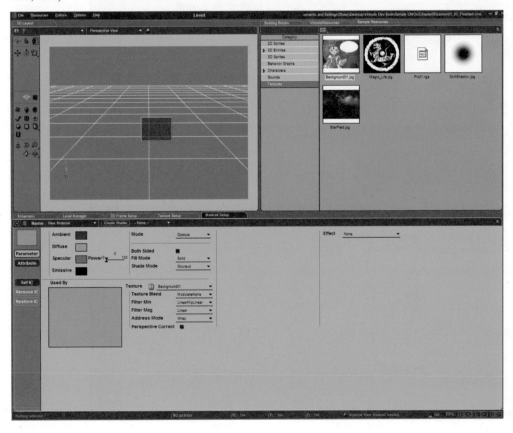

3) Open the 2D Frame Setup panel and change its Material to New Material. Set the X and Y Position to "0" and set the Width to "320" and Height to "240".

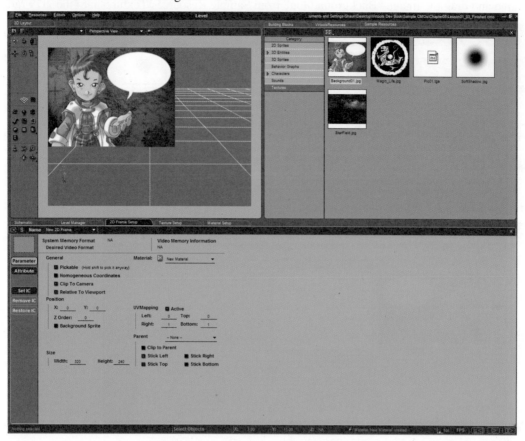

4) Now, create a new Level Script and add the Text Display BB from Building Blocks\Interface\Text.

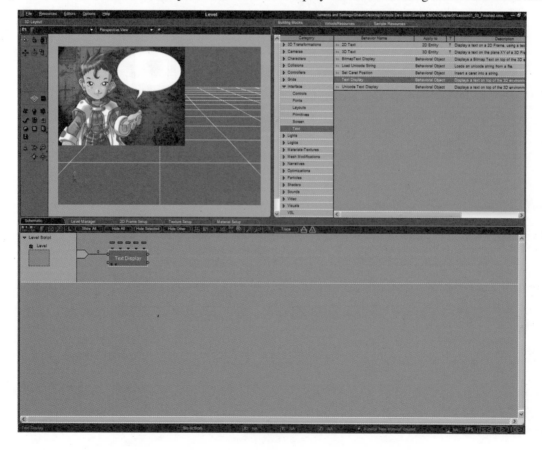

5) Open the Edit Parameters dialog of the Text Display BB and set "Offset" as "X=70, Y=30", "Color" as "R=92, G=75, B=50, A=255" and set the Alignment to Center. Click the Expand icon next to the Text Parameter and add following text (make sure you keep the same number of words per line);
"Welcome…"
"This is some test"
"text using the Text"
"Display BB"

6) Click Play and the text doesn't show up on screen. This is because our 2D Frame is in Layer 1 and the text is in Layer 0. To fix this we need to move the 2D Frame to the layer behind the text.
Open the 2D Frame Setup panel and change the Z Order parameter to -1, which effectively places the 2D Frame behind the text.

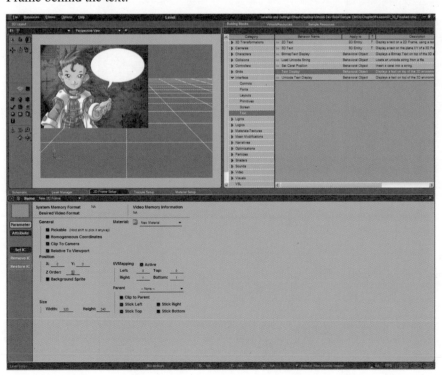

7) Click Play again and you can see some of the text appears in the dialogue area of the picture. However, the lower half of our text has been cut off.

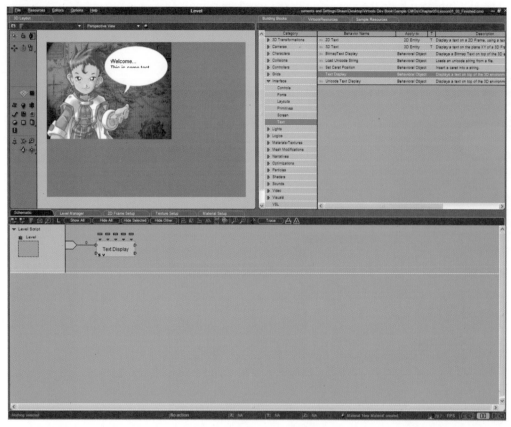

8) This problem is due to the text sprite not being large enough. Right click the Text Display BB and select Edit Settings from the popup menu.

9) In the Edit Settings dialog, change the Y value of the Sprite Size parameter to 200. This will effectively 'expand' the canvas that we can use to write text on.

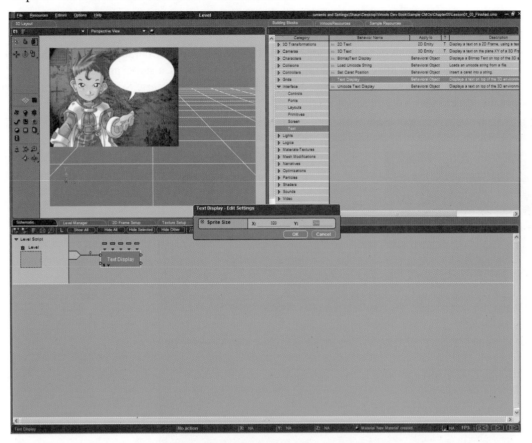

10) Click Play and the text will be displayed correctly in the dialogue area.

2.0 In-Game Dialogues

2.1 Creating a Two Character Dialogue

1) Start by adding the following resources to the scene; From Sample Resources\Characters\Scenes add Scene02. Adjust the view so that the scene appears centered in the viewport and at a good angle for viewing. Now add the Sun WuKong and YinJiao characters from Sample Resources\Characters. Scale and position the two characters as per the screenshot.

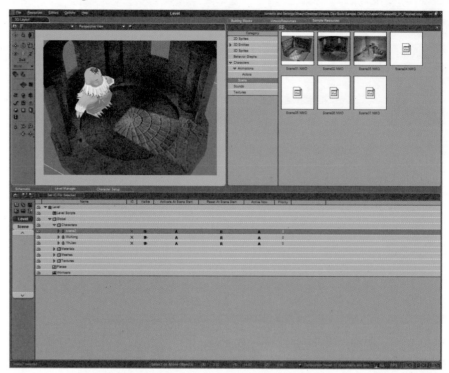

2) Create a new light and position it above the characters in the center of the room. Next add the Shadow Caster Receiver attribute for both the Floor and Wall objects and add the Floor attribute for the Floor object.

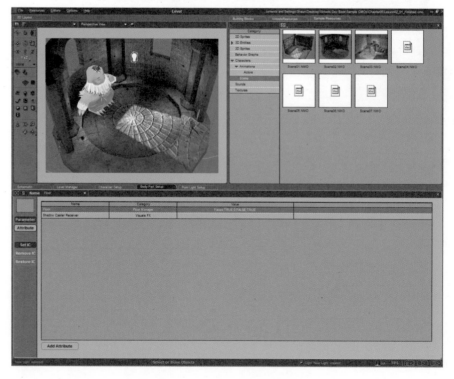

3) Add the Wait, Run, Attack and Back animations to WuKong. Create a script for WuKong and add the Enhanced Keep Character on Floor, Keyboard Controller, Character Controller and Shadow Caster BB's to the script. Connect each BB to the Start Node and configure them as we did in Chapter 3 Lesson 2.1 (Creating Characters and Floors) and Lesson 5.3 (Creating Projected Shadows). Lastly add the Moving Obstacle attribute to the WuKong Character.

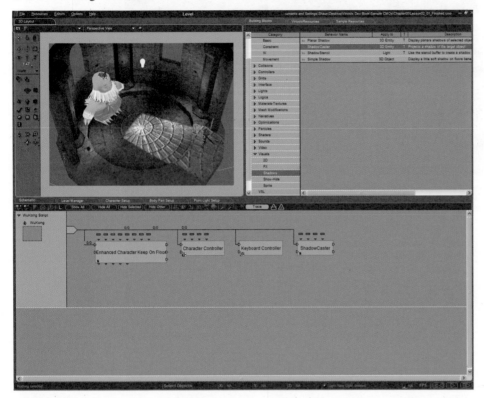

4) Add the Wait animation to YinJiao and then create his Script. Add the Enhanced Keep Character on Floor, Character Controller and Shadow Caster BB's to YinJiao's Script. Connect them all to the Start Node. In the Character Controller Edit Parameters dialog, change YinJiao's Wait animation to Wait.

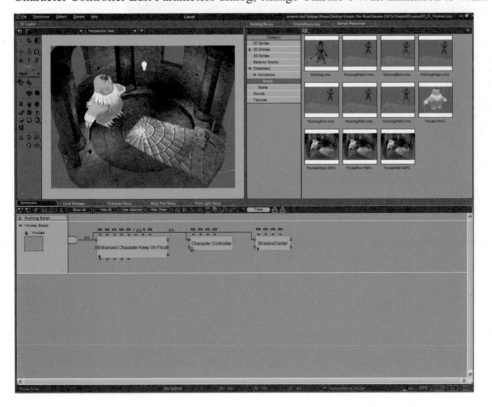

5) Switch to Top View and create a grid over the scene. Use the arrow controls in the Grid Setup window to add more horizontal and vertical blocks to the Grid; a size of 20 x 20 should be sufficient. Create a new layer type called Collision and add it to the Layer list on the left. To finish, fill in all 'blocked' areas of the scene using the Collision layer.

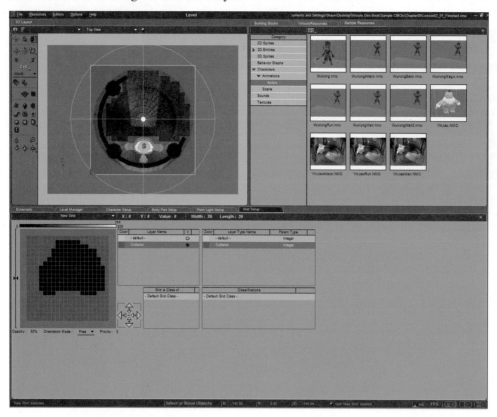

6) Add the Layer Slider BB from Building Blocks\Grids\Basic to the script of WuKong and set the Layer to Slide On parameter to Collision.

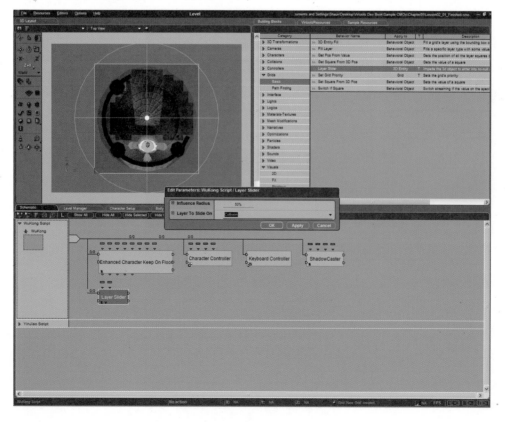

7) Hold down Ctrl+Shift on your keyboard and drag the file "Pic01.tga" from Sample Resources\Textures into the scene to add WuKong's portrait. This will create a 2D Frame and associated Material and Texture. Move the 2D Frame to the bottom left hand corner of the scene, enable Homogenous Coordinates and set the ZOrder to 1. Lastly, rename the 2D Frame to "WuKong Portrait" change the Material Mode to Transparent to enable the alpha channel.

8) Again, hold down Ctrl+Shift on your keyboard and drag the file "Pic02.tga" from Sample Resources\Textures into the scene to add YinJiao's portrait. Move the 2D Frame to the bottom left hand corner of the scene, enable Homogenous Coordinates and set the ZOrder to 2. Rename this 2D Frame to "YinJiao Portrait" and set the Material Mode to Transparent.

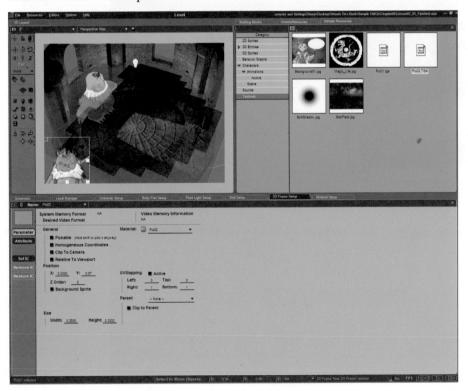

9) Add a 2D Frame to the scene and rename it to DialogueBox. Enable the Homogenous Coordinates and set the Position to X=0.0 and Y=0.8. Now set the Size to Width=1.0 and Height=0.2. Change the ZOrder parameter to -1.

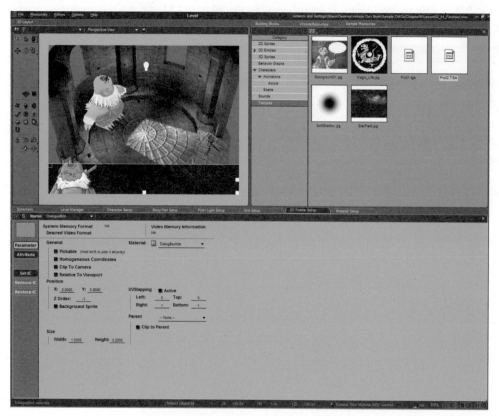

10) Create a new Material and call it DialogueBoxMat. Set the Material Mode to Transparent, the Diffuse Alpha to 175 and the Diffuse Color to Black (RGB 0,0,0). In the 2D Frame Setup Panel for our DialogueBox, set the Material to DialogueBoxMat.

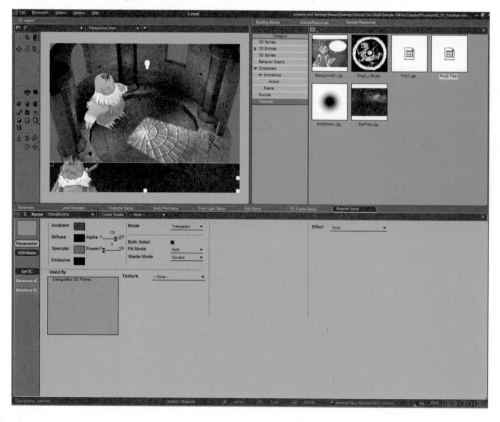

11) In the Level Manager, find the WuKong Portrait 2D Frame and create script for it. Add the Wait Message BB and connect it to the Start Node. Set the Message parameter to "Dialogue". Add Show BB from Building Blocks\Visuals\Show-Hide and connect it with the Wait Message BB. Connect the BOut of the Show BB to the BIn of the Wait Message BB to form a loop.

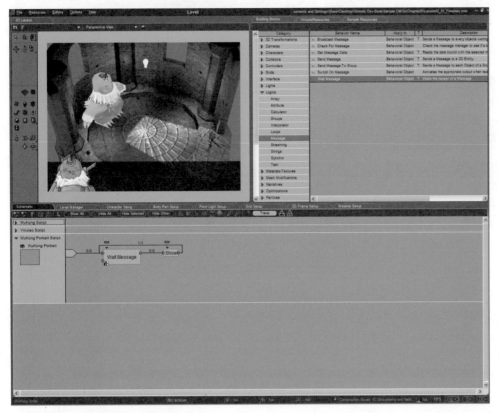

12) Add another Wait Message BB and the Hide BB. Connect them the same way as in the previous step. Set the Message parameter to "Hide"

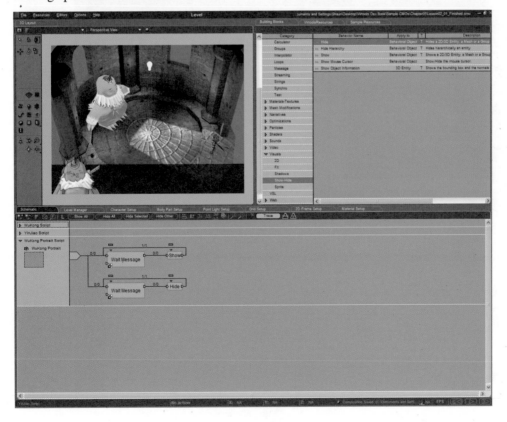

13) Follow the same steps to setup the YinJiao Portrait.

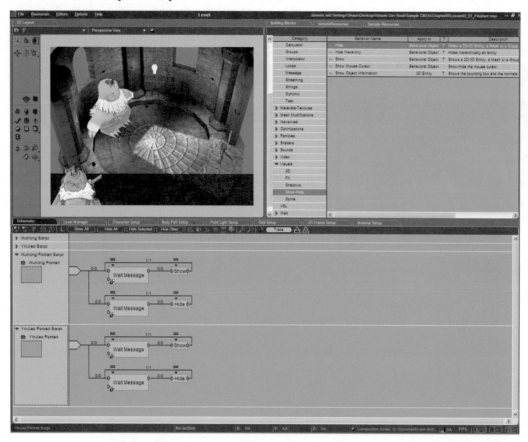

14) We need to do the same again for the DialogueBox but in this case we don't loop the Show BB back to the Wait Message BB.

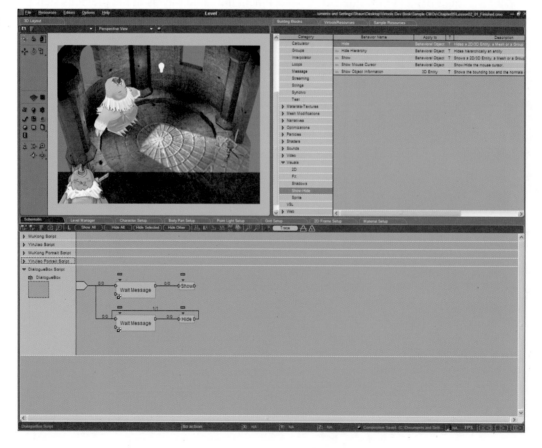

15) In Level Manager, highlight the three 2D Frames WuKong Portrait, YinJiao Portrait and DialogueBox. Right click them and select Place Selected in New Group. Call the new group "DialogueControl".

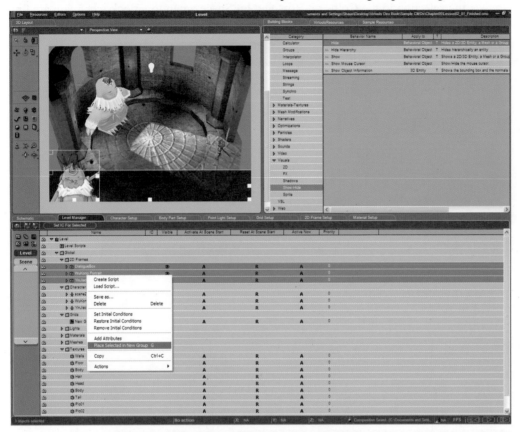

16) Click the 'Eye' icon next to each of the three 2D Frame to set them to invisible. Highlight the three objects, right click and in the popup menu, select Set Initial Conditions.

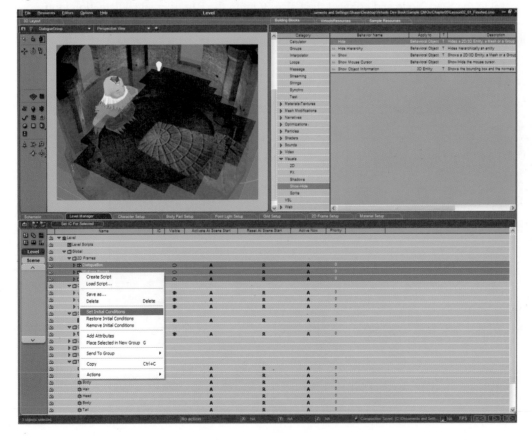

17) Add the object Collision Box from Sample Resources\3D Entities to the scene. Scale the object to approximately the width of the room. To avoid accidentally selecting other objects when you are scaling, hit the Spacebar to lock the selection to the Collision Box, and hit Space again to unlock when you are finished. Lastly, add the attribute Fixed Obstacle in the Collision Manager category.

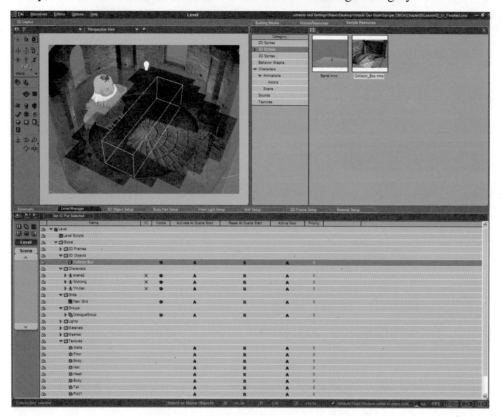

18) Create a script for the Collision Box and add the Collision Detection BB from Building Blocks\Collisions\3D Entity. Connect it to the Start Node and connect the False BOut to the BIn to create a detection loop.

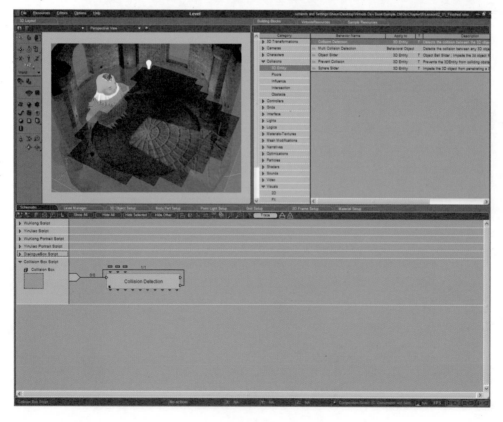

19) Add two "Send Message" BB's and connect them to the "True" BIn of the Collision Detection BB. Set both the Send Message BBs to "Dialogue", then set the Destination to DialogueBox and YinJiao Portrait respectively.

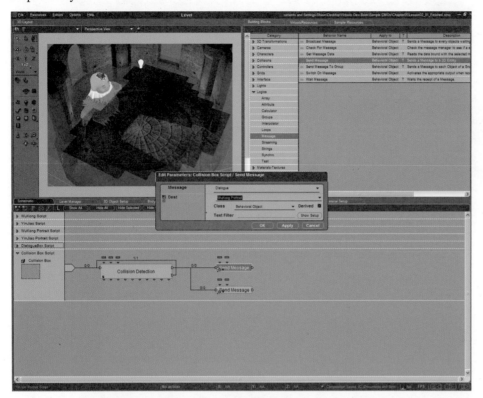

20) Create a Level Script. Add the Set Background Color BB from Building Blocks\World Environments\ Background and set the color to Black. Next add the Key Waiter BB from Building Blocks\Controllers\ Keyboard and add the Send Message to Group BB from Building Blocks\Logics\Message. Connect the Key Waiter BB to the Start Node and to the Send Message to Group BB. Connect the Out BIn of Send Message to Group to the BIn of Key Waiter to form a loop.

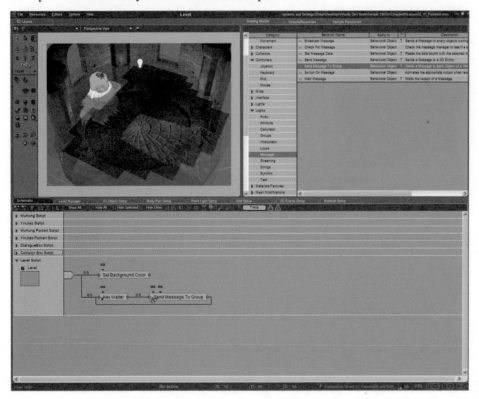

21) Set the Key parameter as "Space" for the Key Waiter BB. Set the Message as "Next Sentence" and Group as "Dialogue Group" for the Send Message to Group BB.

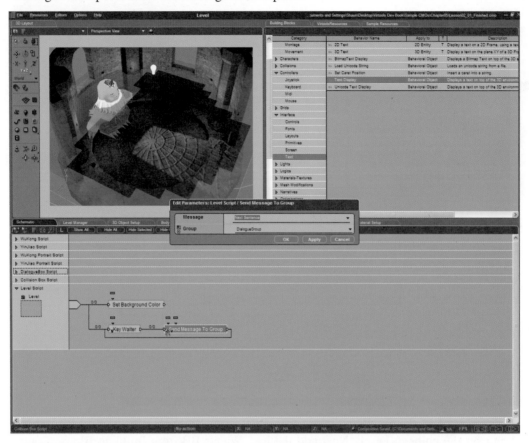

22) Add a Text Display BB in the Dialogue Box script and connect it to the Show BB.

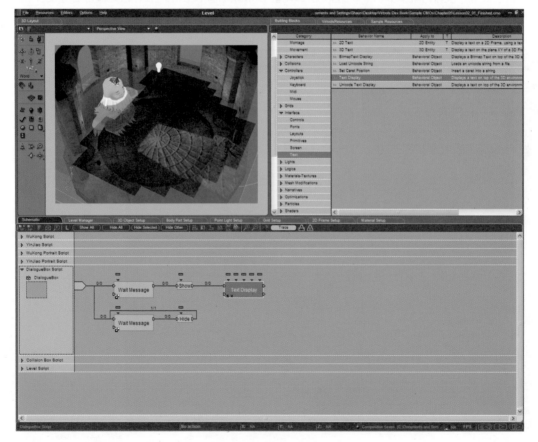

23) Open the Edit Parameters dialog and set Offset to X=170, Y=340 and Size=10". Type the dialogue for YinJiao into the Text field.

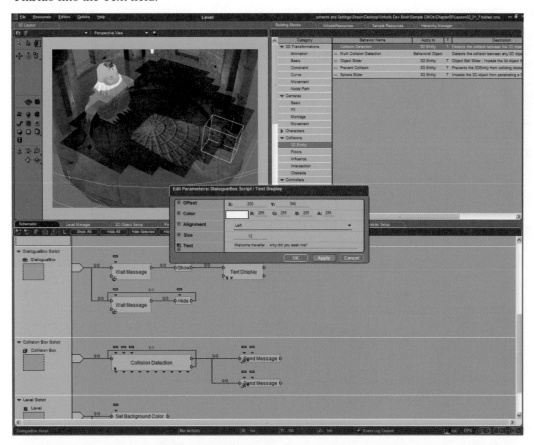

24) Click Play and walk toward YinJiao. The YinJiao Portrait, DialogueBox and Text message appear.

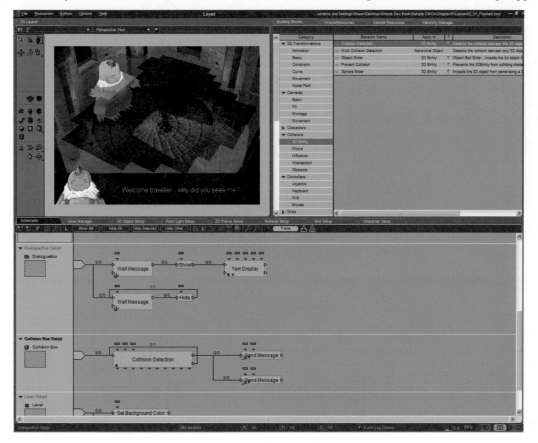

25) Insert a Wait Message BB after the Text Display BB and connect them. Set the Message parameter of the Wait Message BB to "Next Sentence". Connect its BOut to the Off BIn of the Text Display BB. This will clear the text when the "Next Sentence" message is received.

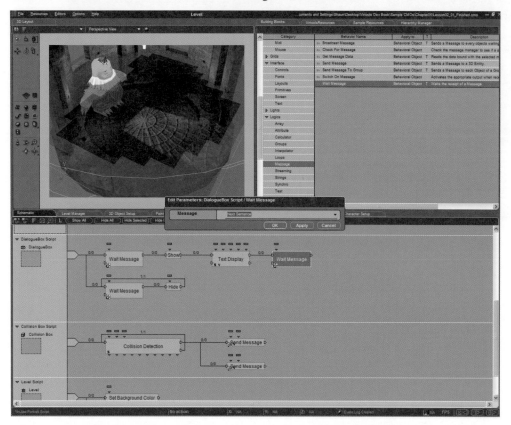

26) Add two Send Message BB's to the script and set them as follows; the first to send the "Hide" message to the YinJiao Portrait and the second to send the "Dialogue" message to the WuKong Portrait.

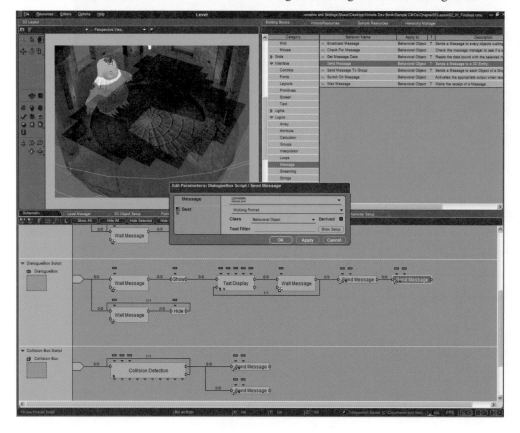

27) Now, add another Text Display BB with exactly the same parameters as the first except change the Text to be that of our WuKong character. Connect it with the Send Message BB.

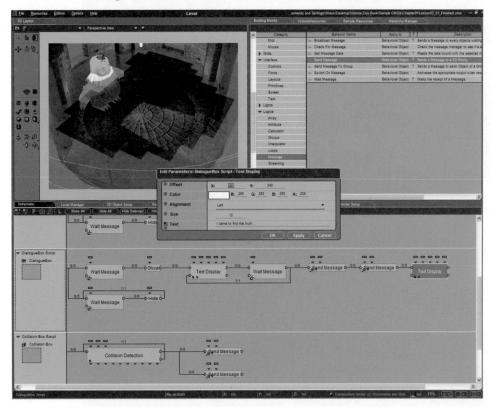

28) To avoid the messages skipping too quickly if the Spacebar is held for a longer period of time, we need to delay the script for a few milliseconds using the Timer BB. So, add the Timer BB from Building Blocks\ Logic\Loops and also add a Wait Message BB. Connect the last Text Display BB to the Timer BB and the Timer BB to the Wait Message BB. Lastly connect the Loop In and Loop Out pins of the Timer BB to form a loop.

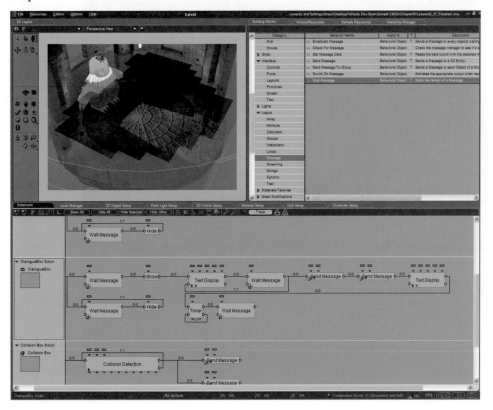

29) Open the window of "Timer" and set the duration as "Ms: 500".

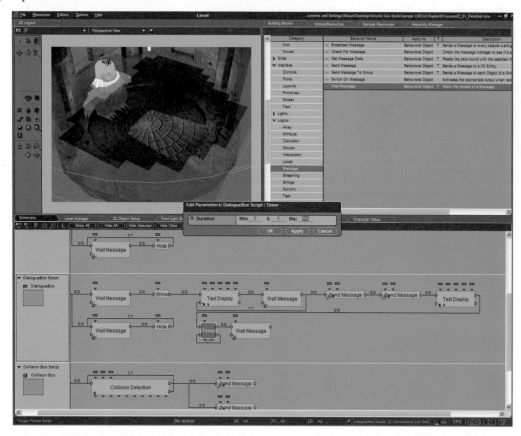

30) By following the same steps, we can create a final dialogue for YinJiao. Add two Send Message BB's and a Text Display BB and configure them accordingly. Don't forget to connect the Out BOut of the last Wait Message BB to the Off BIn of the previous Text Display BB to turn off the last characters text.

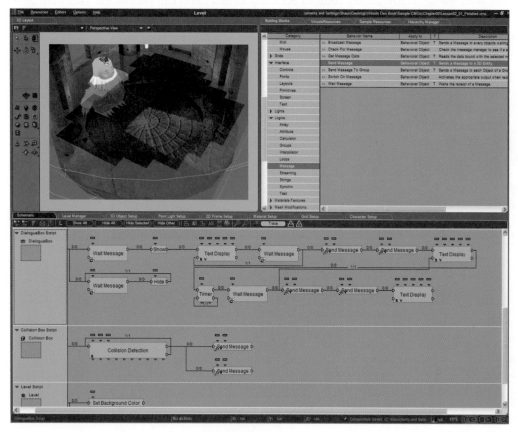

31) Finally, when the dialogue is over we need to clean up and hide all of the dialogue objects. Add a Timer BB, Wait Message BB and a Send Message to Group BB. Connect the Timer BB and Wait Message BB as per the previous steps and set the Send Message to Group BB to "Hide" the "Dialogue Group".

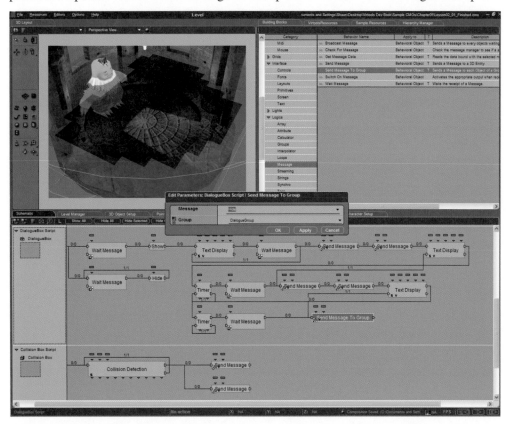

32) In the Level Manager, select the Grid object and make it invisible, this will give us a better view of our scene. Click Play to test the scene.

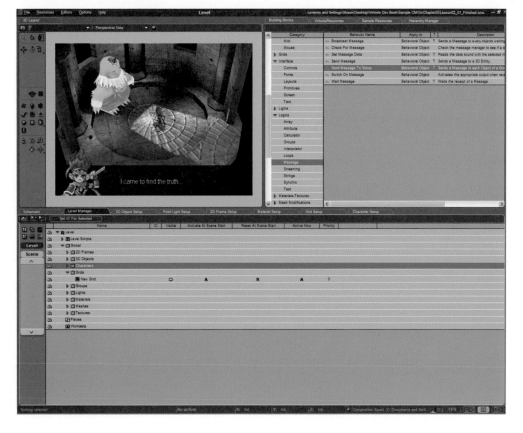

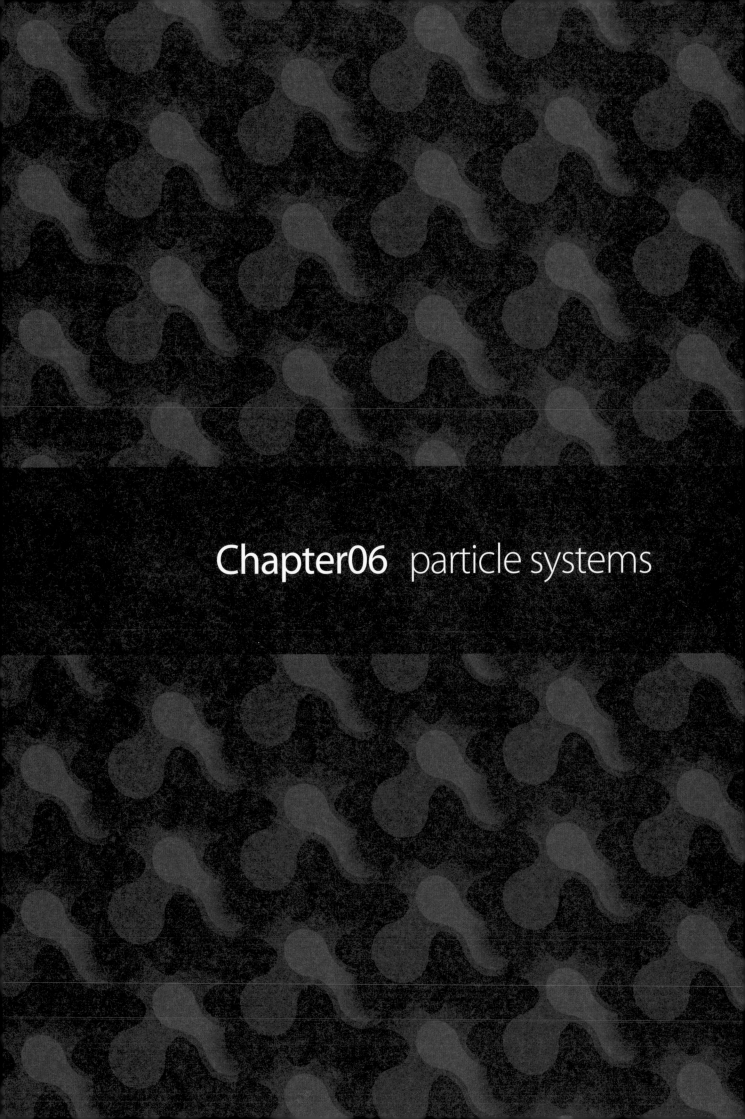

Chapter06 particle systems

1.1 Introducing the Particle Emitter

The Particle System feature in Virtools is an extremely versatile tool that can be used to create various special effects and stimulating visuals with just a little imagination.

Virtools contains a total of 9 types of Particle Emitters, the BB that is responsible for creating the particles. Each type basically emits the particles using a different shape or surface such as a Sphere, Disc or 3D Entity. You can then configure a number of parameters to change the way the particles are emitted, for instance you can adjust the speed, direction, color and size.

In fact, the Particle Emitter BB's have so many configurable parameters that we will only cover the basics in this chapter.

Next, we introduce some special entities in Virtools called Particle Interactors and Deflectors that are used to 'modify' the output of one or more Particle Emitters.

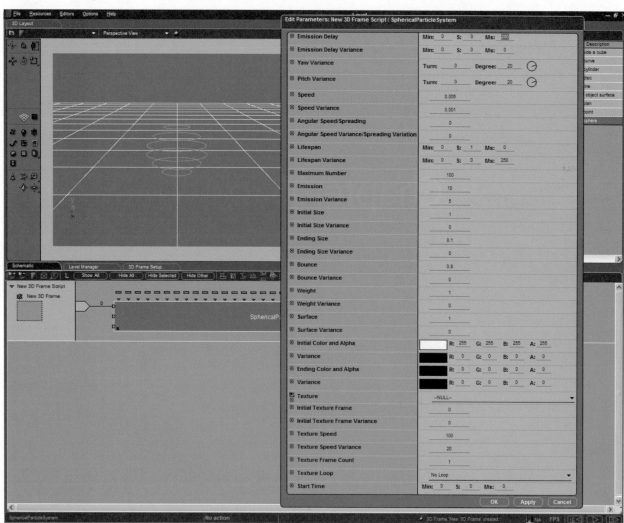

1.2 Introducing Particle Interactors and Deflectors

In addition to the Particle Emitter BB which is used to create or generate particles in our composition, there are another two members of the Particle System family which can be thought of as 'modifiers'. These two types of modifiers appear in Virtools as Attributes that can be applied to entities (for the most part, 3D Frames).

The first type, called Deflectors basically act as obstacles to block or deflect particles. There are six different types including Plane, Sphere and Object deflectors that do the same job but differ in their surface shape. For example, when a group of particles are deflected off a Plane type deflector they would likely bounce back in the opposite direction; however with a Sphere type deflector they would disperse according to the angle of the spheres surface.

The second type, called Interactors has a total of ten variations. Particle Interactors differ from Deflectors in the fact that they modify particles (not only speed and direction, but also the visual properties). Interactors can provide simulations for Particle Emitters like Wind, Gravity, Mutation and Projection.

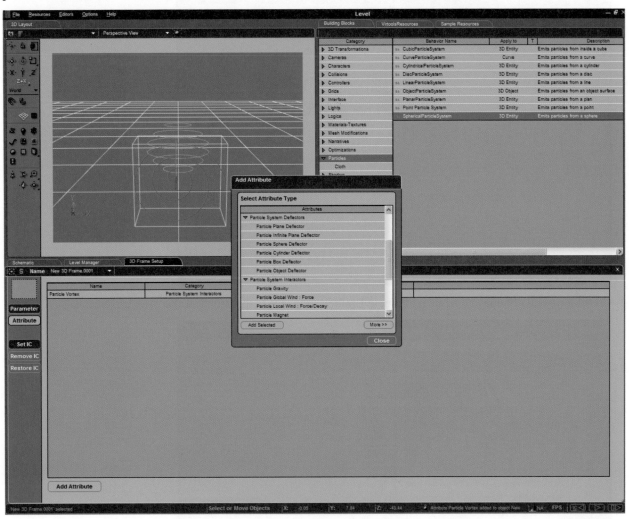

2.0 Using Particle Systems

2.1 Configuring a Particle Emitter

1) Drag Treasure Chest from "Sample Resources\Characters" into the 3D Layout window. Configure its size and position then set its initial conditions. Create a Script for the object and using the Bezier Progression BB, Rotate BB and a ParamOp animate the Lid of the Treasure Chest to Open.

You can refer to Chapter 02, Lesson 2.3 or you can open the file in Sample CMO's called Lesson02_01_Start. CMO.

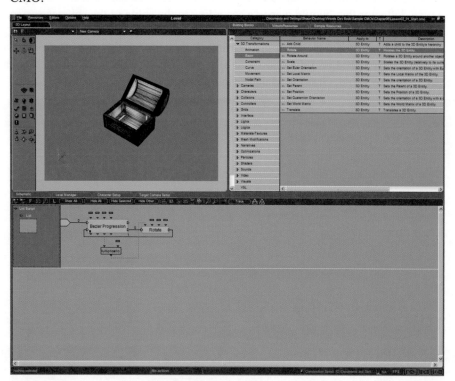

2) Create a new 3D Frame and name it "Particle Emitter". Place it in the center of the Treasure Chest.

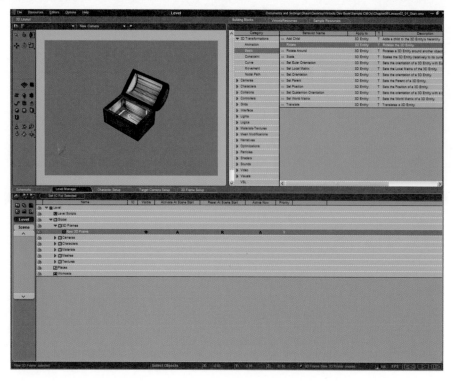

3) Drag Numbers.jpg from Sample Resources\Texture\Particles into 3D Layout window.

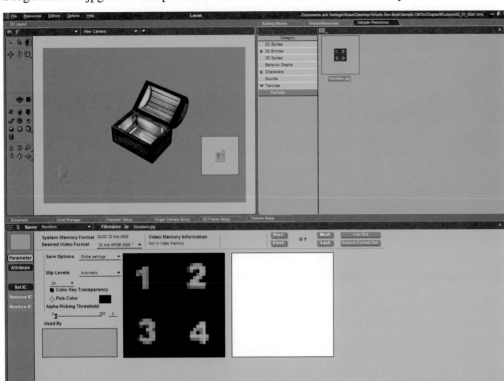

4) Create a script for the Particle Emitter object and drag the Point Particle System BB from Building Blocks\ Particles into its script. Connect it with the Start Node.

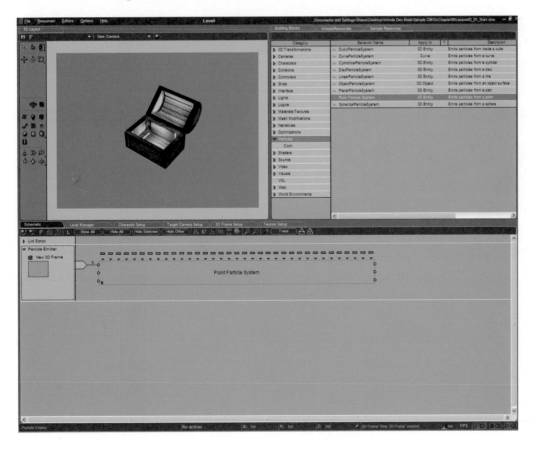

5) Rotate the Particle Emitter object around the X axis by 90 degrees so that the emitter arrowhead is pointing upwards. You may need to scale the emitter if it is too small. Set its Initial Conditions.

6) In the Particle Emitter script, double click the Point Particle System BB to open the Edit Parameters window. Set the parameters as follows; Speed=0.01, Initial Size=1, Ending Size=10, Texture=Numbers. Now click Play to test the scene.

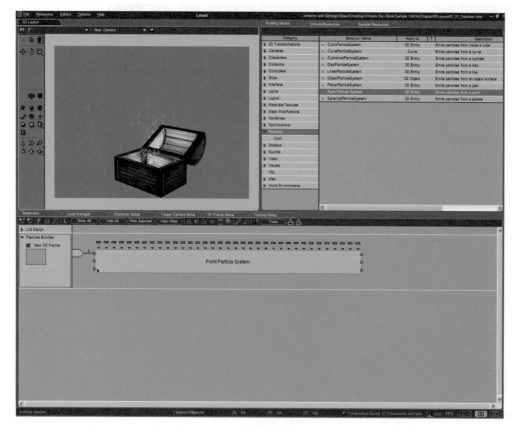

7) Again, open the Edit Parameters window. Set Texture Speed=500, Texture Speed Variance=300, Texture Frame Count=4, Texture Loop=Loop. Click Play and the particles will initially emit as "1" then count to "4" as they get to the end of their life. Note: When animating a texture with the Particle Emitter, the texture must be square. The resolution doesn't matter, but the length and width must be equal. i.e. 2x2, 3x3 or 4x4 etc.

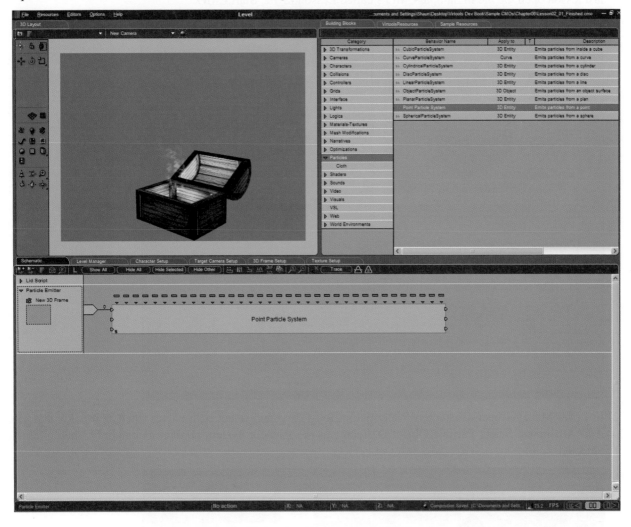

2.2 Creating Particle Collisions

1) Drag the Watermelon object from Sample Resources\Characters into the 3D Layout window. Configure it so that it hangs directly over the Treasure Chest then set its initial conditions. If you aren't continuing from the last lesson open the file in Sample CMO's called Lesson02_02_Start.CMO

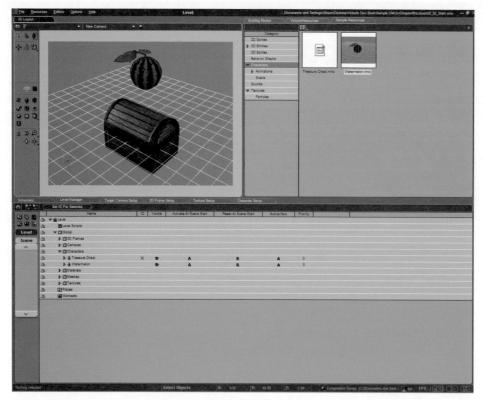

2) In Level Manager open Characters\Watermelon\Body Parts and select both halves, then right click and select Add Attributes. Select Particle Object Deflector in the Particle System Deflectors category, then click Add Selected.

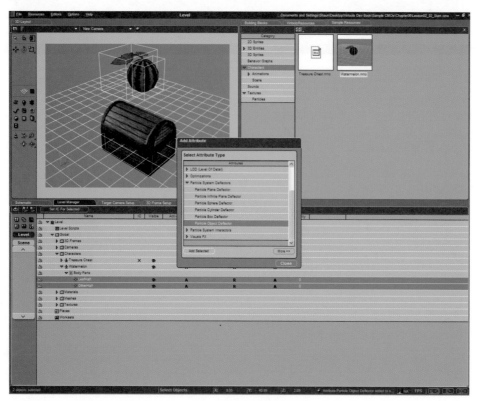

3) In the script of the Particle Emitter object, open the Edit Parameters dialog and set Speed=0.01, Bounce Variance=0.3. Click Play and we can see the Watermelon now deflects the particles emitted from the Treasure Chest.

Note: Move the Watermelon closer to the Treasure Chest if you can't see the effect clearly.

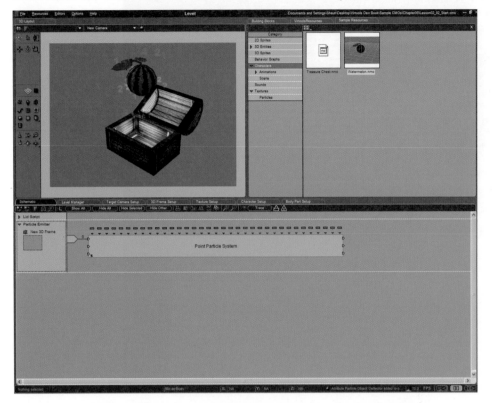

2.3 Using Interactors to Make Particles Track an Object

1) Continuing on from the last lesson, add Path02 from Sample Resources\3D Entities to the scene. Adjust the size and position of the curve so that it is located over the Treasure Chest.

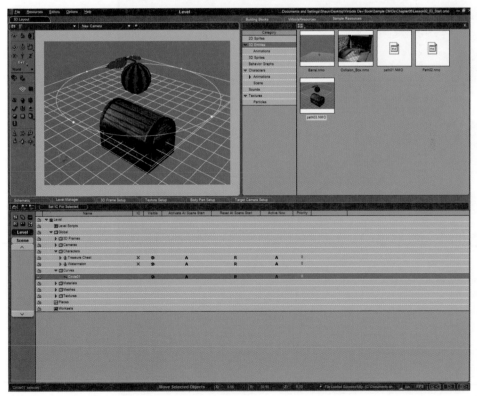

2) We need to make the Watermelon move along the curve. To do this, add a script to the Watermelon and add a Bezier Progression BB from Building Blocks\Logics\Loops and a Position On Curve BB from Building Blocks\3D Transformation\Curve.

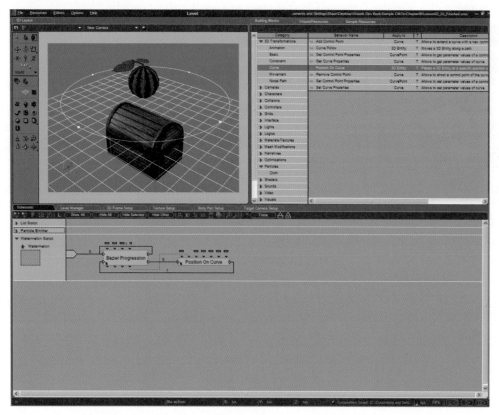

3) Create a new 3D Frame and name it "Magnet". Create its script and then drag the Set Position BB from Building Blocks\Basic into the script. Set the reference object as Watermelon and connect it to the Start Node. Now, connect the Out pin with the In pin to form a loop.

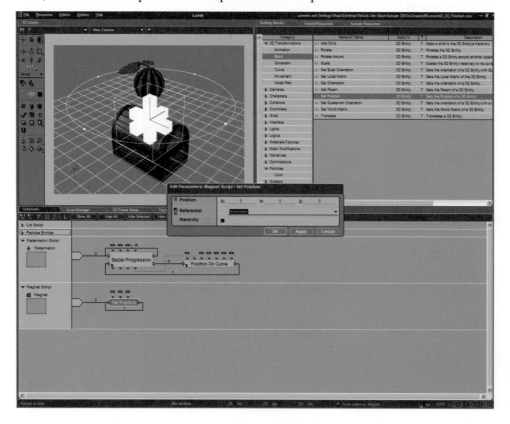

4) Open the Attributes panel for our Magnet object and add the attribute Particle Magnet from the category Particle System Interactors. Double click the attribute to open its configuration dialog and set the value to 10. This will increase the strength of our magnet.

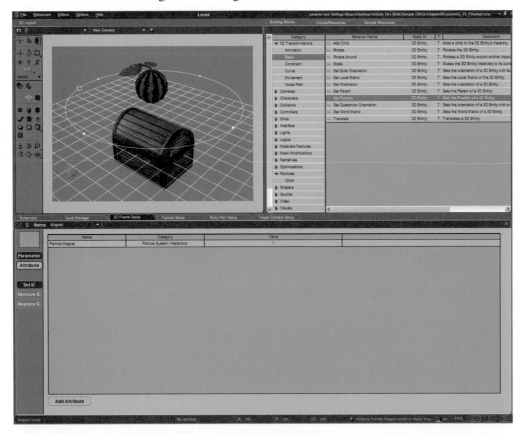

5) Now, click Play and as the Watermelon circles the Treasure Chest, the particles are pulled toward it.

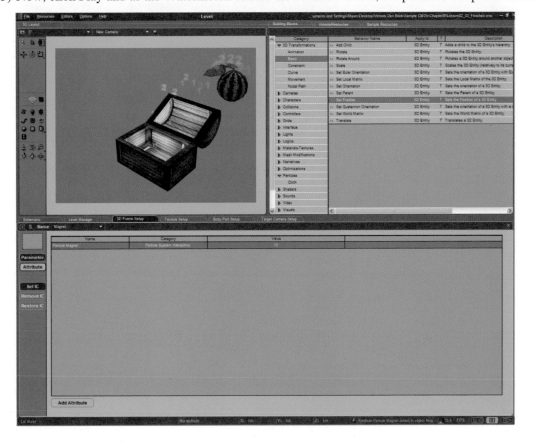

Chapter07 arrays and events

1.0 Using Arrays in Virtools

The use of Arrays in your Virtools projects will greatly determine the overall quality and depth of the product. You can develop a wide variety of systems within your game by effectively taking advantage of the power of Arrays. If you don't have any previous experience in programming, the concept of Arrays may be a little hard to understand at first, but in reality the application of an Array is a very logical process. In Virtools, Arrays are 2-dimensional and consist of Rows and Columns. Think of an Array like a large spreadsheet, but the cells can contain many other types of data (even objects) besides just text and numbers.

In this chapter, we will give a step by step introduction to the basic creation, modification and application of Arrays within Virtools.

1.2 Creating an Array

1) In the Level Manager, click the Create Array button and an empty Array will be created and Virtools will automatically open the Array Setup panel.

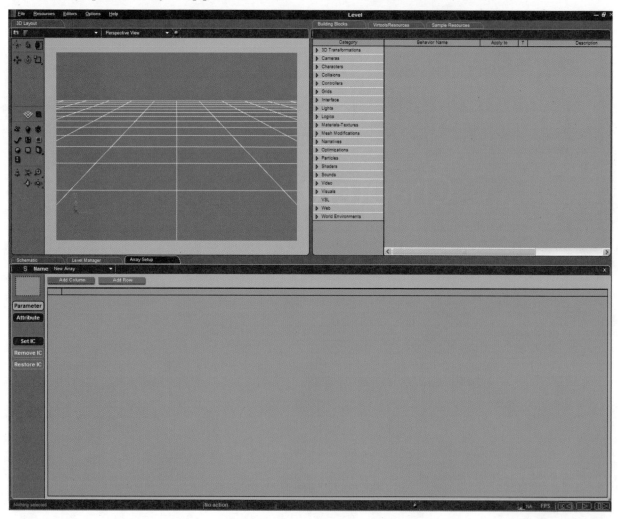

2) Click Add Column and the field setup dialog will open. In the Name field, type "CharName" and set the Type to String. Note that the Parameter setting can only be used if you set the Type to Parameter. Click OK to finish.

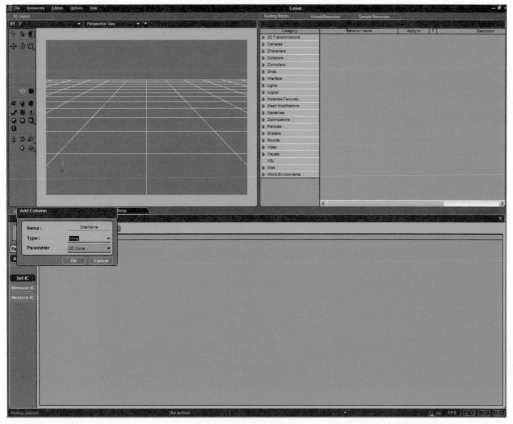

3) Let's add some data to the Array. Click Add Row and a new row will be created. The number on the left represents the ID that Virtools has assigned to the row and cannot be changed.

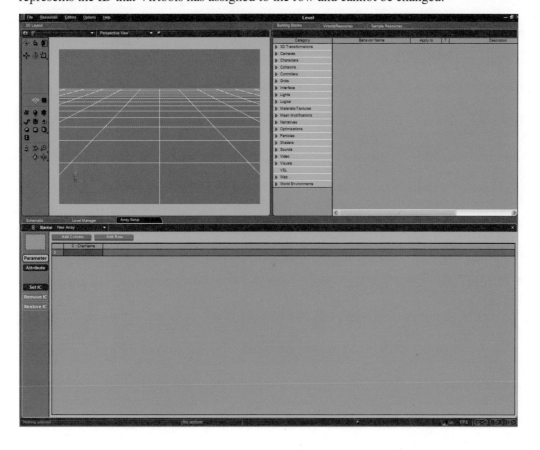

4) You can see our row doesn't contain any data, so double click the blank cell under CharName and type in "WuKong".

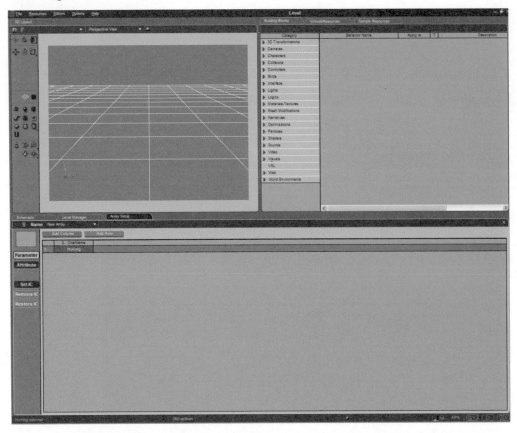

5) Click Add Column and name the new column "Life" and set the type to Integer. This column will hold the amount of life, or hit points of our character. Double click the Life cell and set it to 200.

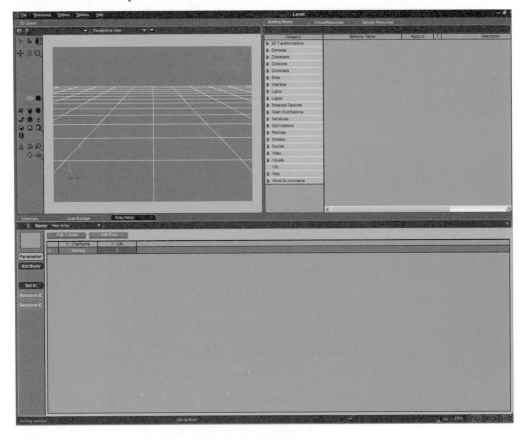

6) Using the steps above, try creating some more statistics for the characters (like Magic, Gold, and Experience etc) and try creating a new row to hold data for another character.

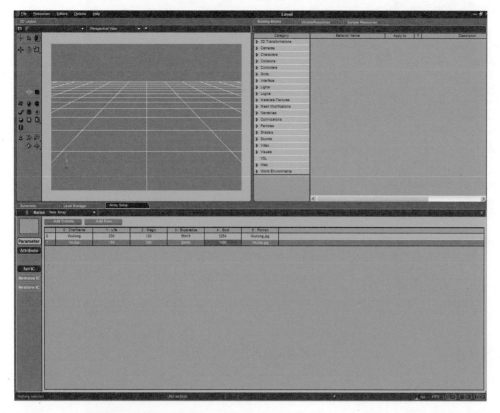

1.3 Getting Array Data

1) To start this lesson, open the composition Sample CMOs\Chapter07\Lesson_01_03_Start.CMO. Then, open the Array Setup panel for the Array called characters. You can see we have a set of stats, including portrait data, for our WuKong and ShaWuJing characters.

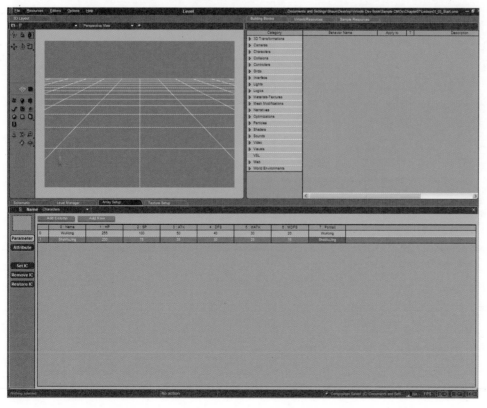

2) Now, in Level Manager, create a Level Script.

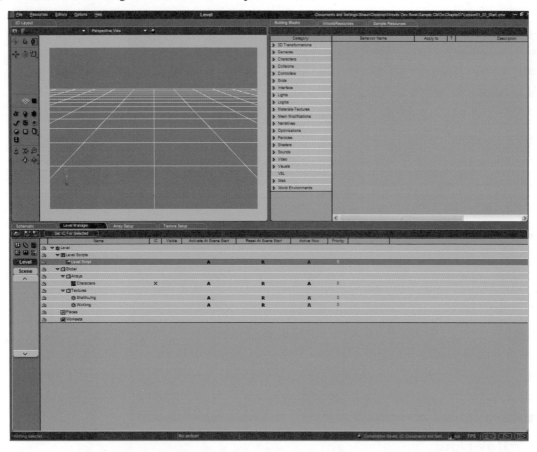

3) Add the Get Row BB from Building Blocks\Logics\Array and connect it to the Start Node.

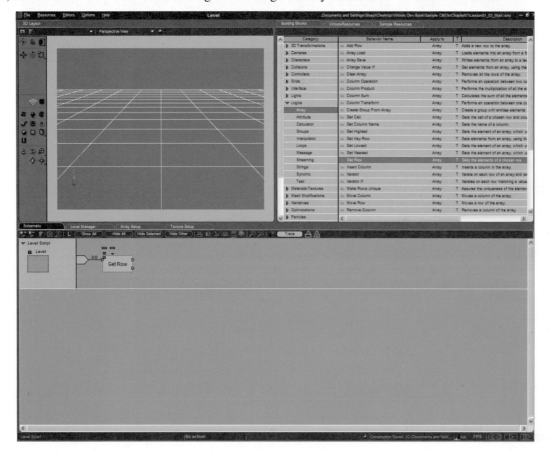

4) Open the Get Row BB Edit Parameters dialog and set the Target (Array) to Characters. When you click OK, a new set of POuts will be added to the bottom of the Get Row BB corresponding to the columns we have in our Character Array.

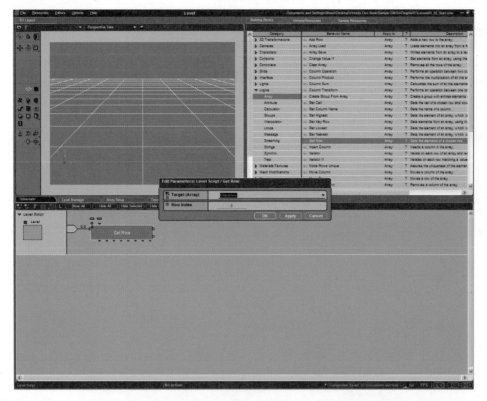

5) Create a new 2D Frame. Set its size to 320x240, its position to 0,0 and its ZOrder to –1. Rename the Frame to ArraySkinFrame. Next, drag the Texture ArraySkin.tga from Sample Resources\Textures into the Scene and create a new Material. Rename the new Material to "ArraySkinMat". Set the Material's texture to Arrayskin and set the 2D Frame's Material to the new material ArraySkinMat. Make sure you set the Materials Mode to Transparent and set the Diffuse color to White.

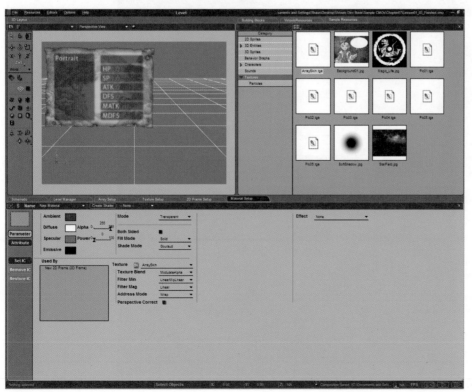

6) Create another 2D Frame and call it PortraitFrame. Set its Size to 128x128. Create a new Material called PortraitMat but don't assign any texture. Just change the Mode to transparent and Diffuse color to White. Position the PortraitFrame in the bottom of the portrait area of the ArraySkinFrame and set its Material to PortraitMat.

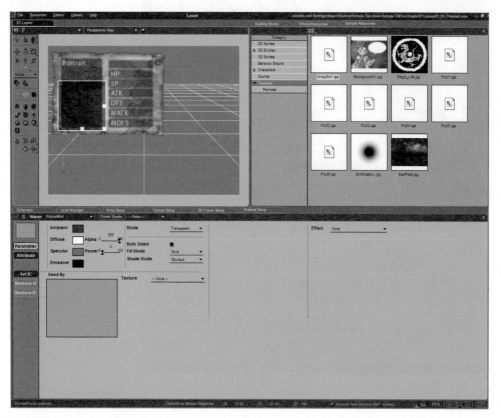

7) Since our array contains seven data fields and one texture field we need to add seven Text Displays BB's from Building Block\Interface\Text and one Set Texture BB from Building Block\Material-Textures\Basic.

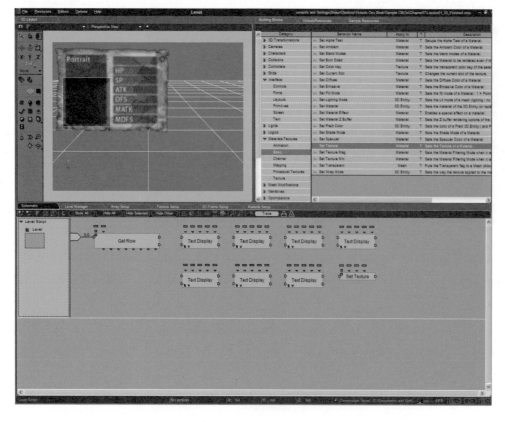

8) Link the first Output POut (Name) of Get Row to the Text Input PIn of the first Text Display BB. Connect the Found BOut to the In BIn of the Text Display BB. Click Play and the characters name will display in the top left of the 3D Layout Window. Open the Edit Parameters dialog of the Text Display BB and adjust the offset to correctly position the text.

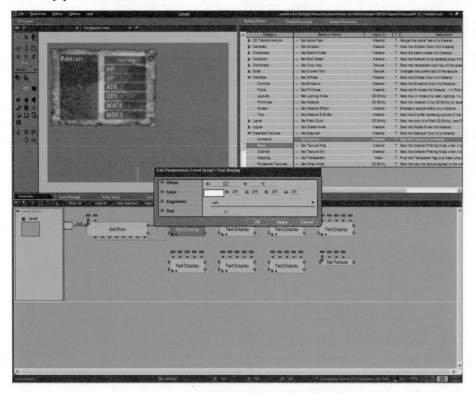

9) Using the same method, connect the second Text Display BB Text In PIn to the second POut of the Get Row BB. Connect the Out BOut of the first Display Text BB to the In BIn second Display Text BB. Open the Edit Parameters dialog of the second Text Display BB and set the Alignment to Right. We do this to ensure the Integer fields all align on the right. Click play (you can do this with Edit Parameter dialog still open) and adjust the Offset of the text to line up with the ArraySkinFrame.

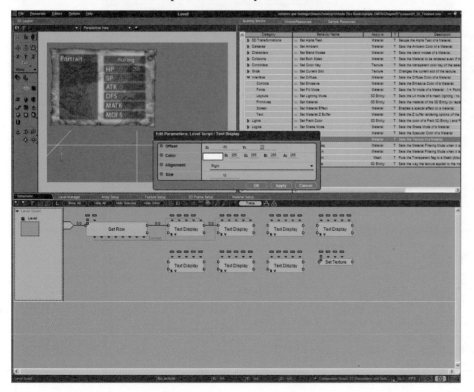

10) Next, setup the rest of the Text Display BB's using the same method.

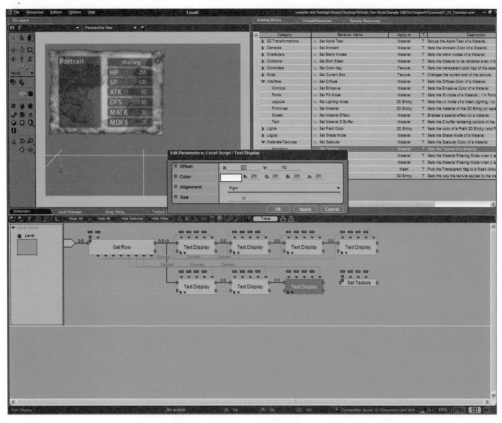

11) Finally, link the Set Texture BB with the Out BOut of the last Text Display BB. Link the Texture PIn of the Set Texture BB to the Texture POut of the Get Row BB. Open the Edit Parameters dialog of the Set Texture BB and set the Target (Material) to PortraitMat. Click Play and the characters portrait will appear in the PortraitFrame.

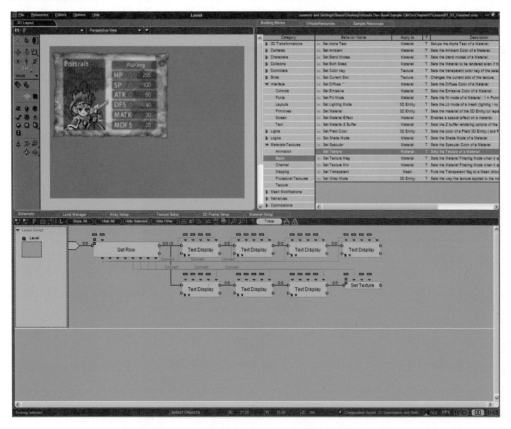

1.4 Creating a Data Switch using an Array

1) Continuing on with our composition from the last lesson add the Switch On Key BB from Building Blocks\
Controllers\Keyboard and connect it to Start Node.

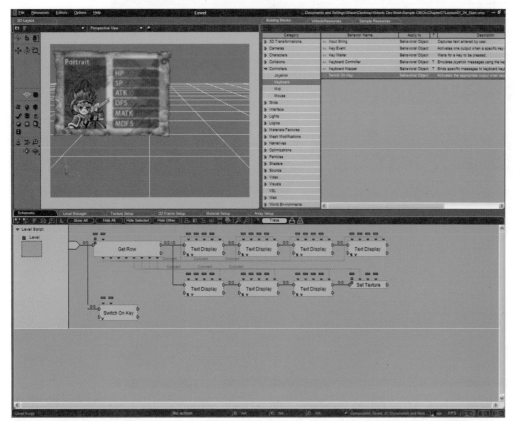

2) Open the Edit Parameters dialog and set the Key parameters to "1" and "2" respectively.

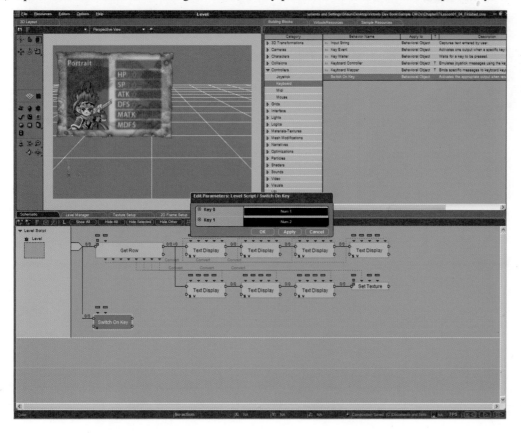

3) Add two Set Cell BB's from Building Block\Logics\Array and connect their In BIn's to the first and second Switch On Key BB outputs.

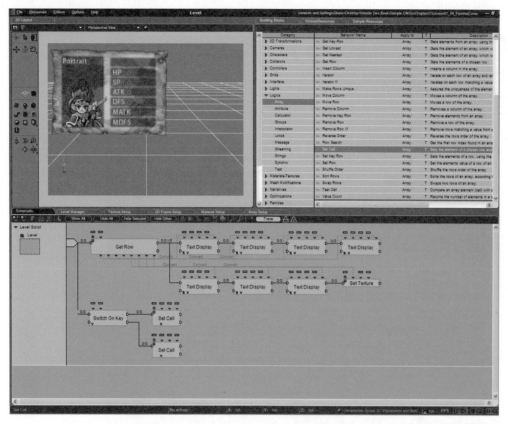

4) In Level Manager, create a new Array called Interface. Add a single column called CharacterNum and lastly add a single row. This array will be used to tell our Character array which row it should read when we push either "1" or "2" in our keyboard.

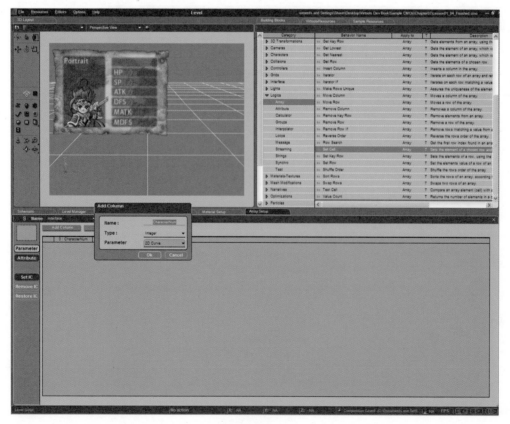

5) In the script schematic, open the Edit Parameters dialog of the first Set Cell BB and set the Target (Array) to Interface. Leave the rest of the parameters as "0". This will set the cell in the first column and first row to "0" which corresponds to the first Character in the Character Array. Next open the Edit Parameters dialog of the second Set Cell BB and set the Target (Array) to Interface and set the Value to "1". This will change the cell value to "1" which corresponds to the second character in the Character Array.

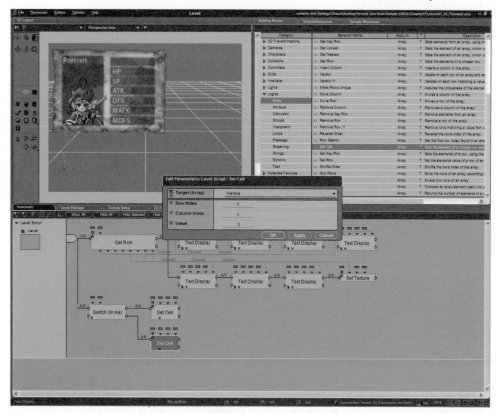

6) Add the Get Cell BB from Building Block\Logics\Array and connect it to the Start Node.

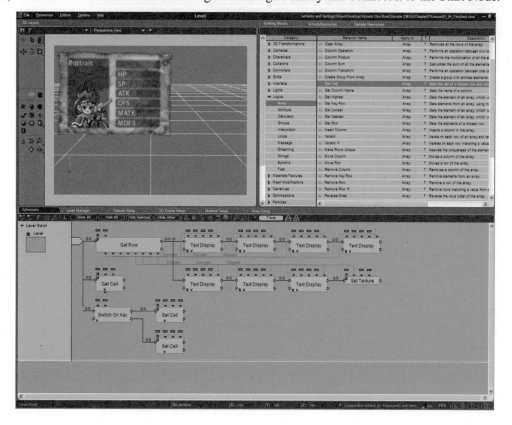

7) Open the Edit Parameters dialog of the Get Cell BB and set Target (Array) to Interface.

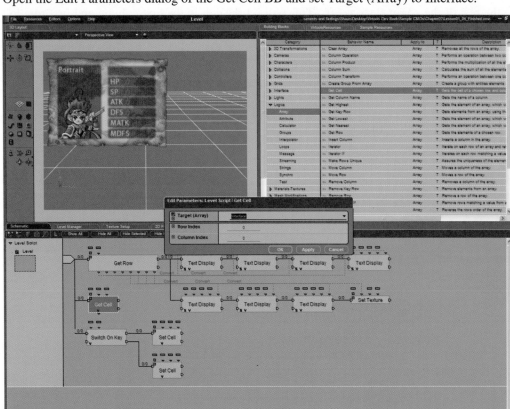

8) Connect the Output POut of the Get Cell BB to the Row Input PIn of the Get Row BB. Delete the Get Row BB's link to the Start Node and connect it with the Found Out BOut of the Get Cell BB.

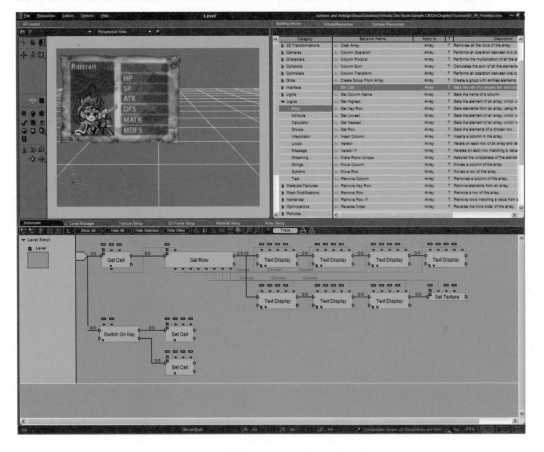

9)   Now connect the Found BOut's of the two Set Cell BB's to the BIn of the Get Cell BB. This will make the script get the data from the array every time we press either the "1" or "2" key.

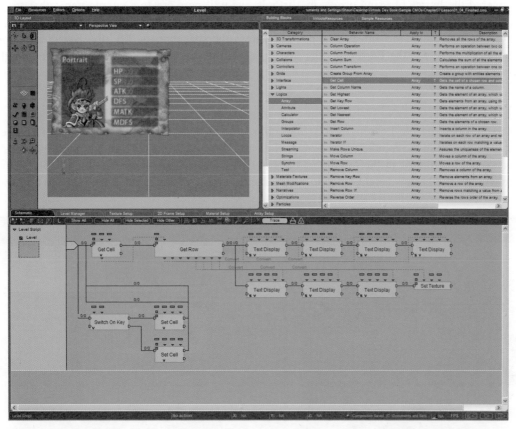

10) Click Play and press the "1" and "2" keys on your numeric keypad. The data and images on screen will update according to the data in the Characters Array.

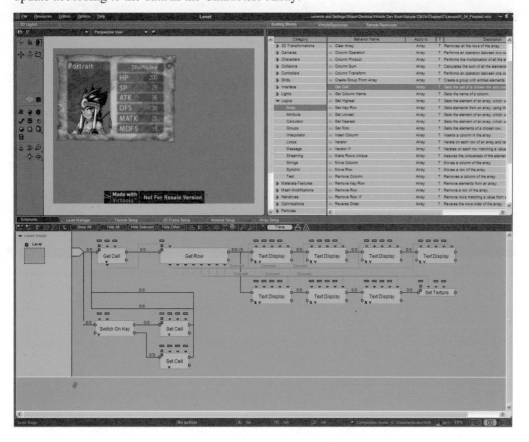

2.0 Event Control

Now that we've covered the basics of using arrays in Virtools, we will now create a simple game that triggers a "Win" or "Lose" event based on the positional value of an object. The game will involve a Barrel that is constantly falling toward the floor, the aim is to repeatedly press the spacebar to "lift" the Barrel and stop it crashing to the ground. You lose if the Barrel hits the floor, you win if you can hit the spacebar fast enough to raise the Barrel to a height of 10.

2.1 Creating an Event Driven Game

1) To begin this lesson, open the file Lesson_02_02_Start.cmo from Sample CMOs\Chapter07. You will see a floor object has been placed in the middle of the scene. Now add the Barrel object from Sample Resources\3D Entities into the scene. Position it in the middle of the floor and set its Y position (height) to "3.0" This is important as we will use the barrels height value to determine the result of our game. Lastly, create a script on the Barrel object.

2) The "Win" condition depends on the Height value of the Barrel, so we first need to know what the Barrels current height is. Add a ParamOp and set the left input to 3D Entity and click the lock icon. Set the Operation parameter to GetY and click OK.

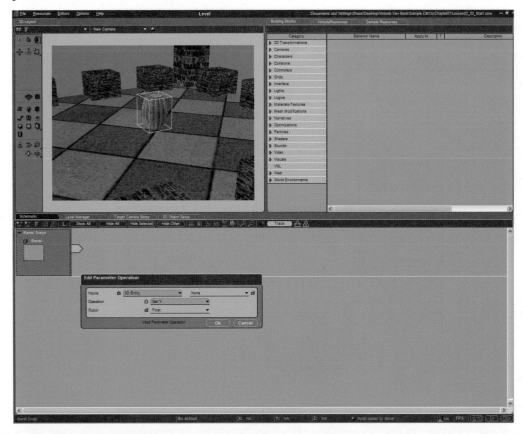

3) Double Click the ParamOp which is now called GetY and set the Local0 parameter to Barrel.

4) Add the Per Second BB from Building Blocks\Logics\Calculator and the Translate BB from Building Blocks\3D Transformations\Basic. Connect the Per Second BB to the Start Node and the Translate BB to the Per Second BB.

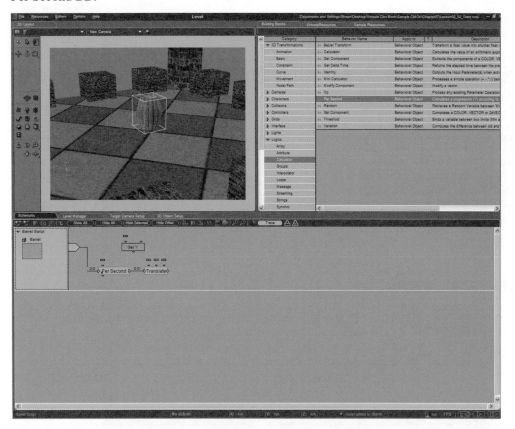

5) Double click the pOut0 POut of the Per Second BB and set its Parameter Type to Vector. Click Ok and then double click the Per Second BB to open the Edit Parameters Dialog. Set the Y value to "-1".

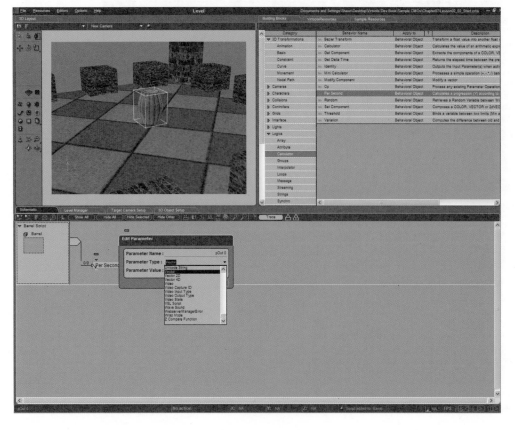

6) Add the Text Display BB and connect the Text Pin to the POut of the GetY ParamOp. This will output the current Y value of the Barrel to the screen so we can see how close we are to winning or losing. Don't forget to connect the Text Display BB to the Translate BB.

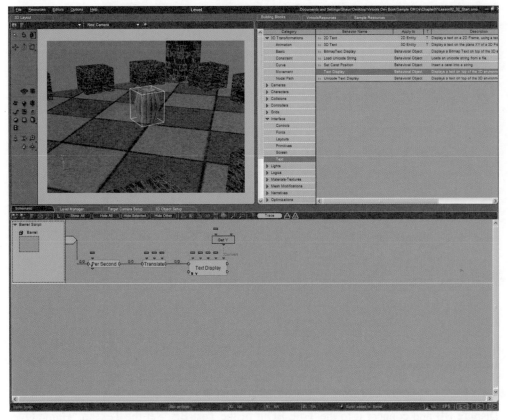

7) Add the Test BB from Building Blocks\Logics\Test and connect it to the Text Display BB. Connect the POut of the GetY ParamOp to the A PIn (the middle pin) of the Test BB.

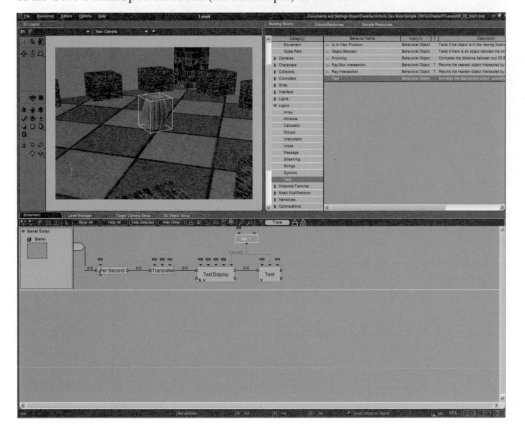

8) Double click the Test BB and set the Test Parameter to Less or Equal. This will check to see if the Barrel is at a height of 0 or lower.

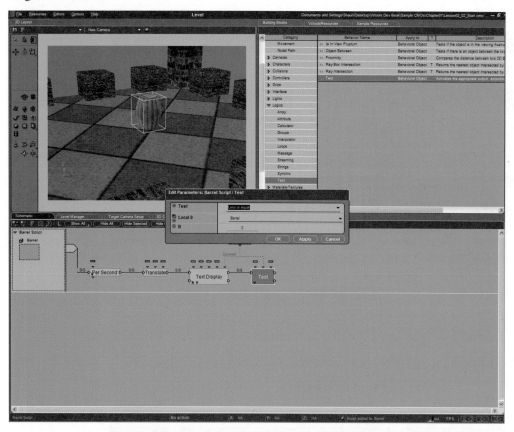

9) Add another Text Display BB and connect it to the True BOut of the Test BB. Set the Text to "Game Over!". This will display a game over message if the Barrel reaches a height of 0 or less.

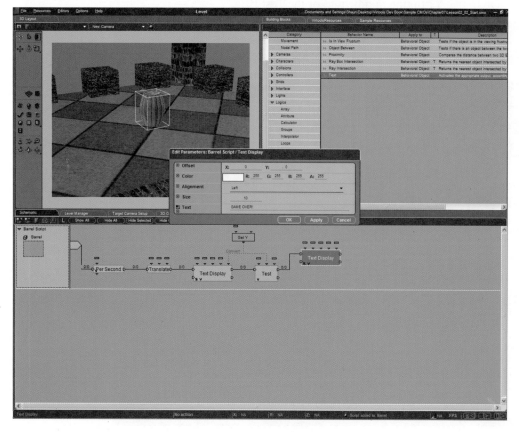

10) Add another Test BB and connect it to the False BOut of the first Test BB. Connect it to the GetY ParamOp in the same way as the first and set its Test parameter to Greater or Equal.

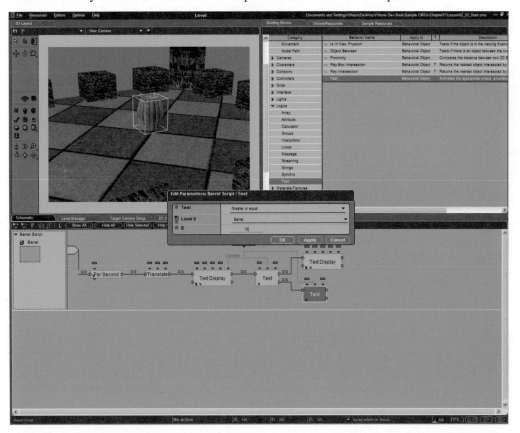

11) Add a Text Display BB and connect it with the True BOut of the second Test BB. Set its Text parameter to "You Win!". When the height of the Barrel reaches 10 or more, the "You Win" text will be displayed.

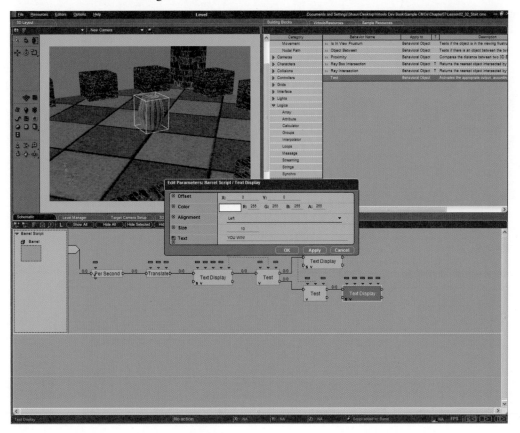

12) Connect the False BOut of the second Test BB to the BIn of the Per Second BB. This will keep the Barrel moving down while its height is higher than 0 and lower than 10.

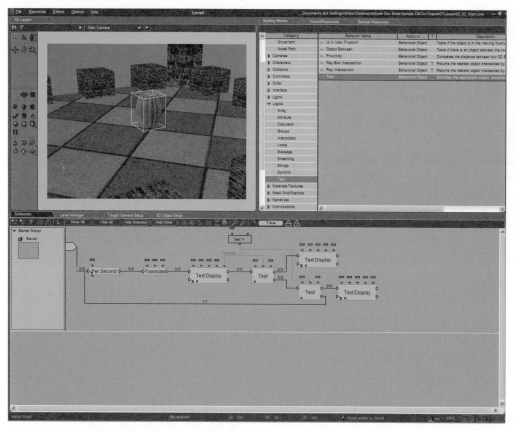

13) To finish this part of the script, connect the True BOut's of both the Test BB's to the Off BIn of the first Text Display BB to turn off the display of the Barrels height when either the win or lose condition is true.

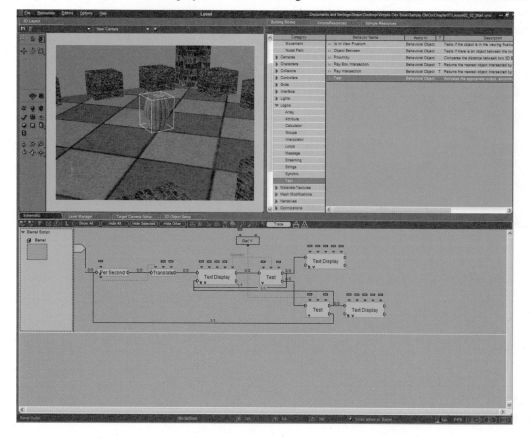

14) In the next part of our script we add the behaviors to make the Barrel move up whenever the spacebar is pressed. Add the Key Event BB from Building Blocks\Controllers\Keyboard and connect it to the Start Node.

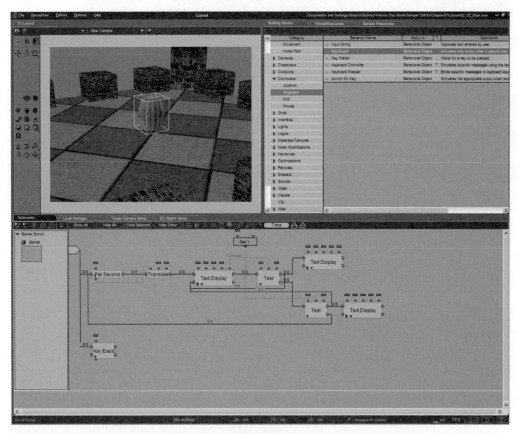

15) Double click the Key Event BB and set the Key Waited parameter to Space.

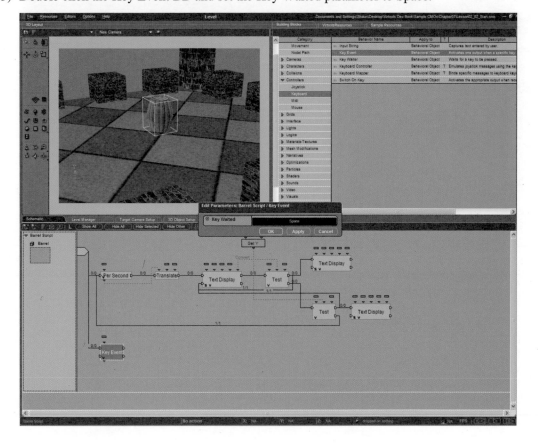

16) Now add a Translate BB and connect it to the Released BOut of the Key Event BB. Set the Translate Vector Y parameter to "2".

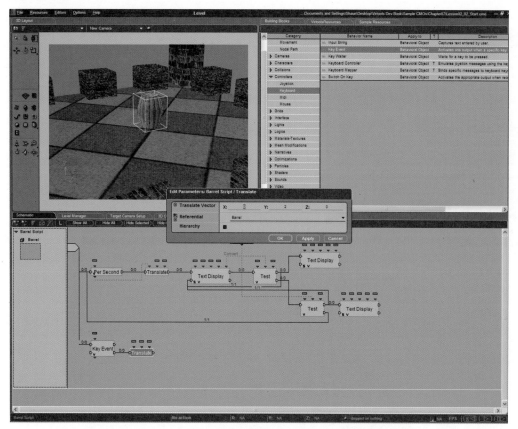

17) Lastly, let's add a shadow to the Barrel to get some feeling of its height in relation to the floor. Use the same method used in Chapter 03 Lesson 5.3 (Creating Projected Shadows).

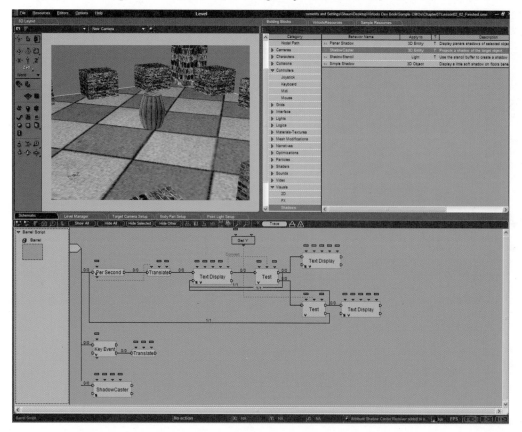

18) Click Play and test the scene.

Chapter08 sound

1.0 Using Sound in Virtools

Using Virtools, you can play regular Wave ('.WAV') or MP3 files, CD Audio tracks and Midi files. There are a variety of building blocks supplied with Virtools to configure the way the sound is played; for example, you can use the 3D Sound BB's to create positional sounds and the Get Sound Spectrum BB to analyze a specific sound frequency range at a point in time. In this chapter we will go through the basic steps of setting up a sound that is attached to an object that rotates around the viewer, or listener in this case.

1.1 Creating 3D Positional Sounds

1) Drag the Barrel object into the scene and set its position to X=0, Y=0 and Z=0. Make sure you set its Initial Conditions.

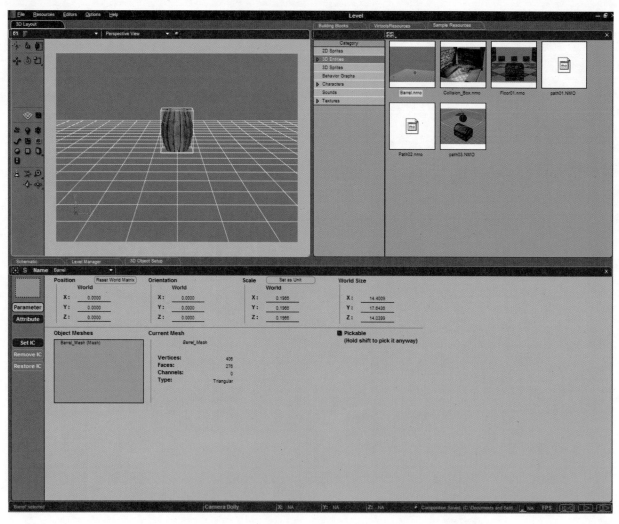

2) Create a new 3D Frame and set its position to X=0, Y=0 and Z=-80.

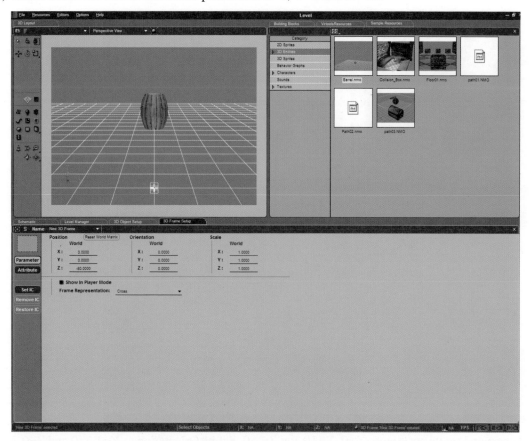

3) Create a script on the Barrel and add the Rotate Around BB from Building Blocks\3D Transformations\Basic. Connect it to the Start Node, then connect it's In and Out pins to form a loop.

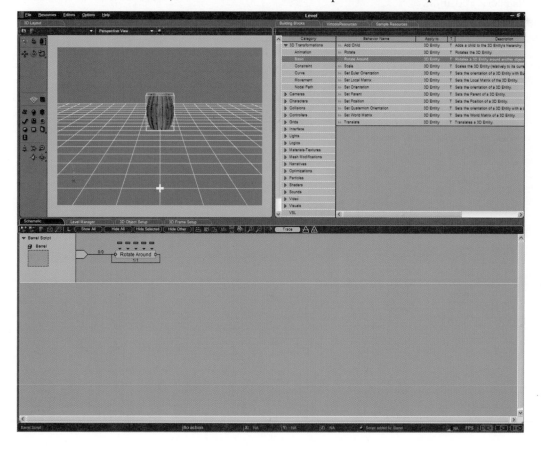

4) Open the Edit Parameters dialog of the Rotate Around BB and set the Reference to New 3D Frame.

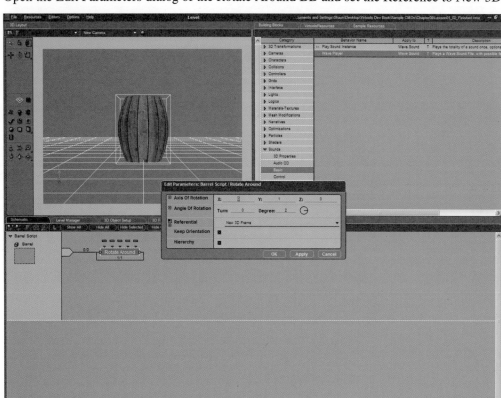

5) Create a new Camera and set its position to X=0, Y=10 and Z=-80. Set its Orientation to X=1,Y-0 and Z=0. We set our Camera to roughly the same position as our 3D Frame as we will use the 3D Frame as a reference for our player (or 'listeners') position.

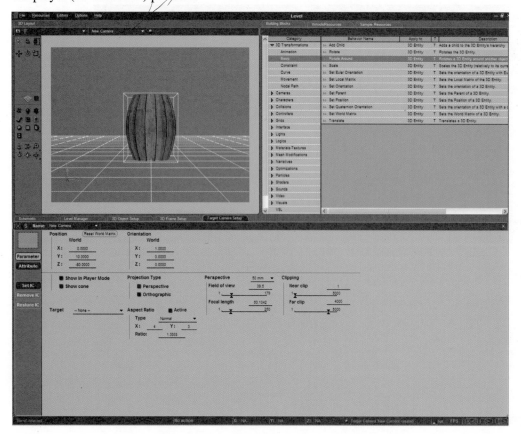

6) Drag the file Water01.wav from Sample Resources\Sounds into the Scene.

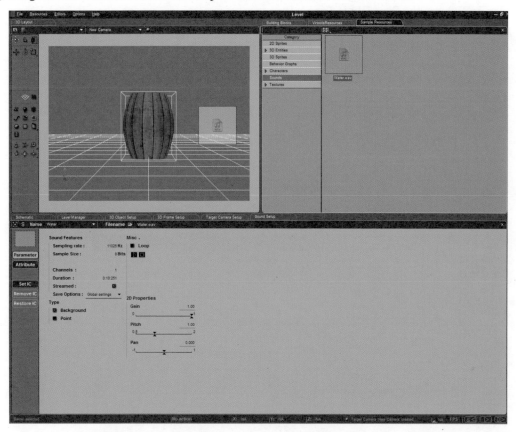

7) In the Sound Setup panel, change the Sound Type to Point. In the 3D Properties section, change the attached object to Barrel to link the sound with the Barrels position. Lastly, in Min and Max Perception Distances set the Max parameter to 3.

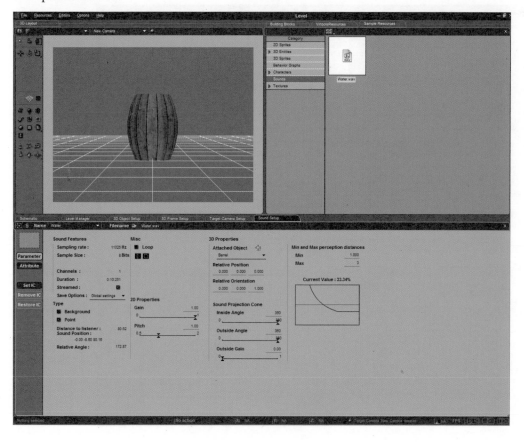

8) In the Barrel Script, add the Wave Player BB from Building Blocks\Sounds\Basic. Connect it to the Start Node and link the End Playing BOut to the Start BIn to form a loop.

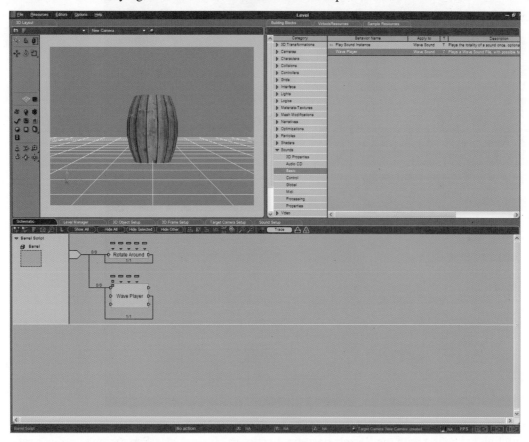

9) Open the Wave Sound BB Edit Parameters Dialog and set the Target (Wave Sound) to Water.

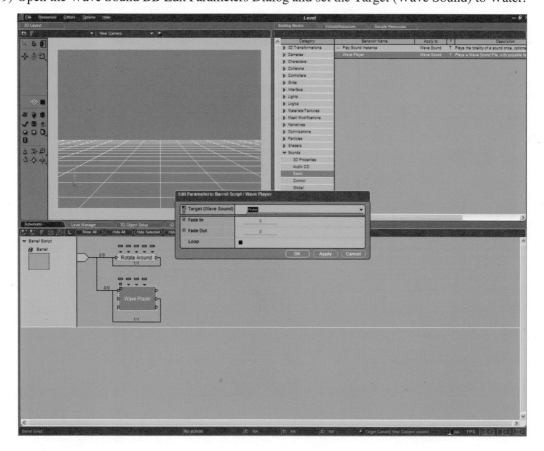

10) Make sure the 3D Layout view is set to use the camera you created. Click Play to test the scene and you will hear the sound change position relevant to the current location of the barrel.

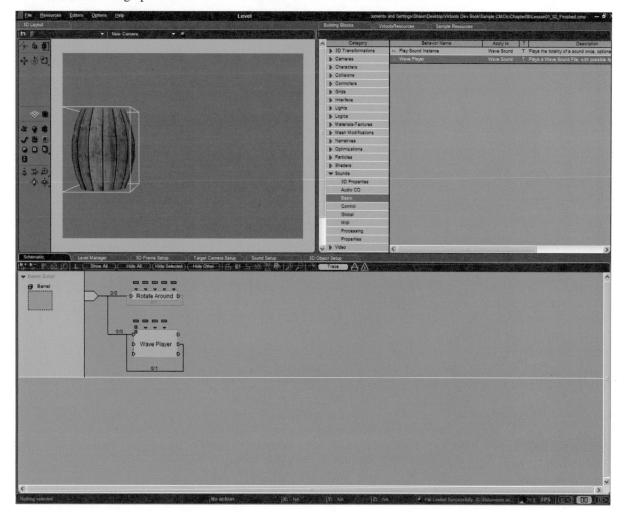

Chapter09 special effects

1.0 Basic Special Effects

Sometimes it's the small details that can make the difference between a plain, boring-looking level and an exciting, living world. In this chapter we cover a few basic special effects which can help to add a more dynamic element to your composition. We teach you how to create common effects like fog and mesh explosions, which can be easily implemented using very few BB's. We also look at some other features like picture-in-picture (for creating map windows or alternate views within the main view) and glowing trails that can be attached to moving objects to create some cool effects.

1.1 Creating Lens Flare

1) Start by dragging the texture Sun02.tga into the Scene.

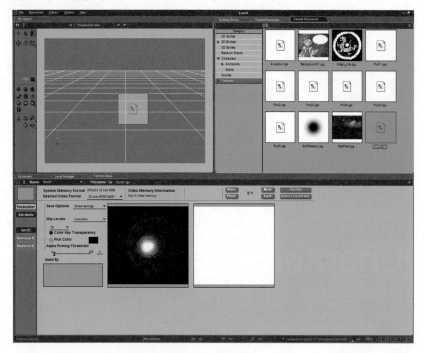

2) Right click on the Alpha Preview window in the Texture Setup panel and select the Get Alpha from Diffuse option.

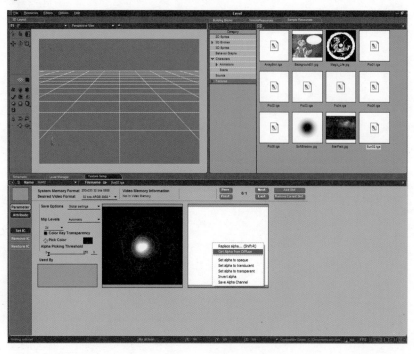

3) Add the file Scene04.nmo from Sample Resources\Characters\Scenes. Position your viewing angle so that the tree is at the back of the scene and you are looking out over the pond.

4) Create a light and set its position to X=150, Y=20, Z=0.

5) Create a Level Script and drag the Lens Flare BB from Building Blocks\Lights\FX into the script. Connect it with the Start Node.

6) Open the Edit Parameters dialog of the Lens Flare BB and set Target (Light) parameter to New Light and the Flare Texture to Sun02.

7) Click Play and try moving the camera around. The lens flare is locked to the position of the light and reacts according to your viewing angle.

1.2 Creating Fog

1) Continue on with the scene from the last lesson or open the file Lesson01_02_Start.cmo from the Sample CMOS\Chapter09 folder. Add the Set Fog BB from Building Blocks\World Environments\Global to the Level Script. Connect it with the Start Node.

2) Open the Edit Parameters dialog of the Set Fog BB and set the Fog Start to 50, the Fog End to 500 and the Fog Color to White (R255,G255,B255,A255).

3) Click Play to see the effect the fog has on the scene.

4) Try changing the Fog End parameter to a smaller value (like 200 for example) to see its effect; Click play to test again.

1.3 Creating a Picture-in-Picture Effect

1) Continue on with the scene from the last lesson or open the file Lesson01_03_Start.cmo from the Sample CMOS\Chapter09 folder. Create a 2D Frame and call it MapWindow. Set its position to X=0, Y=0 and its Size to 120x90.

2) Create a new Texture and Material. Rename the texture to "MapWindow" and the material to "MapWindowMat". In the Material Setup panel, set the Texture to MapWindow and set the Diffuse color to White (R255,G255,B255).

3) Set the Material to MapWindowMat in the 2D Frame Setup panel of MapWindow.

4) Create a new 3D Frame and set its position to X=0, Y=20, Z=0.

5) Create a new camera and rename it "MapWindowCamera". Create its Script.

6) Add the Rotate Around and Look At BB to the Script. Connect them in sequence from the Start Node and then connect the BOut of Look At to the BIn of Rotate Around to form a loop. Set the Rotate Around BB's parameters to Degree=0.3 and Referential=New 3D Frame. Set the parameters for the Look At BB to Referential=New 3D Frame.

7) Create a script for the 2D Frame MapWindow. Add the Render Scene in RT View BB from Building Blocks\Shaders\Rendering. Connect it with the Start Node and loop its In and Out pins.

8) Open the Edit Parameters window. Set the Render Target to MapWindow (this is the texture that the scene will be rendered to) and set the Camera to MapWindowCamera.

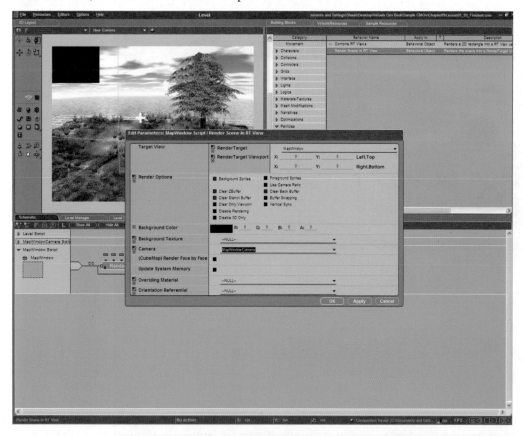

9) Make sure your 3D Layout window is using the Default Camera (New Camera) and click Play to test the scene. The scene will be rendered from the MapWindowCamera's viewpoint as a texture in the 2D Frame.

1.4 Object Motion Blur

1) Continue on with the scene from the last lesson or open the file Lesson01_04_Start.cmo from the Sample CMOS\Chapter09 folder. Add the Watermelon object to the scene and set its position to X=0, Y=20, Z=0.

2) Add Path03.nmo to the scene and set its height to 20 using the same method as we did with the Watermelon.

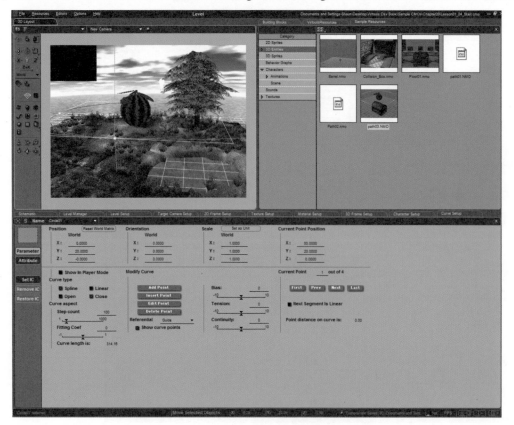

3) Create a Script for the Watermelon. Add the Bezier Progression and Position On Curve BB's and configure them to make the Watermelon follow curve in a loop.

4) In Level Manager, open the Body Parts menu of the Watermelon to view the two halves of the object; one called Leaf Half, one called Other Half. Create Scripts for both of these objects and add the Motion Blur BB to each from Building Blocks\Visuals\FX. Link them both to the Start Node.

5) Click Play to test the scene. The Watermelon will revolve around the scene with a trail behind it. You can open the Edit Parameters dialog of the Motion Trail BB and set the number (length) of trails to increase the visibility of the effect; be careful not to overdo it though as too many trails can consume a lot of processing power.

1.5 Glowing Trails

1) Continue on with the scene from the last lesson or open the file Lesson01_05_Start.cmo from the Sample CMOS\Chapter09 folder. Add the WuKong Character and his corresponding animations for Wait, Run, Attack and Walk Back to the scene. Create a script on the character and configure the Keyboard Controller, Character Controller and Enhanced Character Keep On Floor BB as per Chapter 03 Lesson 2.1.

2) Find the object called King Stick in characters Body Part list and create its Script. Insert the Solid Trail BB from Building Blocks\Visuals\FX. Connect it to the Start Node.

3) Open the Solid Trail BB's Edit Parameters dialog and set the color to Yellow (R255, G255, B0). Leave the other settings as default.

4) Click Play and move WuKong around, you will see the trail behind his weapon. Try adjusting the parameters of the Solid Trail BB to see what effect they have on the appearance of the trail.

1.6 Mesh Explosions

1) Continue on with the scene from the last lesson or open the file Lesson01_06_Start.cmo from the Sample CMOS\Chapter09 folder. Add the Crystal01 object from Sample Resources\3D Entities to the Scene and create a script for it. Position it over the lake and make it a little smaller. Finally set its Initial Conditions.

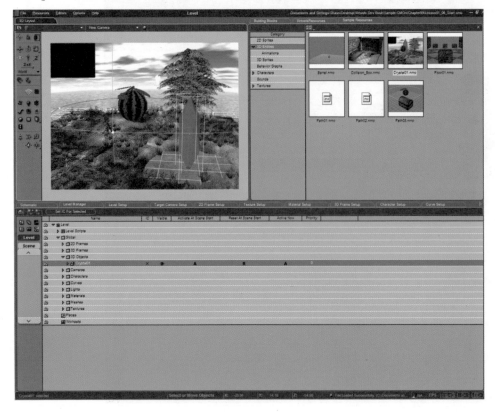

2) Add the Rotate and Collision Detection building blocks and connect them as shown. Don't forget to add the Moving Obstacle Attribute to WuKong.

3) Insert the Explode BB from Building Blocks\Mesh Modifications\Deformation and connect it with the True BOut of the Collision Detection BB. Connect the Collision Detection BB's False BOut to the BIn to form a loop. Because the object will disappear after exploding, add the Show BB from Building Blocks\Visuals\Show Hide before the Collision Detection BB. This will unhide the object when we restart the scene.

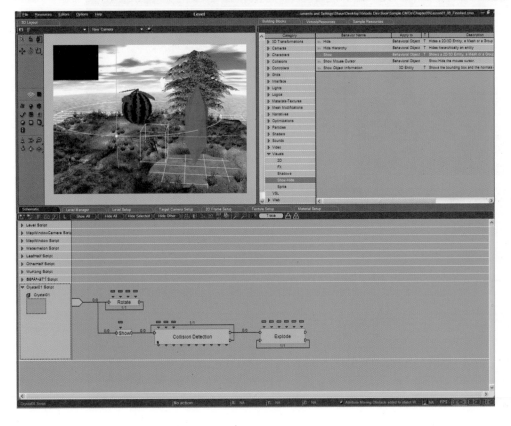

4) Open the Edit Parameters dialog of the Explode BB and set the Duration to 2000.

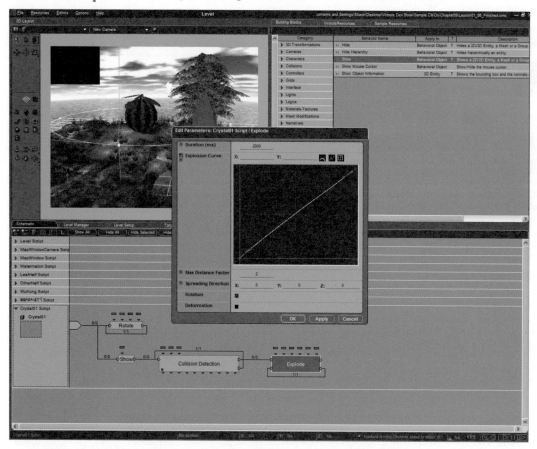

5) Click Play and move WuKong into the crystal and it will explode.

1.7 Simulating Wave Motion

1) Continue on with the scene from the last lesson or open the file Lesson01_07_Start.cmo from the Sample CMOS\Chapter09 folder. In Level Manager, find the body part named Water in Scene04 and create its script.

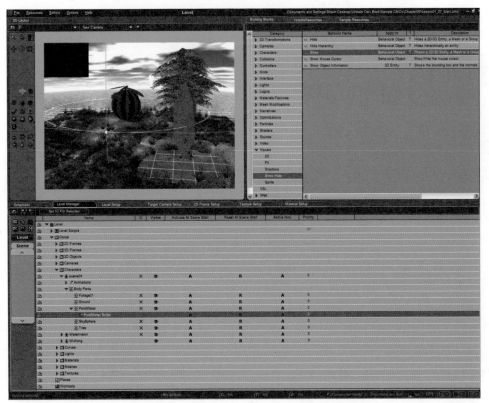

2) Insert the Bezier Progression BB and then the Noise BB from Building Blocks\Mesh Modifications\ Deformation. Connect the Bezier Progression BB to the Start Node and connect the Noise BB to the Loop Out of the Bezier Progression BB. Create loops for both the BB's as shown below.

3) Connect the "Value" POut of Bezier Progression with the "Scale"PIn of Noise.

4) Open the window of Edit Parameters: Water Script\Bezier Progression. Set the Duration to 10s, A to 0.01 and B to 0.02. Set the Bezier Curve to match the one in the picture; it doesn't need to be exact, but the start and end point must be at the same height on the curve.

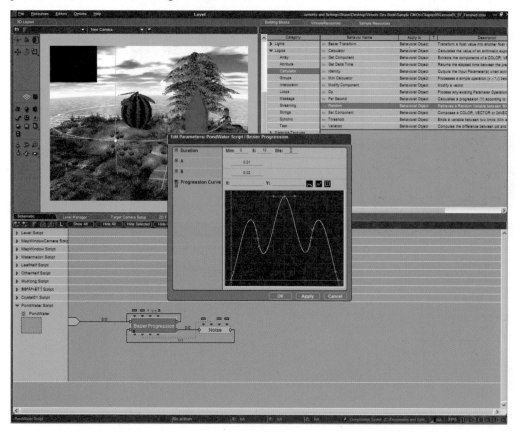

5) Open the Edit Parameters dialog of the Noise BB and set Axis to X=10, Y=10, Z=10. Ensure Reset Mesh is enabled.

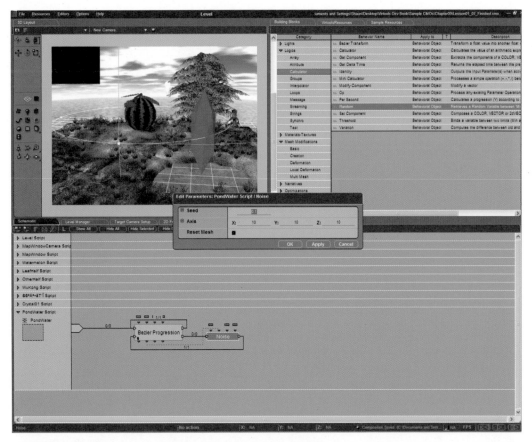

6) Click Play and the water will ripple slowly back and forth.

Chapter10 buttons and web navigation

1.0 Creating 2D Buttons

In this first lesson we show you how to create 2D Buttons within Virtools. You will need a recent version of Adobe Photoshop™ installed on your computer and at least some basic knowledge of how to use layers and export images in PNG format.

Buttons are relatively easy to setup in Virtools and only require a few additional resources, such as textures and materials, to give you basic 'rollover' and 'click' effects.

You can combine Buttons and the techniques you learned in Chapter 5 Text Messages to create User Interfaces and Control Panels for your applications; to take this idea further, you can group sets of buttons together and start creating tab-style panels that show and hide based on which has 'active' focus.

1.1 Preparing the Button Image

1) We will use Photoshop (but you can use any image editor) to create an image with a transparent background to use as our button. You can create your own button, or you can open the file ButtonSkin.PSD located in Sample CMO's\Chapter10. You can see the layers in the image represent the 3 different states of the button; Released (or normal), Over and Pressed. The other layers contain the various text labels we will use later.

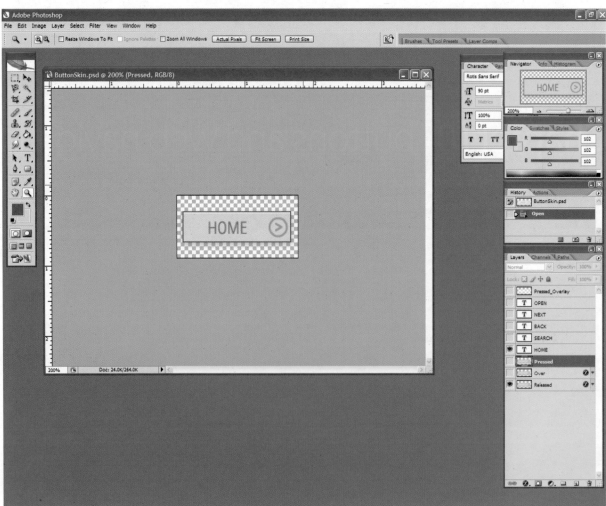

2) Leave the layer configuration as is and select File \ Save for Web. In the Export pop-up that appears, change the Preset selection to PNG-24 and Click Save.

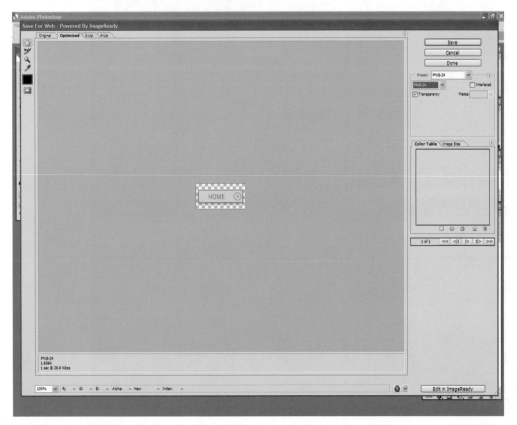

3) In the Save dialog, navigate to your Virtools sample resources directory (the default location is C:\Program Files\Virtools\Virtools Virtools 4.0\Documentation\VirtoolsResources) and open the Textures folder. Name the file "Home_Released.png" and click Save.

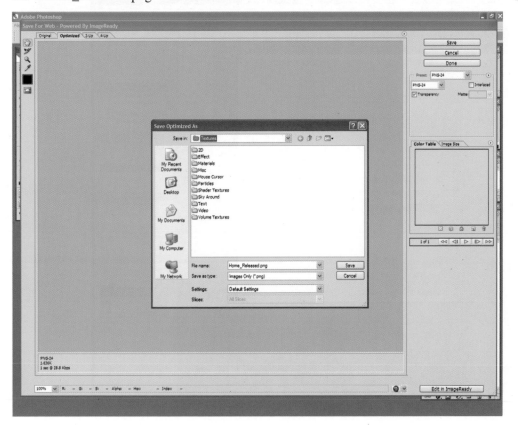

4) Now, switch to Virtools and check the Virtools Resources\Textures folder to make sure your button is there.

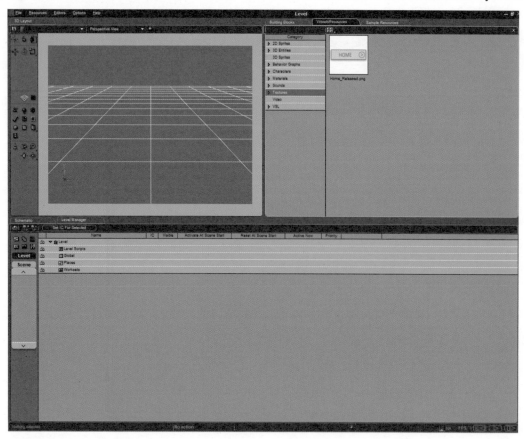

5) To finish off, we need to export the other states of the button (Over and Pressed) in the same way. Switch back to Photoshop and turn off the layer called Released and turn on the Over layer.

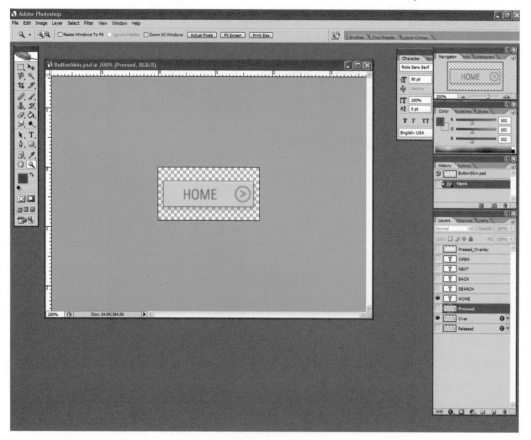

6) Export the image using the Save For Web command and save the file in the same folder as the first. Call this image "Home_Over.png"

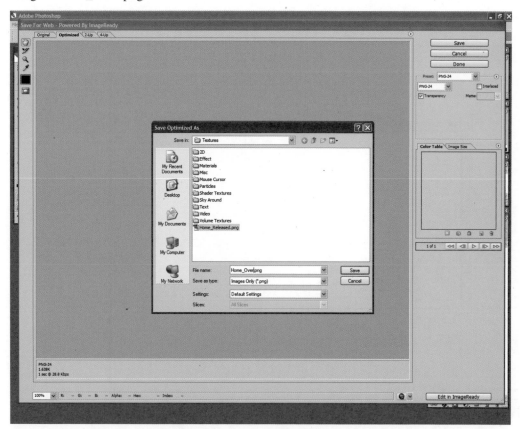

7) Now, turn off the Over layer and turn on the Pressed and Pressed_Overlay layers. The button appears a little brighter which will give a blinking effect when we click.

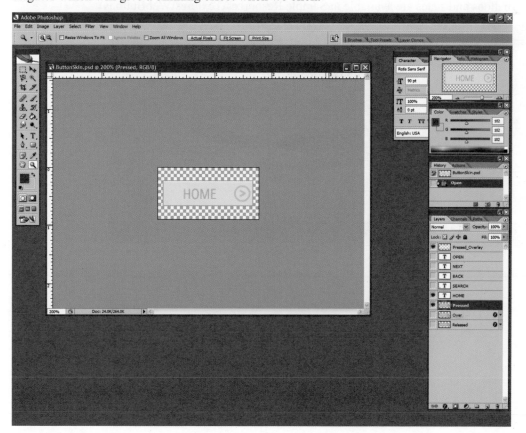

8) Again, use Save For Web to export the image and save it in the same folder. Call the image "Home_Pressed. png".

9) Now, when you switch back to Virtools and look in the Virtools Resources\Textures folder you should see all 3 button images. If you don't, make sure you saved the images in the correct path. (If you have trouble with the above steps, the buttons and states are available in Sample Resources\Textures\WebButtons)

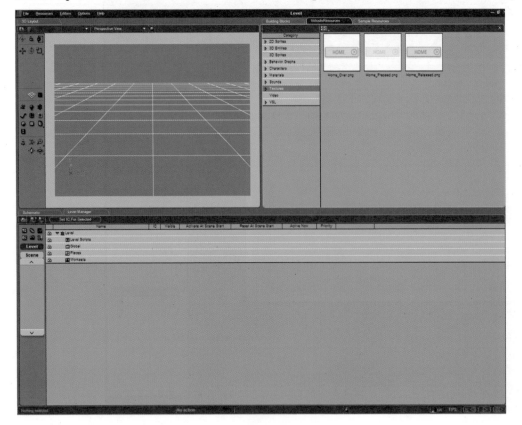

1.2 Making the Button Interactive

1) In this step we will make the button interact with the mouse. Start by creating a 2D Frame and set it to the same size as your button image. If you are using the sample button's we supplied, the image size is 128x64.

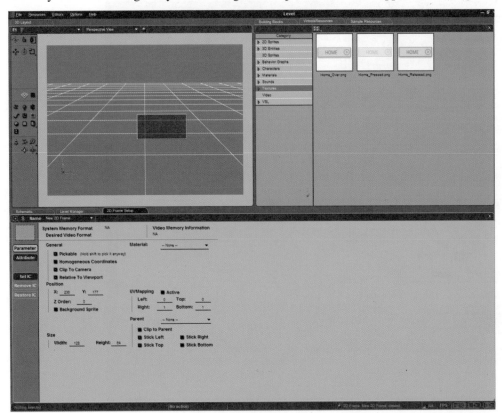

2) Next, drag the 3 button images into the 3D layout window (don't drag them into the 2D Frame, just to a blank area of the window). 3 new textures will be created with the same names as the buttons.

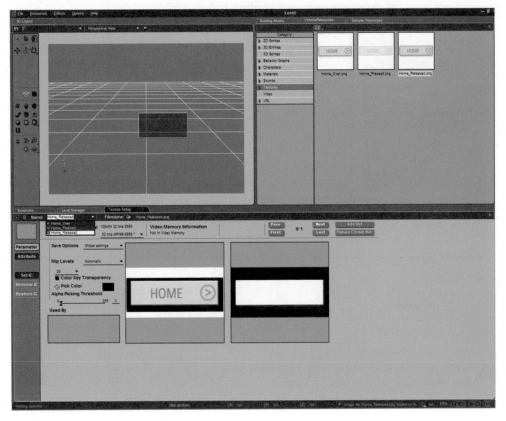

3) Now, we need to create corresponding materials for the buttons. Create 3 new materials and name them according to the texture they will hold (i.e. Home_OverMat etc). Remember to set the diffuse color to White, the Mode to Transparent and the Texture to the right texture for the material.

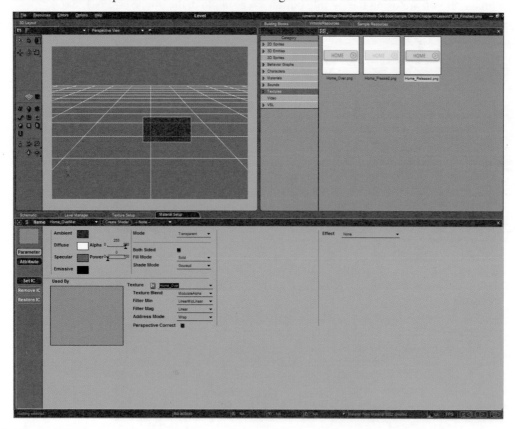

4) For each texture, set the Filter Mag setting to Nearest. This will stop the texture being smoothed (blurred) by the video card.

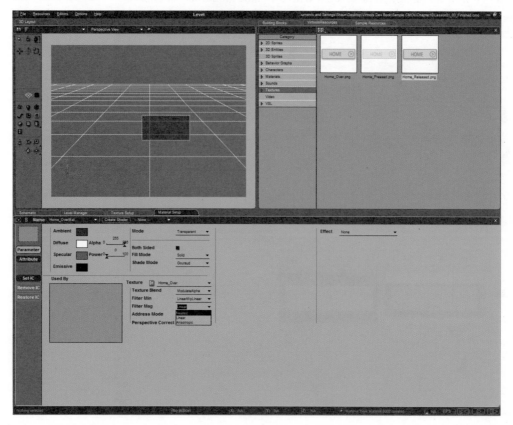

5) Now, create a script for our 2D Frame and add the Push Button BB from Building Blocks\Interface\Controls. Connect it to the Start Node.

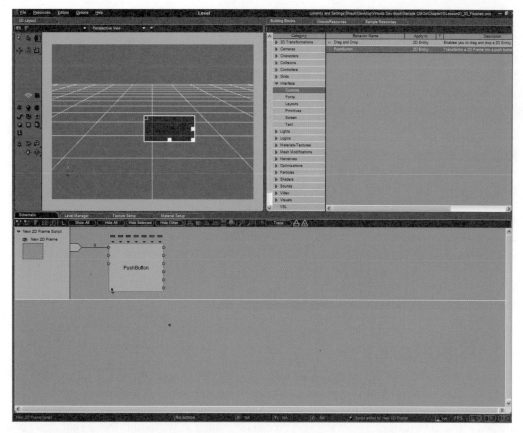

6) Open the Edit Parameters dialog of the PushButton BB and set the Released, Pressed and Rollover parameters to the corresponding materials and set the Pressed Offset to X=0 and Y=0.

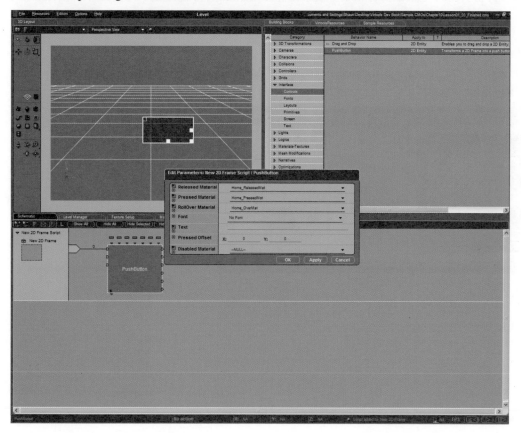

7) Click Play and test the button. It will change texture when you rollover and click it.

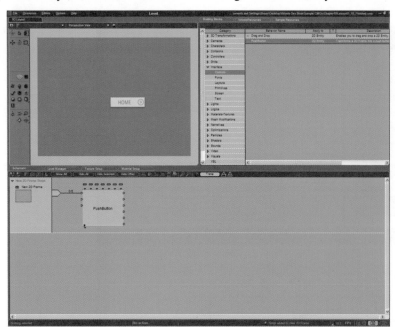

2.0 Creating 3D Buttons

In this lesson we show you how to create 3D buttons that interact with the mouse. We use a special BB called 2D Picking which uses the 2D coordinates of the mouse cursor to determine which 3D object is currently being 'selected' by the mouse. This BB is extremely powerful and can be used for much more than just buttons as any 3D object can be selected using 2D Picking; for example, you can determine a 'waypoint' that a character should walk to, an enemy to attack or item to pickup, all using the mouse. This can help to make your composition much more user-friendly and provide a better overall experience than making the user have to learn a myriad of key combinations.

2.1 Creating the Mouse Over Effect

1) Open the file Lesson02_02_Start.cmo located in Sample CMOs\Chapter10. You will see a crystal button floating in star field. This object will serve as our basic 3D button.

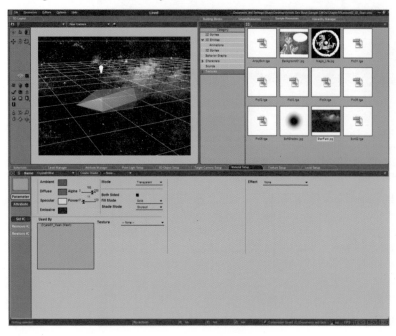

2) Create a script for the Crystal and add the Mouse Waiter BB from Building Blocks\Controllers\Mouse. Connect it with the Start Node.

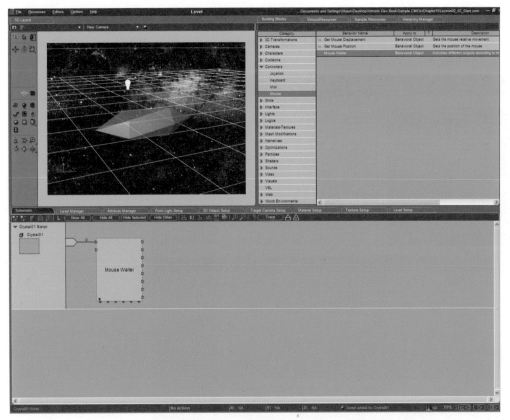

3) Now add the 2D Picking BB located in Building Blocks\Interface\Screen and connect it with the Mouse Move BOut of the Mouse Waiter BB. Together, these two BB's will allow us to check if the mouse is currently over the Crystal.

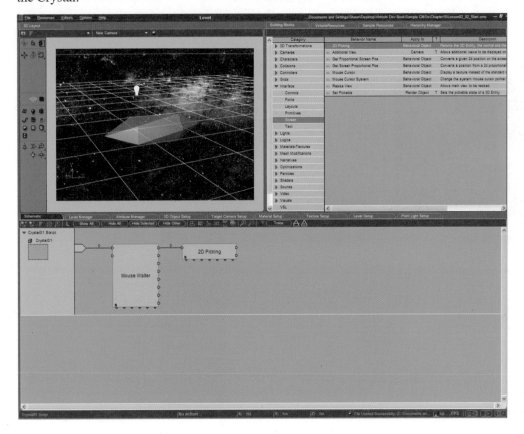

4) It is important to note that for every pixel the mouse moves, the 2D Picking BB will be triggered. That means we have to be careful which BB's we connect to it as they will also be triggered every frame. To allow us to only trigger the Mouse Over event on a change, we use 2 Boolean BB's to check the state of the 2D Picking BB to see if it has changed from the last frame. Add the Binary Memory and Boolean Event from Building Blocks\Logics\Streaming to the script. Connect both BIns of the Binary Memory BB to the BOut's of the 2D Picking BB, making sure they are in parallel.

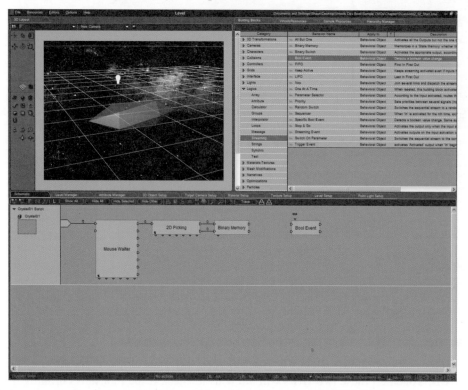

5) Now, connect both of the Binary Memory BOut's to the Boolean Event In BIn. Connect the Binary Memory BB's POut to the Boolean Event BB's PIn. This will pass the True\False data to the Boolean Event BB at runtime.

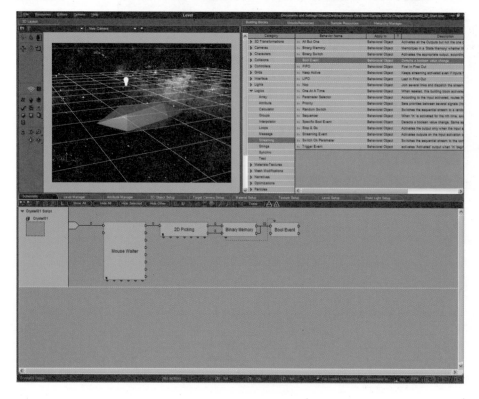

6) We need to change the state of the Crystal if it is 'hit' by the mouse. Since it can only have 2 states (over or not over) we use the Sequencer BB to swap the state of the button when a received from our Boolean Event BB. Add the Sequencer BB from Building Blocks\Logics\Streaming to the script. Connect the Boolean Event BB's Change Detected BOut to the Sequencer BB's BIn. Since there are two states, we need to add another BOut for the second state to the Sequencer BB. Right click the BB and select Construct\Add Behavior Output.

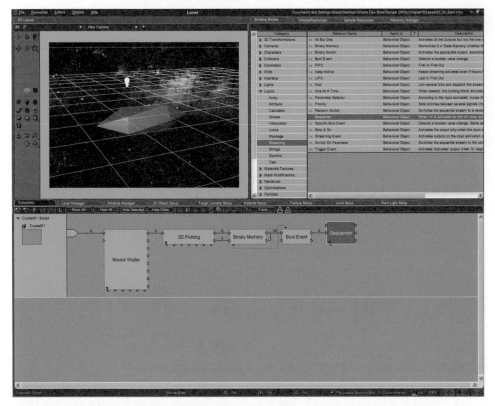

7) Add two Set Diffuse BBs from Building Blocks\Materials-Textures\Basic and connect them to the second and third BOut's of the Sequencer BB.

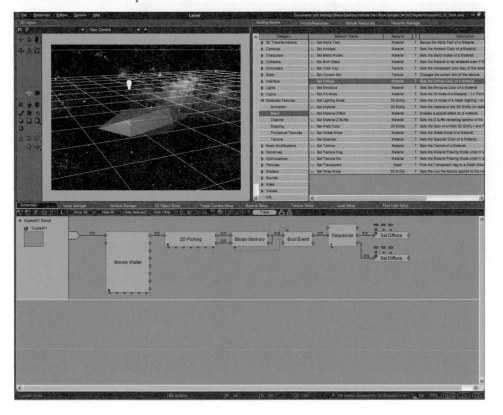

8) Set the first Set Diffuse BB's parameters to Target (Material) = Crystal01Mat, Diffuse Color = R156, G=79, B=79, A=255 and turn off the Keep Alpha Component checkbox. Lastly, set the second Set Diffuse BB's parameters to the same values except change the Diffuse Color to R=156, G=79, B=79, A=180.

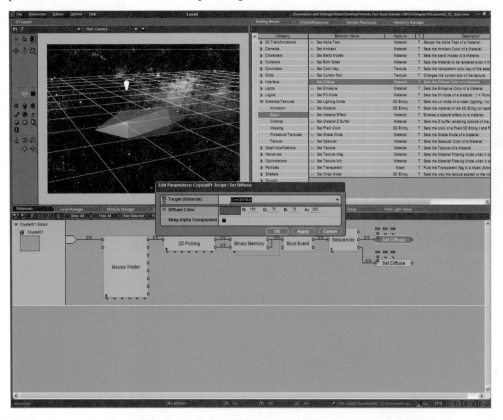

9) Click play and rollover the Crystal, it will become solid when the mouse is over it and transparent when you roll out. Also, make sure the Trace button is enabled in the Schematic view. You can see that the Set Diffuse BB's are only enabled when a Change event is triggered by the Boolean Event BB.

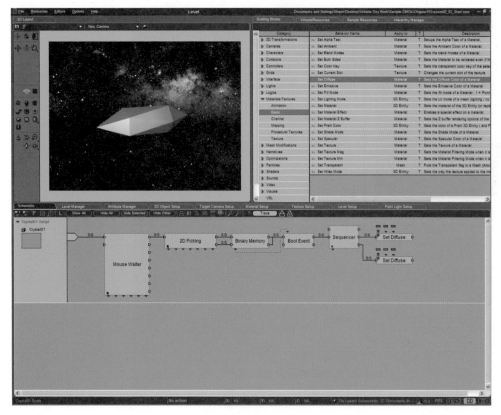

2.2 Creating the On Click Effect

1) You can continue with your scene from the last lesson or open the file Lesson02_02_Start.cmo located in Sample CMOs\Chapter10. To add the On Click effect we basically use a combination of the BB's we used in the last lesson. Hold the Control key and click the 2D Picking, Sequencer and both Set Diffuse BBs. Then Right Click any of the BB's and select copy from the popup menu.

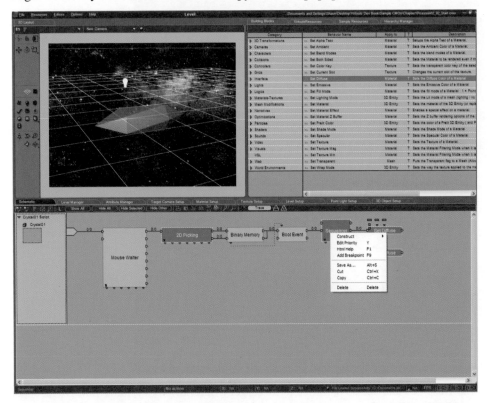

2) Right click in a blank area of the script window and select paste; the BB's will be pasted into the script window in the same layout as they were copied. Re-arrange them below the top row of BB's.

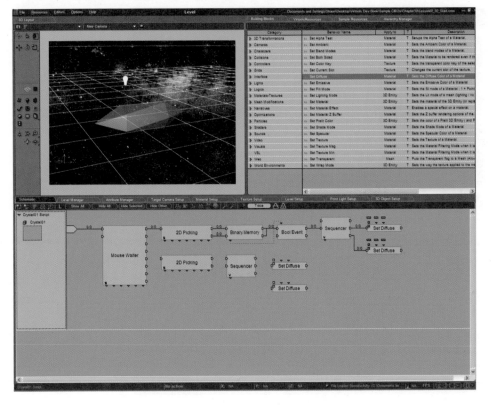

3) You will notice that when you pasted the BB's they lost their Parameter Inputs (Pins). Don't worry, we don't want to use the same parameters as we will configure our own. Connect the 2D Picking BB to the Left Button Down Received BOut of the Mouse Waiter BB. Connect the True BOut of the 2D Picking BB to the In BIn of the Sequencer and the 2 Set Diffuse BBs to the 2nd and 3rd BOut's of the Sequencer BB.

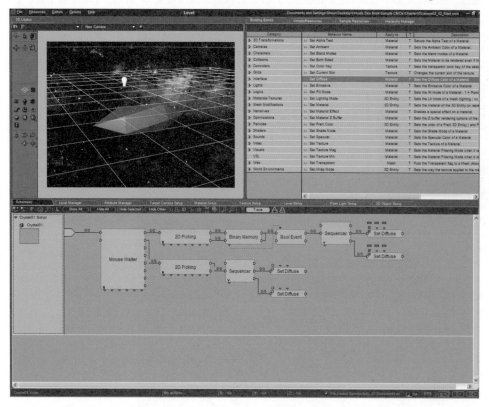

4) Double click the first Set Diffuse BB and set its parameters to Target (Material) = Crystal01Mat, Diffuse Color R=147, G=156, B=78, A=255. Lastly, set the second Set Diffuse BB's parameters to the same values except change the Diffuse Color to R=84, G=55, B=179 A=255.

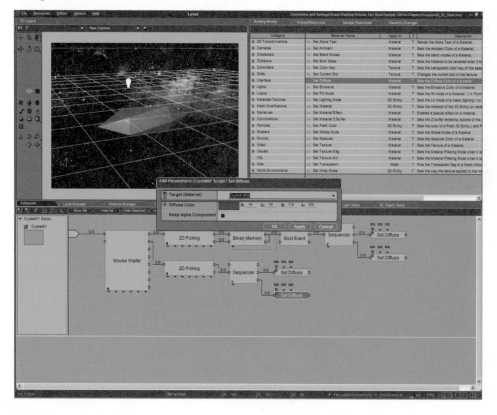

5) Click play and try clicking the Crystal, it will change color according to the sequencer state.

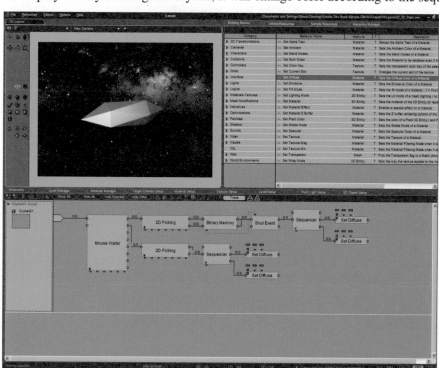

3.0 Web Page Navigation

3.1 Creating a Web Browser Toolbar

1) Open the file Lesson03_01_Start.cmo located in Sample CMOs\Chapter10. There are a set of 6 2D Frames in the Scene, 5 being button frames and one the background. In Level Manager, open the Materials folder and you can see each button has a material for each of its 3 states with a total of 15 materials cover all the states of all the buttons.

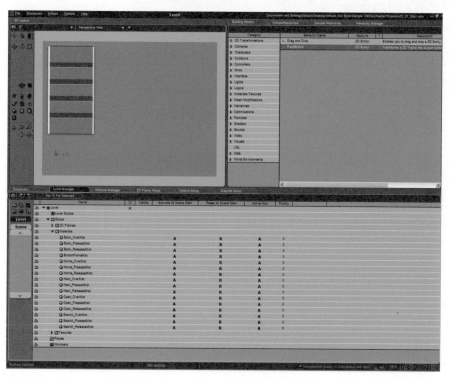

2) In the Schematic View, open the script for the BackButton 2D Frame and add the Back BB from Building Blocks\Web\Navigation. Connect it to the Pressed BOut of the PushButton BB.

3) Double click the Schematic Tab to maximize the workspace and open the script windows for the remaining buttons. Add the following BB's to the scripts; HomeButton = Home BB, NextButton = Next BB, OpenButton = Go To Web Page BB and SearchButton = Search BB. Connect each with the Pressed BOut of the PushButton BB. (Note: The Go To Web Page BB defaults to the URL 'http:\\www.virtools.com; feel free to change this any site you like).

4) We have finished the scripting component of this lesson, but to test this composition we need to view it within our web browser. Select the File\Create Web Page option.

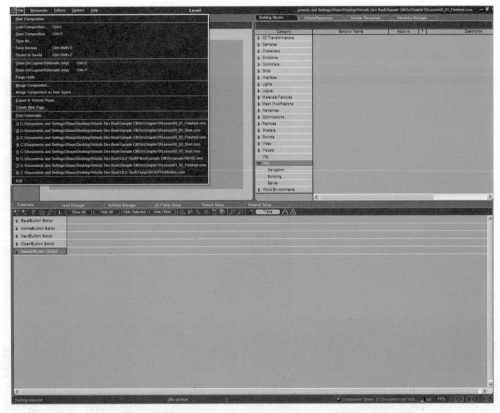

5) In the Save dialog that appears, click Choose Destination and select a location to store the files (try to use a location that you can find easily, like the desktop). Now change the Window Size to 640x480 and click OK. Virtools will create two files; a VMO which is a non-editable runtime version of a CMO and a matching HTML page.

6) Switch to Windows Explorer and open the newly created HTML file in Internet Explorer. Try clicking the buttons; the Home button for example will open your default homepage. Note that the Back and Next buttons won't be active until you have browsed some pages.

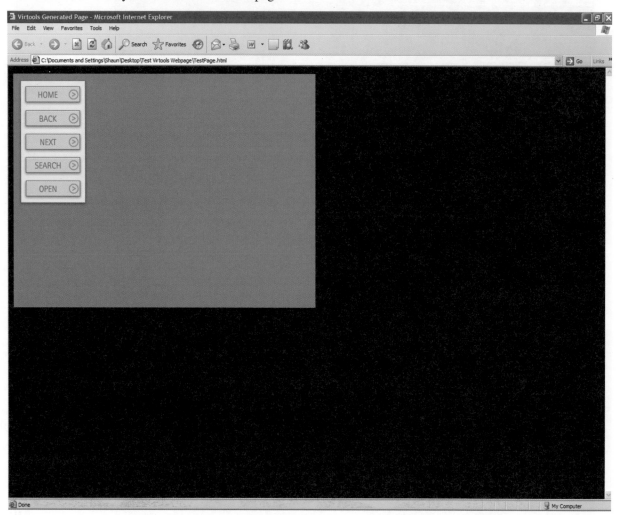

Chapter11 creating a game

1.0 Project Planning

1.1 Overview

In this chapter we take a step back from Virtools and look at what it takes to create a game from scratch. We discuss some of the planning and prototyping tasks that are involved in game production including concept art, workflows, character definition and modules of the game etc. In section 2.0, we start on creating a single level of our game using some of the scenes and characters described in this section.

We will use an outline for a fictional game called "Journey to the West" based on an ancient Chinese story of the same name. Even though we are just making a game demo, the actual planning phase for a real game is very similar (although we wont cover business topics like financials, human resources, marketing and publishing).

Any kind of software development needs to have some preliminary planning regardless of whether the project is big or small, and games are no different. Let's start by covering the back story to set the scene for our demo.

1.2 The Game Story

The destiny of the entire world is controlled by a magical device called the Cosmosphere. The Cosmosphere is balanced by eight magical stones that represent the eight attributes of the universe. But because of the greed and self-indulgence of the human race, the power of the black stone has become too strong causing a catastrophic imbalance in the Cosmosphere. With the disparity caused by the conflicting forces, the Cosmosphere eventually could no longer contain the power of the stones and they were scattered to different regions of the kingdom. Once outside of the Cosmosphere, the stones returned to their daemon form and began to wreak havoc on the world; the final days of mankind were fast approaching.

Our story begins in the ancient Chinese province of Chang'an; Tripitaka the Master is a notorious thief at large in the city. Together with his loyal companions Sun WuKong the Monkey, Sha the Monk and Ba Jie the Pigsy they rob the cities wealthy residents using the old catchphrase "looting the rich to give to the poor". One day, they thought they would try their hands at ransacking the Royal Government Museum, but it turned out to be more than they could handle and they soon besieged by the Royal Army. Whilst trying to escape they fell into secret room in an ancient section of the museum where they met a mighty White Dragon.
The White Dragon was a herald sent from heaven and had already predicted all the events leading up to the present. He told the band of thieves about the plight of the eight stones and offered them a chance of freedom if they would capture the daemons and return them to the Cosmosphere. Of course, the four refused immediately, knowing that the powerful daemons would surely guarantee them a swift and painful death. Thus the White Dragon gave them a final offer; if the four can successfully retrieve the daemons and return them to the Cosmosphere they can keep the golden incarnations that would be left after the daemons transformation back to stone form. Tripitaka and his three companions finally accepted the offer.

The White Dragon cast a magic spell called Jiang Shen on Tripitaka. With this power he could weaken the daemons so that they could not call on help from other animals. Then the White Dragon gave the Sky Scroll to Sun WuKong; the Sky Scroll would allow the daemons to be captured and returned to the Cosmosphere. As long as our band of makeshift heroes can capture the eight daemons and return them to the Cosmosphere the mission will be complete. And so the quest to save the world begins.

1.3 The Game Fundamentals

Our game will consist of 3 different fundamental elements or parts;
1) Part I is the World Map, an overall view of the Middle Kingdom where our player can choose their mission.
2) Part II is the Combat mission. Our player proceeds through the game by winning battles against various enemies. Each mission consists of three battles. Altogether there are eight combat missions.
3) Part III is the Boss Combat mission, which happens at the end of each Combat mission. The player has to fight against one of the Cosmosphere daemons in order to win this mission.

1.4 The Players

Our player can select to play as any one of the four heroes including;
4) Tripitaka the Master
5) Sun WuKong the Monkey;
6) Sha the Monk;
7) Ba Jie the Pigsy

The enemies include the eight daemons;
1) Black Wind (Hei Feng)
2) Gold Horn (Jin Jiao)
3) Silver Horn (Yin Jiao)
4) Fire Boy
5) Skeleton
6) The Minister
7) Princess with the Iron Fan
8) The Ox
We also have other enemies which include eight kinds of Imps and four kinds of Goblins.

1.5 The Game Modules

Our game has 5 basic modules, or modes of operation;
1) The Main Menu
2) Hero Selection
3) The Middle Kingdom Map
4) Main Mission \ Combat Mode
5) And Movie (or Story) Mode

1.6 Game Types and Special Features

1) Game type
   The game will have two versions;
   a.The first will be a downloadable Internet version. Each file must be less than 2Mb in size to ensure smooth game flow and minimal delay for our player. The quality and fidelity of the images, textures and sounds will be lower than normal.
   b.The second will be a PC based version. In this edition we will include movies, high quality audio and larger textures. This version will require more disk space and a more powerful system.
2) Techniques
   Each time the player defeats an Imp or Goblin, the enemy may drop some equipment and the player will accumulate magic power points. Once the player has acquired enough magic power points they can use the Jiang Shen spell to transform their incarnation. Each hero has a different incarnation and the Jiang Shen spell can only be accessed after defeating a specific daemon.
3) About the Cosmosphere
   Every time a player defeats a daemon, the daemons stone will fall to the ground. When the player picks up the stone it will automatically be returned to the Cosmosphere. There are 4 special holes in the Cosmosphere and once a hole becomes full there will be certain special features unlocked according to the order the player collects the stones.
4) Multi-Threaded Storyline
   The player can select a main mission on the map that contains multiple sub-missions. The player can only choose one and the choice will affect the content of the mission.
5) Multiplayer
   The game will support LAN and Internet-based play with a maximum number of four simultaneous players. However, multiplayer functionality will not be available in the Demo.

1.7 Summary of Characters

Below is an example table which contains a summary of the elements we need to compose our game Demo. This kind of table is very useful when trying to give others an overview of your game elements and assigning tasks to team members. It is also a useful tool for you to track your progress.

Journey to the West: Game Elements Estimate				
Item Name	Category	Information	Level of Detail	Priority
WuKong (Standard)	Player Character	Run, Attack a; Attack b; Jump; Back off; Use stunts; Unique skill; Injured; Dead	<30 surfaces	High
WuKong (Low Res)	Player Character	Run, Attack a; Attack b; Jump; Back off; Use stunts; Unique skill; Injured; Dead	<10 surfaces	High
Imp A	Enemy	Run; Attack a: Attack b; Injured	<10 surfaces	High
Imp B	Enemy	Run; Attack a: Attack b; Injured	<10 surfaces	High
Imp C (Change color)	Enemy	Run; Attack a: Attack b; Injured	<10 surfaces	High
Imp D (change color)	Enemy	Run; Attack a: Attack b; Injured	<10 surfaces	High
The Ox (Standard)	Daemon	Run, Attack a; Attack b; Jump; Back off; Unique skill; Injured; Dead	<30 surfaces	High
The Ox (Low Res)	Daemon	Run, Attack a; Attack b; Jump; Back off; Unique skill; Injured; Dead	<10 surfaces	High
Spider Queen (Standard)	Daemon	Run, Attack a; Attack b; Jump; Back off; Unique skill; Injured; Dead	<30 surfaces	High
Spider Queen (Low Res)	Daemon	Run, Attack a; Attack b; Jump; Back off; Unique skill; Injured; Dead	<10 surfaces	High
WuKong (High Res)	Cut Scene Character	Actions will vary according to specific events	<50 surfaces	Medium
BaJie (High Res)	Cut Scene Character	Actions will vary according to specific events	<50 surfaces	Medium
Tripitaka (High Res)	Cut Scene Character	Actions will vary according to specific events	<50 surfaces	Medium
Sha (High Res)	Cut Scene Character	Actions will vary according to specific events	<50 surfaces	Medium
Spider Queen (High Res)	Daemon	Actions will vary according to specific events	<50 surfaces	Medium
The Ox (High Res)	Daemon	Actions will vary according to specific events	<50 surfaces	Medium
World Map	Main Scene	3D World Map; Player selects mission	<20 surfaces	High
Spider's Cave A	Combat Scene	The Team must fight the 1st Spider Boss	<1M for low <10M for high	High
Spider's Cave B	Combat Scene	The Team must fight the 2nd Spider Boss	<1M for low <10M for high	High
Spider's Cave C	Combat Scene	The Team must fight the 3rd Spider Boss	<1M for low <10M for high	High
Spider's Cave Daemon Battle	Boss Combat Scene	The Team must fight the Spider Queen	<1M for low <10M for high	High
Mount Flame A	Combat Scene	The Team must fight the 1st Flame Boss	<1M for low <10M for high	High
Mount Flame B	Combat Scene	The Team must fight the 2nd Flame Boss	<1M for low <10M for high	High
Mount Flame C	Combat Scene	The Team must fight the 3rd Flame Boss	<1M for low <10M for high	High
Mount Flame Daemon Battle	Boss Combat Scene	The Team must fight the Flame Boy Daemon	<1M for low <10M for high	High
Title Screen	User Interface	Start Game, Story, Credits and Exit Options	<1M for low <2M for high	High
Hero Selection	User Interface	4 x Hero Options	<1M for low <5M for high	High
Character Info Panel	Popup U.I.	Statistics; Life value; Cosmosphere Status		
Cut Scene A	Non-Interactive Scene	The team arrive at the Spider Queen's cave	<10M	Low
Cut Scene B	Non-Interactive Scene	The Spider Queen appears	<10M	Low
Cut Scene C	Non-Interactive Scene	The Ox appears and captures Tripitaka the Monk	<10M	Low
Cut Scene D	Non-Interactive Scene	The Ox appears	<10M	Low
Cut Scene E	Non-Interactive Scene	The Demo ends	<2M	High
Game Website	Website	Viewers can get an introduction to the game, play online or download the full version	<2M	High
Music A	Sound	For the Title menu and Website	Midi file	Medium
Music B	Sound	For Hero Selection	Midi file	Medium

Music C	Sound	For the Middle Kingdom Map	Midi file	Medium
Music D	Sound	For the Spider's Queen's cave	Midi file	Medium
Music E	Sound	For Mount Flame	Midi file	Medium
Music F	Sound	Demo End Scene	Midi file	Medium
Special Effect A	Sound	For WuKongs Special Attack	Wave file	High
Special Effect B	Sound	For WuKong transforming his incarnation	Wave file	High
Special Effect C	Sound	For Spider Queen's unique skill	Wave File	High
Special Effect D	Sound	For the Ox's unique skill	Wave file	High
Item's 2D drafts	Concept	Make use of existing concept artwork	N/A	High
Scene Design Drafts	Concept	2 missions and 8 figures in total	N/A	High

1.8 Sketches and Concept Art

Concept art is essential in the preparation of your game. It not only conveys the overall look and feel of your game, but also gives a good starting point for creating the 3D versions of your models.

Below is some of the concept art for our game, Journey to the West.

1. Sun WuKong
the Monkey

2. Tripitaka the Master

3. Ba Jie the Pigsy

4. Sha the Monk

5. Yang 3 Eyes

6. The Ox

7. Princess with
the Iron Fan

8. Flame Boy

9. Golden Horn (Jin Jiao)

10. Silver Horn
(YinJiao)

11. Spider Queen

12. Scene –
Concept Sketch

13. Scene –
Colorized Concept

14. Concept Sketch
of BaJie and the
Spider Queen

15. Triptaka's
JiangShen Incarnation

16. Scene
Concept Sketch

17. Poster Concept

1.9 Game Flow Chart

Designing a flow chart that outlines the entire game will have a big effect on the success of your design and development process. The chart will ensure that project managers can grasp the overall structure, the programmers understand the underlying systems and rules and the designers know all the game's graphical elements and their relationship. Therefore, as the game designer you need to put some effort into designing your flowchart carefully. Below is the flowchart of our demo game for your reference.

Journey to the West: Game Flowchart

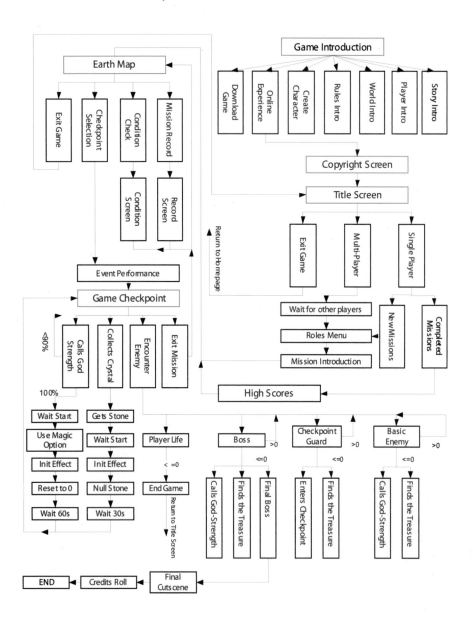

2.0 Setting Up the Scene

2.1 Basic Setup

1) Open the file Lesson02_01_Start.CMO located in Sample CMO's\Chapter11. Adjust the 3D Layout Window to match the view shown in the screenshot.

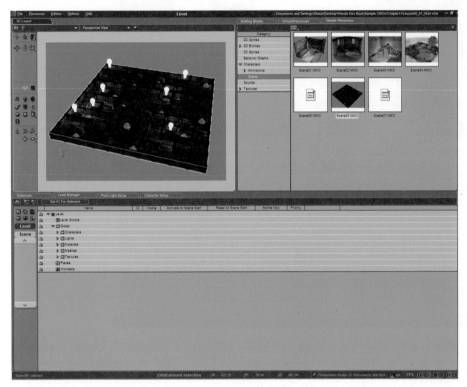

2) In Level Manager, select the Floor and FloorTrigger Body Parts of Scene06 and add the Floor and Shadow Caster Receiver attributes.

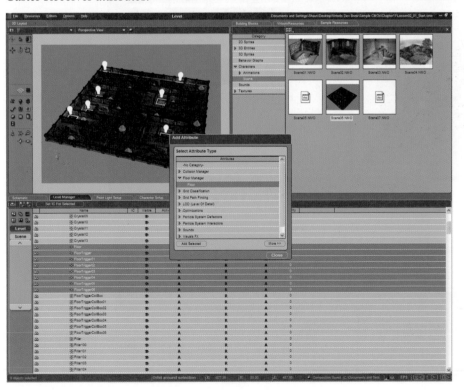

3) Next, select all of the FloorTriggerCollBox, Pillar and Wall body parts and add the Fixed Obstacle attribute. Add the Shadow Caster Receiver attribute to just the Pillar and Wall body parts.

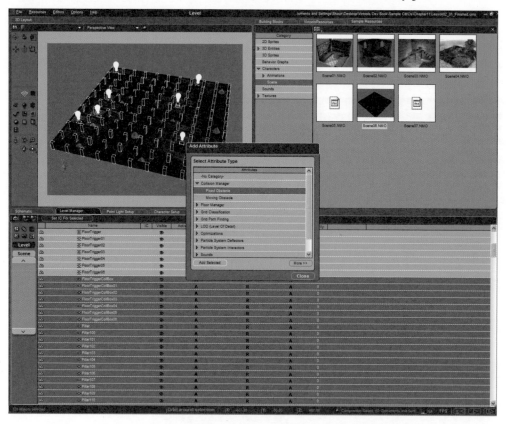

4) Select all the Crystal objects and right click the selection. Use the Place Selected in New Group command to create a new group called Crystals. Do the same for all the Pillar and Wall objects creating two new groups called Pillars and Walls respectively.

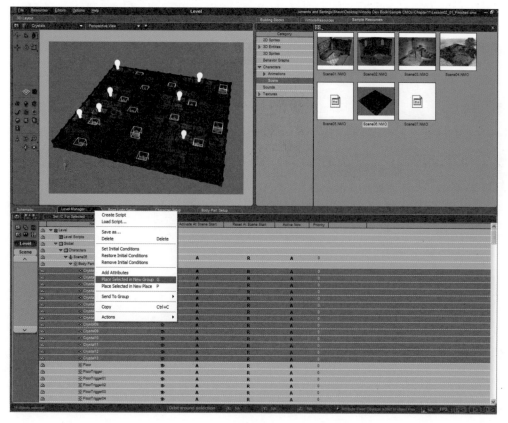

2.2 Making the Crystals Glimmer

1) Continue from the last lessons progress or open the file Lesson02_02_Start.CMO located in Sample CMO's\Chapter11. Start by creating a new Level Script and adding the Bezier Progression, Interpolator and Set Diffuse BB's into the Script.

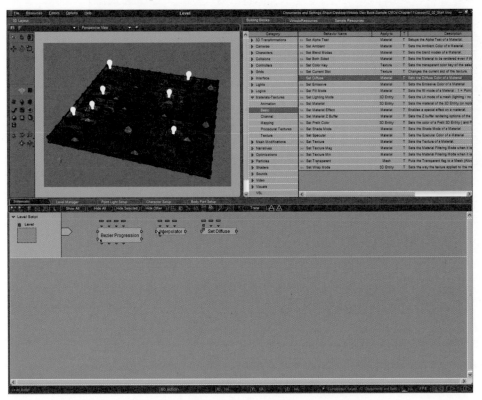

2) Connect the Bezier Progression BB to the Start Node and connect the remaining BB's in consecutive order with the Loop Out BOut Bezier Progression BB. Connect the Set Diffuse BOut with the Bezier Progression Loop In BIn to form a loop.

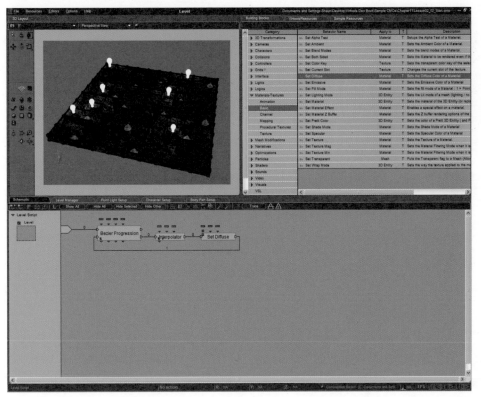

3) Connect the Output POut of the Bezier Progression BB to the Value Pin of the Interpolator BB

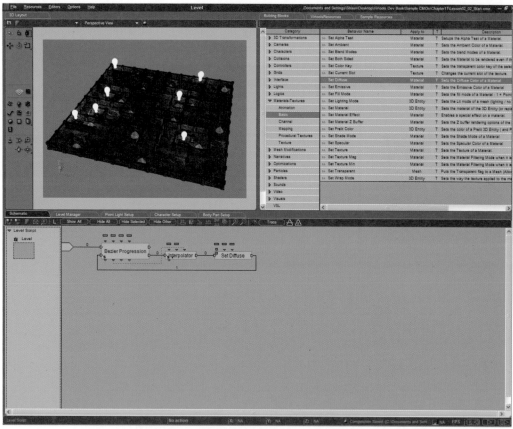

4) Double click the POut of the Interpolator BB and set its Parameter Type to Color. Connect it to the Set Diffuse Color Pin.

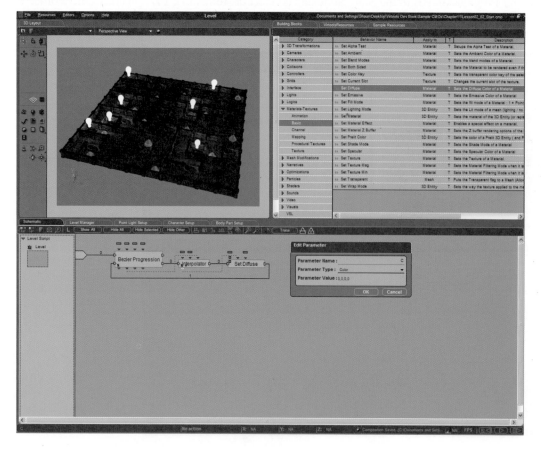

5) Double click the Interpolator BB and set the color values to A = R0, G0, B0, A0 and B = R255, G255, B255, A255.

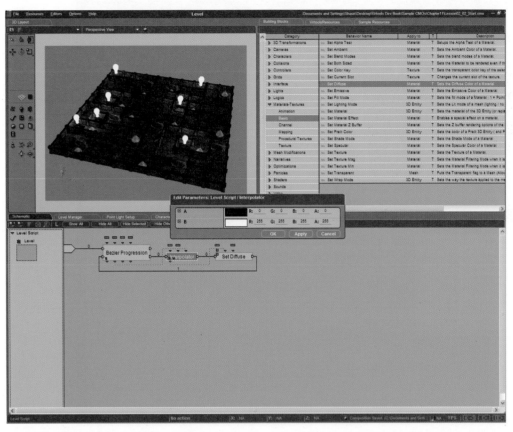

6) Double click the Set Diffuse BB and set the Target (Material) to CrystalMat and uncheck the Keep Alpha Component checkbox.

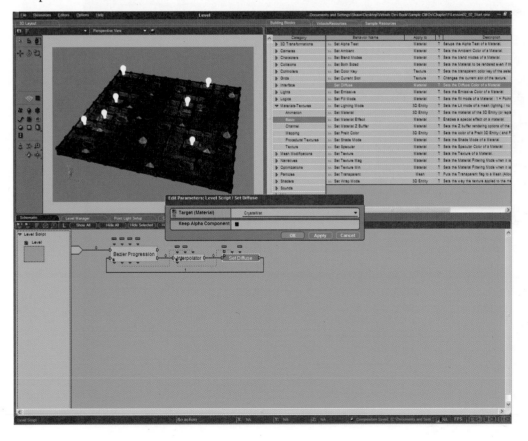

7) Right click in a blank area of the script window and select Draw Behavior Graph from the popup menu

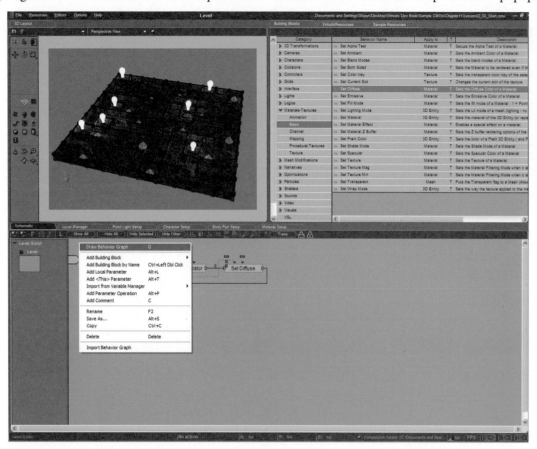

8) Click and drag a rectangle around the 3 BB's making sure you completely capture them all within the frame.

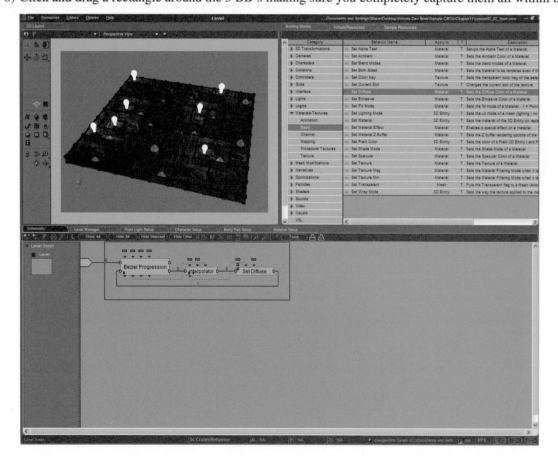

9) A new Behavior Graph will be created for the 3 BB's. Connect the Bezier Progression BIn to the Behavior Graphs BIn.

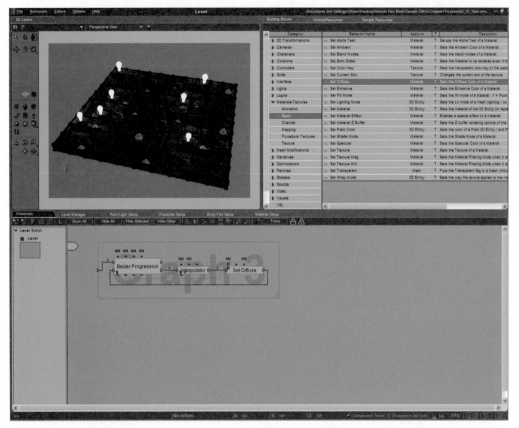

10) Right click in a blank section of the Behavior Graph and in the popup menu select Construct \ Add Behavior Output.

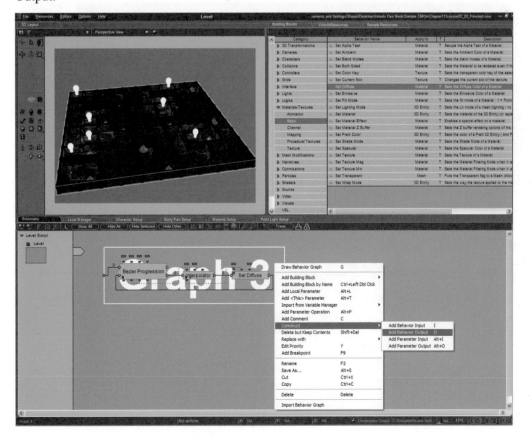

11) Connect the BOut of the Bezier Progression BB to the Behavior Graphs newly created BOut.

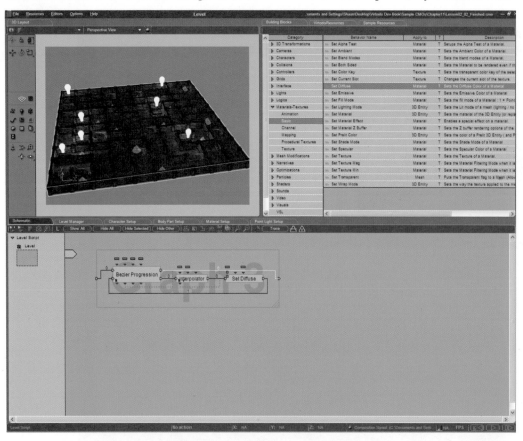

12) Double click a blank area in the Behavior Graph and it will collapse into a small BB. Select the BB and press F2 to rename it. Call the BB Alpha In. Connect it to the Start Node.

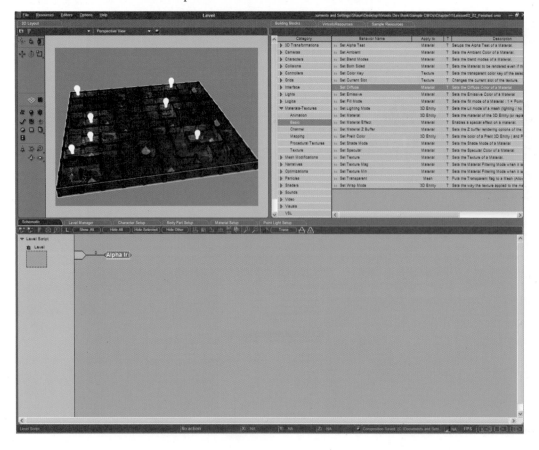

13) The Alpha In Behavior Graph makes the Crystals shine brighter, but we need to counter this with a second Behavior Graph that will set the Crystals back to their default state; this will give us a smooth glimmering effect. First right click the Alpha In BG and copy and paste it. Rename the copied Alpha In BG to Alpha Out. Connect it with the Alpha in BG.

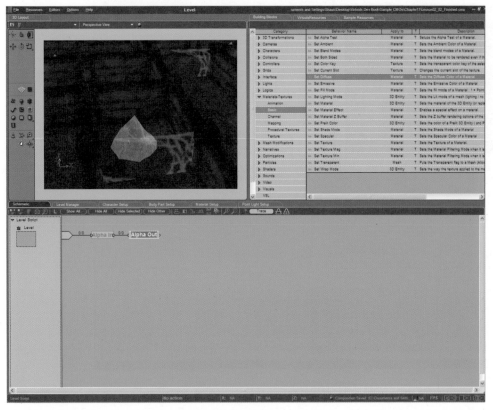

14) Now, double click the Alpha Out BG to view the BB's it contains. Open the Edit Parameters dialog of the Interpolator BB and swap the A and B colors.

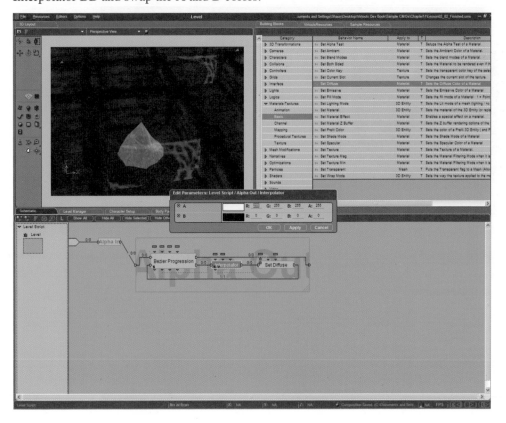

15) Finally close the Alpha Out BG and connect its BOut with the Alpha In BG's BIn. Click Play and you will see the crystals faintly glimmer over a 6 second period.

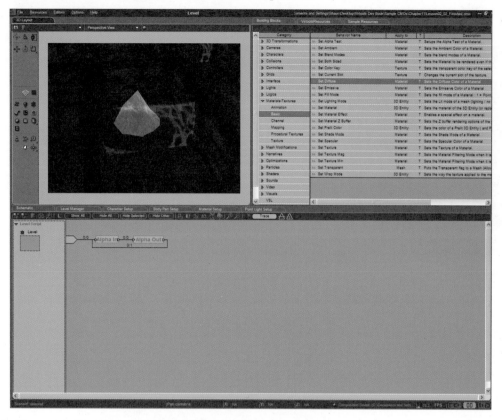

2.3 Crystal Collision Explosion Effect

1) Continue from the last lessons progress or open the file Lesson02_03_Start.CMO located in Sample CMO's\Chapter11. Start by creating a new Script for one of the Crystals.

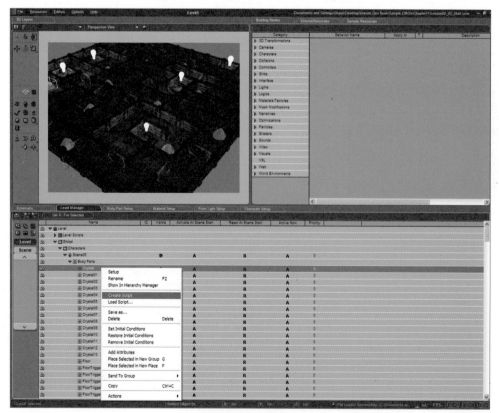

2) Add the Wait Message and Collision Detection BB's to the Script. Connect the Wait Message BB to the Start Node and connect its BOut to the Collision Detection BIn. Connect the False BOut of the Collision Detection BB to the BIn of the Wait Message BB to form a loop. Double Click the Wait Message BB and set the Message Parameter to Attack.

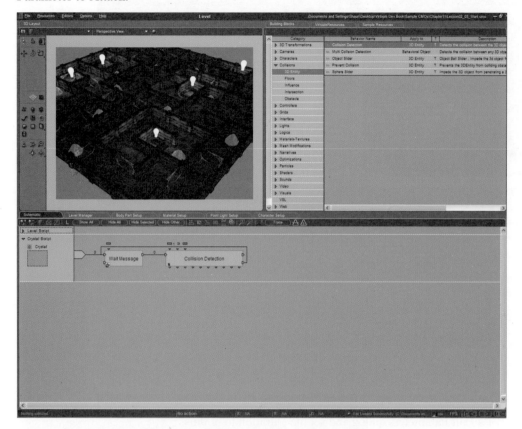

3) Add the Explode, Wave Player and Move To BB's to the Script.

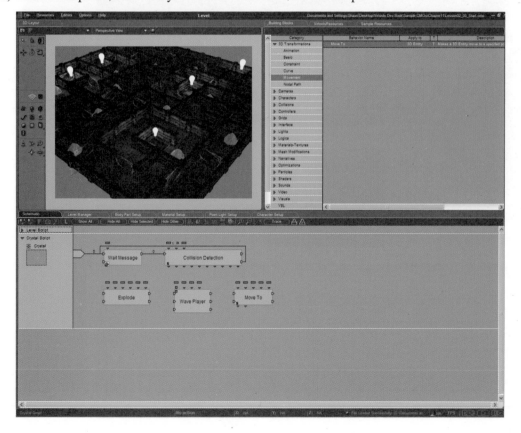

4) Connect the Explode BB to the Collision Detection BB's True BOut and create a loop between the Explode BB's Loop In and Loop Out pins as shown in the screenshot.

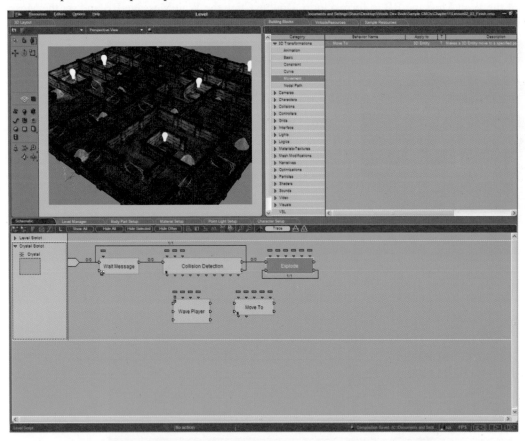

5) Open the Explode BB's Edit Parameters dialog and set the Duration to 500ms.

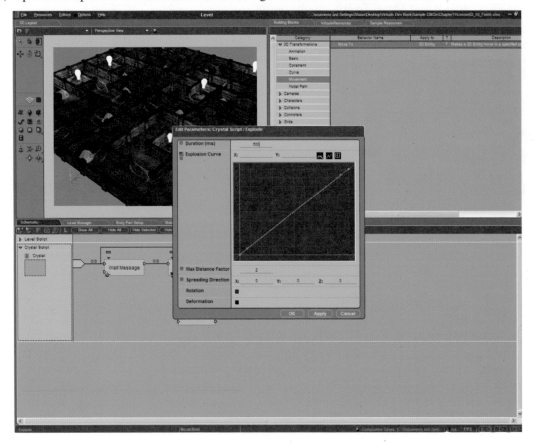

6) Connect the Wave Player Play BIn to the Collision Detection True BOut.

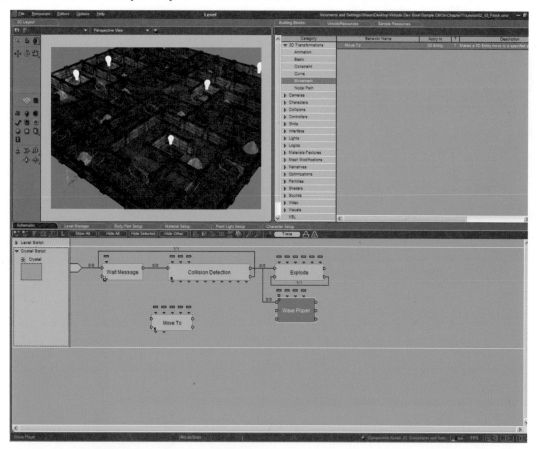

7) Add the file Explode.wav from Sample Resources \ Sounds to the scene.

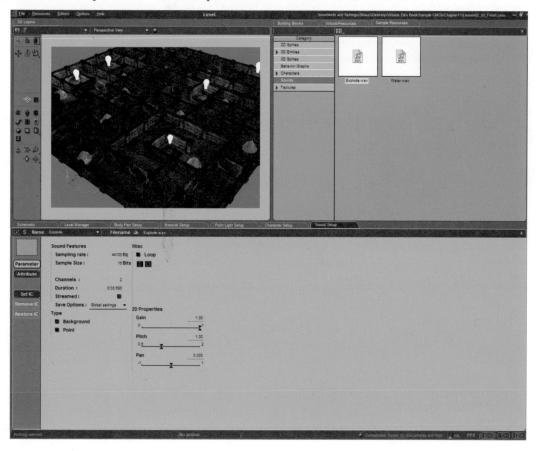

8) Double click the Wave Player BB and set the Sound to Explode.

9) Next, press Alt+T on your keyboard to add a parameter called "This". The This parameter allows you to reference the object the script is currently running in thus avoiding having to keep changing the reference if you copy and paste your script to other objects.

Note: The This parameter will be created under your mouse pointer, so make sure your mouse is within the Script Window.

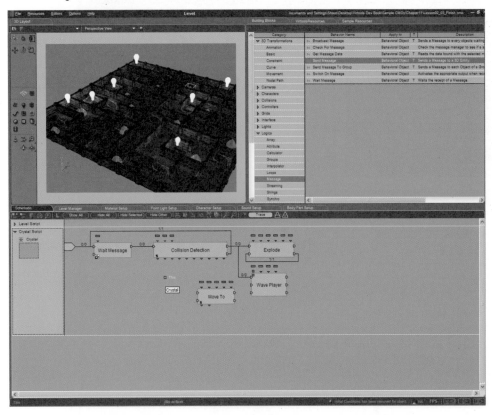

10) Now connect the This parameter to the Referential Pin of the Move To BB. Connect the BIn of the Move To BB to the True BOut of the Collision Detection BB and Loop its Loop In and Loop Out pins.

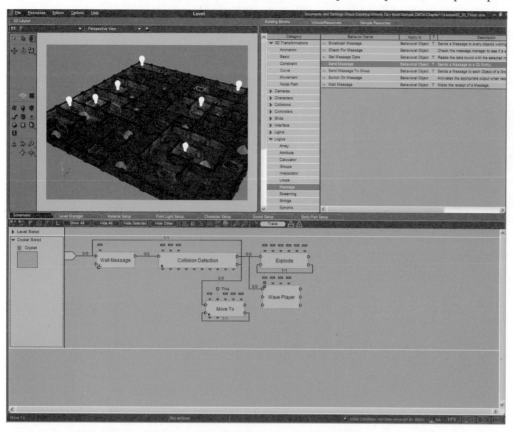

11) Lastly, open the Edit Parameters dialog of the Move To BB and set the Destination Point X=0, Y=-20 and Z=0 and set the Duration to 500ms. Our Explosion script is complete.

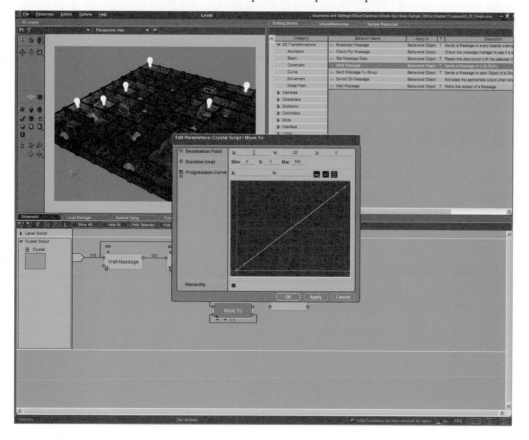

12) The final step of this lesson is to convert these various BB's into a single Behavior Graph. Using the techniques we covered in the last lesson, create a new BG called Crystal Explosion and connect it to the Start Node. Don't forget to connect the Wait Message BIn to the BG's In BIn.

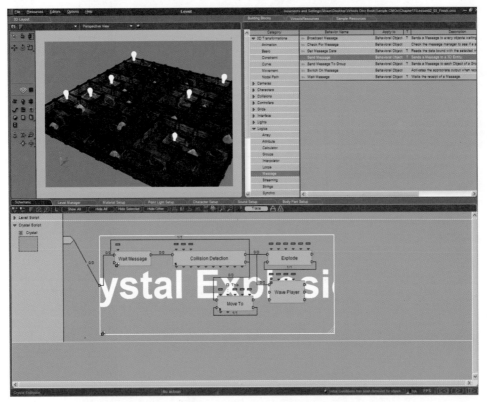

13) Now, create Scripts for the remaining Crystals and copy and paste the Crystal Explosion BG into their Scripts. Remember to connect the BG's with the Start Node. One important step to remember is to set the Initial Conditions for each of the Crystals, otherwise, when the Crystal Explosion event is triggered, the crystals will not reset back to their original position when you restart the level.

2.4 Creating the Floor Trigger Actions

1) Continue from the last lessons progress or open the file Lesson02_04_Start.CMO located in Sample CMO's\Chapter11. In Body Parts list of Scene06 select the 3 entities FloorTrigger, FloorTriggerCollBox and SecretWall and create their Scripts.

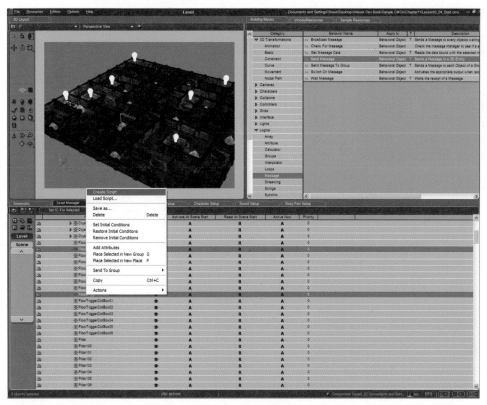

2) We will first create the script that will detect our characters collision with the trigger. In the FloorTriggerCollBox Script, add a Collision Detection and 2 Send Message BB's

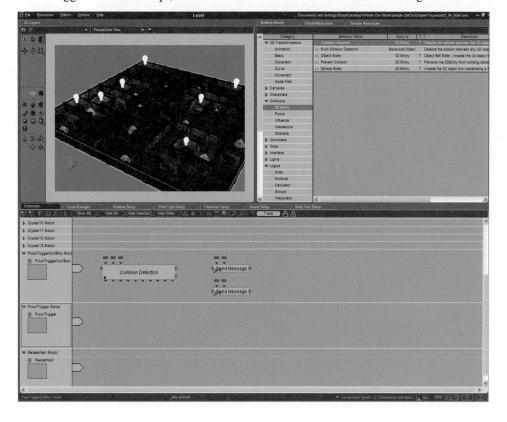

3) Connect the Collision Detection BB to the Start Node and loop it internally by connecting the False BOut to the BIn. Connect the True BOut to the two Send Message BB's.

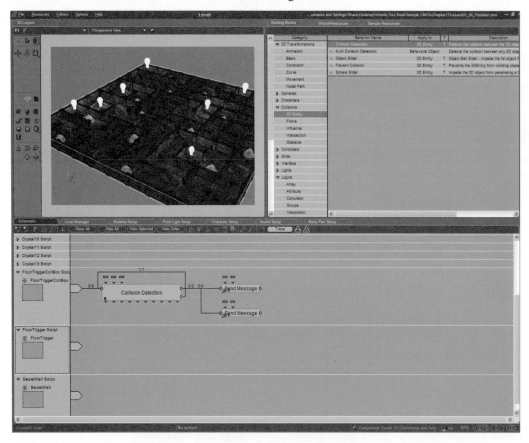

4) Set the first Send Message BB's Parameters to Message="Open Sesame" and Destination=FloorTrigger.

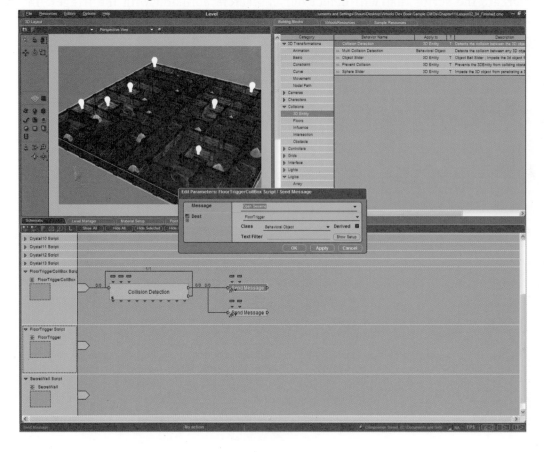

5) Set the second Send Message BB's Parameters to Message="Open Sesame" and Destination=FloorTrigger.

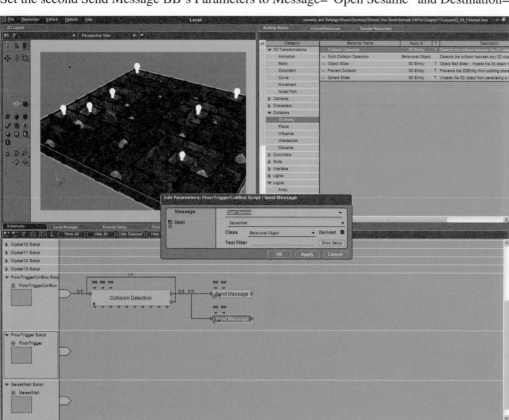

6) That's it for our detection script, now we will create the falling animation of our Floor Trigger. Start by adding the Wait Message BB into the FloorTrigger Script. Set the Message parameter to Open Sesame.

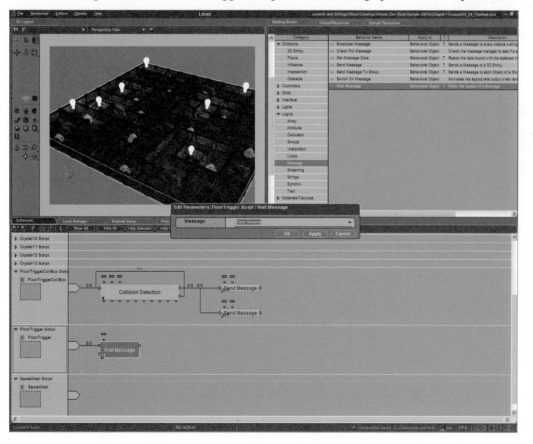

7) Next, add the Move To BB and create the This parameter by pressing Alt+T. Connect the This parameter to the Referential PIn on the Move To BB. Open the Edit Parameters dialog and set the Destination Point to X=0, Y=-2, Z=0 and the Duration to 1 Second. Connect the BB to the Start Node and connect its Loop In and Loop Out pins.

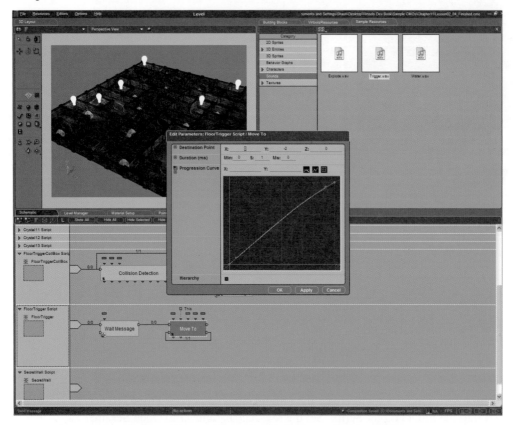

8) Add the Wave Player BB and connect it to the Wait Message BB's BOut.

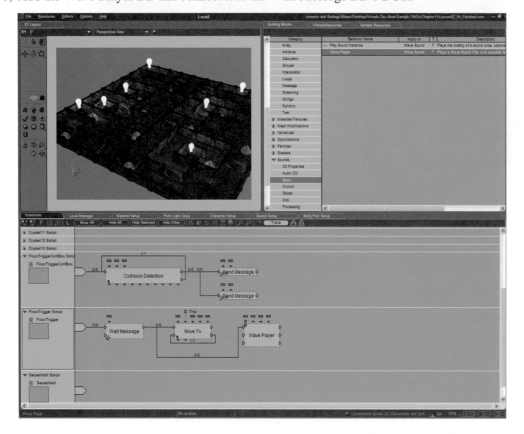

9) Add the file Trigger.wav from the Sample Resources \ Sounds to the scene.

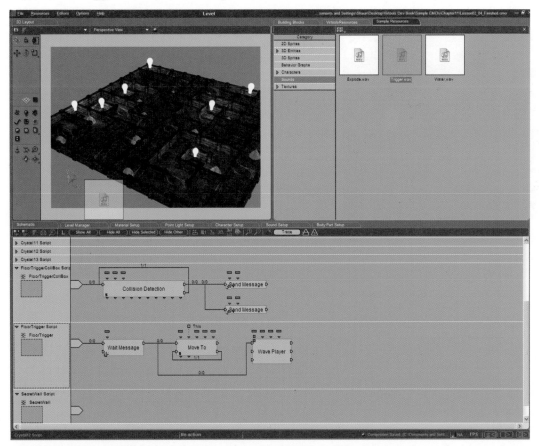

10) In the Wave Player BB's Edit Parameter dialog, set the Sound to Trigger.

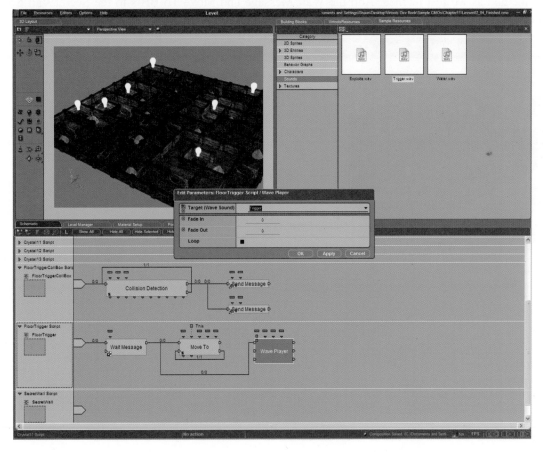

11) Add a Hide BB to the script and link it to the Move To BB's Out BOut; this will hide the object once it has sunk below the floor and save some valuable CPU power.

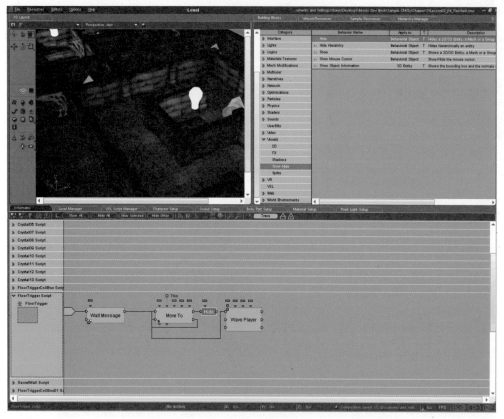

12) We have finished with the actions for the Floor Trigger; now all that's left is hiding the Secret Wall. Using the same method as we just learned, Add the Wait Message and Move To BB's to the SecretWall Script. Connect them in the same way as the last script and set the Wait Message BB's Message to Open Sesame.

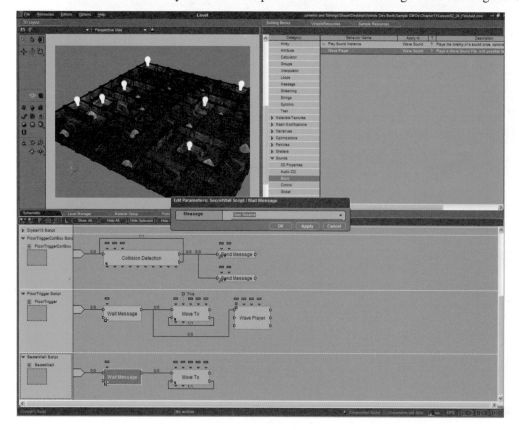

13) Add the This parameter and connect it to the Move To BB's Referential PIn. Open the Edit Parameters dialog of the Move To BB and set the Destination Point parameter to X=0, Y=0 and Z=-5. Leave the Duration as 3 Seconds.

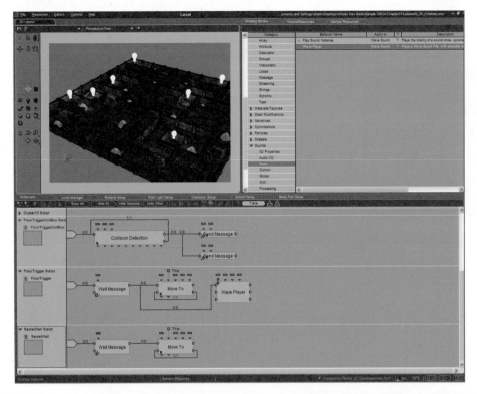

14) Lastly, to finish the task we will convert each scripts BB's into a Behavior Graph that we can use to create the actions for the rest of the Floor Triggers. We then will create scripts for the rest of the Floor Triggers, Trigger Collision Boxes and Secret Wall and copy and paste the BG's to the scripts. Since this is a rather time consuming process, you can open the file Lesson02_04_Finished.cmo and have a look at the finished result.

Note: There is no SecretWall06 to match the FloorTrigger06 object as this is the last trigger that will allow the character to successfully complete the level.

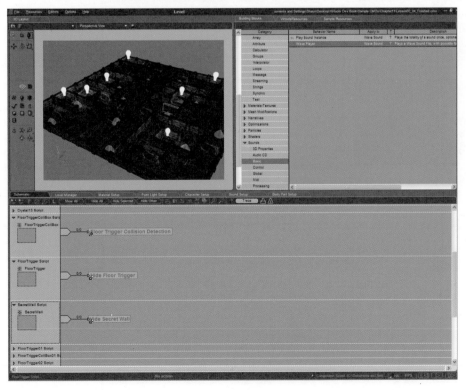

2.5 Creating the Start Point Magic Effect

1) Continue from the last lessons progress or open the file Lesson02_05_Start.CMO located in Sample CMO' s\Chapter11. Add the file Magic01.nmo from Sample Resources \ Characters to the Scene and position it at the Starting Point (World Position X=-933, Y=7, Z=-37).

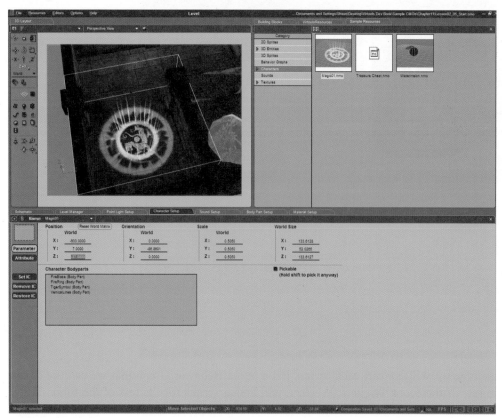

2) Create scripts for the 3 Body Parts FireBlaze, TigerSymbol and FireRing.

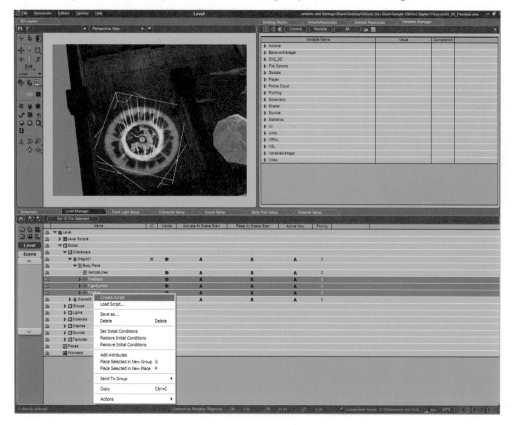

3) Add a Rotate BB to each of the Scripts, connect it to the Start Node and loop it internally.

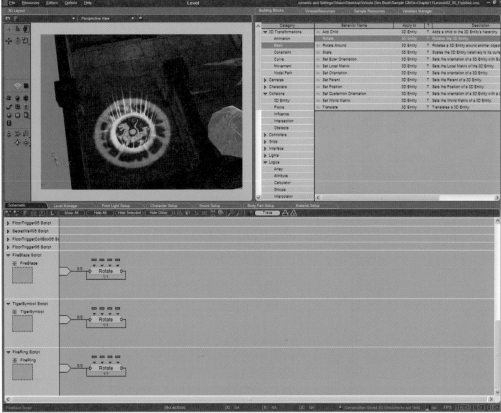

4) We need to make the elements of the magic ring rotate at different speeds to make the effect more convincing. In the Edit Parameters window of each of the Rotate BB's set the Angle Of Rotation to Degrees=-0.6 for the FireBlaze, 0.4 for the TigerSymbol and 0.8 for the FireRing.

5) Click play and the magic ring will spin with each component moving at a different speed.

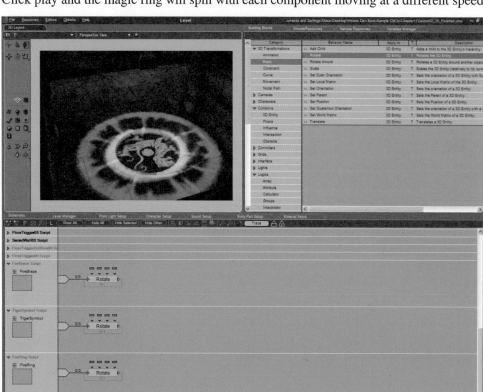

2.6 Creating the Floor Reflection

1) Continue from the last lessons progress or open the file Lesson02_06_Start.CMO located in Sample CMO's\Chapter11. Firstly, Create a Script for the Floor Body Part of the Scene06 Character.

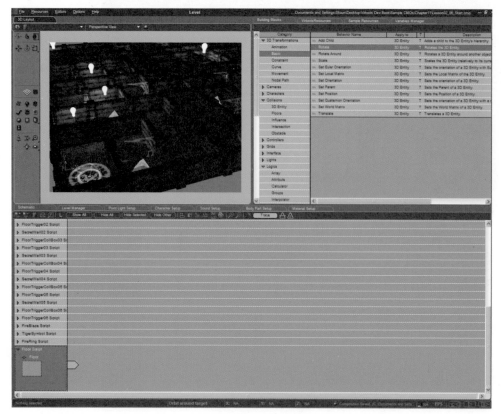

2) Add the Planar Reflection BB to the Script and connect it with the Start Node.

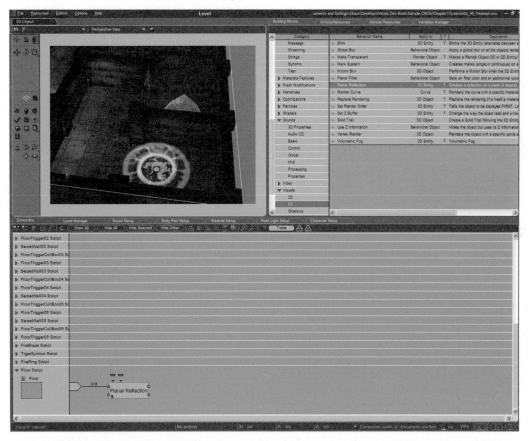

3) In Level Manager open the Groups list and open the Crystals Group. Right click the Objects icon and click the Select Children option. Then right click on the selected objects and click Add Attributes from the popup menu.

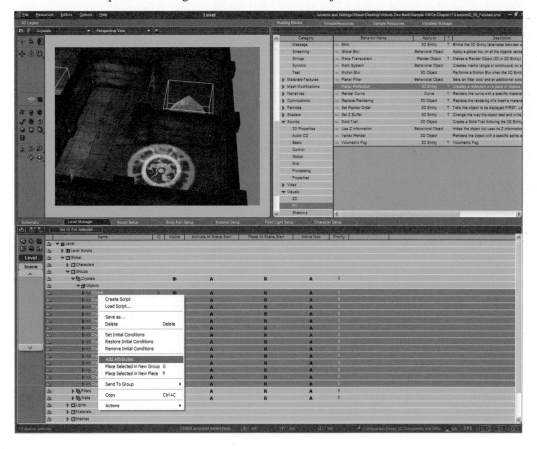

4) Add the Reflected Object attribute from Visuals FX. Repeat the same process for the Walls and Pillars groups.

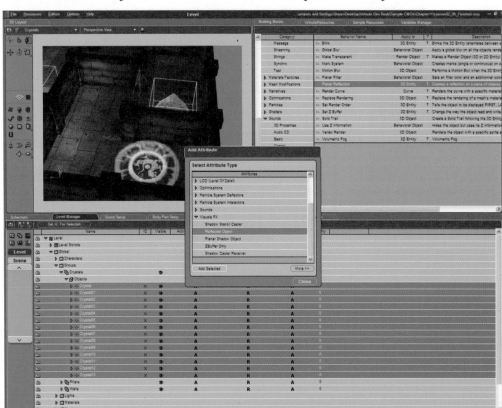

5) Lastly, in the Materials rollout, double click the FloorMat to open its setup panel. Set the Material Type to Custom. In the new option panel that appears on the right, set the Alpha Test checkbox to True and the Blend checkbox to True. Set the Source Blend to SrcAlpha and the Dest Blend to SrcColor.

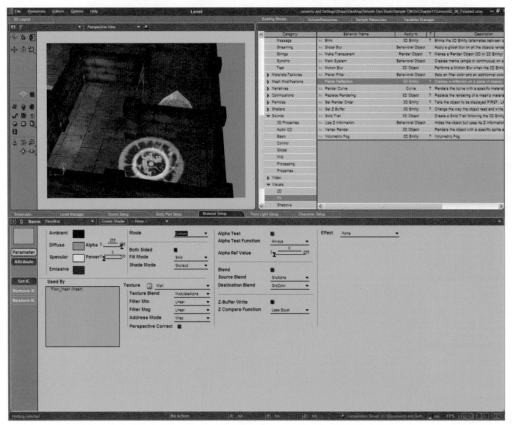

6) Click play to test the Planar Reflection. You should see the Walls, Pillars and Crystals mirror reflected on the Floor.

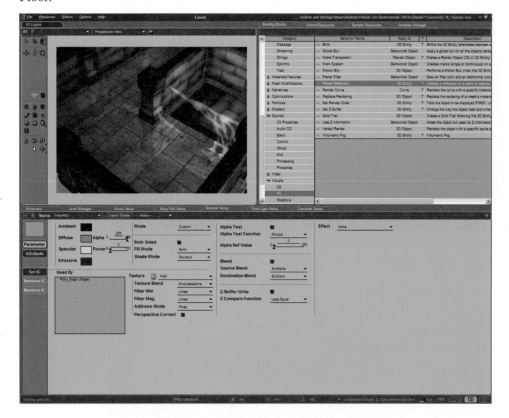

2.7 Creating the Crystal Reflection

1) Continue from the last lessons progress or open the file Lesson02_07_Start.CMO located in Sample CMO's\Chapter11. Firstly, drag the texture Water01.bmp from Sample Resources \ Textures into the Scene.

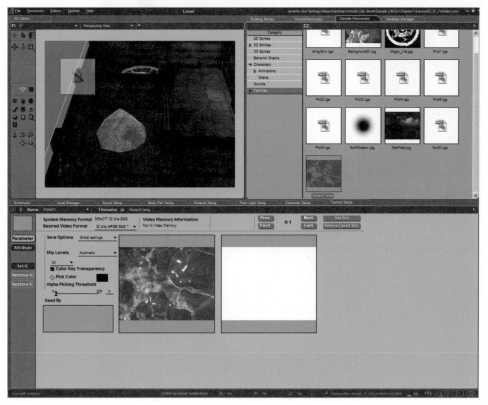

2) Open the Material Setup panel and select the CrystalMat material. Set the Texture to the newly added Water01 texture.

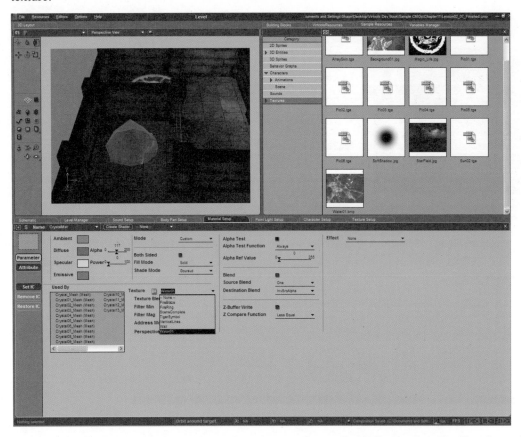

3) Now, on the furthest right hand column there is an option called Effect, select TexGen from the dropdown box. A button called TexGen Type will appear below, click it and select Reflect from the dropdown box.

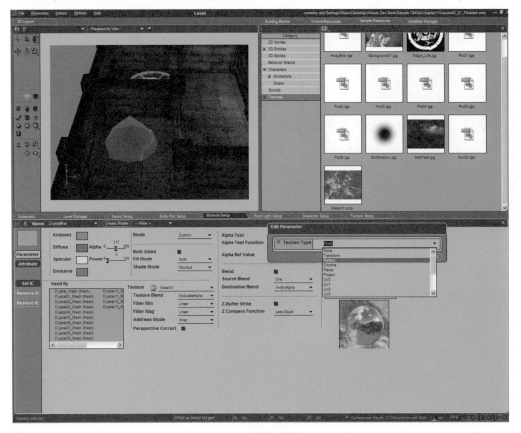

4) When you select Reflect, you will notice the color of the Crystal will change. Try moving the camera around the scene to get a feel for the effect; the crystals surface will have a kind of reflective effect that resembles the Water01 texture.

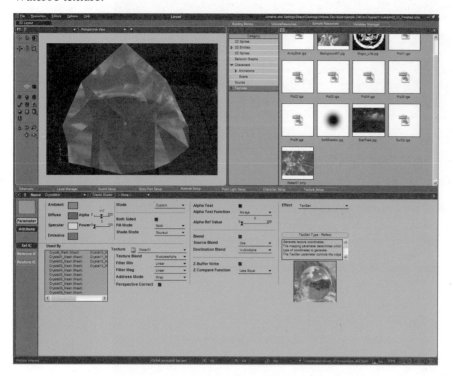

3.0 Creating the Player Character

3.1 Basic Action Configuration

1) Open the file Lesson03_01_Start.CMO located in Sample CMO's\Chapter11. Add our main character WuKong from Sample Resources\Characters\Actors to the scene. Position and scale WuKong as shown in the screenshot and set his Initial Conditions. Create a script on the character.

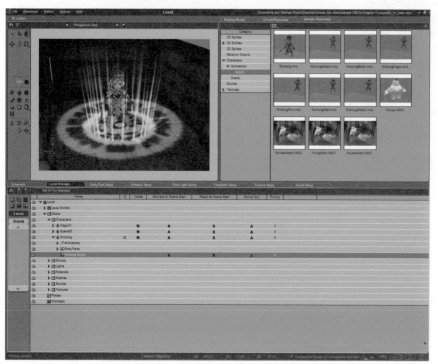

2) Add all of WuKong's animations by dragging them from the resources panel and into the Animations category of the WuKong character in Level Manager.

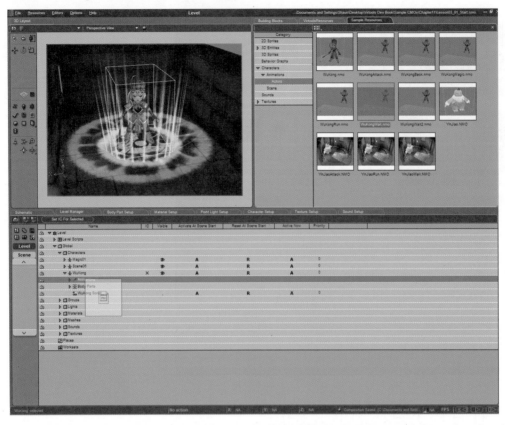

3) Now, add the Unlimited Controller BB from Building Blocks \ Characters \ Movement to the script and connect it to the Start Node. We won't use the Character Controller BB in this case as the Unlimited Controller gives us access to more advanced settings.

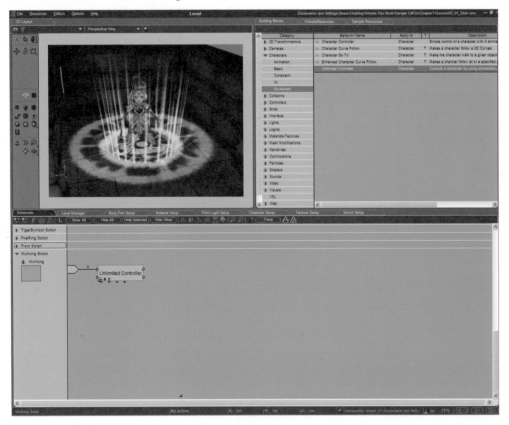

4) Double click the Unlimited Controller to open its Edit Parameters dialog. Add a new animation and set its Order to 3. Set the Joy_Up and Joy_Down animations to Run and Back respectively. Set the Message for the 3rd item to Attack and the Animation to Attack. Set the 4th items animation to Wait and set the Rotation Angle at the bottom to 7.0.

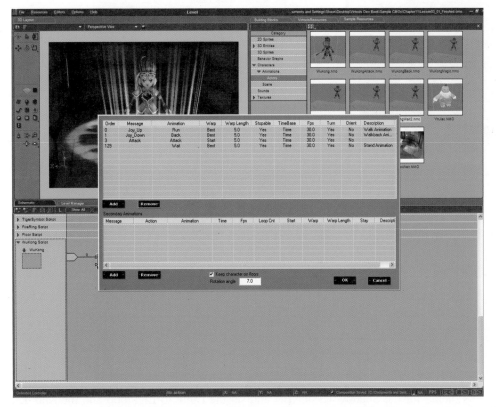

5) Using the unlimited controller we can adjust the frame rate and blending of each animation. Set the FPS values for the Attack and Wait animations to 15Fps and set the Stoppable parameter of the Attack action to No (this will avoid the incomplete playback of the attack animation).

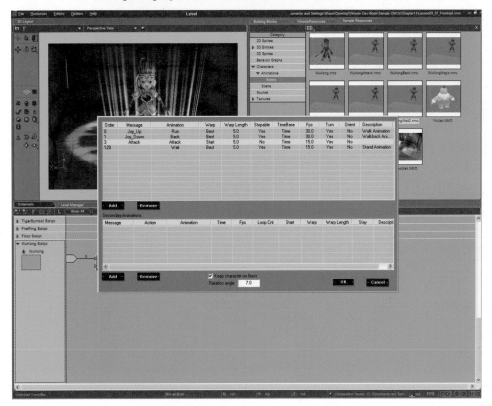

6) Add the Keyboard Controller and Shadow Caster BB's to the script. Connect both to the Start Node.

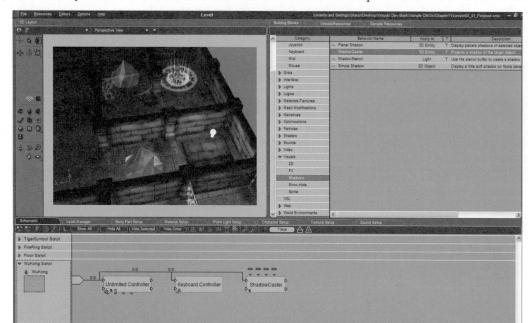

7) Open the Edit Parameters dialog for the Shadow Caster BB and set the Light to Light006 and the Max Light Distance to 200.

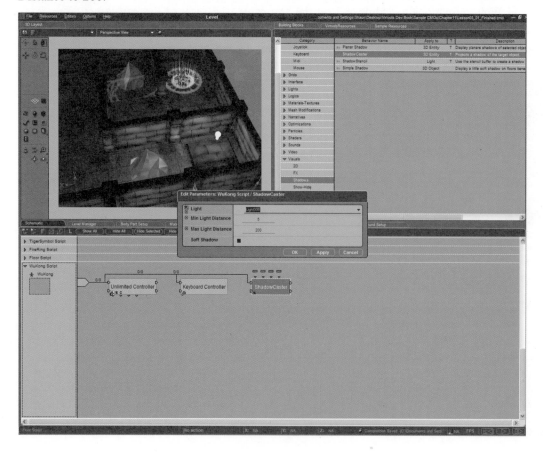

8) Click Play and walk WuKong towards the closest light as shown in the screenshot. He should cast a shadow within the lights range of influence.

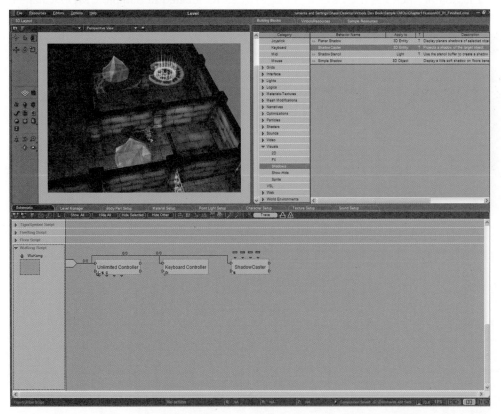

9) You will note that we only created one Shadow Caster for the light closest to WuKong. If you have a reasonably powerful video card, you can create Shadow Casters for the remaining lights in the scene. When you play the scene and walk into an area that is influenced by more than one light, WuKong will cast multiple shadows.

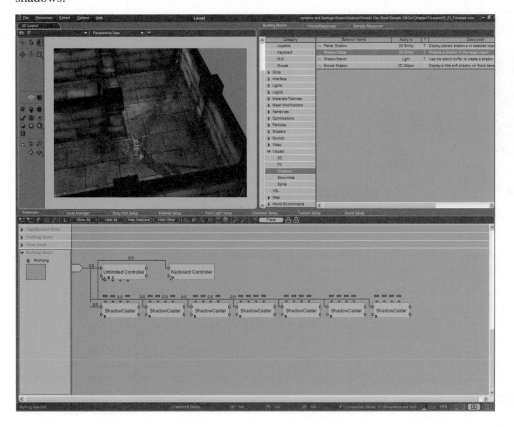

3.2 Setting Up the Characters Collisions

1) Continue from the last lesson or open the file Lesson03_02_Start.CMO located in Sample CMO's\Chapter11. Add a Prevent Collision and 3 Object Slider BB's to WuKong's Script. Connect each BB to the Start Node.

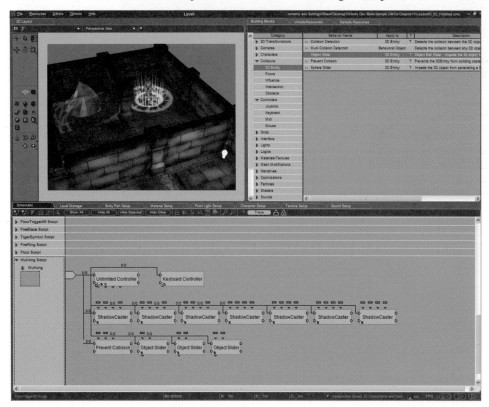

2) Open the first Object Slider BB's Edit Parameters dialog and set the Radius to 25 and the Group to Crystals. Set the remaining Object Slider BB's parameters to 30 for the Pillars group and 25 for the Walls group. Click Play and test if WuKong can walk through the Walls, Pillars or Crystals.

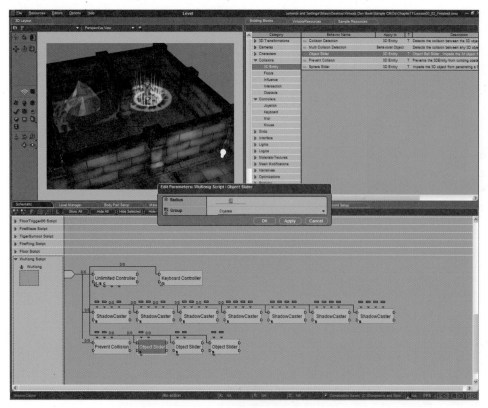

3.3 Creating the Characters Attack Actions

1) Continue from the last lesson or open the file Lesson03_03_Start.CMO located in Sample CMO's\Chapter11. Add a Key Event and 2 Send Message BB's to the Script. Connect the Key Event BB to the Start Node and connect the 2 Send Message BB's to the Key Event BB's Pressed BOut.

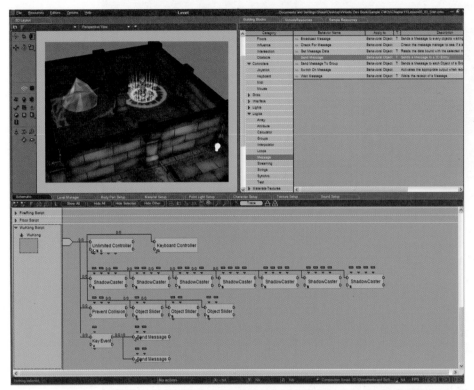

2) We use the Key Event BB rather than the Key Waiter BB as the Key Event BB is runs only once when the key is pressed opposed to the Key Waiter which continuously activates the Pressed BOut for every frame it detects the key is down; thus causing multiple messages to be sent. Open the Key Event BB's Edit Parameters dialog and set the Key to Q.

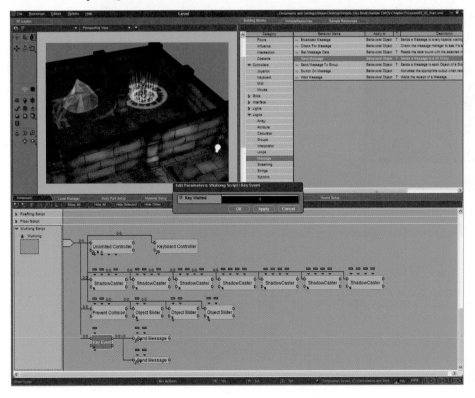

3) Set the first Send Message BB's parameters to Message = Attack and Destination = WuKong.
   Set the second Send Message BB's parameters to Message = Attack and Destination = WuKongWeapon. This will be used later to add some special effects to the weapon when the attack animation is playing.

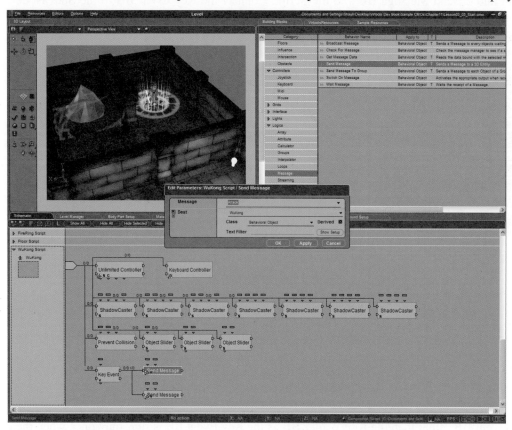

4) Click Play to test the Attack actions we just created. Press Q and WuKong's attack animation will play.

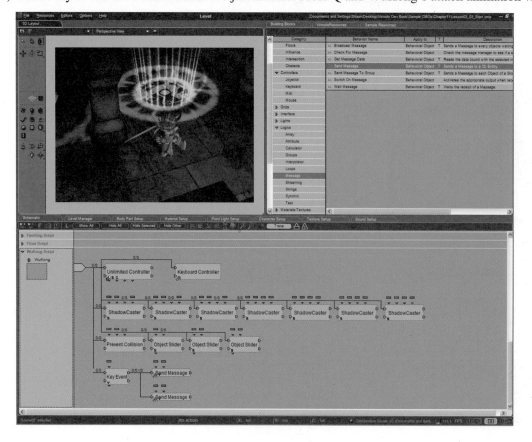

3.4 Attack Special Effects

1) Continue from the last lesson or open the file Lesson03_04_Start.CMO located in Sample CMO's\Chapter11. Create a Script for the Body Part WuKongWeapon.

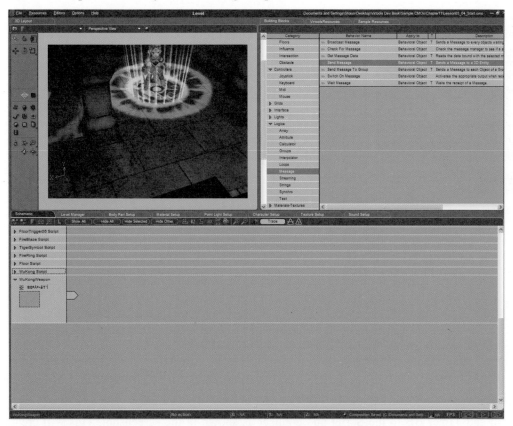

2) Add a Wait Message BB and set its Message parameter to Attack.

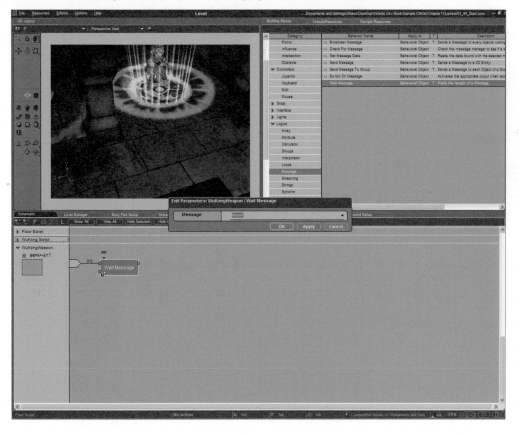

3) Add the Sound Fight.wav from Sample Resources\ Sounds to the Scene. Now add the Play Sound Instance BB to the Script and connect it to the Wait Message BB. Loop its BOut to the Wait Message BB's BIn, this will make the Wait Message BB "rewait" after the attack has finished. Lastly set the Target parameter of the Play Sound Instance BB to Fight.

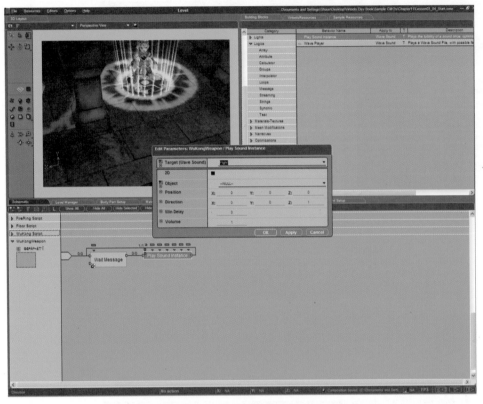

4) Add the Solid Trail and Timer BB to the Script and connect as shown in the screenshot. This will create a glowing trail that follows the weapon only while the Attack animation is playing (i.e. for a limited time as set the by the Timer BB).

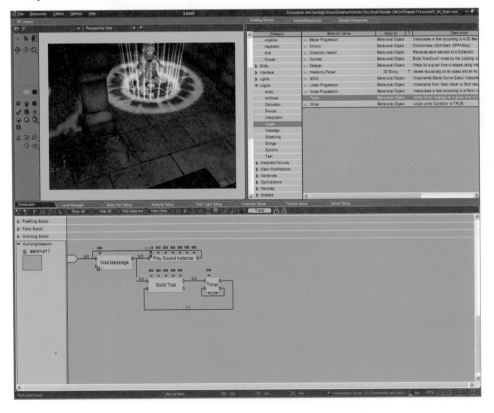

5) Set the Solid Trail BB's parameters to your own preference and set the Timer BB's Time parameter to 1 Second.

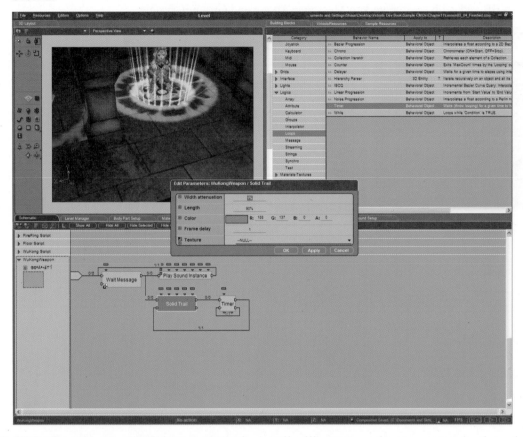

6) Click play and press the Q button to attack. A trail will appear as the weapon moves through its animation and will disappear after 1 second.

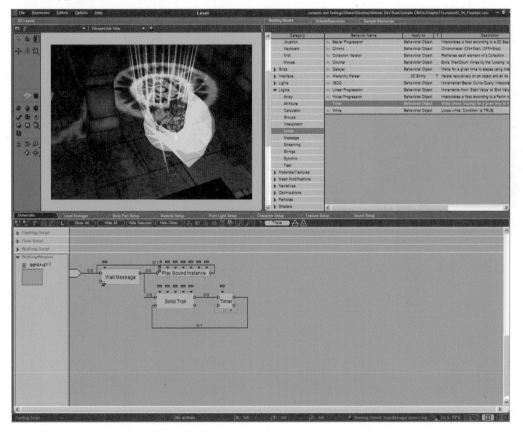

7) To finish off, we need to send a message to the Crystals when we attack to initiate a check and perform the explode action if we detect a collision between WuKongs Weapon and the Crystal. To do this, add the Send Message to Group BB and set its parameters to Message=Attack and Group=Crystals.

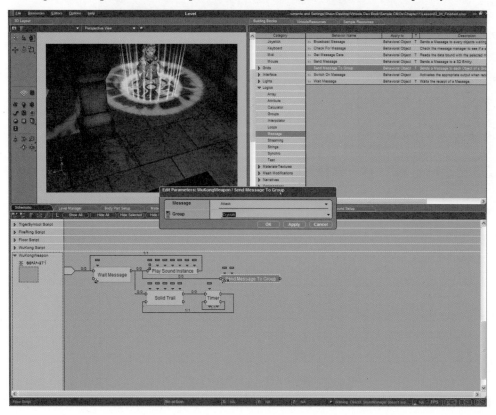

8) Click play and move WuKong over to one of the Crystal and press Q. WuKong will attack and the crystal will explode. You may need to attack the Crystal a few times in order to trigger the collision as we haven't refined the detection settings in this Demo.

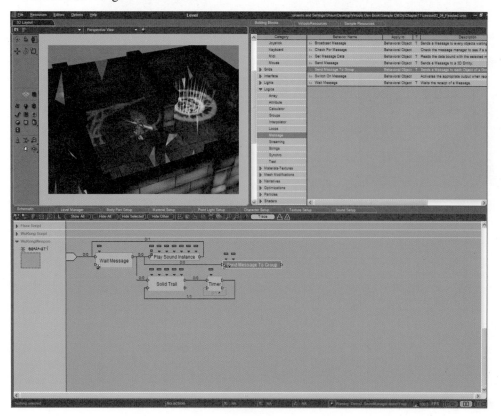

4.0 Database Configuration

4.1 Setting up the Database Array

1) Open the file Lesson04_01_Start.CMO located in Sample CMO's\Chapter11. In Level Manager, create a new Array and call it CharacterInfo.

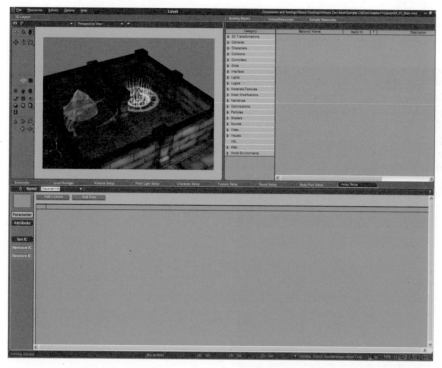

2) Create 4 columns in the Array as follows;
   1 – CharName (Type = String)
   2 – HitPoints (Type = Integer)
   3 – AttackPwr (Type = Integer)
   4 – DefensePwr (Type = Integer)

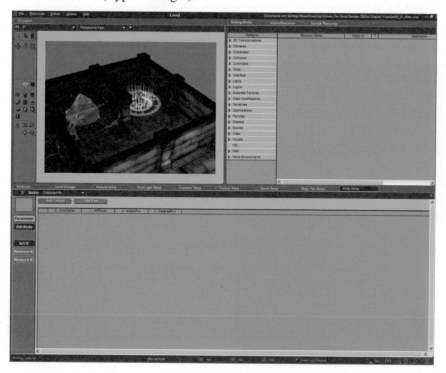

3) Now add 8 new rows and fill them with the following data;

CharName	HitPoints	AttackPwr	DefensePwr
SunWuKong	500	45	6
BossYinJiao	2500	25	8
SmallYinJiao	420	12	5
SmallYinJiao	400	15	4
SmallYinJiao	420	14	3
SmallYinJiao	600	13	5
SmallYinJiao	500	18	6
SmallYinJiao	520	20	4

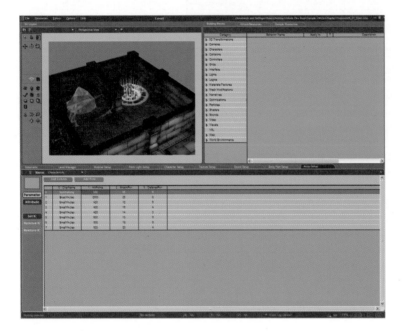

5.0 Stage Prop Creation

5.1 Creating the Point Crystals

1) Continue from the previous lesson or open the file Lesson05_01_Start.CMO located in Sample CMO's\Chapter11. Add the Crystal02 object from Sample Resources \ 3D Entities to the Scene and create its Script.

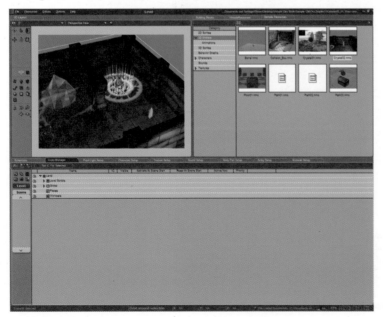

2) Add a Rotate BB, connect it to the Start Node and loop it internally.

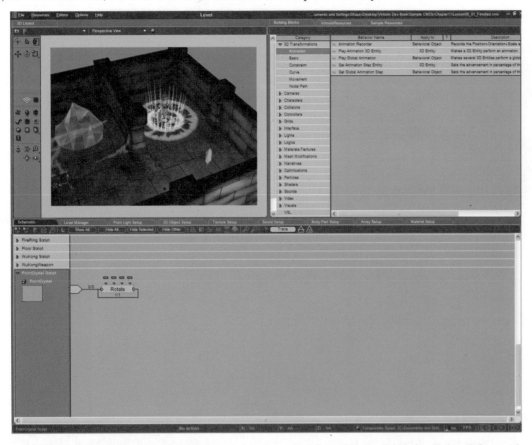

3) Add a Collision Detection BB and connect it to the Start Node. Link its False BOut to its BIn to make it continually check for collision.

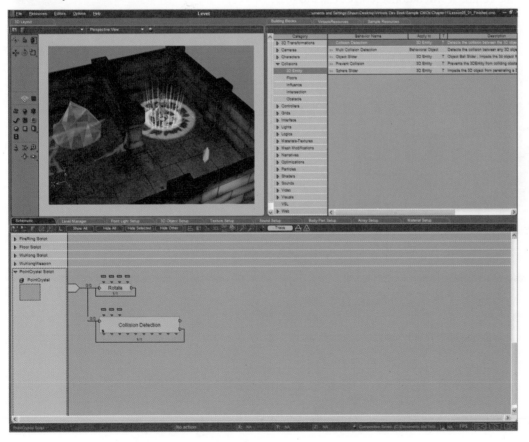

4) Add the Get Cell BB to the Script and connect it with the True BOut of the Collision Detection BB.

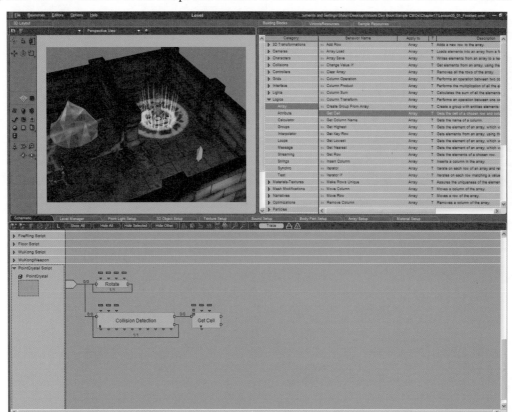

5) Now, create a new Array and call it PointCrystals. This array will keep a count of the number of Point Crystals WuKong collects during the game. Add a single column called CrystalCount of the Integer type. Add a row and leave it blank (the cell data will automatically be set to 0).

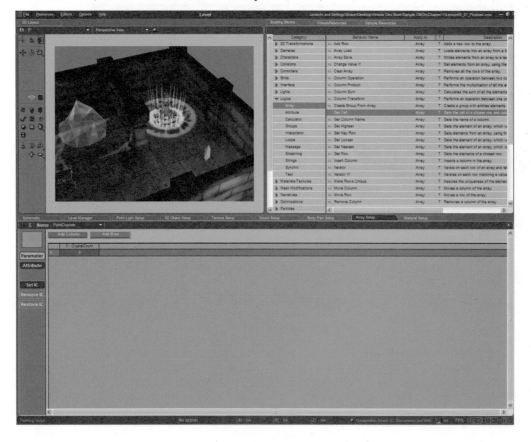

6) Go back to the Script of our PointCrystal and set the Get Cell Array parameter to PointCrystals.

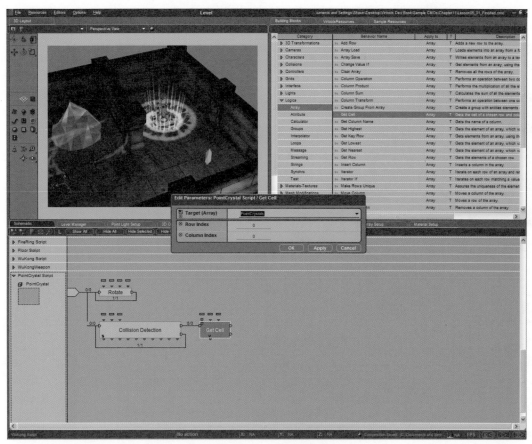

7) Click on the first PIn (it is called Target (Array). It will highlight and a help balloon will popup.

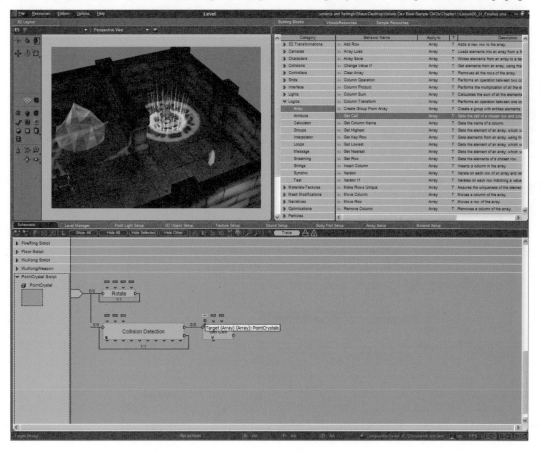

8) We can change the display type of any BB's Parameter In. This will let us see which parameters we are linking to without having to open up the Edit Parameters dialog of the BB. To do this, press the spacebar twice. The parameter display will change to show the name of the Array we are linking to.

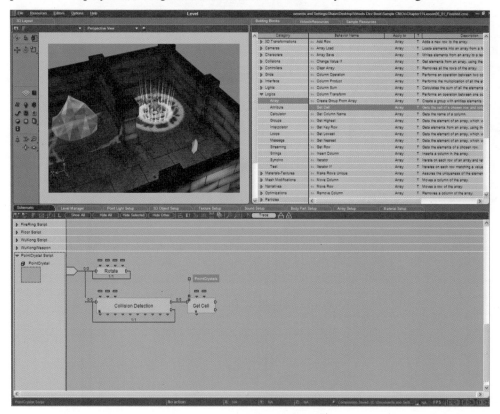

9) Now, add a ParamOp to the Script (you can press Alt+P instead of using the menu) and configure it to perform an Integer Addition. We will use this to add 1 to the current value of the CrystalPoints cell every time WuKong collects a crystal.

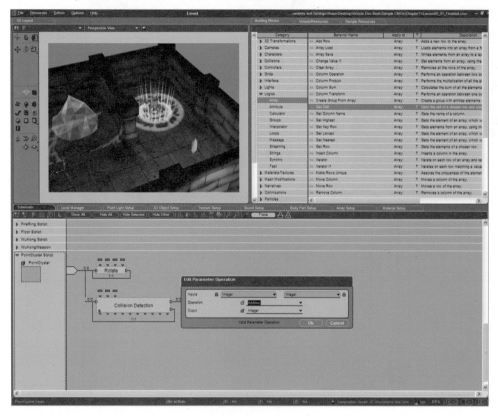

10) Connect the ParamOp's left PIn to the POut of the Get Cell BB and set the right PIn to 1. This will perform the addition using the Get Cell data and the fixed value of "1".

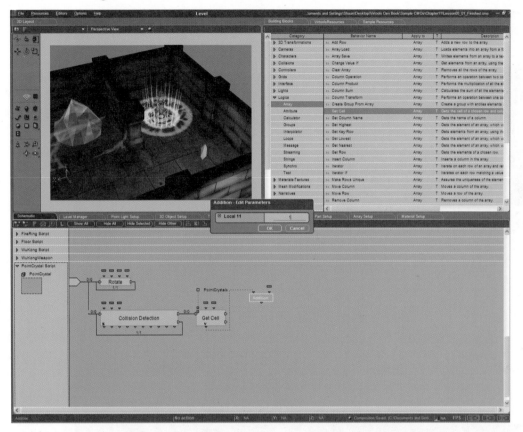

11) Add a Set Cell BB and connect its BIn with the Get Cell BB's Found BOut. Connect the Target (Array) PIn (the first pin) to the PointCrystals parameter and connect the Value PIn to the ParamOp's POut.

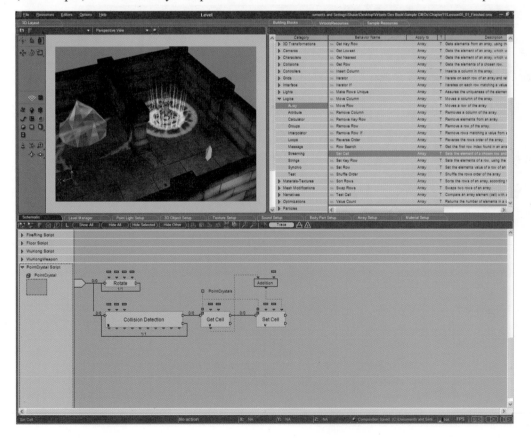

12) Add the Explode and Play Sound Instance BB's. Connect them both to the Set Cell BB's Found BOut and internally loop the Explode BB.

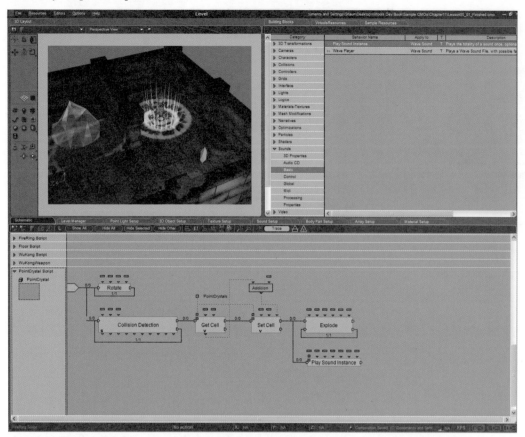

13) Add the CollectCrystal.wav file from Sample Resources \ Sounds to the scene.

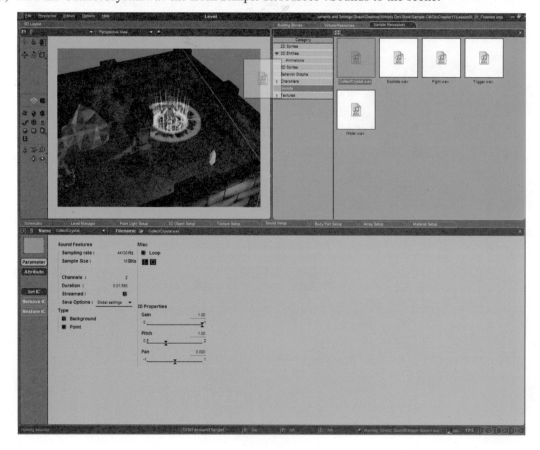

14) Set the Play Sound Instance BB's Target (Wave Sound) parameter to CollectCrystal and ensure the 2D checkbox is checked.

15) Click play to test the scene. When WuKong touches the Point Crystal it will explode, play a sound and increment the CrystalPoints cell value by 1. You will notice however that the Rotate BB is still looping even though the crystal is no longer visible; this is a waste of our systems resources.

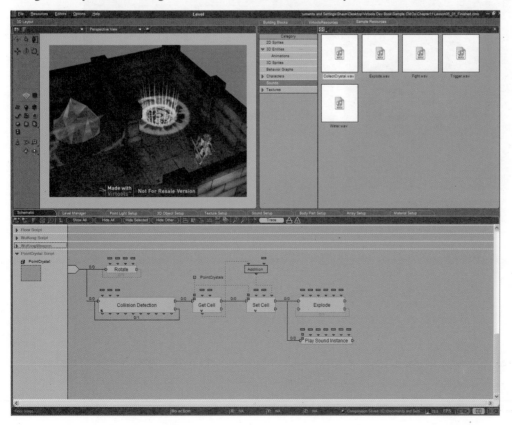

16) To fix this, we simply connect the Rotate BB in line with the Collision Detection BB's "False" loop as shown in the screenshot. This means that the Crystal will rotate only when it has not been collided with, thus the Rotate BB is "disabled" when the collision result is True.

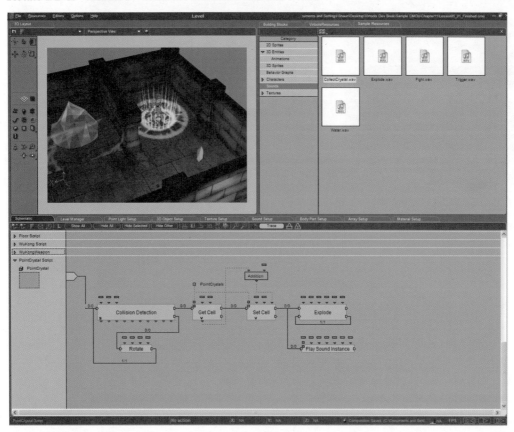

17) Click Play again to test the result. The Rotate BB is no longer active after the Crystal's explosion.

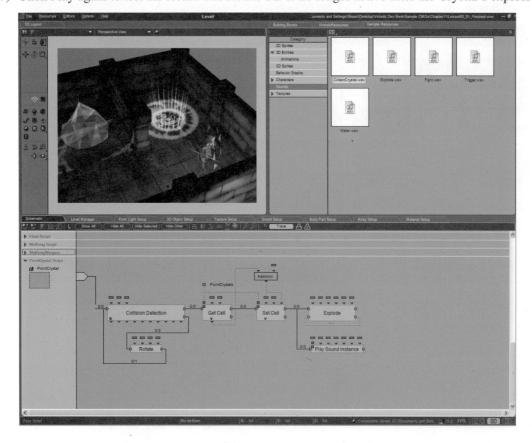

18) Open the 3D Object Setup panel for the PointCrystal and add the Reflected Object Attribute.

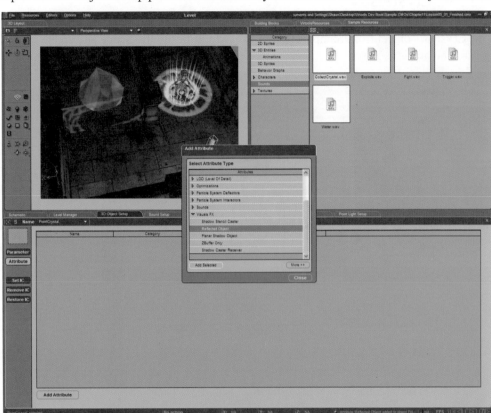

19) The next step is to duplicate the Point Crystals throughout the maze. You can use the Duplicate command that appears when you right click the Point Crystal and drag the new objects one or many at a time to different areas of the maze. Since this is a time consuming process, you can simply open Lesson05_01_Finished.cmo from Sample CMO's to see the result.

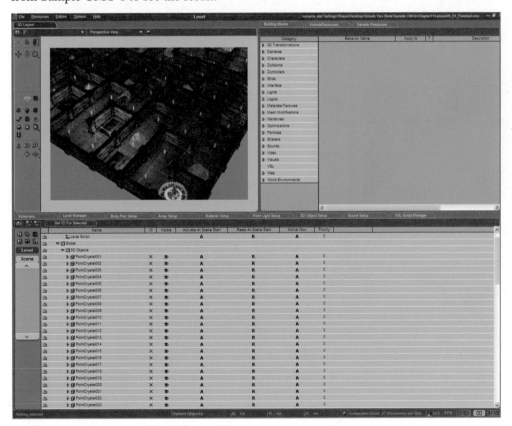

5.2 Creating the Life Crystals

1) Continue from the previous lesson or open the file Lesson05_02_Start.CMO located in Sample CMO's\Chapter11. Add the Crystal01 object from Sample Resources \ 3D Entities to the Scene and create its Script if you are continuing from the previous lesson.

2) Add the Rotate and Collision Detection BB's and link them in the same way as the previous lesson.

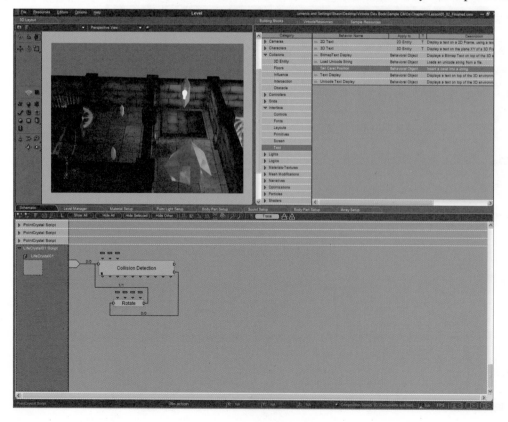

3) Add the Get Cell and Set Cell BB's and a ParamOp. Configure the BB's the same as in the previous lesson, except set the Target (Array) to CharacterInfo.

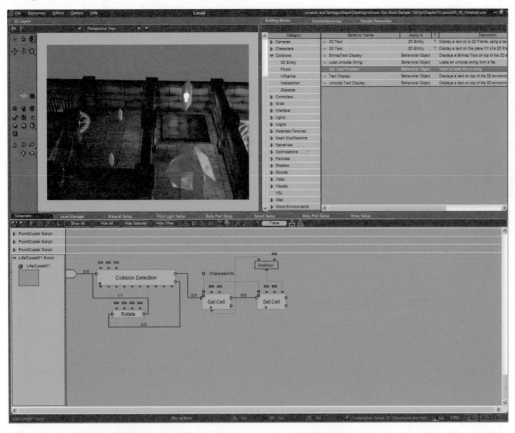

4) The idea is when WuKong collects a Life Crystal, 200 Hit Points will be added. So firstly we need to change the Addition ParamOp to add 200 to the current cell value.

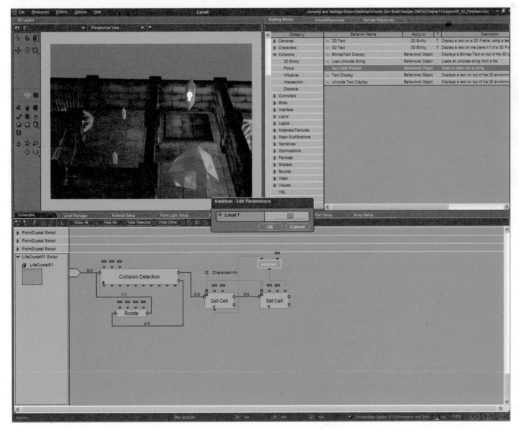

5) We now need to point the Get Cell and Set Cell BB's to the correct cell in the Array. If you switch to the Array Setup panel you can see which cell contains WuKong's Hit Points. It is Row 0, Column 1.

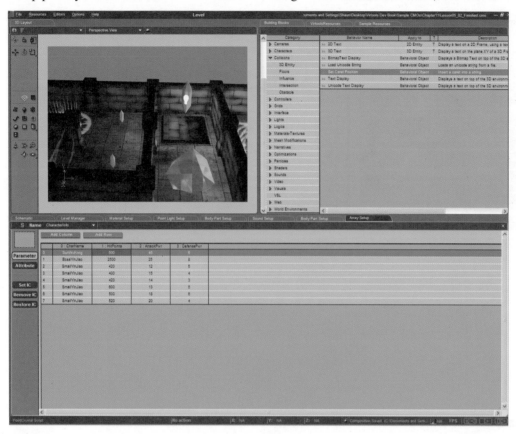

6) Open the Edit Parameters dialog of the Get Cell BB and set Row = 0, Column = 1. Do the same for the Set Cell BB.

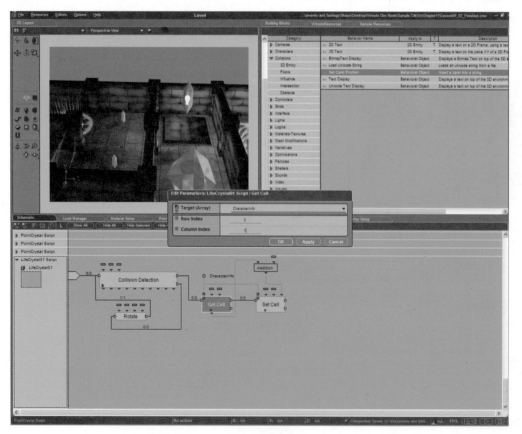

7) Add the sound LifeCrystal.wav from Sample Resources \ Sounds to the Scene.

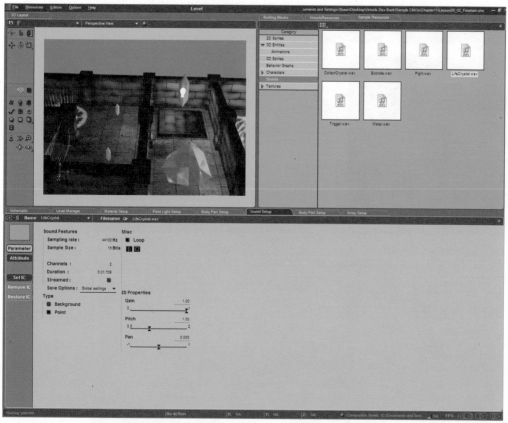

8) Add the Explode and Play Sound Instance BB's to the Scene and connect them to the Set Cell Found BOut. Configure the Play Sound Instance BB's parameters to Target (Wave Sound) = LifeCrystal and make sure the 2D checkbox is checked.

9) Click Play and walk WuKong over to the Life Crystal. When you get close enough, the crystal will explode, the sound will play and if you check the Array WuKong's Hit Points will have increased by 200.

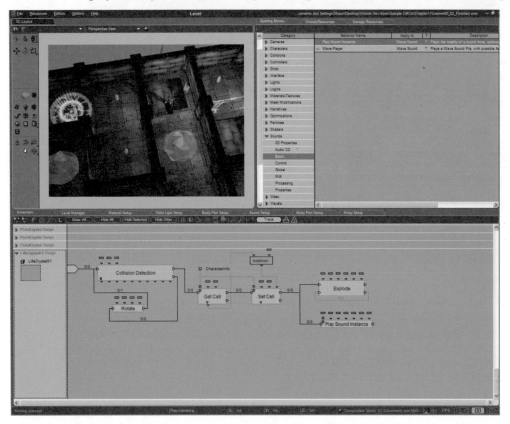

10) Lastly, using the same method as the last lesson, place a life Crystal over each of the Floor Triggers except for the trigger in the top left corner which is our special "End Game" trigger. To save time, you can open the file Lesson05_02_Finished.cmo from Sample CMOs\Chapter11 to see the final configuration.

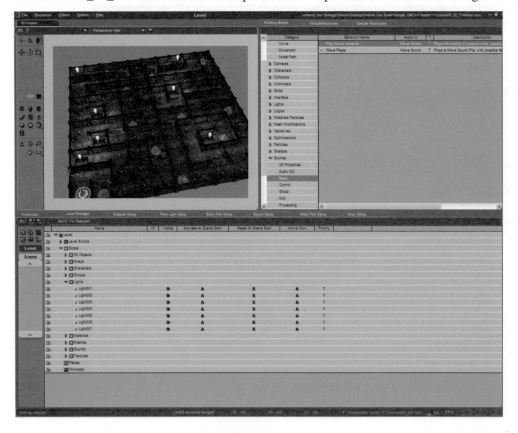

6.0 Creating the 2D User Interface

6.1 Setting up the Panel Backgrounds

1) Continue from the previous lesson or open the file Lesson06_01_Start.CMO located in Sample CMO's\Chapter11. Hold down Shift+Ctrl on your keyboard and drag the texture HPCrystals.png from Sample Resources \ Textures into the scene. This will create a 2D Frame, Texture and associated Material using the HPCrystals texture and name.

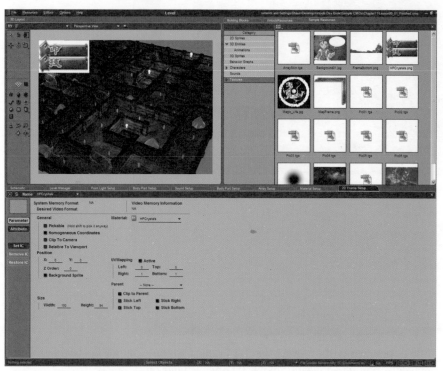

2) Go to the HPCrystals Material Setup Panel and set the Material Mode to Transparent. Set the Filter Min mode to Anisotropic to sharpen up the image a little.

3) Following the same procedure, add the FrameBottom.png and MapFrame.png textures to the Scene. Set their position according to the screenshot below and adjust their material properties.
   Note: The game will be played at a resolution of 640x480, so we have adjusted our 3D Layout window to match the final game resolution. You can change the 3D Layout window size by selecting Options \ General Preferences from the Top Menu.

4) To make editing our level a little easier, we will "freeze" the 2D Frames so they cannot be selected using the mouse. This will avoid accidental selection when we edit other 3D objects later on.
   In each frames 2D Frame Setup panel, uncheck the Pickable checkbox.

6.2 Creating the Text Display Frames

1) Continue from the previous lesson or open the file Lesson06_02_Start.CMO located in Sample CMO's\Chapter11. Create two new 2D Frames called HPText and PointCrystalsText. In the 2D Frame Setup panel, set their ZOrder to 1 to make them appear in front of the background frame. Set the HPText position to X=74, Y=16 and its size to Width=70, Height=30. Set the PointCrystalsText position to X=74, Y=55 and its size to Width=70, Height=30.

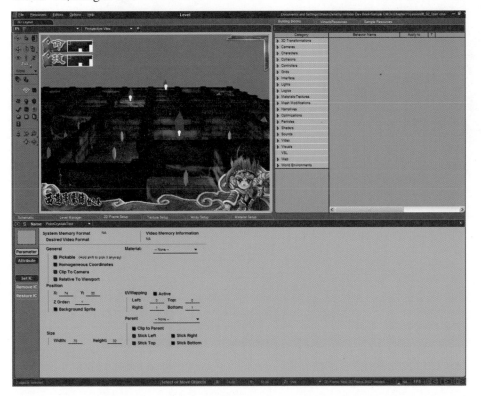

2) Create a new level script called Text Display. Add the Create System Font and Set Font Properties BB's to the script. Connect the Font POut of the Create System Font BB to the Font PIn of the Set Font Properties BB.

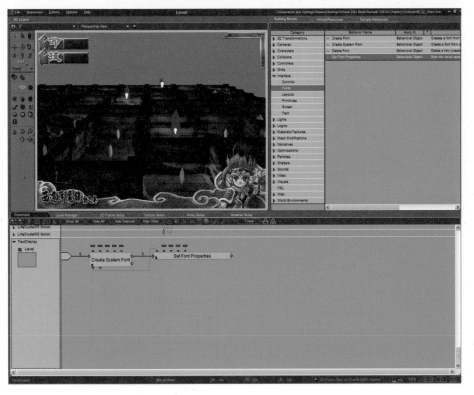

3) Set the Create System Font BB's Font Weight parameter to Bold. This will make the text thicker and easier to read on screen.

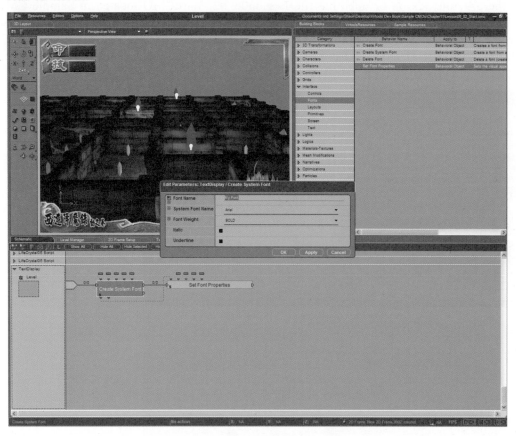

4) Add a Get Cell and 2D Text BB to the script. Connect them in a loop as shown in the screenshot. Set the Get Cell BB's parameters to Array=CharacterInfo, Row=0, Column=1.

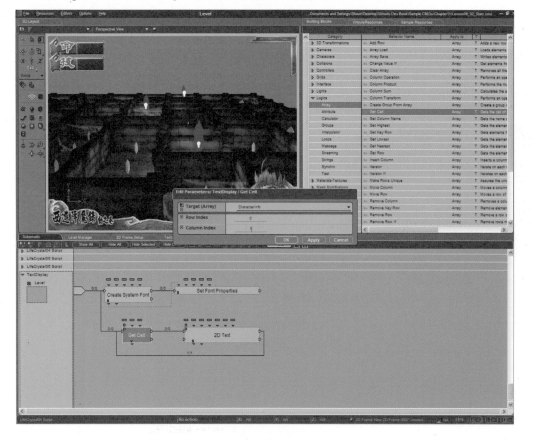

5) Link the Get Cell BB's Value POut to the 2D Text BB's Text Pin. Next, link the Create System Font BB's Font POut to the 2D Text BB's Font PIn. Open the 2D Text BB's Edit Parameters window and set the Target (2D Entity) to HPText.

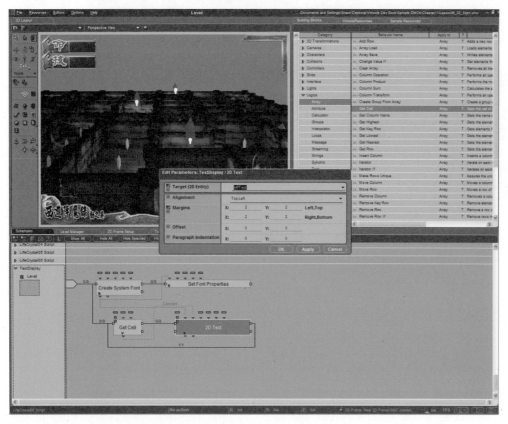

6) Copy the Get Cell and 2D Text BB's and configure them in the same way as we just did. Set the Get Cell BB's Target (Array) parameter to PointCrystals, Row to 0 and the Column to 0.

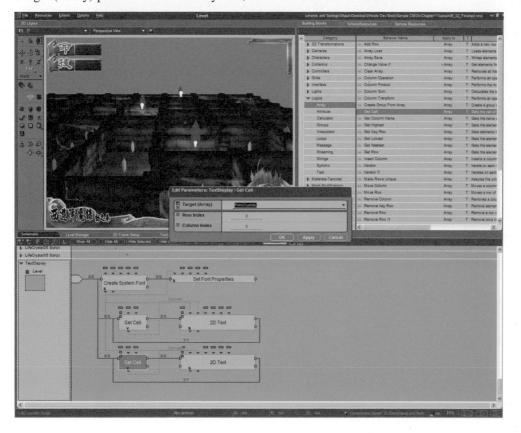

7) Set the 2D Text BB's Target (2D Entity) to the PointCrystalsText.

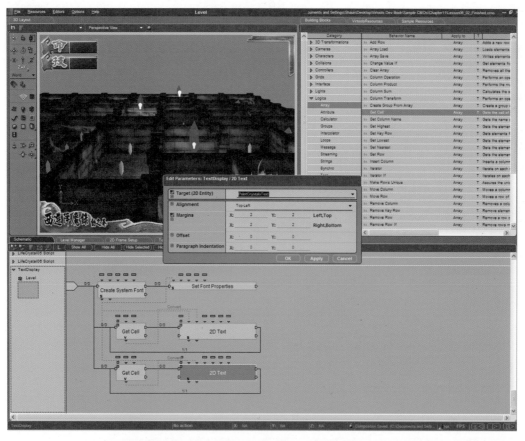

8) Click Play and try collecting a few Point Crystals and Life Crystals. The two values should automatically increase according to the data in the array.

7.0 Enemy AI

7.1 Basic Enemy Configuration

1) Continue from the previous lesson or open the file Lesson07_01_Start.CMO located in Sample CMO's\Chapter11. Add the YinJiao character from Sample Resources\ Animations\Actors to the scene. Resize and position YinJiao in front of the first trigger plate. Add YinJiao's Wait, Run and Attack animations and create his script. Set the Characters Initial Conditions.

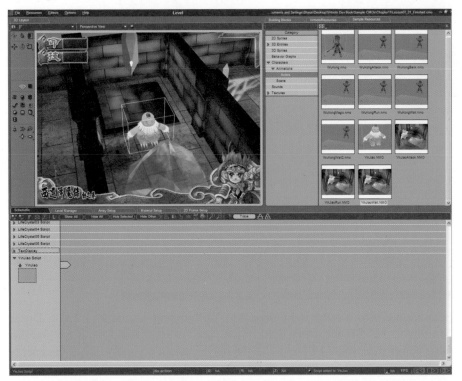

2) Add the Unlimited Controller BB to YinJiao's script and set the parameters as per the screenshot.

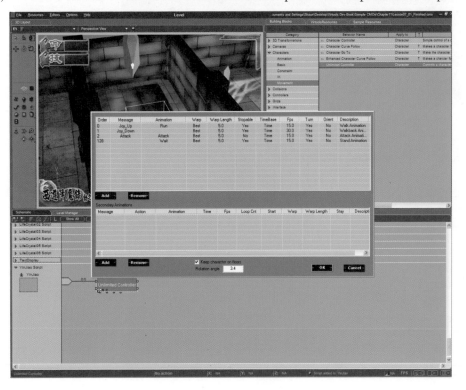

3) Add the Prevent Collision and 3 Object Slider BB's. Refer to the 3 Object Slider BB's in WuKong's script to get the correct configuration parameters.

4) Add the Shadow Caster BB, configure it to use the light closest to YinJiao and set the Max Light Distance to 200. We will not add a Shadow Caster BB for every light in the scene as this would require a significant amount of additional processing power that would be wasted as the player would normally defeat the enemy in its 'local' area.

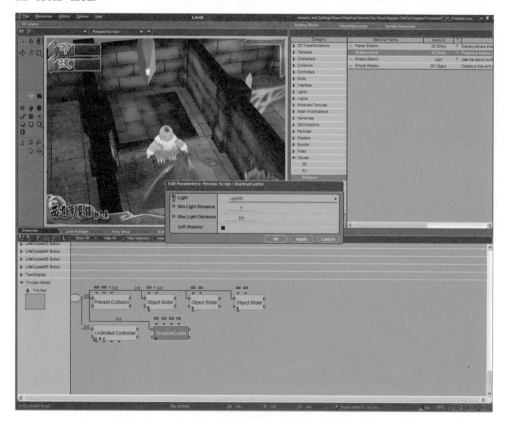

5) Add the Moving Obstacle and Reflected Object attributes the character.

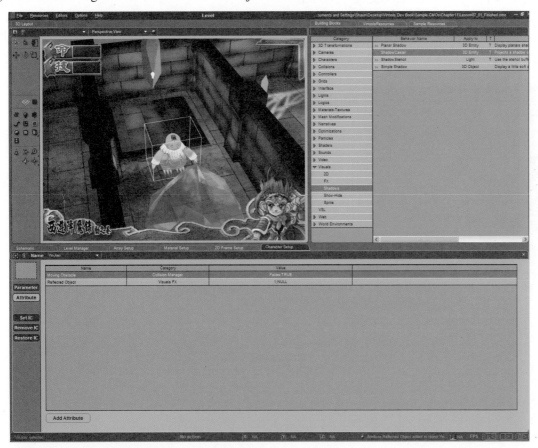

6) Click play to test the changes we just made.

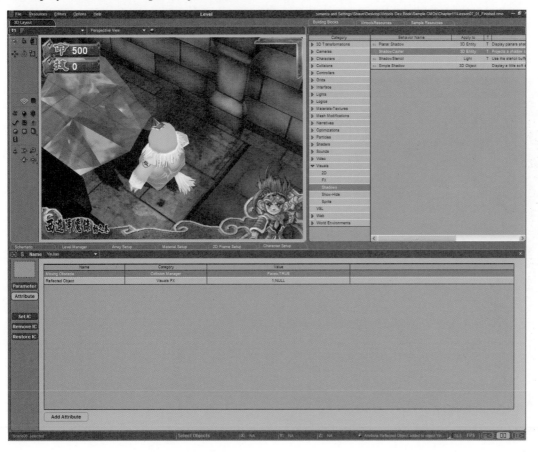

7.2 Enemy and Player Distance Testing

1) Continue from the previous lesson or open the file Lesson07_02_Start.CMO located in Sample CMO's\Chapter11. We need to test the distance between the enemy and the player before we trigger any of the enemies' actions. Add a new ParamOp and set the two input values to 3D Entity, the Operation to Get Distance and Output to Float.

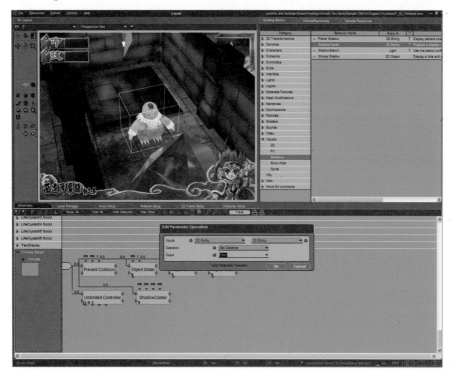

2) Use the Alt+T combination to add the This parameter to the script. Link it to the left hand Pin of the Get Distance ParamOp. Set the right hand Pin to our WuKong character then click the Local Parameter on the right of the Get Distance ParamOp and press the spacebar twice. This will change its display type to show the 3D Entities name, which in this case is WuKong. Whenever the POut of this ParamOp is called by a BB, it will trigger the calculation of the distance between the scripts object and the WuKong character.

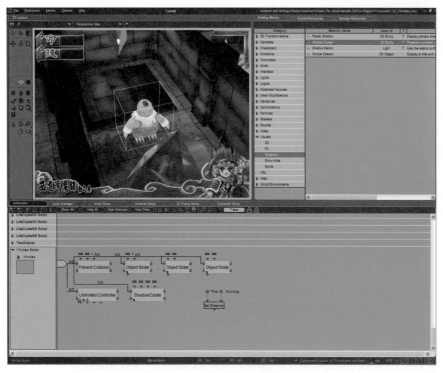

7.3 Enemy Attack Test

1) Continue from the previous lesson or open the file Lesson07_03_Start.CMO located in Sample CMO's\Chapter11. Double click the Get Distance ParamOps POut and change the name to DistanceToWuKong. Next Add the Test BB and connect it to the Start Node.

2) Right click the Get Distance ParamOps POut and select copy from the Popup menu

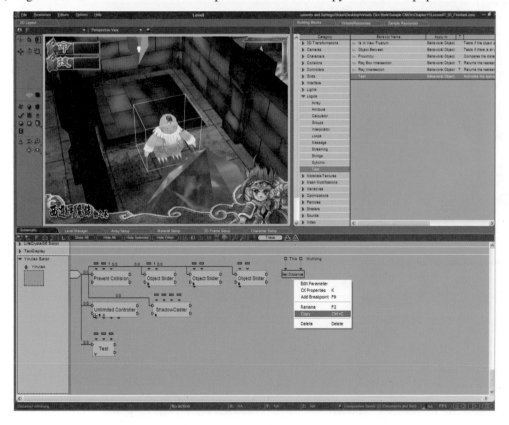

3) Right click a blank area in the script window and select Paste As Shortcut from the popup menu. Press the Spacebar to show the Parameters Name.

4) Link the DistanceToWuKong parameter to the Test BB's A Pin. Set the Test Parameter to Less Than and the B value to 100.

5) Connect the Test BB's False BOut to its BIn to make it loop internally. Add a Character Go To BB and link it to the Test BB's BOut.

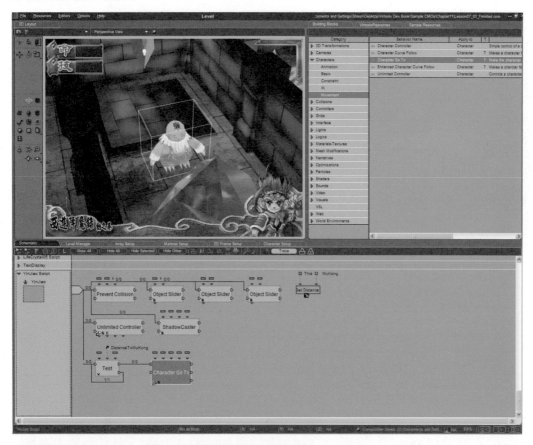

6) Set the Character Go To BB as shown in the Screenshot.

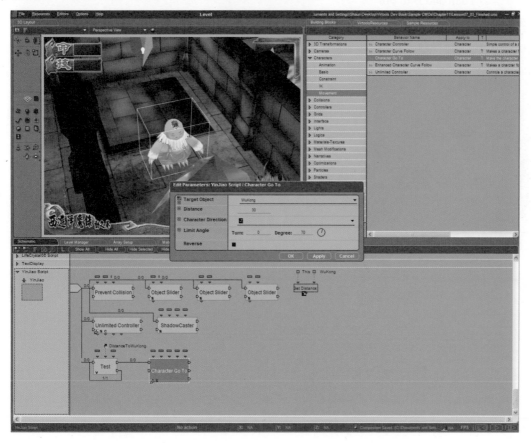

7) Loop the Character Go To BB internally and add another Test BB. Connect the new Test BB to the Character Go To BB's Arrived BOut.

8) Create another shortcut for the DistanceToWuKong parameter and connect it to the Test BB's A Pin. Set the Test parameter to Less Than and B to 30.

9) Loop the Test BB's False BOut back to the first Test BB's BIn. Add a Send Message BB to the script and connect it with the Test BB's True BOut.

10) Add a This parameter and connect it to the Destination PIn of the Send Message BB. Set the Message parameter to Attack.

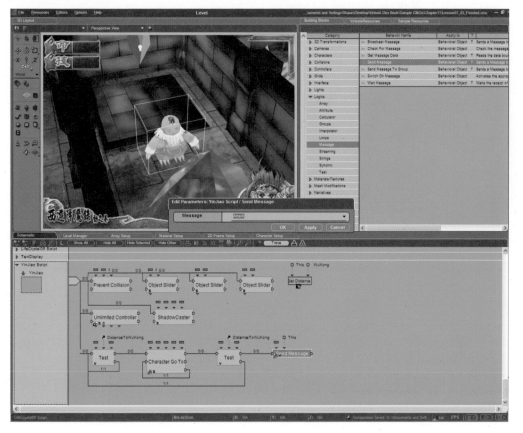

11) Add a Timer and Test BB and connect them sequentially after the Send Message BB. Connect the Timer BB's Loop In and Loop Out pins and set the Duration to 1 Second.

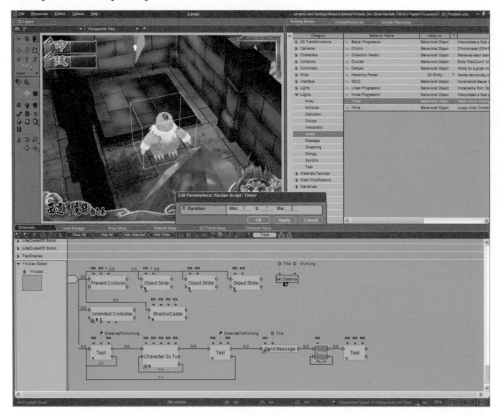

12) Configure the Test BB in exactly the same way as the previous one. Link its False BOut to the first Test BB's BIn. In this step we are making our script wait for 1 Second and then recheck to see if WuKong is still less than 30 units away from the enemy, if so, we can move onto the next action (WuKong has been hit). If not, go back to the first Test BB (WuKong dodged the attack).

7.4 Player Hit Actions

1) Continue from the previous lesson or open the file Lesson07_04_Start.CMO located in Sample CMO' s\Chapter11. Add the 3D Sprite FXB01.jpg to the scene. Set its Size and Position as shown in the Screenshot.

2) Add the other animation images to the texture using the Add Slot button. For each of the slots, right click in the Alpha Preview panel and select Get Alpha from Diffuse. Lastly, set the 3D Frame's Material Type to Transparent.

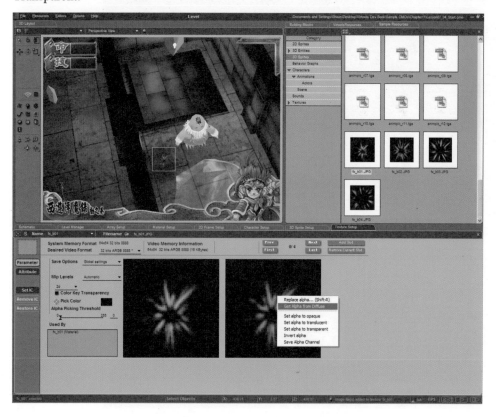

3) Create a Script on the 3D Frame and add the Wait Message, Show and Set Position BB's. Set the Message parameter to Attack for the Wait Message BB.

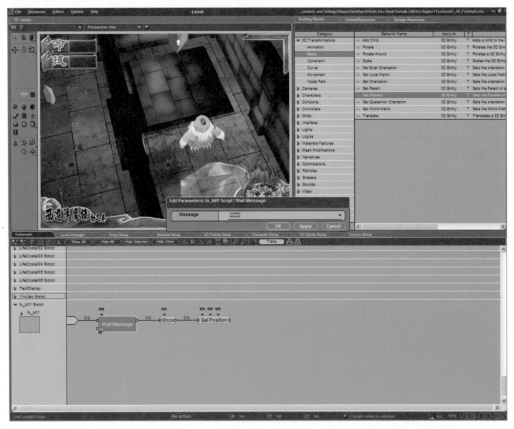

4) Set the Referential parameter of the Set Position BB to the WuKong character and set Position to X=0, Y=50, Z=0.

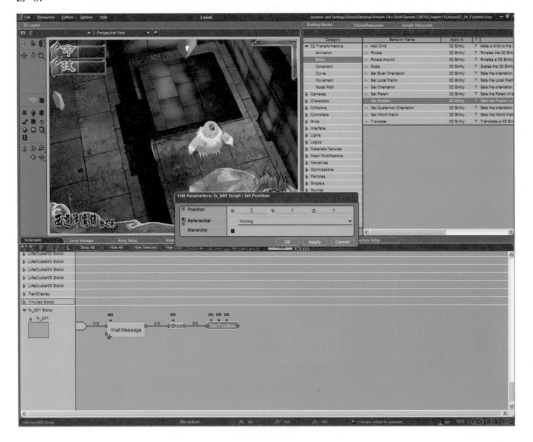

5) Add a Movie Player BB and set the parameters as shown in the Screenshot.

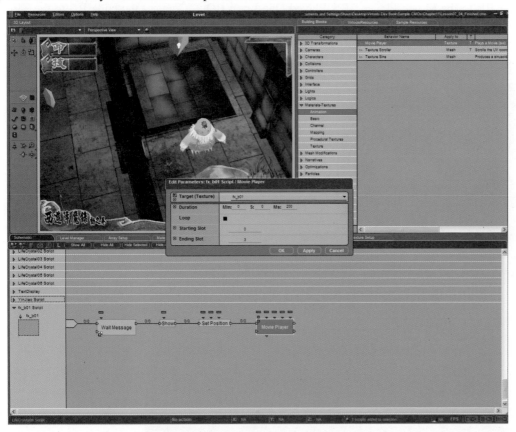

6) Add the Play Sound Instance BB to the script and connect it to the Set Position BOut. Add the sound Attack. wav from Sample Resources \ Sounds. Set the Play Sound Instance Target (Wave Sound) parameter to Attack and make sure the 2D box is checked.

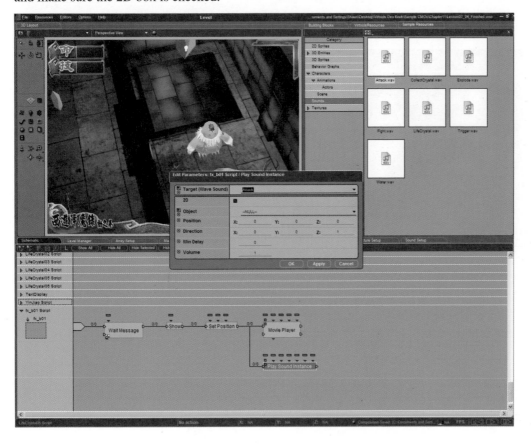

7) Lastly, loop the Movie Player BB so that it stops after one loop. Add a Timer and Hide BB to the Script and connect the Timer BB to the Movie Player BB's Played One Loop BOut. Connect the Hide BB to the Timers BOut. Loop the Timer internally and set the Duration to 500Ms. Connect the Hide BB's BOut back to the Wait Message BB's BIn to create a loop for the entire script.

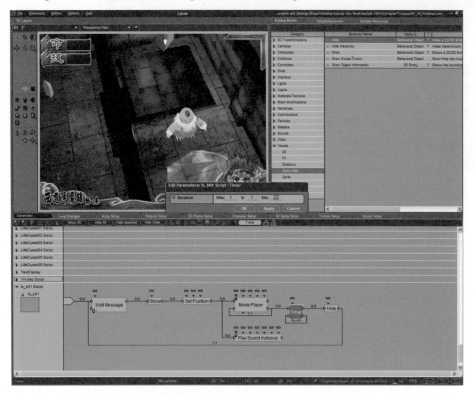

7.5 Creating the Player Hit Point Loss Event

1) Continue from the previous lesson or open the file Lesson07_05_Start.CMO located in Sample CMO's\Chapter11. Add a Send Message BB and connect it to the True BOut of the last Test BB. Set it to send the Attack message to the FX_B01 3D Sprite.

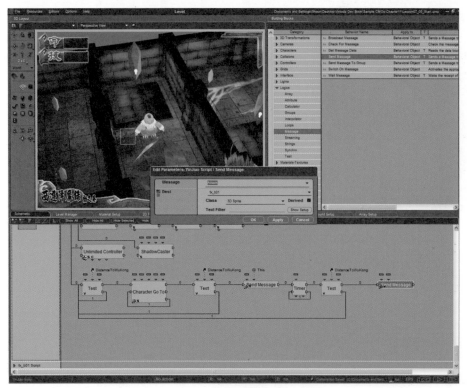

2) Add a Get Row BB and set the Target Array to our CharacterInfo table and the Row Index to 2 (which is the first non-boss enemy characters data). Change both the Get Cell BB's PIn's to show their values on screen by pressing the spacebar twice when the PIn is selected.

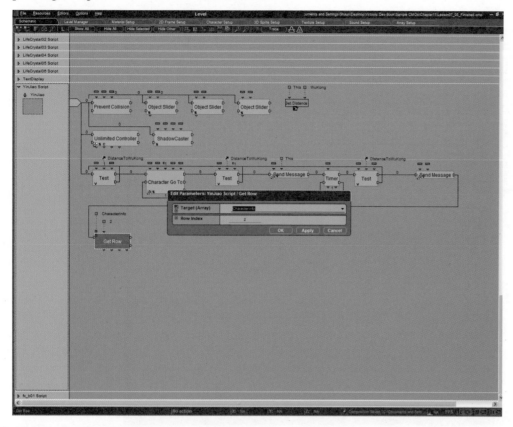

3) Add another Get Cell BB and use the existing CharacterInfo PIn as the Target Array and set the Row to 0 (which is the row containing WuKong's character stats)

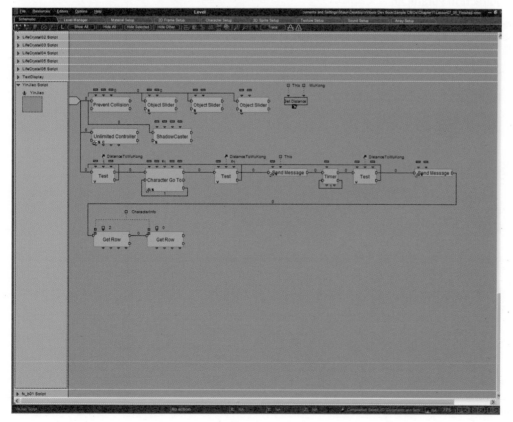

4) Create a new ParamOp that performs an Integer\Integer subtraction and connect the left PIn to the AttackPwr of the Enemy. Connect the right PIn to the Defense Power of the WuKong Get Row BB. This will calculate the amount of points to subtract from WuKongs Hit Points based on the enemies attack power versus WuKong's defense power.

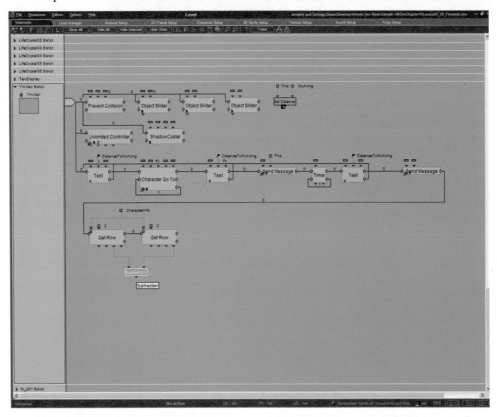

5) Add a second Subtraction ParamOp and connect the left PIn to WuKong's Hit Points and the right Pin to the result of the first Subtraction ParamOp.

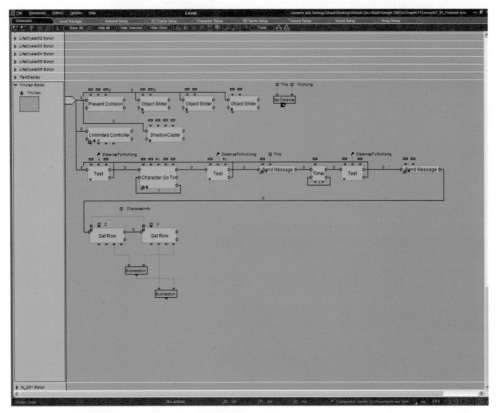

6) Add a Set Cell BB and connect it to the Found BOut of the last Get Row BB. Connect the Target (Array) PIn to the CharacterInfo local parameter and connect the result of the last Subtraction ParamOp to the Value PIn (furthest pin on the right). Open the Set Cell BB's Edit Parameters dialog and set the Row Index to 0 and the Column Index to 1 (this where we store WuKongs HitPoints).

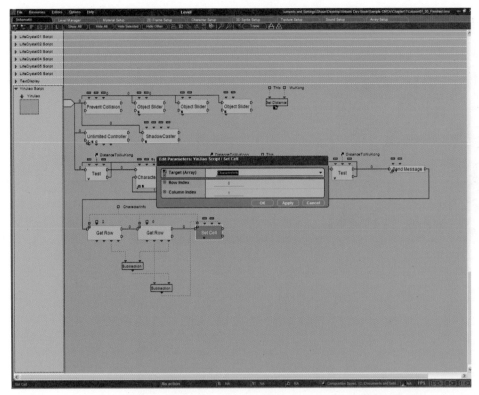

7) Finally, add a Test BB and connect the last Subtraction ParamOp's result to the Value A PIn. Set the Test parameter to Less or Equal and leave B at 0. This will test if WuKongs Hit Points are less than or equal to 0 and perform the relevant action. Connect the False BOut back to the very first Test BB's BIn to create a complete loop.

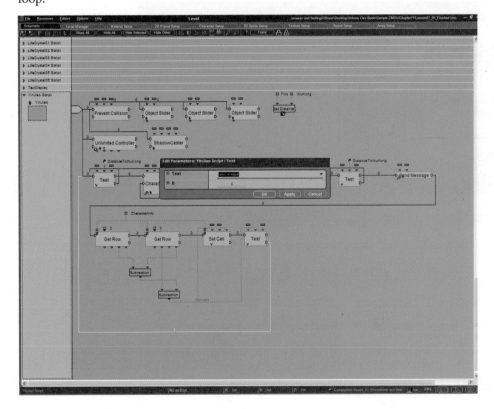

7.6 Creating the Enemy Hit Point Loss Event

1) Continue from the previous lesson or open the file Lesson07_06_Start.CMO located in Sample CMO's\Chapter11. Open the WuKongWeapon script and add a Send Message to Group BB. Connect it to the first Send Message to Group BB's BOut.

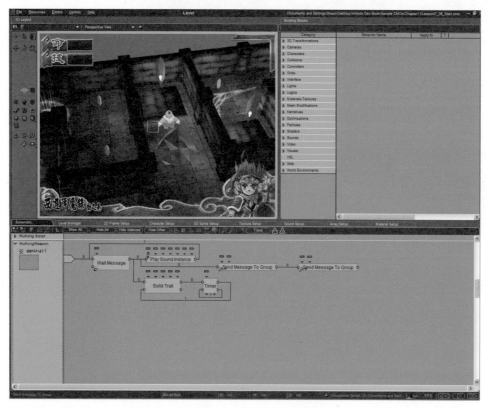

2) In Level Manager, select the YinJiao character, right click and select Place Selected in New Group. Call the group 'Enemies_YinJiao'. This group will be used as a container for all the YinJiao enemies in this level.

3) Now, in the WuKongWeapon script, set the new Send Message BB's parameters to Message=WuKongAttack and Group=Enemies_YinJiao.

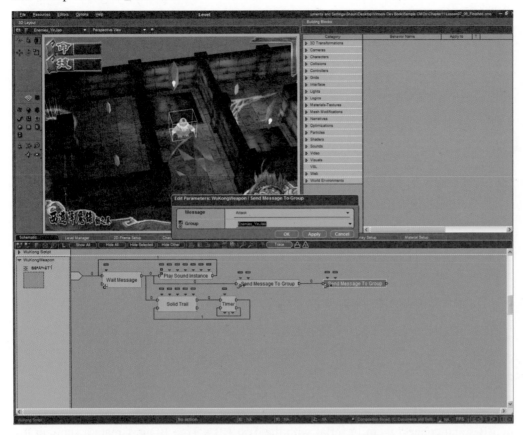

4) Go back to YinJiao's Script and add a Wait Message and Test BB. Connect the Wait Message BB to the Start Node and connect its BOut to the Test BB. Set the Wait Message BB to Message=WuKongAttack.

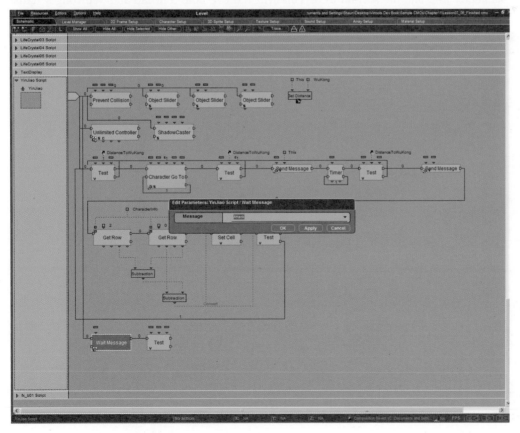

5) Connect the False BOut of the Test BB back to the Wait Message BIn to form a loop. Create a Shortcut to the DistanceToWuKong local parameter and connect it to the Test BB's A value PIn. Set the Test BB's parameters to Test=Less Than and B=30.

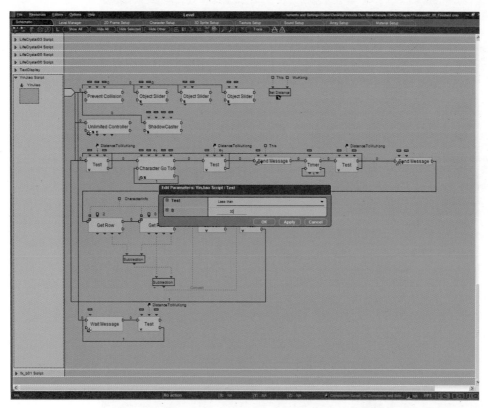

6) Add two Get Row BB's and connect them in serial with the Test BB's True BOut. Create a shortcut to the CharacterInfo local parameter and link it to the Target (Array) PIn for both the Get Row BB's. Set the first Get Row BB's Row parameter to 2 and the second to 0. This will retrieve both YinJiao and WuKong's statistics from the array.

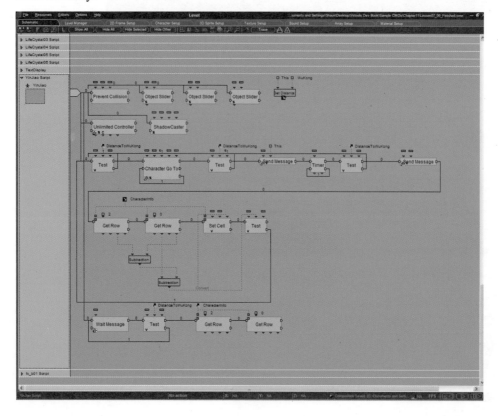

7) Create another Subtraction ParamOp and connect the left PIn to WuKong's AttackPwr. Connect the right PIn to YinJiao's DefensePwr.

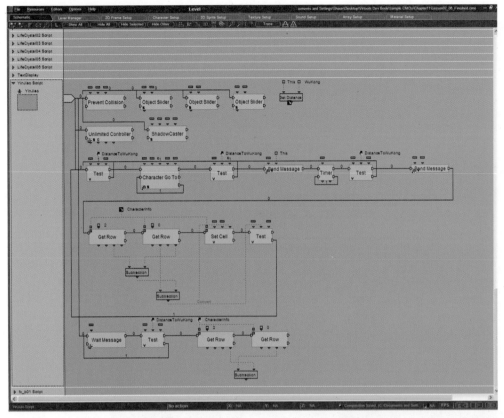

8) Create a second Subtraction ParamOp (just copy and paste the first) and connect the left PIn to YinJiao's HitPoints. Connect the right PIn to the first Subtraction ParamOp's POut. The POut of the second Subtraction ParamOp will give us the total remaining hit points of YinJiao after a successful hit by our player, WuKong.

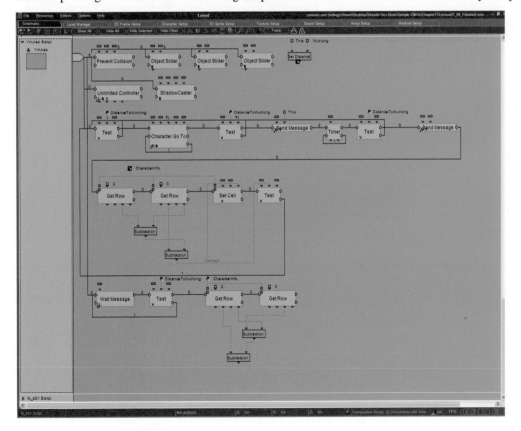

9) Add a Set Cell BB and connect it to the last Get Row BB's Found BOut. Set the Target (Array) to CharacterInfo using a shortcut and connect the second Subtraction ParamOp's POut to the Set Cell BB's value PIn. Set the Set Cell BB's Row Index to 2 and the Column Index to 1.

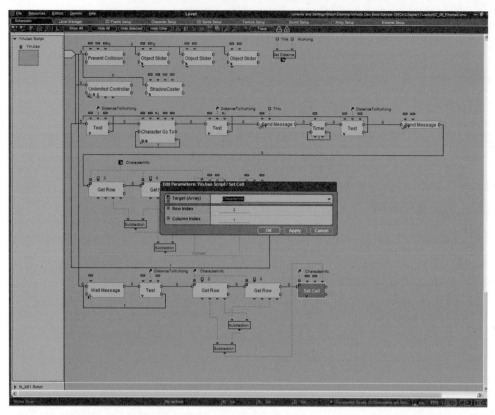

10) Create a new Array called AttackTarget. Create a new column called Enemy. Set its Type to Parameter and Parameter to Character. We will use this array to send the enemies we are currently attacking's position to another script.

11) Add the This local parameter and another Set Cell BB to the script. Set the Set Cell's Target (Array) to AttackTarget. Double click the Value PIn and change its parameter type to Character. Connect the new Set Cell BB to the Found BOut of the previous Set Cell BB.

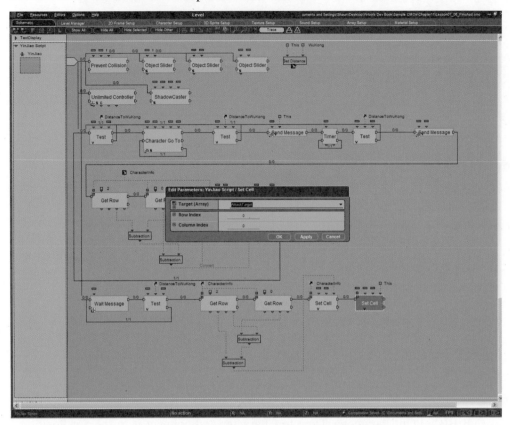

12) In Level Manager, make a copy of the being hit FX sprite. Make sure its script is called something you can easily recognize (avoid any duplicate names as it will confuse you later).

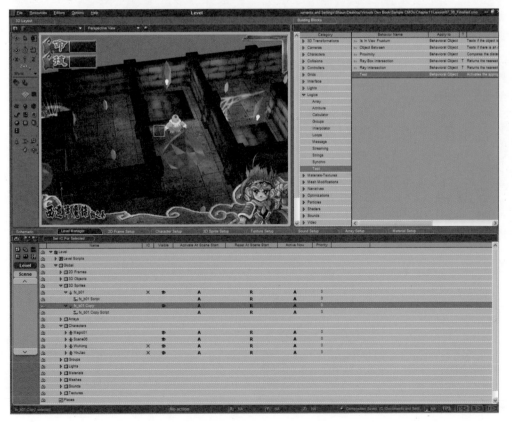

13) Delete the Play Sound Instance BB and insert and Get Cell BB between the Show and Set Position BB's. Set its Target (Array) to AttackTarget and leave the other settings as default.

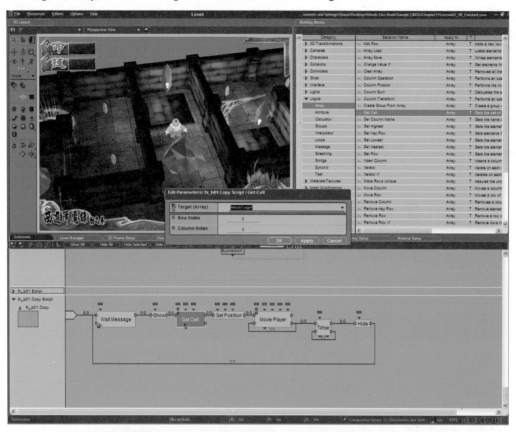

14) Change the Get Cell BB's POut Parameter Type to Character and connect it to the Set Position BB's Referential PIn.

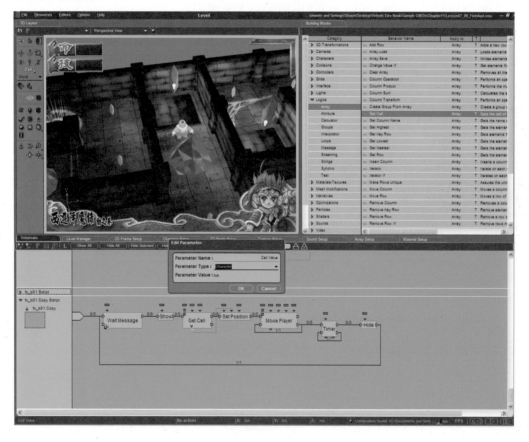

15) Go back again to YinJiao's Script and add a Timer and Send Message BB. Connect the Timer to the last Set Cell BB's Found BOut and connect its Loop In \ Loop Out pins. Connect the Timer BB's BOut to the Send Message BB. Lastly, set the Timer BB's Duration parameter to 500Ms.

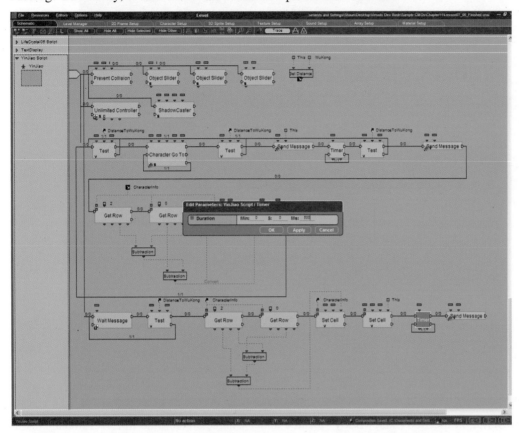

16) Set the Send Message BB to Message=Attack and Destination=FX_B01.Copy.

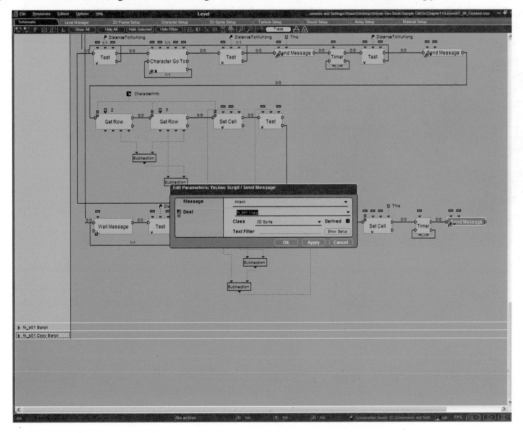

17) Add a Test BB and connect it to the Send Message BB. Connect it's A value PIn to the second Subtraction ParamOps result and set Test=Less or Equal and B=0.

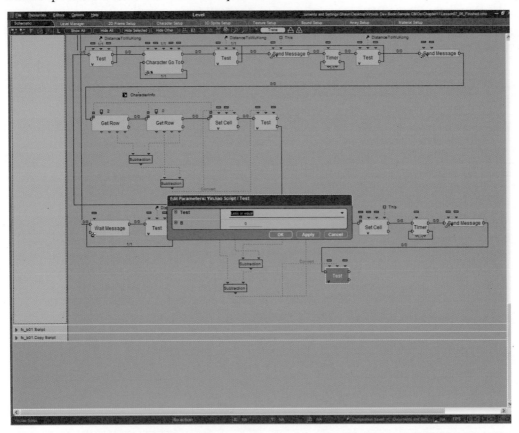

18) Create a new Script on the Body Part "Body" located under Characters\YinJiao in Level Manager. Call the script YinJiao Die and add a Wait Message BB. Set the Message parameter to YinJiao_Die.

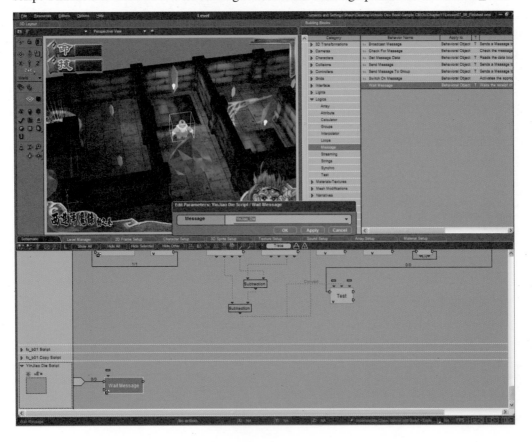

19) Add the Deactivate Script BB from Building Blocks\Narratives\Script Management and an Explode BB. Set the Deactivate Script BB's Script parameter to YinJiao Script.

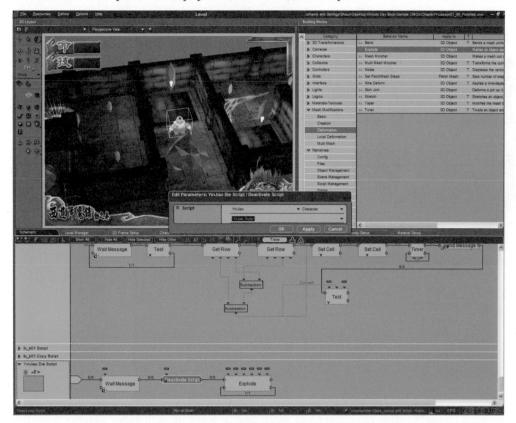

20) Back in YinJiao's script, add another Send Message BB and connect it to the True BOut of the last Test BB. Connect the last Test BB's false BOut back to the original Wait Message BB's BIn (check the screenshot if you are not sure). Set the Message to YinJiao_Die and the Dest to the "YinJiao_Body" Body Part.

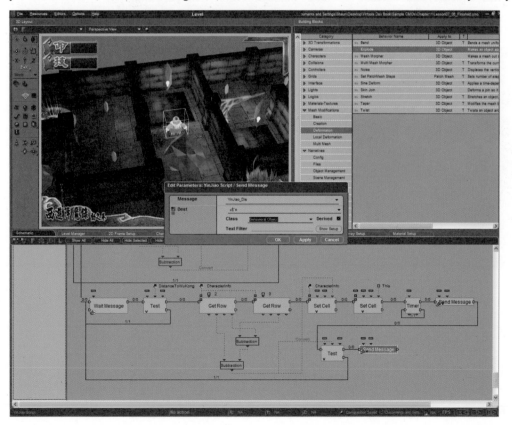

21) Click Play and try attacking the first YinJiao. You will see that if you stand still YinJiao will constantly attack and your hit points will decrease. If you attack YinJiao you can periodically check the CharacterInfo array to see his current hit point level. When it falls to 0 or less, he will explode.

22) Lastly, duplicate each of the YinJiao characters and place one in front of each Floor Trigger object. Don't forget to change the Row Index to match the YinJiao in the CharacterInfo array.

For the final Floor Trigger (the one that will let us finish the level) set the Row Index for that YinJiao to BossYinJiao (Row Index 1) and increase his size to make him look more boss-like.

Note: If you get stuck or find the duplication process too difficult, open the sample CMO called Lesson07_06_Finished located in Sample CMO's \ Chapter11.

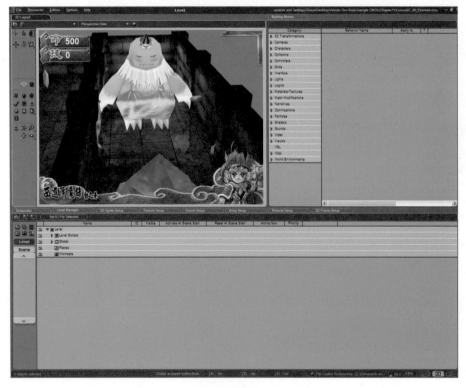

8.0 Special Features

8.1 Creating the Mini-Map

1) Open the file Lesson08_01_Start.CMO located in Sample CMO's\Chapter11. Holding Ctrl+Shift on your keyboard, drag the Icon_Map.png texture from Sample Resources\Textures into the Scene. Position it under the Map Frame and set the related materials Mode to Transparent.

2) Add a Get Cell and Test BB; connect them as shown in the screenshot. Set the Get Cell Target (Array) to PointCrystals and leave the other parameters as default (as our Crystal in stored in cell 0,0). Connect the Get Cell BB's POut to the Test BB's A Value PIn and set the Test BB's parameters to Test=Greater or Equal and B Value to 3. This will test to see if WuKong has collected 3 or more Point Crystals.

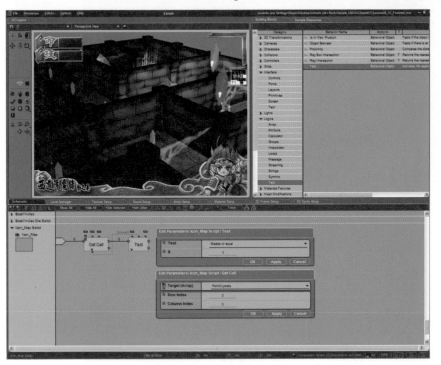

3) Add the Show and Hide BB's to the script; link the Show BB to the Test BB's True BOut and the Hide BB to the False BOut. Link them both back to the Get Cell BB's BIn to form a loop.

4) Add a Wait Message BB and connect it to the Show BB's BOut. Set the Message parameter to ShowMiniMap.

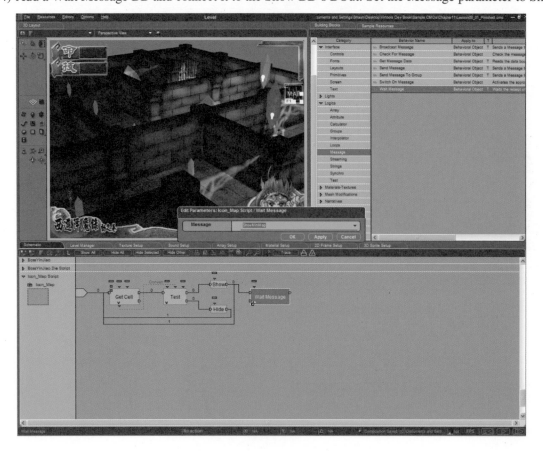

5) Open the Level Script and add a Key Waiter and Send Message BB. Configure them to wait for the F1 key to be pressed and send the Message ShowMiniMap to the Icon_Map 2DFrame.

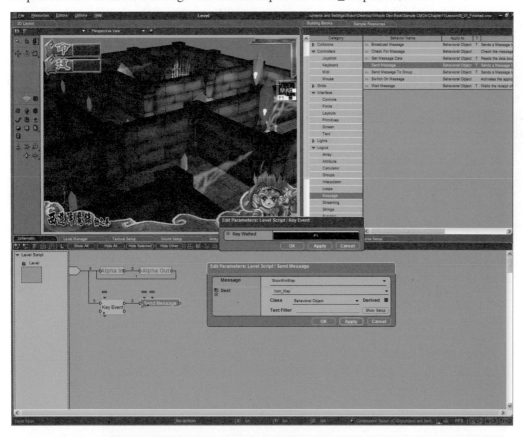

6) Back in the Icon_Map script, copy the first Get Cell and Test BB's and create the same configuration to get the number of crystals WuKong has collected.

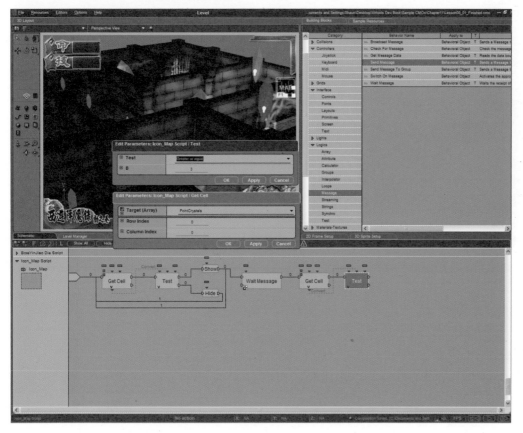

7) Add a Set Cell BB and connect it to the Found BOut of the Test BB, set its Target (Array) to PointCrystals. Create a Subtraction ParamOp and configure it to subtract 3 from the Get Cell BB's POut (the total number of Point Crystals). Connect the result of the Subtraction ParamOp to the Value PIn of the Set Cell BB.

8) Connect the Test BB's False BOut back to the first Get Cell's BIn to form a loop.

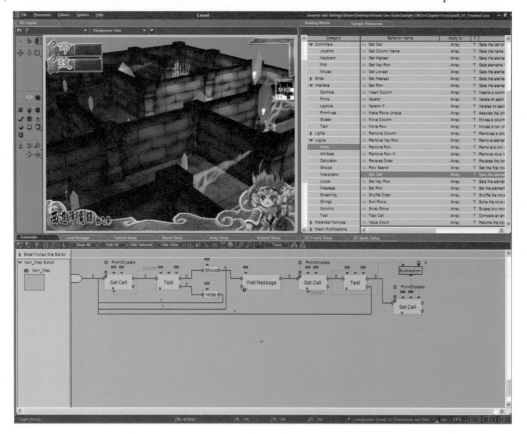

9) Add a Play Sound Instance BB and connect it to the True BOut of the Test BB. Add the Space.wav sound to the scene. Configure the Play Sound Instance BB to Sound=Space and make sure the 2D checkbox is on.

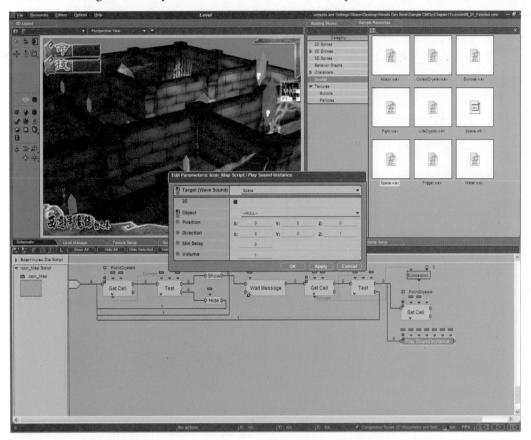

10) Create a new Camera called MiniMapCamera and create its script.

11) Configure the Camera so that it looks directly down over the level. Set the Orientation to X=90, Y=0, Z=0.

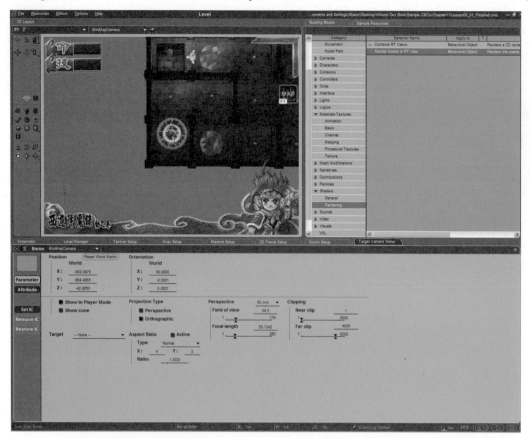

12) In the MiniMap Camera's script, add a Set Position BB and set its parameters to Position X=0, Y=2000, Z=0 and Referential=WuKong.

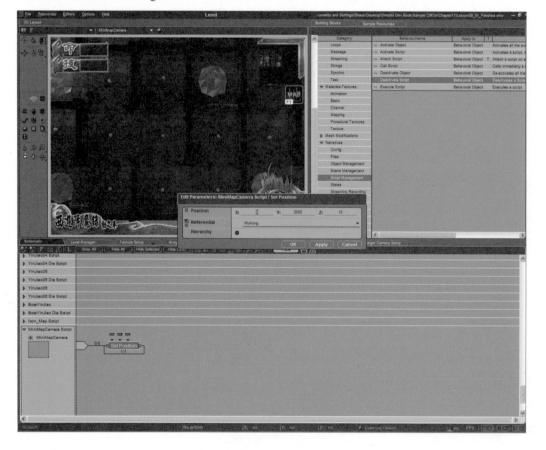

13) Create a new 2D Frame called MiniMapFrame and create a corresponding material and texture called MiniMapMat and MiniMapTex respectively. Assign the texture to the material and the material to the 2D Frame. Set the Size of the 2DFrame to 96x96 and position it to fit within the MapFrame (the border in the top right hand corner). Don't forget to set the Material Type to Transparent as we will need the Alpha component for the Fade In action.

14) Create a script on the MiniMapFrame and add the Set Diffuse BB. Connect it to the Start Node and set its Target (Material) to MiniMapMat, the Diffuse Color to Black with an Alpha value of 0 and the Keep Alpha Component checkbox should be unchecked.

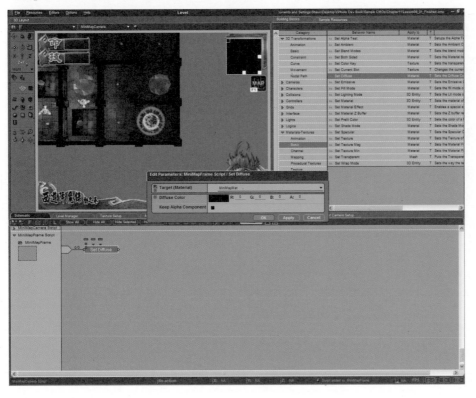

15) Add a Wait Message BB and set it to wait for the ShowMiniMap message.

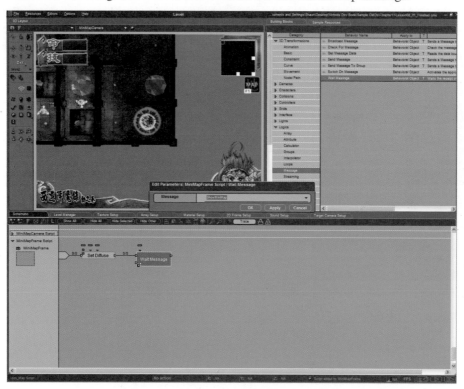

16) To perform the Fade In event when the MiniMap is activated, add a Bezier Progression, Interpolator and Set Diffuse BB. Connect the 3 in series after the Wait Message BB making sure you connect the Interpolator BB to the Bezier Progression BB's Loop Out BOut and the Set Diffuse BB's BOut to the Bezier Progression BB's Loop In BIn. Set the Bezier Progression BB's Duration to 2 Seconds. Double click the Interpolators POut and change the Parameter Type to Color. Set the Interpolators first color to Black with 0 Alpha and the second color to White with an Alpha of 255. Change the Set Diffuse BB's Target (Material) to MiniMapMat and turn off the Keep Alpha Component. Finally connect the Bezier Progression BB's Value POut to the Interpolator's Value PIn and connect the Interpolators Value (Color) POut to the Set Diffuse BB's Color PIn.

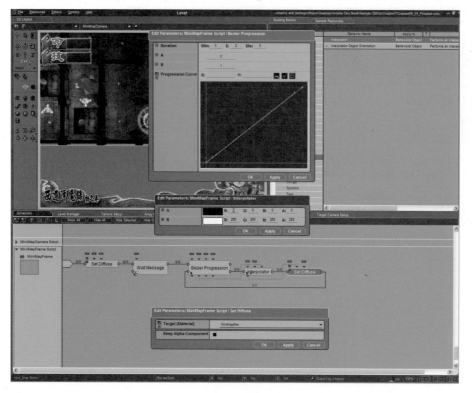

17) Add the Render Target in RT View BB from Building Blocks \ Shaders \ Rendering to the script. Connect it to the Wait Message BOut. Open its Edit Parameters dialog and set the RenderTarget to MiniMapTex and the Camera to MiniMapCamera. Make sure Use Camera Ratio is Disabled.

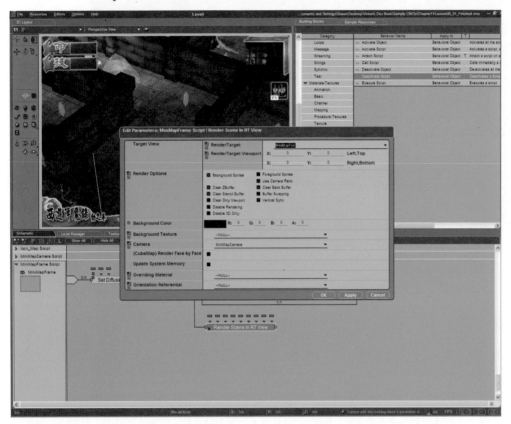

18) Back in the Icon_Map script, add a new Send Message BB and connect it to the Set Cell BB's Found POut. Set its parameters to send the ShowMiniMap message to the MiniMapFrame.

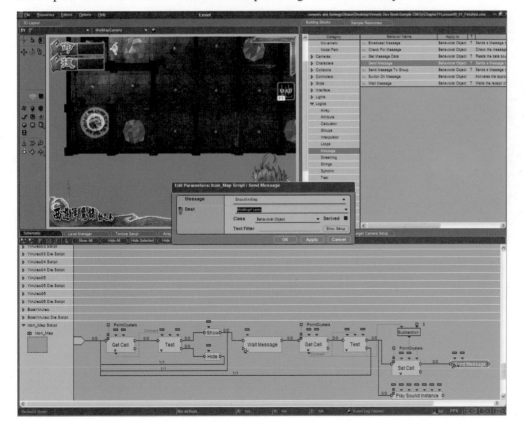

19) Add the Hide and Deactivate BB's to the script and connect them in series with the Play Sound Instance BB's BOut. Set the Deactivate Script BB's script parameter to the Icon_Map script.

20) Finally, its time to test our work. Click Play and collect 3 Point Crystals, then press the F1 key to bring up the MiniMap. It should fade in slowly and playback the sound instance we added earlier. After the sound has finished playback, the MiniMap icon should disappear.

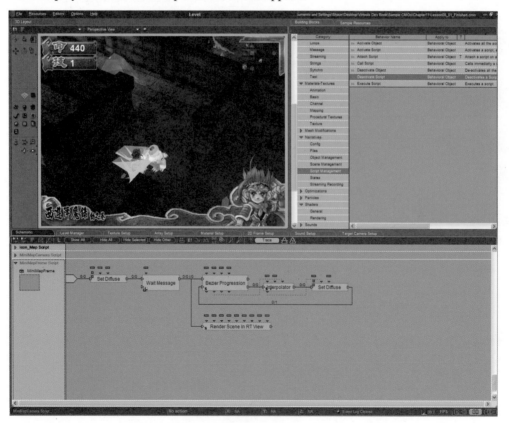

8.2 Creating the Hit Point Restoration Feature

1) Open the file Lesson08_02_Start.CMO located in Sample CMO's\Chapter11. Holding Ctrl+Shift on your keyboard, drag the Icon_Life.png texture from Sample Resources\Textures into the Scene. Position it under the Map Icon and set the related material's Mode to Transparent.

2) Create the sequence of BB's as per the MiniMap Icon script. Configure the Test BB to check if WuKong has collected more than 5 Crystals. Set the Wait Message BB to wait for the HPRestore message and set the Subtraction ParamOp to reduce the number of crystals by 5.

3) In the Level Script window, add another Key Event and Send Message BB. Set the Key Event BB's Key parameter to F2 and the Send Message BB's Message to HPRestore with the Destination as the Icon_Life 2D Frame.

4) Add another Get Cell, Set Cell BB combination and connect it to the Found BOut of the last Set Cell BB. Set the Target (Array) for both to the CharacterInfo Array and the Row=0 and Column=1. Create an Addition ParamOp, connect its left PIn to the Get Cell BB's POut (WuKongs current HP value) and set the right PIn to 100 (Add 100 HP). Connect the ParamOp's POut to the Value PIn of the Set Cell BB.

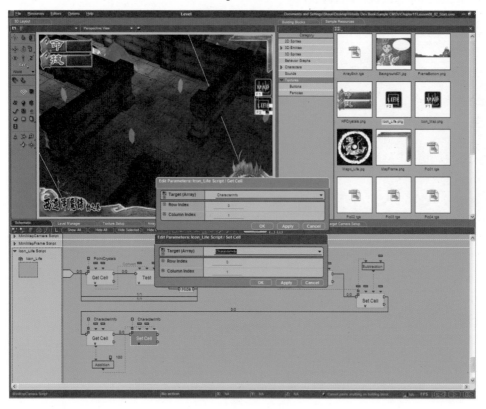

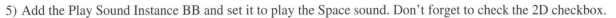

5) Add the Play Sound Instance BB and set it to play the Space sound. Don't forget to check the 2D checkbox.

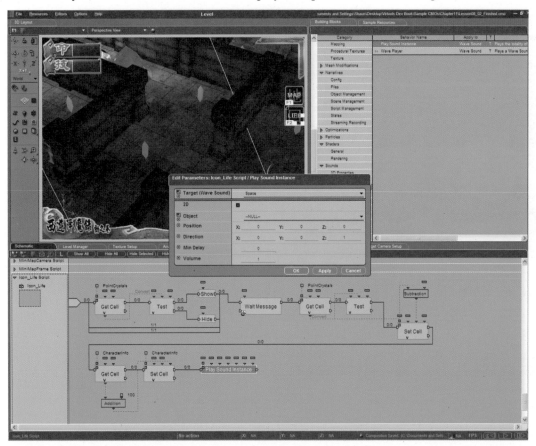

6) Connect the Set Cell BB's Found BOut to the first Get Cell BB's BIn to create a full script loop.

7) Add the curve Path01 to the Scene from Sample Resources\3D Entities.

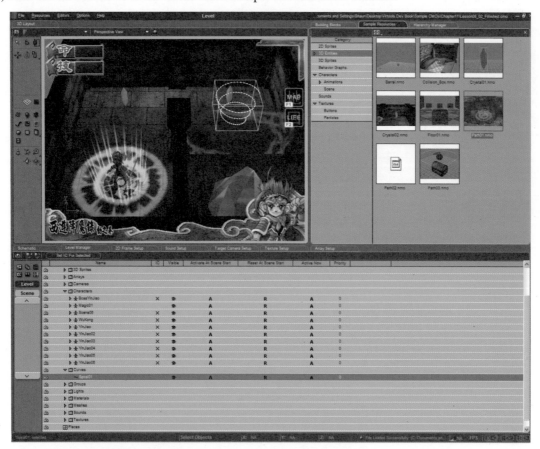

8) Now add the LifeMagic object from Sample Resources\Characters.

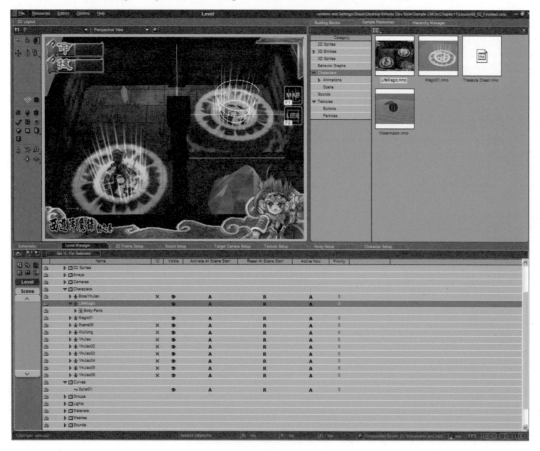

9) Create a script for the LifeMagic object. Add the Hide, Wait Message, Show, Set Position and Timer BB' s to the script. Link them as shown in the screenshot. Set the Message parameter to HP Restore for the Wait Message BB. Configure the Set Position BB to X=0, Y=-15, Z=0 and set the Referential to WuKong. Configure the Timer to loop for 2 seconds.

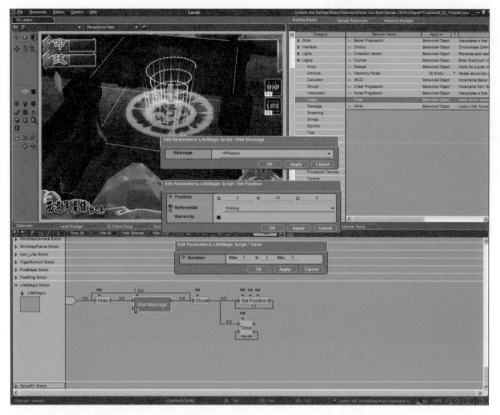

10) Create a script for the Spiral01 curve and add a Set Position BB. Configure the Set Position BB to Position X=0, Y=60, Z=0 and Referential=WuKong.

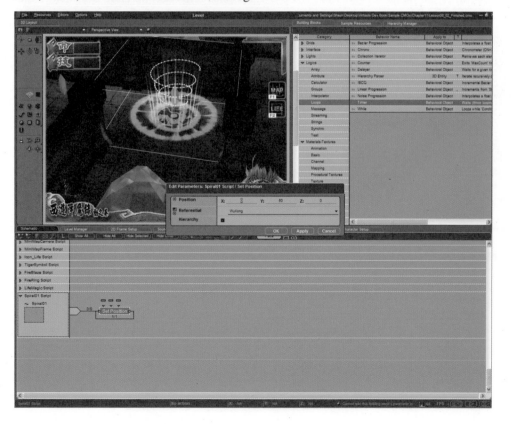

11) Create a new 3D Frame called LifeRestoreSparkle and create its script.

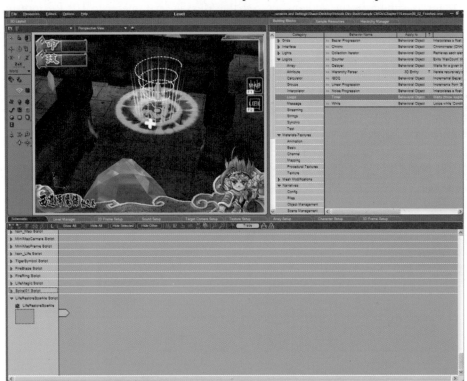

12) Add a Hide and Point Particle System BB to the Script. Connect them as shown. Now add a Wait Message, Show, Bezier Progression and Position on Curve BB. Connect the Wait Message BB to the Start Node, and connect the remaining BB's in series. Remember to connect the Position on Curve BB to the Bezier Progression BB's Loop Out BOut and back to its Loop In BIn. Connect the Percentage POut of the Bezier Progression BB to the Position on Curve BB's Progression PIn and set the Curve to Sprial01. Add another Hide BB and connect it to the Bezier Progression BB's BOut. Connect the second Hide BB back to the Wait Message BB. This will 're-hide' the particle system once the animation has finished.

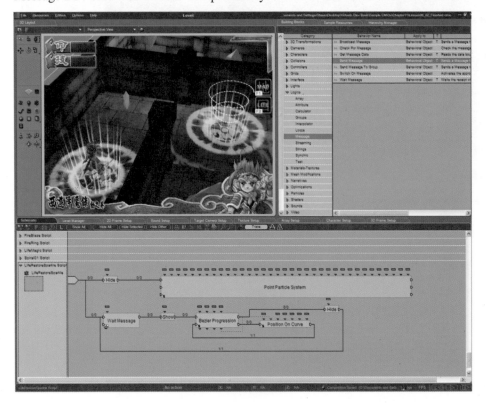

13) Add the texture Sparkle from Sample Resources\Textures\Particles. Open the Point Particle System BB's Edit Parameters dialog and set the values as shown in the screenshot.

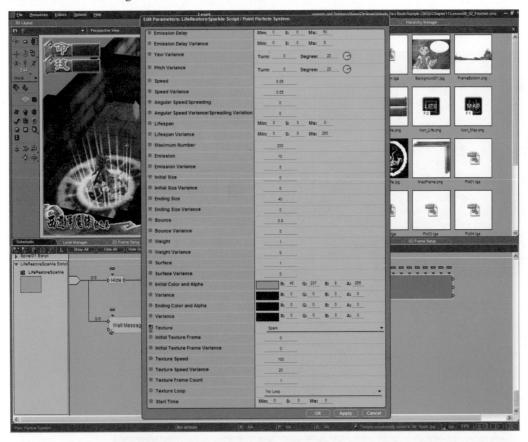

14) Click Play to test the script. When you have collected 5 Crystals you can use the Life Restore magic.

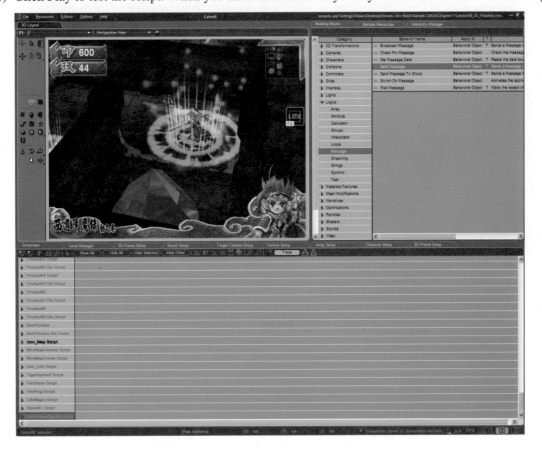

8.3 Creating WuKong's Special Attack

1) Open the file Lesson08_03_Start.CMO located in Sample CMO's\Chapter11. Holding Ctrl+Shift on your keyboard, drag the Icon_Attack.png texture from Sample Resources\Textures into the Scene. Position it under the Life Icon and set the related material's Mode to Transparent. Create a Script on the 2D Frame.

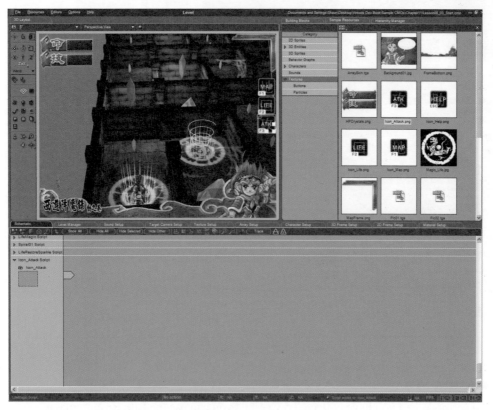

2) Referring to the method in the last 2 lessons, create a script to check if WuKong has 8 or more crystals, wait for the SpecialAttack message and subtract 8 from the total crystal count.

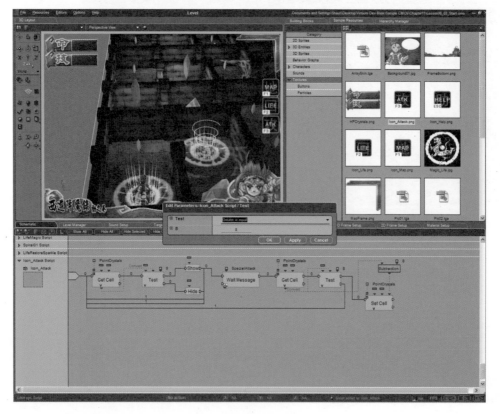

3) Go to the Level Script and add another Key Event and Send Message BB. Set the Special Attack message to the Icon_Attack 2D Frame we just created.

4) In the Icon_Attack script, add a Play Sound Instance BB and set it to playback the Space sound. Connect it to the Set Cell BB's Found BOut. Now, add another Set Cell BB and configure it to increase WuKong's attack ability (AttackPwr) to 80.

5) Create a new 3D Frame and its script. Add the Cylindrical Particle System and a Set Position BB to the script. Connect the Cylindrical Particle System BB to the Start Node, and configure the Set Position BB to keep the 3D Frame on WuKongs Weapon. Remember to loop the Set Position BB.

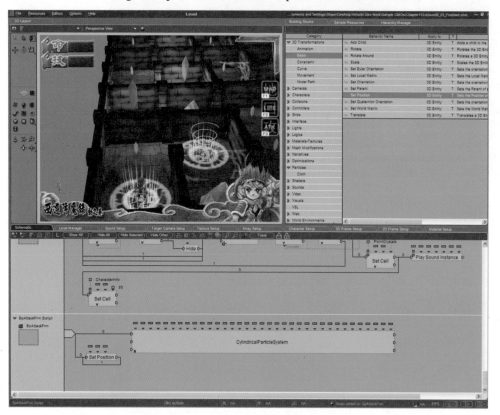

6) Add the texture Fire.jpg to the scene. In the Texture Setup panel, right click the Alpha preview window and select Get Alpha from Diffuse. Now set the Cylindrical Particle System BB's Initial Size=0, Ending Size=40 and Texture=Fire.

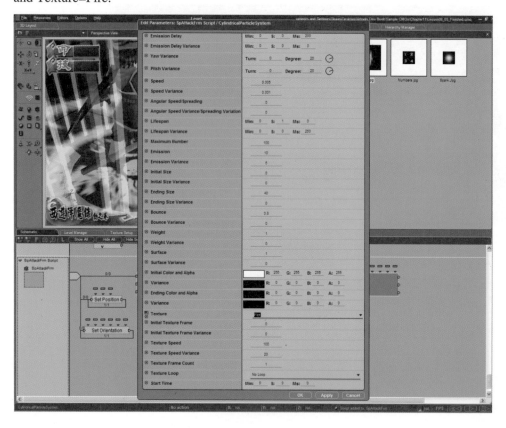

7) Add a Set Orientation BB and set Dir to X=0, Y=1, Z=0, Up to X=0, Y=0, Z=1, Referential to WuKongWeapon and loop it internally. Click Play and then you will see the particles emitting from the weapon, but only from the center. Zoom the camera toward the weapon and scale the cylindrical frame to roughly match the length of the weapon.
Note: Use the Lock Selection to avoid accidentally scaling a background object.

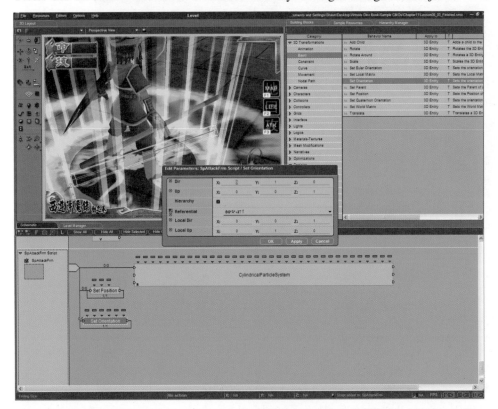

8) Create a new Array called SpecialAttack. Add a single column called SpAtkEnabled and set its type to Integer. Add a single row.

9) In the Icon_Attack script, add a Set Cell BB and Execute Script BB. Connect them in series with the last Set Cell BB. Set the Set Cell BB to Target (Array)=SpecialAttack, Row=0, Column=0 and Value=1. Set the Execute Script to Reset=True and Script to SpAttackFrmScript.

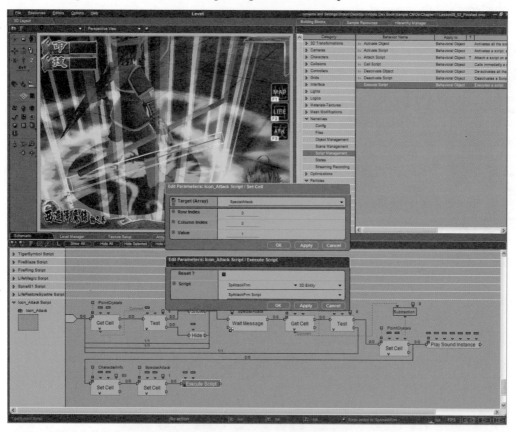

10) Add the 3D Sprite Boom01.bmp to the scene. Scale and position the sprite as shown in the screenshot.

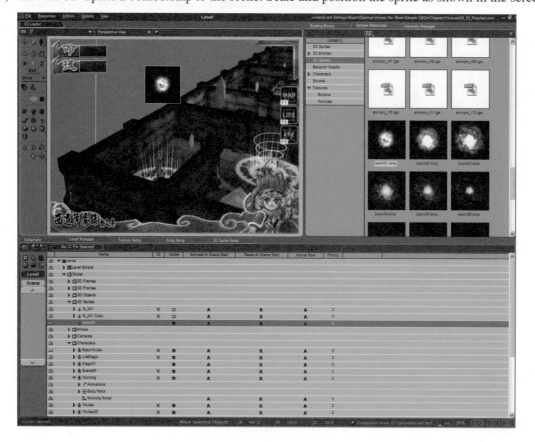

11) Set the Boom01 Material Type to Transparent. In the Texture Setup panel, use the Add Slot button to add the other Boom images to the texture. To remove the black background, right click in the Alpha Preview window and select Get Alpha from Diffuse (you will need to do this for each image).

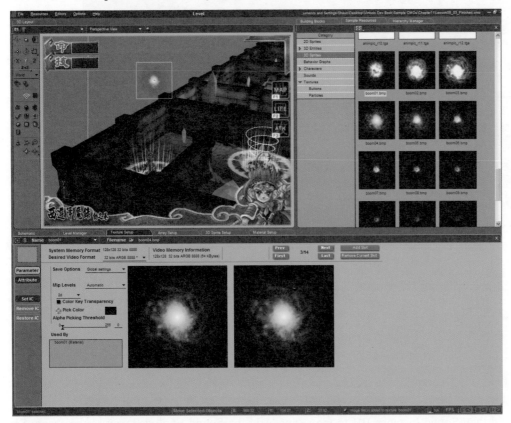

12) Add a script to the Boom01 3D Sprite and add the Wait Message and Timer BB's. Set the Message to SpecialAttack and the Timer Duration to 250Ms.

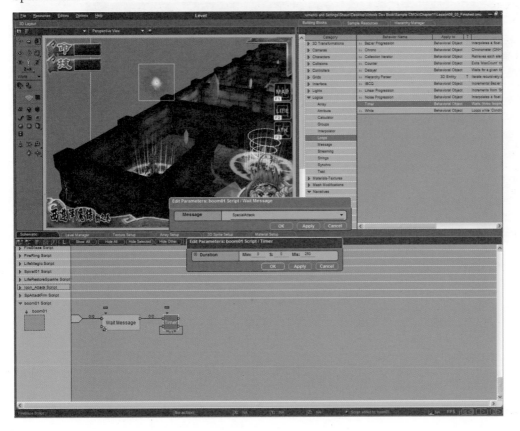

13) Add a Get Cell BB and Test BB to the script. Set the Get Cell BB to retrieve the first cell in the SpecialAttack array. Set the Test BB to check if the Get Cell POut value is equal to 1.

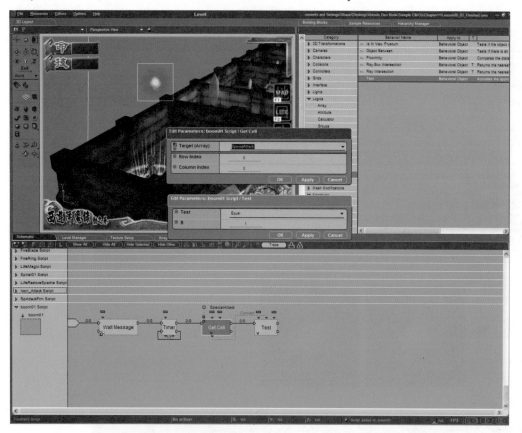

14) Add a Show and Play Sound Instance BB to the script. Add the Sound Explode2.wav to the scene. Set the Play Sound Instance BB to play the Explode2 sound and ensure 2D is turned on.

15) Add a Get Cell and Set Position BB. Configure them to get the position of the enemy from the AttackTarget array and set that value to the Set Position BB's Referential. Remember to change the Get Cell BB's POut to the Character parameter type otherwise you wont be able to connect it to the Set Position BB's Referential PIn.

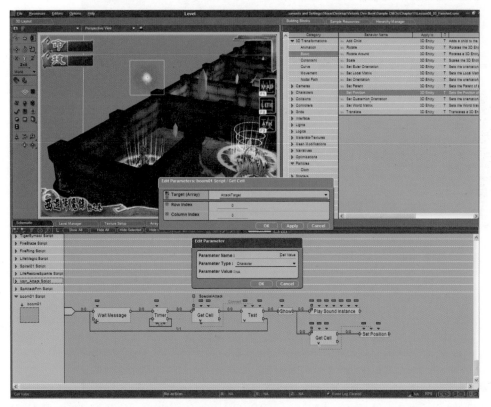

16) Add the Timer, Hide and Movie Player BB's to the script. Connect the Timer and Hide BB's in series with the Set Position BB, loop the Timer BB internally and connect the Hide BB back to the Wait Message BIn to form a complete loop of the script. Connect the Movie Player BB to the Set Position BB.

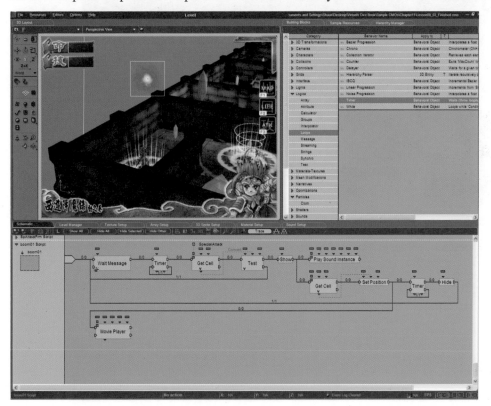

17) Set the Timer BB's Duration to 500Ms. Set the Movie Player to Target (Texture)=Boom01, Duration=500Ms, Loop=False and Ending Slot=14.

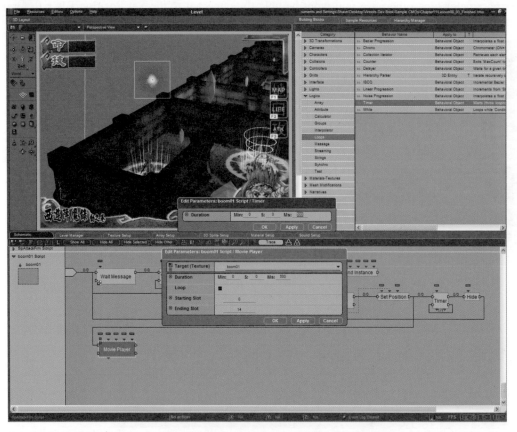

18) Go to the FX_B01.Copy Script and add a Send Message BB. Connect it with the Wait Message BB's BOut. Configure it to send the SpecialAttack message to the Boom01 3D Sprite.

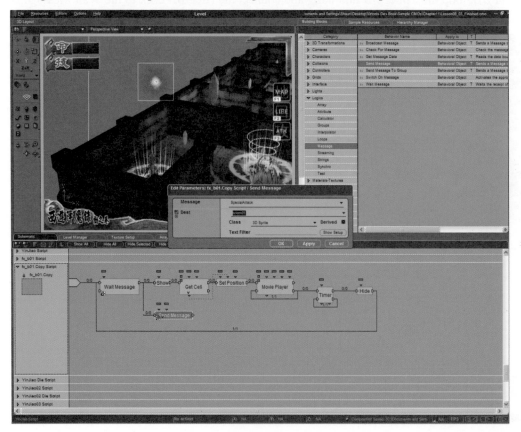

19) Back in the Icon_Attack script, add a Timer and Bezier Progression BB. Connect the Timer BB to the last Set Cell BB and connect the Bezier Progression to loop within the Timer BB. Set the Timer BB's Duration to 3 Seconds and the Bezier Progression BB's Duration to 200Ms.

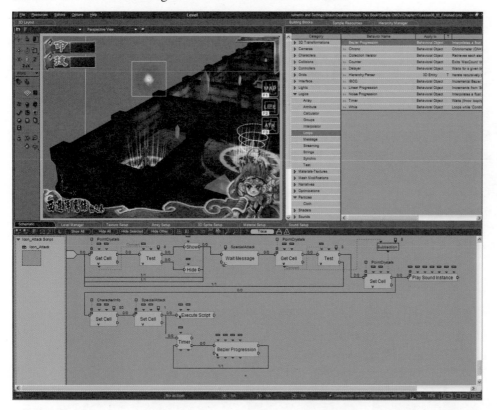

20) Add an Interpolator and two Set Emissive BB's. Loop them in series with the Bezier Progression BB's Loop Out\In pins. Change the Interpolator BB's POut parameter type to Color and set the A color to Black and the B color to White. Since our WuKong character has two materials, we need to set each Set Emissive BB to each of the materials. Set the first to BodyMat and the second to HairMat.

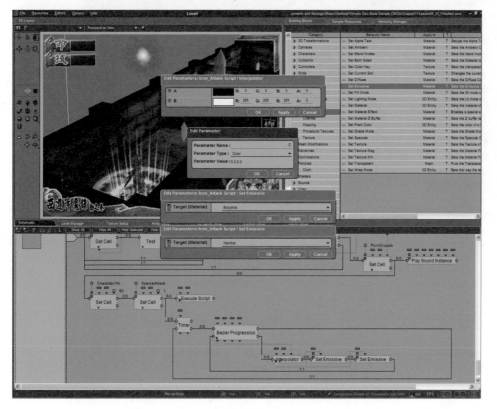

21) Add two Set Cell BB's to the script. Connect them in series with the Timer BB's BOut. Configure the first Set Cell BB to change WuKongs attack ability (AttackPwr) back to 45 and the second to set the SpAtkEnabled value back to 0.

22) Add a Deactivate Script BB to turn off the SpAttackFrm script.

23) Connect the last Get Cell BB back to the first to complete the script loop.

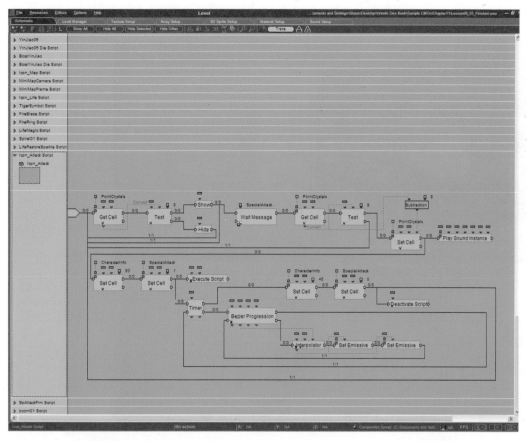

24) Lastly, in Level Manager, set the SpAttackFrm to Deactivated At Start by clicking on the 'A' in the Activate At Scene Start column. Then set the objects Initial Conditions.

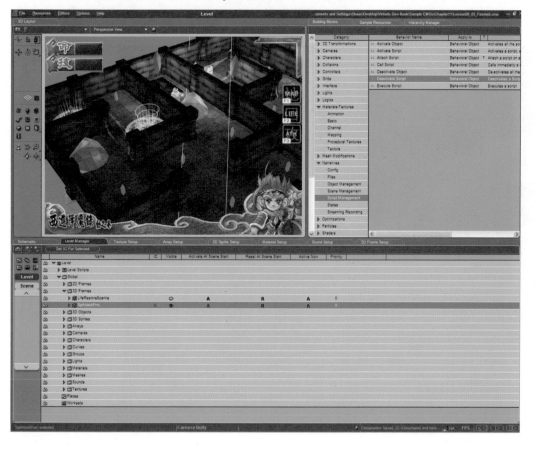

25) Click Play and test the Special Attack. When you press F3 the power up sound will play, WuKongs weapon will glow and he will start blinking. If you check the CharacterInfo array, you will also see WuKongs AttackPwr has increased to 80. After a while the effect will disappear.

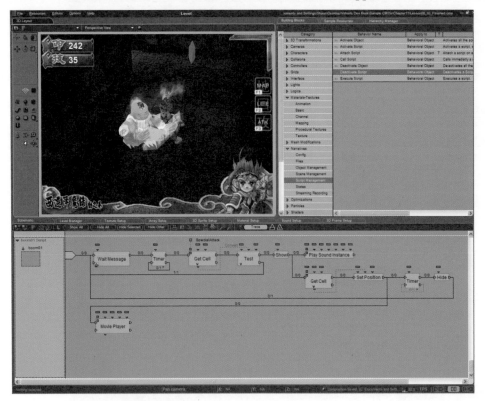

8.4 Creating the Help Screen

1) Open the file Lesson08_04_Start.CMO located in Sample CMO's\Chapter11. Holding Ctrl+Shift on your keyboard, drag the Icon_Help.png texture from Sample Resources\Textures into the Scene. Position it under the Attack Icon and set the related material's Mode to Transparent. Create a Script on the 2D Frame.

2) Create a new 2D Frame called HelpFrame and set its Size to 640x480 and its Position to 0,0. Set its ZOrder to -2.

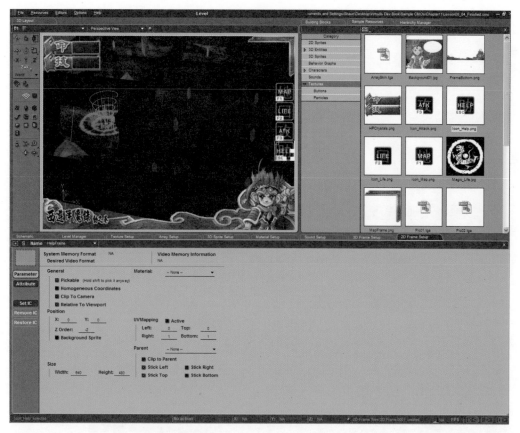

3) Create a new Material called HelpFrameMat. Set its Type to Transparent. Set the HelpFrame's material to HelpFrameMat.

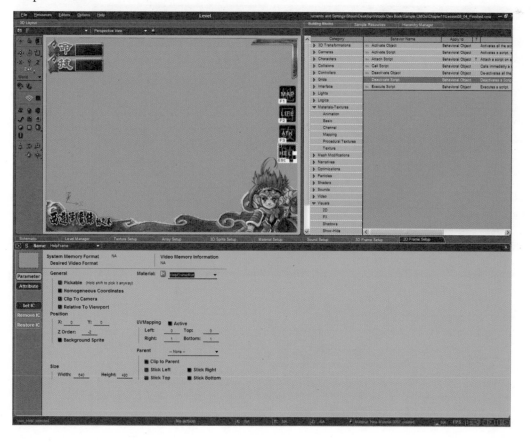

4) In the Icon_Help script, add a Set Diffuse BB and configure it to set the HelpFrameMat material to Black with an Alpha value of 0. Turn off Keep Alpha Component.

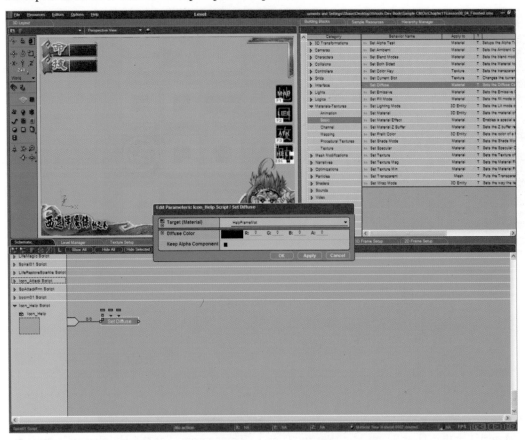

5) Add a Wait Message BB and set it to wait for the ShowHelp message.

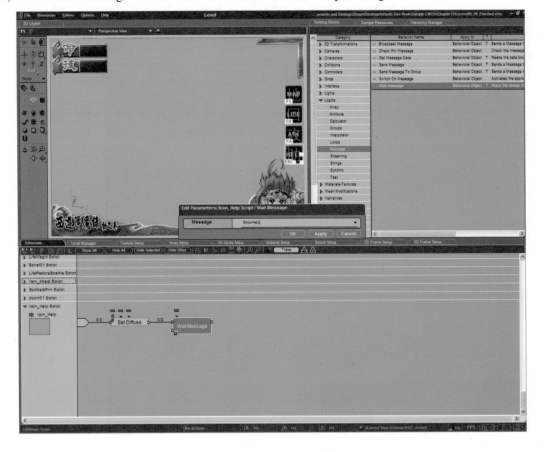

6) In the Level Script, add another Key Event and Send Message BB. Set the Key to ESC and the Message to "ShowHelp" with a Destination of Icon_Help 2D Frame.

7) Add a Sequencer BB and use the Construct menu to add another Behavior Output. Connect its In BIn to the Wait Message BOut.

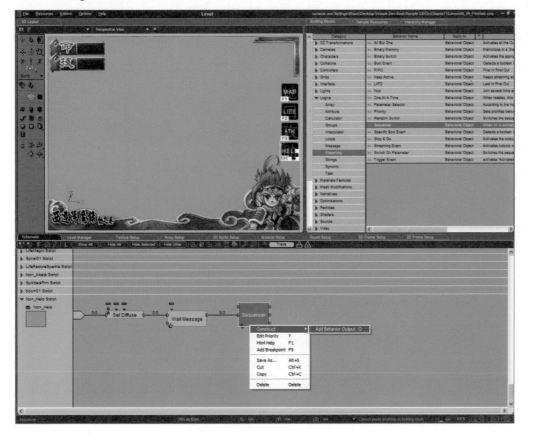

8) Add two Set Diffuse BB's and connect each to one of the Sequencer BB's Out BOut's. Set the first Set Diffuse BB to Black with an Alpha value of 150 and the second to Black with an Alpha value of 0. Make sure both have Keep Alpha Component turned off and the Target (Material) is set to HelpFrameMat. Connect the second Set Diffuse BB back to the Wait Message BIn.

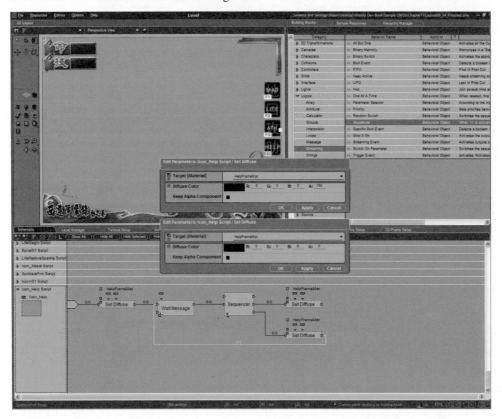

9) Add a Text Display BB. Connect its On BIn to the first Set Diffuse BB and its Off BIn to the second Set Diffuse BB. Connect it's Text Off BOut back to the Wait Message BB's BIn.

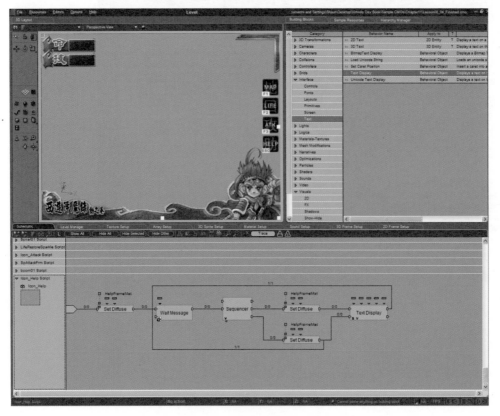

10) Edit the Text Display BB's parameters to set the text to roughly the center of the screen, the font size to 12 and type in some text that explains to players how to control the character.
Important: If your text is getting cut off, it means the sprite being used to 'print' the text onto is too small. Simply right click the Text Display BB and change Sprite Size to a higher resolution.

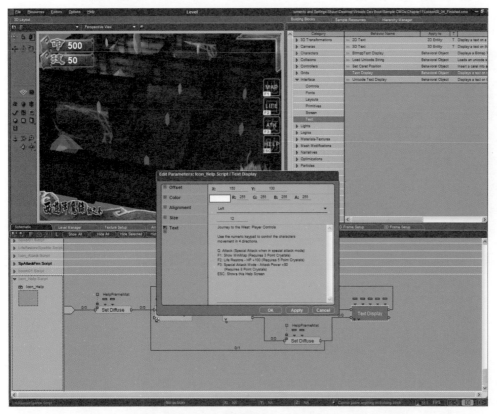

11) Click Play and press the Escape key. The help text will appear. You may need to tweak the Text Display settings to get it looking exactly how you want.

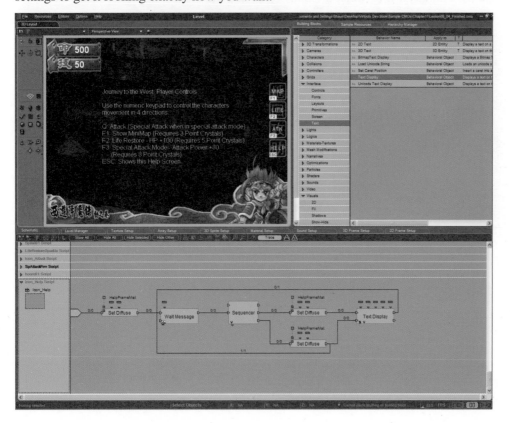

9.0 End Game Events

9.1 Creating Level Cleared Event

1) Open the file Lesson09_01_Start.CMO located in Sample CMO's\Chapter11. Open the script of the Scene06 Body Part called FloorTriggerCollBoxEnd.

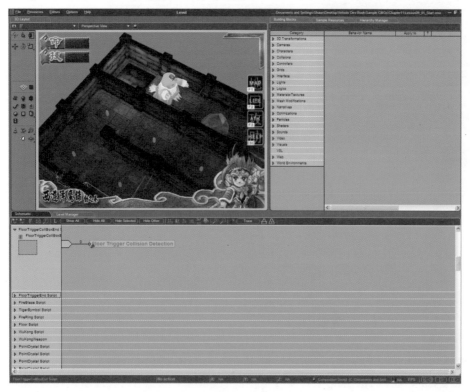

2) Add a Wait Message BB and insert it between the Start Node and the Floor Trigger Collision Detection BG. Set the Message to DefeatedBoss.

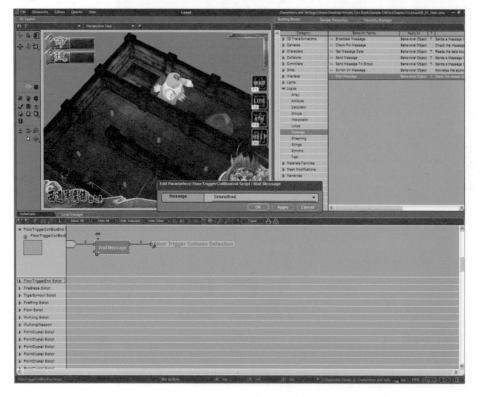

3) Open the script of the character BossYinJiao. At the end of the script there is a Send Message BB that sends a message to the script that makes the character explode. Add a second Send Message BB and connect it to the last Test BB's True BOut. Set the Message to DefeatedBoss and Destination to FloorTriggerCollBoxEnd.

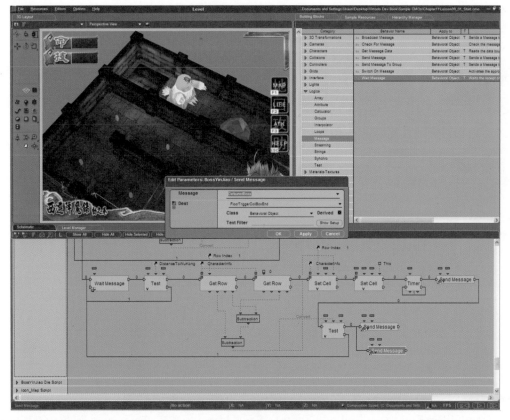

4) Holding Ctrl+Shift, drag the LevelCleared.png texture into the scene. This will create a 2D Frame with a corresponding texture and material. Change the Material Type to Transparent.

5) Create a script for the LevelCleared 2D Frame. Add the Wait Message, Show, Timer and Go To Web Page BB's. Connect them in sequence and internally loop the timer BB. Set the Message to Level Cleared, the Duration to 5 Seconds and the URL to GameMenu.htm.

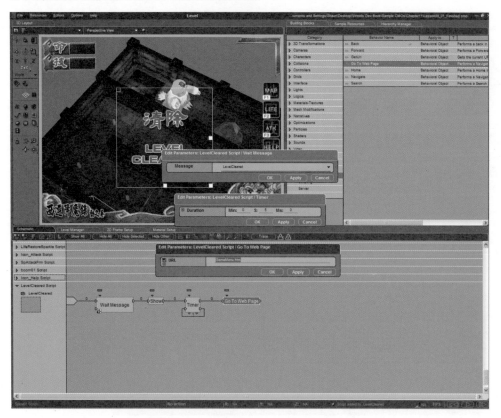

6) Go to the FloorTriggerCollBoxEnd script and add another Send Message BB. Connect it to the Collision Detection BB's True BOut. Set the Message to LevelCleared and the Destination to the LevelCleared 2D Frame.

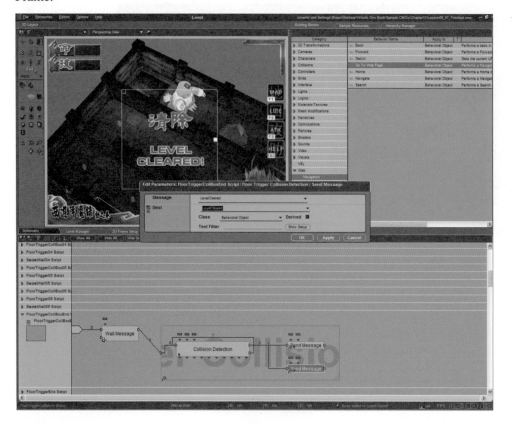

7) Lastly, in Level Manager select the LevelCleared 2D Frame and set its Visible property to Hidden then set its Initial Conditions.

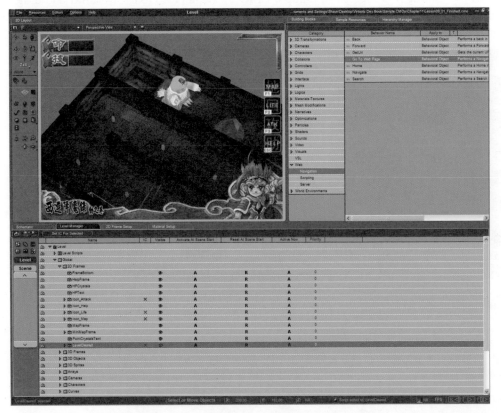

8) Click Play to test the script. Defeat the Boss YinJiao enemy and then walk over the Floor Trigger, then Level Cleared message will appear.

Note: You can move WuKong close to the end of the level to save going through and defeating all of the YinJiao enemies.

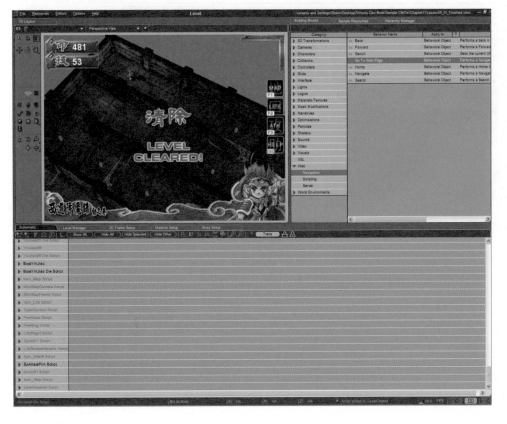

9.2 Creating the Game Over (Player Dies) Event

1) Open the file Lesson09_02_Start.CMO located in Sample CMO's\Chapter11. Hold Ctrl+Shift and drag the GameOver.png texture into the scene to create a new 2D Frame. Set the Material Type to Transparent. Create a script on the 2D Frame.

2) Using the Get Cell and Test BB's create a script to test if WuKong's Hit Points are Less or Equal to 0.

3) Add the Show, Timer and Go To Web Page BB's. Connect them in sequence with the True BOut of the Test BB. Internally loop the Timer BB and set its duration to 5 Seconds. Set the Go To Web Page URL to GameMenu.htm.

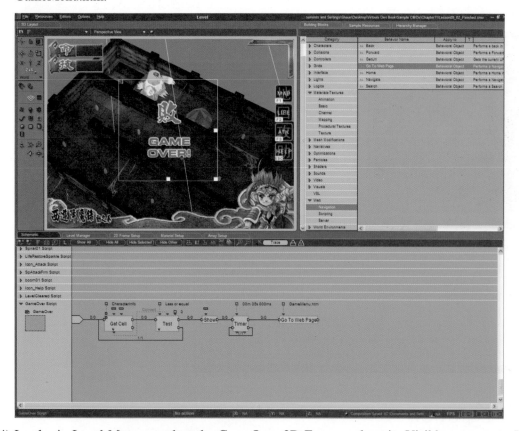

4) Lastly, in Level Manager select the GameOver 2D Frame and set its Visible property to Hidden then set its Initial Conditions.

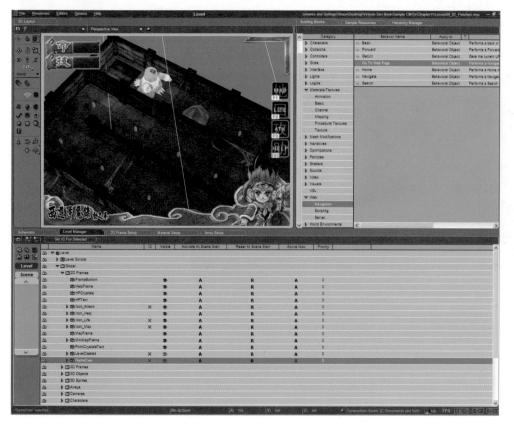

5) Click Play to test the script. When WuKong's Hit Points fall to 0 or below, then GameOver message will appear.

Note: Try improving on the Game Over event by making the WuKong character explode using the same technique as we used for the YinJiao characters.

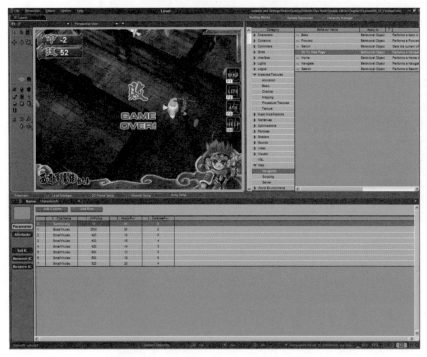

10.0 Final Integration

10.1 Creating a Top Down Camera View

1) Open the file Lesson10_01_Start.CMO located in Sample CMO's\Chapter11. Create a new Camera and add the Look At and Keep At Constant Distance BB's. Configure them using the settings shown in the screenshot. Try adjusting the Attenuation and Following Speed parameters to see the effect it has on the camera.

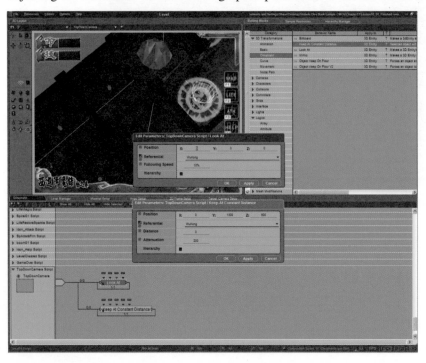

10.2 Creating a Follow Camera

1) Open the file Lesson10_02_Start.CMO located in Sample CMO's\Chapter11. Create a new Camera and add the Look At and Keep At Constant Distance BB's. Configure them using the settings shown in the screenshot.

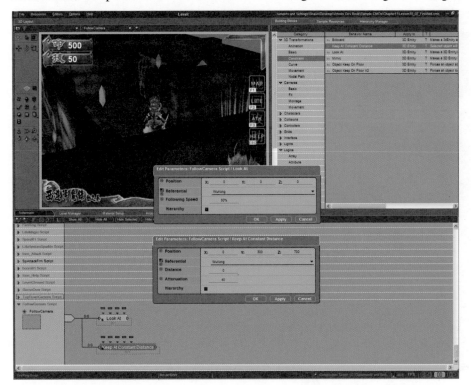

10.3 Creating a Camera Switch

1) Open the file Lesson10_03_Start.CMO located in Sample CMO's\Chapter11. In the Level Script add the Switch On Key and two Set As Active Camera BB's. Configure each Set As Active Camera BB to activate a different view.

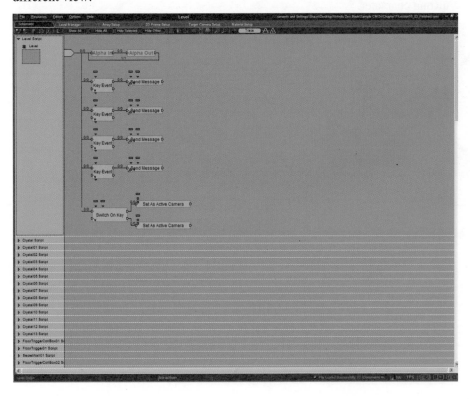

10.4 Setting the Initial Camera

1) Open the file Lesson10_04_Start.CMO located in Sample CMO's\Chapter11. In the Level Script add the Set As Active Camera BB. Configure the camera you want the player to initially use.

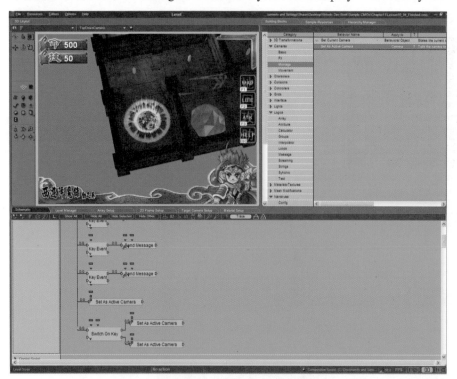

10.5 Setting Up Arrow Key Character Control

1) Open the file Lesson10_05_Start.CMO located in Sample CMO's\Chapter11. Considering most laptops don't have a separate numeric keypad, we need to create the corresponding Arrow key controls. Add the Switch On Key and four Send Message BB's. Add an additional two Behavior Outputs to the Switch on Key BB and setup the relevant arrow keys. Set each Send Message BB to send the relevant Joy_Up, Joy_Down, Joy_Left and Joy_Right message to the WuKong character.

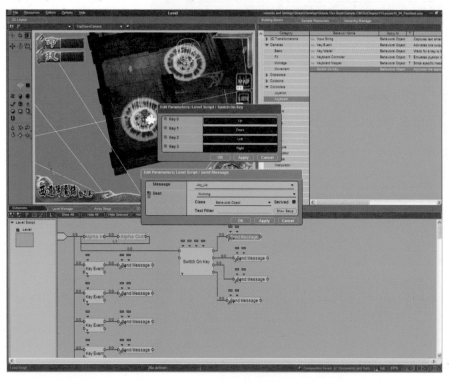

10.6 Setting the Background Color

1) Open the file Lesson10_06_Start.CMO located in Sample CMO's\Chapter11. Add the Set Background Color BB and connect it to the Start Node. Set the Color to Black.

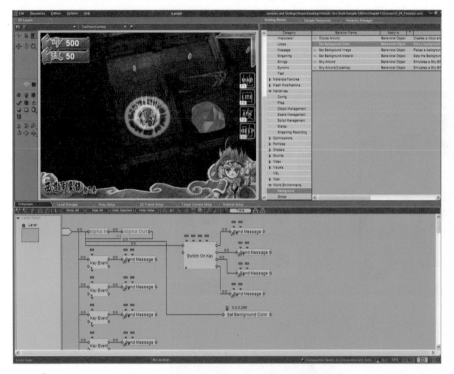

10.7 Creating the Level Fade-In Effect

1) Open the file Lesson10_07_Start.CMO located in Sample CMO's\Chapter11. Add a Bezier Progression and Camera Color Filter BB to the Level Script. Connect the Bezier Progression BB to the first Set As Active Camera and connect the Camera Color Filter BB to loop internally within the Bezier Progression BB. Configure the settings as shown in the screenshot. Remember to delete the camera switching BB's connection to the Start Node and connect them to the end of the Bezier Progression to stop users switching camera while we are fading the scene in.

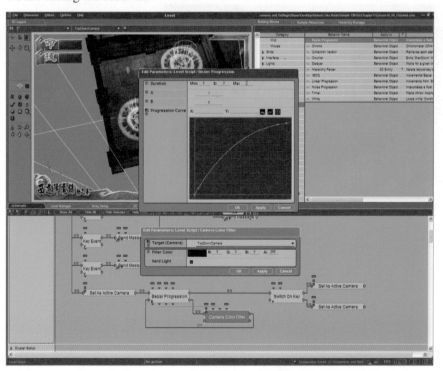

11.0 Creating the Game Menu

11.1 Adding the Title and Character Images

1) Begin by creating a new composition in Virtools. Change the level background color to Black using the Level Setup panel. Next, holding Ctrl+Shift drag the Texture AllCharacters.png from Sample Resources \ Textures into the scene. This will create a new 2D Frame. Set the Material Type to Transparent and set the 2D Frame's ZOrder to -2.

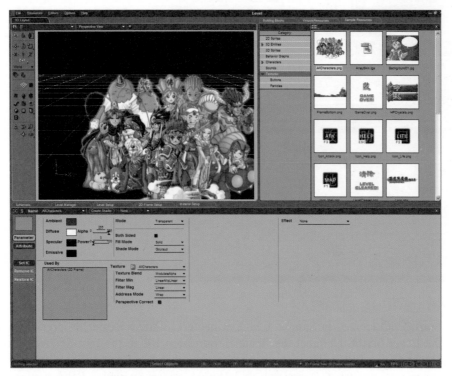

2) Again, hold Ctrl+Shift and drag the texture Logo.png into the scene. Position it at the top-left of the 3D layout panel. Remember to change the Material Type to Transparent.

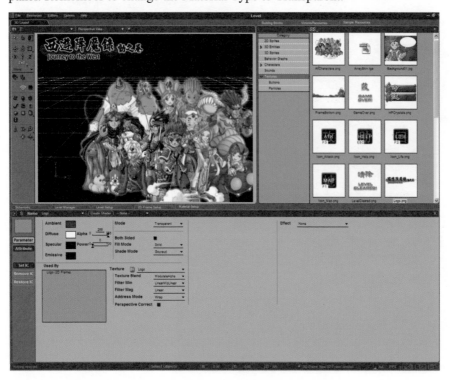

11.2 Adding the Selection Buttons

1) Continue from the last lesson or Open the file Lesson11_02_Start.CMO located in Sample CMO's\Chapter11. Holding Ctrl+Shift drag the Texture Story_Normal.png from Sample Resources \ Textures \ GameButtons into the scene. Set the Material Type to Transparent and set the 2D Frame's zOrder to 1 to make it sit on top of the background images.

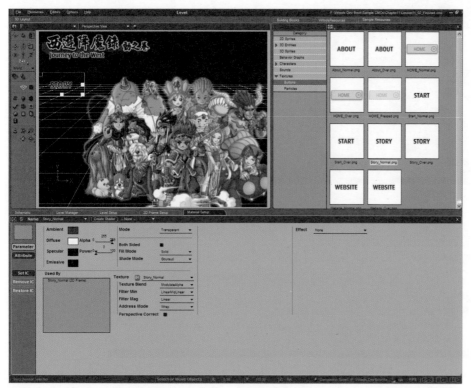

2) Again, holding Ctrl+Shift drag the texture Scroll.png into the 3D Layout window. Set its Material Type to Transparent and ZOrder to -1. Position it over the characters image as this 2D Frame will be used as the background for our story. In Level Manager, set the 2D Frame to Hidden and set its Initial Conditions.

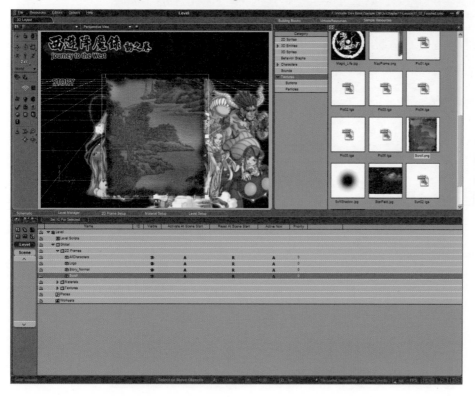

3) Drag the Texture Story_Over.png into the scene and create its associated material. Set the Material Type to Transparent. Select the Story_Normal 2D Frame and set its Material to None.

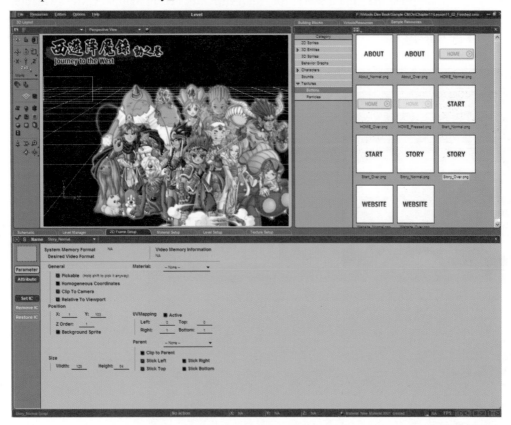

4) Create a script on the Story_Normal 2D Frame and add the Push Button BB. Set the Push Button BB's Released Material to the Story_Normal texture and the Pressed and Rollover Materials to the Story_Over texture. Set the Pressed Offset to 0,0.

5) Add the Show, Hide and Text Display BB's to the script and connect them as shown in the screenshot. The PushButton BB's Enter Button POut should connect to the Show BB and the Exit Button POut should connect to the Hide BB. The Show and Hide BB's POut's should connect to the Text Display's On and Off BIn's respectively. We will use this to show the Scroll frame and text when the mouse is over the button and to hide it when to mouse rolls off the button.

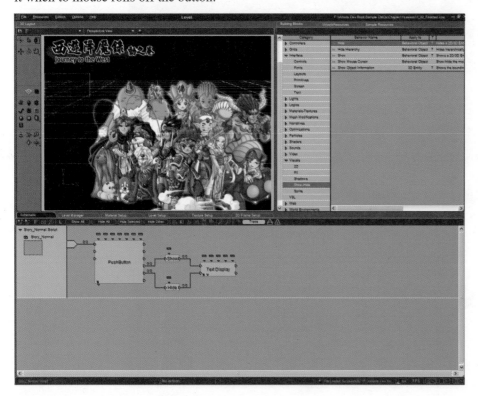

6) We need to tell the Show and Hide BB's what object we want to show and hide. By default it will target the object that contains the script, but we want to target the Scroll 2D Frame. Right click the Show BB and select Add Target Parameter from the popup menu. Set the Parameter to our Scroll 2D Frame. Repeat the process for the Hide BB.

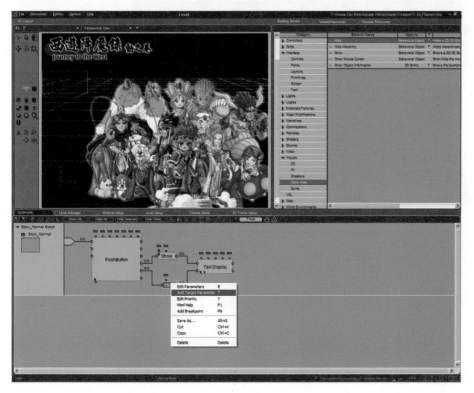

7) Change the sprite size of the Text Display BB to 320x320 by right clicking on the BB and selecting Settings from the popup menu. Next, adjust the Text Display BB's parameters to position the text over the Scroll. You can make the job easier by disconnecting the Hide BB so the text will always show and using the Apply button to see the changes when you play the composition.

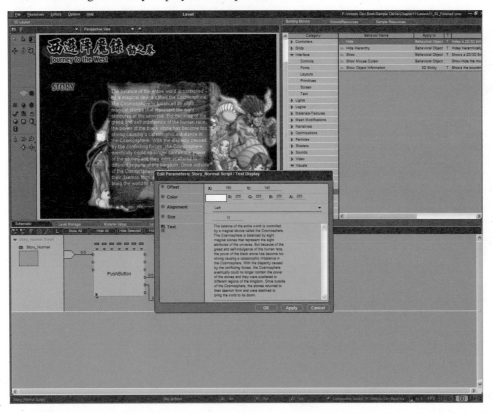

8) Next, holding Ctrl+Shift drag the rest of the buttons (the _Normal versions) into the 3D Layout window. Position them so they line up vertically and have equal distance between each other. Set their zOrder to 1 and the Material Type to Transparent. Add remaining '_Over' Textures to the scene.

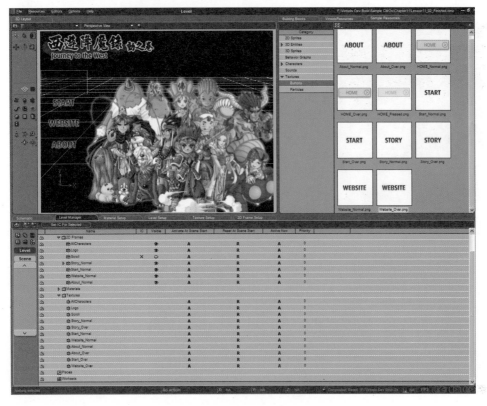

9)   Add three new materials to the scene and name them Start_Over, Website_Over and About_Over. Set their Textures to the respective button '_Over' textures. Set the Diffuse color to White and Mode to Transparent.

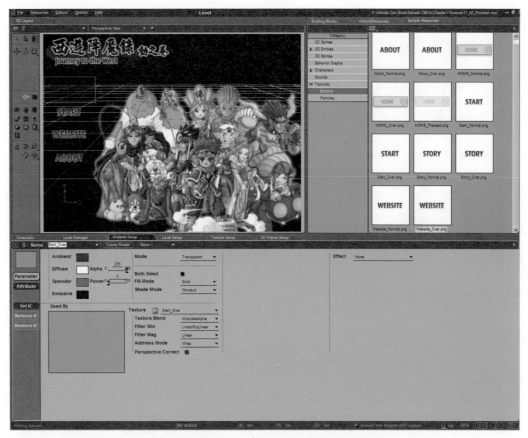

10) Create scripts for each of the 2D Frames and add the Pushbutton BB.

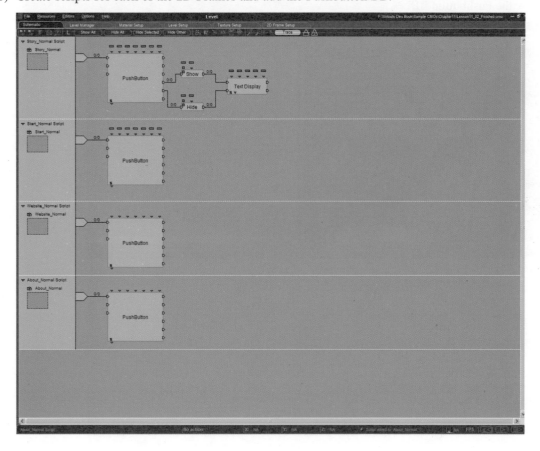

11) For each of the Pushbutton BB's, set the Released, Pressed and Rollover parameters to the matching Materials. Remember to set the Offset to 0,0 to avoid the button moving when the mouse rolls over.

12) In the 2D Frame Setup panel, set each of the three buttons Material to None as this parameter is now controlled by the Pushbutton BB.

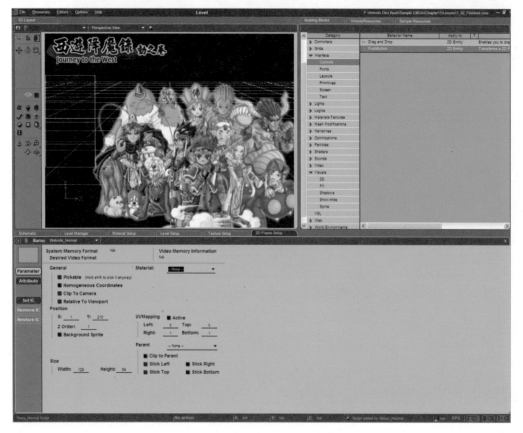

13) Go to the Script for the Start button and add a Go To Webpage BB. Connect it to the Pushbutton BB's Released BOut and set the URL to Game.htm.

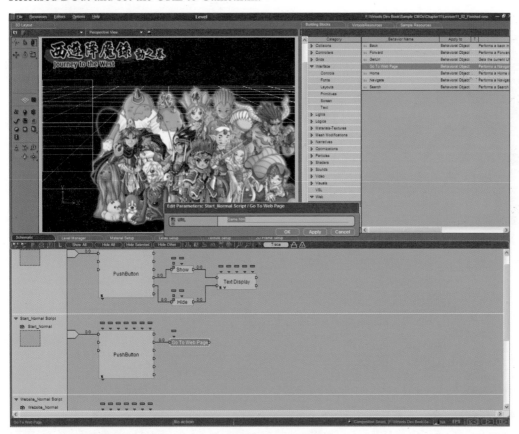

14) Next, add a Go To Webpage BB in the Website button's Script. Connect it to the Pushbutton BB's Released BOut and set the URL to your own website if you have one.

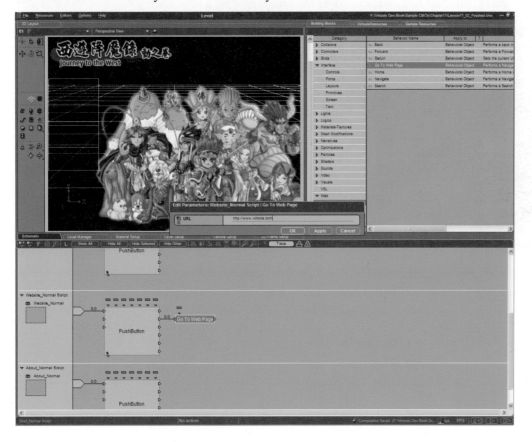

15) Lastly, following the same steps as the Story script to create an About message. You can copy and paste the BB's and local variables from the Story button script and just modify the Text Display's Text parameter.

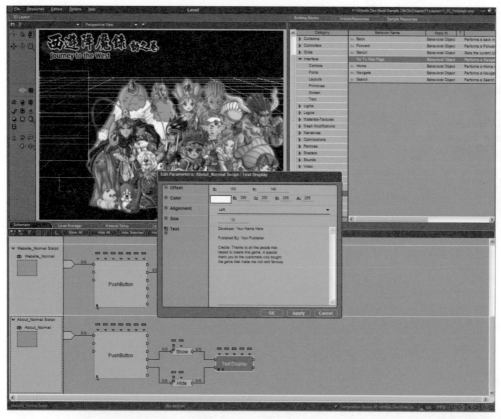

16) Click Play to test the composition. When you roll the mouse over the Story and About buttons the related text should appear. Unfortunately we can't test the Start and Website buttons as we need to export the composition and configure the HTML files first. We will cover the export process a little later.

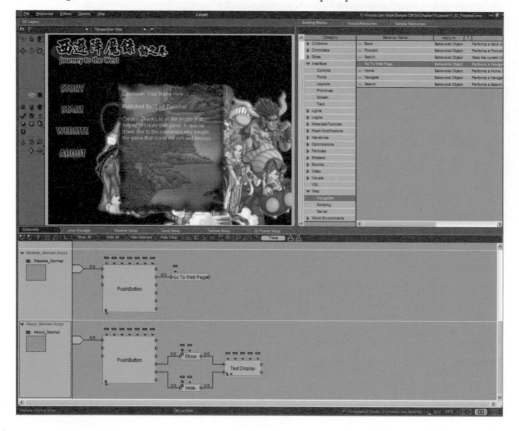

11.3 Adding the Background Scene

1) Continue from the last lesson or Open the file Lesson11_03_Start.CMO located in Sample CMO's\Chapter11. Add Scene05 from Sample Resources \ Characters \ Scenes to the composition. Create a new Camera and position it too look down on the scene.

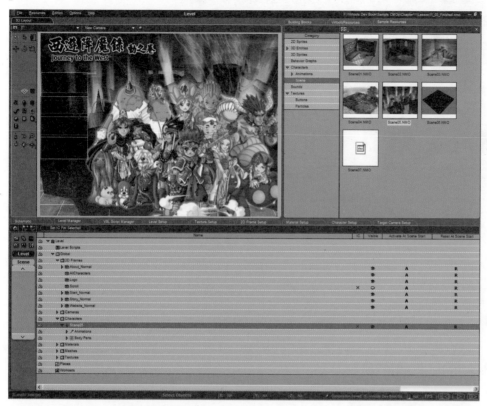

2) Add the Set Active Camera, Look At and Rotate Around BB's and configure them to make the camera fly around the scene and look at the 3D Frame we just created.

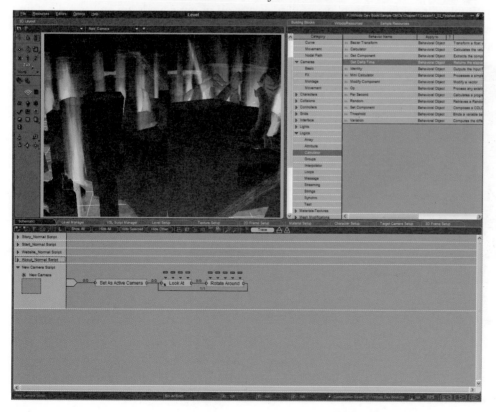

3) Lastly, to create some depth and movement in the scene, use the Texture Scroller and Texture Sine BB's on the LavaFloor, LavaSprial and LavaStream Meshes. You can refer to the file Lesson11_03_Finished.CMO located in Sample CMO's\Chapter11.

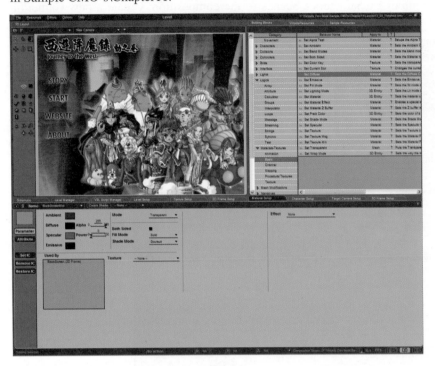

12.0 Exporting the Game

12.1 Exporting the Maze Level

1) Open the file Lesson10_07_Finished.CMO located in Sample CMO's\Chapter11. Since we are exporting the file with the intention of uploading it to the web, we need to ensure all of our sounds are embedded within the final file. Open the General Preferences dialog and select the Miscellaneous Controls preference panel. Set the Sound Files Save Option to Save Inside CMO.

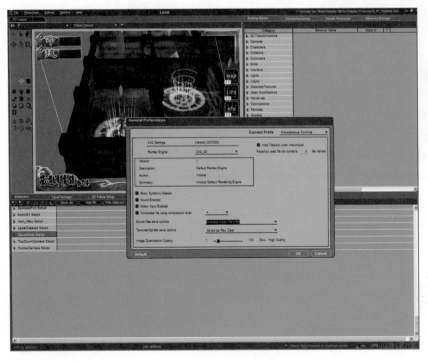

2) Select Create Web Page from the file menu. Create a folder to store all of the game related files that we will export. Use the Choose Directory button to select the folder, set the name of the file to Game.htm. Set the Web Page Title to Journey to the West and the Window Size to 640x480. Click Ok to export. Virtools will create a VMO and matching HTML file in the folder.

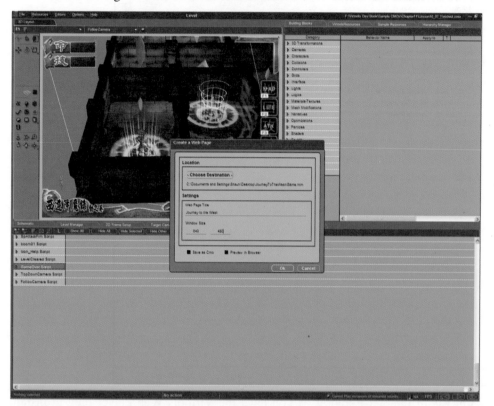

3) Now, open the file Lesson11_03_Finished.CMO located in Sample CMO's\Chapter11. Use the same settings as the pervious step to export the game menu composition. Make sure you set the name of the HTML file to GameMenu.htm otherwise our Go To Webpage BB's wont work.

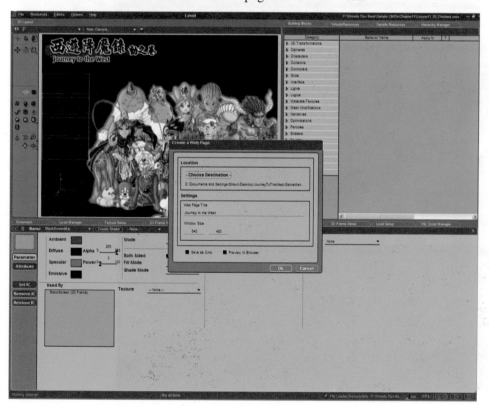

4) To test the export, navigate to the folder you chose to save the files in. There should be a total of four files; 2 VMO files and 2 HTM files.

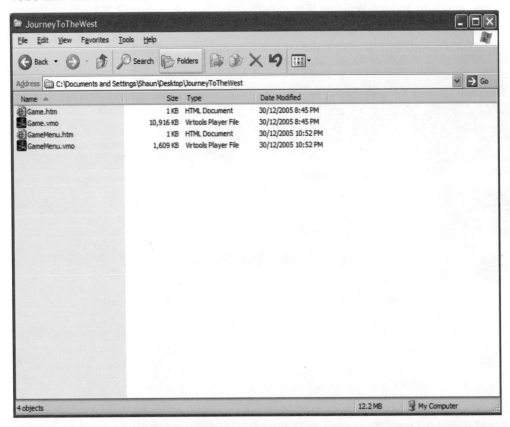

5) Open the GameMenu.htm file in Internet Explorer. If you have the Virtools Web Player plug-in installed, the composition should load immediately. If not, it will automatically connect to the web and download the required components.

6) Test each of the buttons and try playing your game through to the end. Try getting your character killed and see if you are taken back to the main menu. If all works correctly, you are ready to upload you first Virtools game to the web. Congratulations!

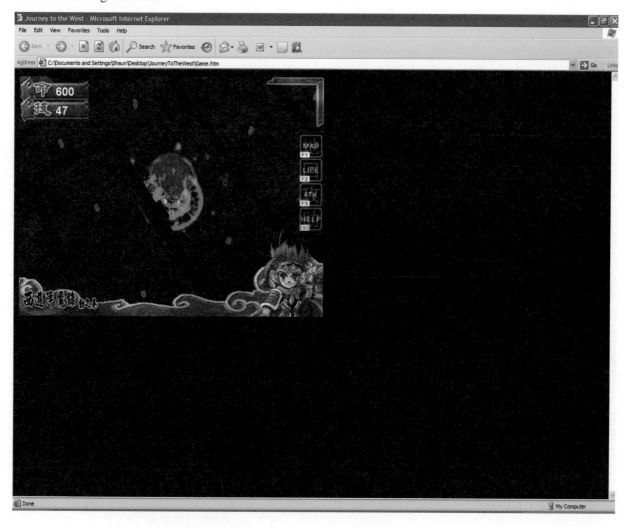

License Agreement / Notice of Limited Warranty

By opening the sealed disc container in this book, you agree the following terms and conditions. If, upon reading the following license agreement and notice of limited warranty, you cannot agree to the terms and conditions set forth, return the unused book with unopened disc to the place where you purchased it for a refund.

License:

The enclosed software is copyrighted by the copyright holder(s) indicated on the software disk. You are licensed to copy the software onto a single computer for use by a single concurrent user and to a backup disk. You may not reproduce, make copies, or distribute copies or rent or lease the software in whole or in part, except with written permission of the copyright holder(s). You may transfer the enclosed disc only together with this license, and only if you destroy all other copies of the software and the transferee agrees to the terms of the license. You may not decompile, reverse assemble, or reverse engineer the software.

Notice of Limited Warranty:

The enclosed disc is warranted by learnvirtools.com to be free of physical defects in materials and workmanship for a period of sixty (60) days from end user's purchase of the book / disc combination. During the sixty-day term of the limited warranty, learnvirtools.com will provide a replacement disc upon the return of a defective disc.

Limited Liability:

THE SOLE REMEDY FOR BREACH OF THIS LIMITED WARRANTY SHALL CONSIST ENTIRELY OF REPLACEMENT OF THE DEFECTIVE DISC. IN NO EVENT SHALL PRIMA OR THE AUTHORS BE LIABLE FOR ANY OTHER DEMAGES, INCLUDING LOSS OR CORRUPTION OF DATA, CHANGES IN THE FUNCTIONAL CHARACTERISTICS OF THE HARDWARE OR OPERATING SYSTEM, DELETERIOUS INTERACTION WITH OTHER SOFTWARE, OR ANY OTHER SPECIAL, INCIDENTA, OR CONSEQUENTIAL DAMAGES THAT MAY ARISE, EVEN IF PRIMA AND / OR THE AUTHOR HAVE PREVIOUSLY BEEN NOTIFIED THAT THE POSSIBILITY OF SUCH DAMAGES EXITS.

Disclaimer of Warranties:

learnvirtools.com AND THE AUTHORS SPECIFICALLY DISCLAIM ANY AND ALL OTHER WARRANTIES, EITHER EXPRESS OR IMPLIED, INCLUDING WARRANTIES OF MERCHANTABILITY, SUITABILITY TO A PARTICULAR TASK OR PURPOSE, OR FREEDOM FROM ERRORS. SOME STATES DO NOT ALLOW FOR EXCLUSION OF IMPLIED WARRANTIES OR LIMITATION OF INCIDENTAL OR CONSEQUENTIAL DAMAGES, SO THESE LIMITATIONS MAY NOT APPLY TO YOU.

Other:

This Agreement is governed by the laws of the Taiwan without regard to choice of law principles. The United Convention of Contracts for the International Sale of Goods is specifically disclaimed. This Agreement constitutes the entire agreement between you and learnvirtools.com regarding use of the software.

Publisher: Axis 3D Technology, Inc.
Associate Marketing Manager: Alex Wu
Managing Editor: Shaun Le Lacheur Sales
Technical Reviewer: Franz Krauth
Cover Design: Shaun Le Lacheur Sales
CD-ROM Producer: Kevin Yeh

Virtools is a registered trademark of Dassault Ssytem in the France and / or other countries. 3D Studio Max is a registered trademark and Discreet is a trademark of Autodesk / Discreet in the USA and / or other countries. All other trademarks are the property of their respective owners.

Important: learnvirtools.com cannot provide software support. Please contact the appropriate software manufacturer's technical support line or Wed site for Assistance.

learnvirtools.com and the author have attempted throughout this book to distinguish proprietary trademarks from descriptive terms by following the capitalization style used by the manufacturer.

Information contained in this book has been obtained by learnvirtools.com from sources believed to be reliable. However, because of the possibility of human or mechanical error by our sources, learnvirtools.com, or others, the Publisher does not guarantee the accuracy, adequacy, or completeness of any information and is not responsible for any error or omissions or the results obtained from used of such information. Readers should be particularly aware of the fact that the Internet is an ever-changing entity. Some facts may have changed since this book went to press.

Printed in Taiwan.
ISBN: 978-986-83208-0-2